The National
Supported Work Demonstration

The National
Supported Work Demonstration

Edited by
Robinson G. Hollister, Jr.,
Peter Kemper,
and Rebecca A. Maynard

The University of Wisconsin Press

Published 1984

The University of Wisconsin Press
114 North Murray Street
Madison, Wisconsin 53715

The University of Wisconsin Press, Ltd.
1 Gower Street
London WC1E 6HA, England

First printing

Printed in the United States of America

For LC CIP information see the colophon

ISBN 0-299-09690-4

In memory of David N. Kershaw

Contents

Tables and Figures

Tables

Figures

Acknowledgments

The research reported on in this volume was conducted over a period of seven years, with many individuals and institutions making significicant contributions. Although each of the chapters involved the work of between one and three authors, the underlying research design, implementation, and analysis, for the most part, represented a team effort. At the Manpower Demonstration Research Corporation (MDRC), which had responsibility for the design and oversight of the Supported Work Demonstration and research effort, William J. Grinker, Judith Gueron, and Gary Walker played key roles, in addition to Joseph Ball, who directed the process research. At Mathematica Policy Research, Inc. (MPR), a subcontractor for the main demonstration evaluation, Robinson Hollister was the principal investigator, with Rebecca Maynard and Peter Kemper managing the impact and benefit-cost studies, respectively. MPR's evaluation was directed initially by Heather Ruth and subsequently by Valerie Leach.

Other key contributors to the evaluation effort include Jean Behrens, Anne Bloomenthal, Randall Brown, Russell Jackson, David Kershaw, David Long, Charles Metcalf, Emmanuel Noggoh, Craig Thornton, Stephen Werner, Christine Whitebread, and Judith Wooldridge, from Mathematica Policy Research, Inc.; Richard Clayton, Lee Friedman, John O'Donnell, and Felicity Skidmore, consultants to Mathematica Policy Research, Inc.; and Katherine Dickinson, Irwin Garfinkel, Rosemary Gartner, Stanley Masters, Philip Moss, and Irving Piliavin from the Institute for Research on Poverty, University of Wisconsin-Madison. In addition, the MDRC Board of Directors, under the chairmanship of Eli Ginzberg, and numerous individuals in the government funding agencies contributed to the design, implementation, and monitoring of the Supported Work programs and the evaluation effort underlying this manuscript.

Preparation of this manuscript was funded, in part, by Mathematica Policy Research, Inc., and by the Manpower Demonstration Research Corporation. The research upon which this book is based was funded by a number of federal agencies through a lead federal agency, the

Employment and Training Administration, U.S. Department of Labor, under grant number 33-36-76-01 and contract numbers 30-36-75-01 and 30-34-75-02. Other agencies contributing funding were the Law Enforcement Assistance Administration, U.S. Department of Justice; Office of Planning Evaluation, U.S. Department of Health, Education and Welfare; National Institute on Drug Abuse, U.S. Department of Health, Education, and Welfare; Office of Policy Development and Research, U.S. Department of Housing and Urban Development; and Economic Development Administration, U.S. Department of Commerce. The national demonstration was also funded by the Ford Foundation.

Researchers undertaking such projects under government sponsorship are encouraged to express their professional judgments freely. Therefore, points of view or opinions stated in this document do not necessarily represent the official position or policy of the federal government or the sponsors of the demonstration.

Contributors

Joseph Ball is a senior research associate at the Manpower Demonstration Research Corporation.

Rosemary Gartner is a specialist at the University of Wisconsin-Madison and is affiliated with the University's Institute for Research on Poverty.

Eli Ginzberg, director of the Conservation of Human Resources at Columbia College, was chairman of the Board of Directors of the Manpower Demonstration Research Corporation during the operation of the Supported Work Demonstration.

Judith Gueron is the executive vice-president of the Manpower Demonstration Research Corporation.

Robinson G. Hollister, Jr., is a professor of economics at Swarthmore College and a senior fellow at Mathematica Policy Research.

Peter Kemper is the director of the Madison office of Mathematica Policy Research.

David A. Long is an economist at Mathematica Policy Research.

Rebecca A. Maynard is a senior economist at Mathematica Policy Research.

Richard Nathan, professor of the Woodrow Wilson School of Public and International Affairs at Princeton University, was treasurer of the Board of Directors of the Manpower Demonstration Research Corporation during the operation of the Supported Work Demonstration.

Irving Piliavin is professor of social work at the University of Wisconsin-Madison and is affiliated with the University's Institute for Research on Poverty.

Felicity Skidmore is an independent economic consultant who works regularly for Mathematica Policy Research.

Robert Solow, institute professor at the Massachusetts Institute of Technology, was vice-chairman of the Board of Directors of the Manpower Demonstration Research Corporation during the operation of the Supported Work Demonstration.

Craig Thornton is a senior economist at Mathematica Policy Research.

The National
Supported Work Demonstration

1 *Robinson G. Hollister, Jr.*

Introduction

The Supported Work demonstration-experiment grew out of a very specific and a very general concern on the part of some key individuals and institutions in the early 1970s. The specific concern was to find and test a new type of program for groups of individuals facing the most severe problems in finding and maintaining employment. The general concern was that, whatever new program concept was initiated, it should be tested in such a way that reasonably unassailable estimates of the effect of the program on the subsequent economic circumstances of the participants would be provided.

Both of these concerns arose from the early assessment of the Great Society program efforts of the 1960s as they related to the labor market. Many employment and training programs had been initiated in the late 1960s and early 1970s,[1] but few had really been tightly designed for, and targeted on, those at the very lowest end of the labor market queue. In addition, it was a common complaint that, although billions of dollars had been spent on employment and training programs, very little was known on a systematic basis about the impact of these programs.[2]

The basic program concept of Supported Work appears to have its roots in an attempt by a small group at the Vera Institute of Justice to alleviate some of the problems of a few alcoholics on the Bowery by putting them to work making toys. This effort failed, but the Vera group, with support from the Special Action Office on Drug Abuse (and later from the National Institute on Drug Abuse) and the Law Enforcement Assistance Administration, developed the concept of a

3

program emphasizing immediate work, rather than training or counseling, as a method of assisting those whose circumstances made it difficult for them to obtain and hold employment. A pilot project for ex-addicts, entitled "Wildcat," was mounted in New York City, with a careful research design attached.[3]

The results of this pilot test were sufficiently encouraging for the Ford Foundation, the U.S. Department of Labor, and a number of other government agencies to begin to organize a larger test of the underlying program concept, spreading it to more cities and testing it with other specific disadvantaged groups, in addition to ex-addicts.[4] They enlisted the assistance of other federal agencies, developed a full demonstration and research effort, and created a special nonprofit organization (the Manpower Demonstration Research Corporation) to direct the demonstration-experiment.

This development, from concept to pilot project to national demonstration-experiment, represents an unusually careful and patient procedure for bringing forward a new initiative for a potential national program. The major research effort associated with the project began in 1974 and ended (more or less) in late 1979. This volume is devoted to issues related to program design and implementation, evaluation design and findings, and lessons and policy conclusions from the national demonstration-experiment.

The demonstration and the research were funded by six federal agencies and the Ford Foundation and directed by the Manpower Demonstration Research Corporation (MDRC). The primary quantitative research was carried out by Mathematica Policy Research, Inc., and the Institute for Research on Poverty of the University of Wisconsin. An additional "documentation research" effort with a more qualitative orientation and aimed primarily at gaining a better understanding of how characteristics and operations of various parts of the demonstration may have affected outcomes was carried out by MDRC's research and operations staff.

The fact that each of the various chapters of this book was written by only one to three individuals is misleading. Almost all of the individual authors participated to a substantial degree in the design, implementation, and analysis of the research in the areas covered by the other authors; only in the final stages of write-up of analyses were the subject areas very clearly separated out. More important, readers should be aware that research of the sort reported here, carried out over five years, involving multiple data collection efforts covering more than 6,000 subjects in 10 cities across the nation, obviously requires a massive team effort. While the names of some of those contributing to the effort appear in the note references to supplementary papers and documents, the list of major participants—from interviewers through programmers to consultants—is far longer than what appears on formal documents.

Readers will find the details of the Supported Work program spelled out in the chapters that follow, so only the most superficial introduction is necessary here. The primary feature of Supported Work was that it provided a limited-duration (12–18 months), subsidized employment opportunity. The work experience was provided in an atmosphere intended to be more supportive and closely supervised than is normally the case for jobs at the lower end of the labor market. Such an atmosphere would be, it was expected, conducive to the acquisition of skills, habits, and credentials that facilitate transition to continued unsubsidized employment. Associated with such employment changes, it was hoped, would be reductions in welfare dependency and, for those with previous crime and drug-abuse histories, lower recidivism rates.

Four target groups were selected for inclusion in the experiment: unemployed ex-offenders, former drug addicts, women who had received welfare payments for a long period, and young school dropouts. (More detailed eligibility criteria for each group are described in the subsequent chapters.) Members of each of these groups clearly were likely to have severe problems in finding and holding more than sporadic employment and, therefore, might be expected to benefit from the sort of experience Supported Work would provide.

Supported Work as a demonstration had sites in 15 cities across the country. In 10 of the sites, an experimental design was imposed which required the creation of control groups through random assignment and required enrollment and periodic follow-up interviews for at least 18 months and up to three years. Most of the research reported below was based on the data for the 10 experimental sites. However, some information on the five nonexperimental sites is provided in selected chapters, particularly chapter 3 on program implementation and chapter 9 on lessons from the demonstration evaluation effort.

There were certain features of the Supported Work program that were similar across the various sites. The participants were employees of the program; they worked at wages that averaged slightly above the minimum wage; and they could be promoted, suspended, or fired on the basis of performance. In addition, there was an attempt to implement the concept of a supportive environment through peer group support, close supervision, and graduated stress. Peer group support took the form of work in crews with persons of similar background (although not necessarily from the same target group). Close supervision was provided by supervisors with skills in the relevant work and with sensitivity to the problems of the individuals in these target groups. Graduated stress was implemented by adjusting work demands over the period of employment from a low initial level to a level at the end which was roughly commensurate with regular employment. Obviously, these features, while similar across sites, were implemented in detail in somewhat different ways.

Partly through necessity and partly through design, the type of work performed varied considerably across sites and, to some degree, even within sites over time. Work ranged from painting and cleaning and sealing abandoned homes, at one end of the spectrum, to manufacturing of basic products and to aiding in a day-care center, at the other end.

This sketchy outline of the development of Supported Work and its characteristics should be sufficient for a general orientation. With this background, a few remarks about the individual papers are in order before sending the reader forward into the details of the full analysis.

Chapters 2 and 3 by Hollister and by Ball, respectively, provide very important information about the background and setting of the program and research. As mentioned above, Supported Work was a national demonstration-experiment. Both Hollister and Ball discuss the ways in which the requirements of these two aspects interacted in the development and implementation of the program and the research. It is important to have these different aspects in mind in reviewing the results reported in the subsequent chapters. For example, an awareness of the different types of work experiences provided in different sites and the variations in labor market conditions both across sites and over time makes it easier to understand why the researchers discussing each target group take great pains to check for differences in program impacts associated with site or time differences.

The design and implementation of the research are discussed by Hollister. The discussion of events in the development of the design helps to explain some of the sources of difficulties that emerged in the analysis stage. In particular, readers may find helpful the brief review of the sample design decisions and the ways these relate to the "cohort problem" which is discussed in subsequent chapters. Hollister stresses the importance of the experimental design, based on random assignment, for the assessment of outcomes, particularly as they differ among target groups. However, he also points out that, while it is usual to think of experiments as being conducted in a relatively "controlled" environment, the changing economic and social context in which Supported Work was carried out complicated the interpretation of the results and required the use of analytic techniques most often associated with nonexperimental analysis. Hollister also provides some brief comments on insights (or lack thereof) derived from the comparison of results across several target groups—a perspective that is mostly missed, in the focus on individual target groups.

Chapter 3 provides an unusually rich description of the context in which the programs operated and the variety of financial and other pressures that shaped the way in which they operated. In most of the previous major social experiments, the nature of the "treatment program" has been relatively simple, controllable, and clear. For Supported Work, however, the "treatment" was neither simple nor readily controllable and, for that reason, the material in Ball's chapter is critical for an understanding of the process that generated the research results reported elsewhere.

The first of these chapters on the individual target groups, by Hollister and Maynard, reports the effects for women with a long history of welfare dependence, referred to as the AFDC (Aid to Families with Dependent Children) group. This is the group for which Supported Work had the greatest employment effects. Members of this target group stayed in Supported Work considerably longer than did those in any of the other groups and, in the postprogram period, their employment, hours of work, and earnings were substantially higher than those of their control group counterparts. In the initial research design, members of this group were followed for up to 27 months after enrollment. After finding a significant postprogram employment effect, it was decided to resurvey this group to obtain a longer postprogram record (up to 45 months for some). Results from this resurvey effort show that employment effects are sustained over this longer period. The chapter goes beyond these overall results to examine outcomes in detail by site and by type of employment to try to gain better insights as to the mechanisms through which the employment gains were obtained. Information about differences in total income and receipt of welfare benefits also yield interesting insights.

The chapter on research findings on the ex-addict target group is provided by Skidmore. The analysis for ex-addicts yields some strong results, some equivocal results, and some difficult analytic problems. There is a significant and substantial effect of Supported Work in reducing arrests and incarcerations among the ex-addict group. The results for postprogram employment are more difficult to interpret. Here the "cohort phenomenon" becomes important, as the statistically significant postprogram employment gains appear only among the cohort enrolled early in the program development period. Further, these results occur after a period in which there is no employment difference between experimentals and controls and in a period when we do not have follow-up data for the later cohorts. The findings indicate no overall effect of Supported Work on drug use among ex-addicts. While a substantial portion of both experimentals and controls reported using some drugs in any 9-month period (20–38 percent), the majority did not use drugs, and there was no significant difference between the proportion of experimentals and controls either during or after the in-program period. In looking at results by site and subgroup, or after the in-program period. In looking at results by site and subgroup, Skidmore reports that, generally, Supported Work tended to be more effective, the worse off the subgroup control counterpart; that is, the lower the employment or the higher the crime or drug use among the controls, the more likely it was that some indication of Supported Work effects would be found.

Chapter 6 by Piliavin and Gartner reviews the results for ex-offenders. Overall, the conclusion would seem to be that Supported Work had little long-term effect for this group, but there were problems in the analysis related again to "cohort differences." There were no sizable overall effects on employment and crime, although there was some indication of effects on drug use. When they looked at subgroups, Piliavin and Gartner found some indication of effects on crime for those over age 35 and those with dependents, and they theorize about possible reasons for these special effects.

The youth group results are reported in the chapter by Maynard. She found no postprogram effects on employment and no effects on crime or drug use. Most interesting in this chapter is the careful attention paid to the control group experiences. Employment among the youth controls grew more rapidly over the period in which they were interviewed than did the employment of controls in other target groups. Thus, the failure to find employment effects would appear not to be due to a failure of the Supported Work youths to find employment, but rather that those without Supported Work experience found jobs at an equally high rate. One might be tempted to conclude that the program was not tightly targeted enough on youths with serious employment problems; yet Maynard's comparison of Supported Work controls with other youth groups suggests that they were, in fact, a group with significant problems. These findings, while negative, are equally important for policy, suggesting that youth employment problems may not yield easily to program intervention.

Data from a follow-up survey of the sample youth did yield evidence that the overall negative conclusions from this main study were the result of Supported Work leading to large adverse impacts on youths who stay in the program for relatively long periods of time before being terminated for negative reasons. On average, other youths who were not terminated negatively benefited significantly from the program. As Maynard points out, the challenge then is to target resources on this latter group.

The eighth chapter reports on the benefit-cost analysis carried out by Kemper, Long, and Thornton. Readers will find this not only an extremely careful and thorough piece, but a very helpful medium through which to pull together the many results reported in the preceding chapters. The analysts evaluate benefits and costs for each target group and do so from three different perspectives: that of society as a whole (the perspective usually preferred by economists), that of the nonparticipant (the perspective usually preferred by politicians), and that of the participants (the view usually preferred by participants).

While all benefits and costs cannot be easily quantified, Kemper, Long, and Thornton have carried the process a long way. Many have expressed misgivings about such attempts at quantification, as it inevitably requires a large number of assumptions. It is a strength of the study that the assumptions made are clearly laid out and, more importantly, that extensive sensitivity analyses were carried out to determine how the overall results would change with alterations in key assumptions. Fortunately, the overall benefit-cost conclusions for three of the target groups are quite robust when subjected to these sensitivity tests; while the estimates of the absolute magnitude of social benefits minus social costs changes with reasonable change in assumptions, the conclusion as to whether the overall payoff was positive or negative does not. The benefit-cost analyses confirm that Supported Work was most successful for the AFDC group, that its benefits exceeded its cost for the ex-addict group, and that its costs exceeded its benefits for youth. For ex-offenders, the overall benefit-cost conclusions shift negative to positive with some extreme shifts in assumptions.

The reasons for the variations in results by target groups are far from being well understood, and there are many other interesting questions raised by the research reported here which are unresolved. Still the diversity and robustness of the main research results stand out. It would appear from the research reported here that the basic approach to program development supported by rigorous research was justified; while it took time and resources, solid findings, both negative and positive, were provided about possibilities of program interventions to alleviate employment problems for the four disadvantaged groups that were the focus of the Supported Work Demonstration.

There is a natural tendency to focus exclusively on the research outcomes from a demonstration or experiment. Yet the scope and nature of the outcomes, if not their specific content, are shaped by the decisions about design and processes of implementation which bring the demonstration into being. Chapters 2 and 3, as discussed above, provide some information on these decisions and processes. However, one innovative aspect of the National Supported Work Demonstration which deserves special attention in this regard was the creation of a special agency, interposed between funding sources and operational and research organizations, to manage and monitor the entire demonstration and research associated with it. This agency was, and is, the Manpower Demonstration Research Corporation, and in chapter 9 Gueron discusses some of the lessons drawn from the experience of the agency in guiding the Supported Work project. She discusses and evaluates the problems of balancing the forces generated by the interests of the funding agencies, the requirements of the research design and concerns of research contractors, and the desires and difficulties of those operating the programs at the local level.

The description of the operation of the demonstration from the perspective of this unique oversight agency helps one both to understand why various aspects of the demonstration were shaped as they were and to evaluate the role such intermediary agencies might play in any future demonstration-experiment of magnitude similar to Supported Work.

As suggested at the beginning of this introduction, the Supported Work Demonstration should not be viewed as an isolated event, but rather as part of the general effort in the 1970s to improve understanding of the effects of social policies in employment, training, and welfare, and through that understanding to improve the policy making process. In chapter 10, the specific lessons from the Supported Work Demonstration are related to this broader policy context. The authors of the chapter, Ginzberg, Nathan, and Solow, were involved in the demonstration as members of the group that first served as advisors to the funding agencies during the design phase and then became the Board of Directors of the Manpower Demonstration Research Corporation. Their discussion draws upon their direct experience with Supported Work as well as their broader involvement in the development of social policy at the national level.

The general discussion in this chapter of the uses of research in the formulation of social policy provides a broader context for understanding the factors which led to the creation of the Supported Work Demonstration—factors which they specifically describe—and the concrete contributions the Supported Work experience makes to the re-search-policy nexus, in terms of both research outcomes and organizational structures. The authors stress the importance of federal, state, and local relationships both for the formation of social policy in the employment and welfare area and for the design and implementation of research in that domain.

Readers will find refreshing, we believe, the strong sense of realism in this final chapter about the ability of research to influence policy, combined with a stress on the importance of persisting in the effort to meet the requirements for high-quality research which can enhance the understanding of the effects of social policies; the authors help us neither to overestimate the possibilities of the first nor to underestimate the difficulties of the second.

We hope a similar sense of realism and high standards pervades this volume as a whole; we have sought to claim no more for Supported Work as a program and a research effort than could be well supported by the data, but where the evidence of success is strong we hope to bring it, hereby, to greater public attention, and perhaps, in time, into policy action.

Notes

1 See Ginzberg (1980) for a brief description of employment and training policies from 1962 to 1979.
2 See, for example, Goldstein (1972), O'Neill (1973), and National Academy of Sciences (1974).
3 National Institute on Drug Abuse (1978).
4 The key people involved in these activities were Mitchell Sviridoff and William Grinker of the Ford Foundation; William Kolberg and Howard Rosen at the Department of Labor; William Morrill and Michael Barth at the Department of Health, Education, and Welfare; Donald Santorelli and Charles Work at the Law Enforcement Assistance Administration; and Robert DuPont at the National Institute on Drug Abuse.

2 *Robinson G. Hollister, Jr.*

The Design and Implementation of the Supported Work Evaluation

Work status is the central defining characteristic in the American social structure. A basic presumption of most social commentators has been that low work status generates social ills—bad health, alienation, disintegrating family structure, crime. Those of a more skeptical bent have reversed the order of causation, hypothesizing that penchant for antisocial behavior has, for certain individuals, precluded attainment of a stable position in the workforce.

The Supported Work Demonstration was a project designed to test how these fundamental propositions apply to some of the groups in our society which are in the most desperate circumstances. It was a demonstration program which provided a direct work opportunity for former criminals, ex-drug addicts, young school dropouts, and women who had been receiving welfare for long periods of time. Appended to the demonstration was a major research component designed to

In some places in this chapter I have drawn heavily on *Summary and Findings of the National Supported Work Demonstration*, by the Board of Directors, Manpower Demonstration Research Corporation (1980), just as the authors of that volume drew upon drafts by the project researchers, including myself. However, much of the description herein is highly subjective, and it should not be presumed that others involved in the demonstration and the research endorse this account of events and interpretations of findings.

In the five years of research effort, many have suffered and sustained, but, in particular, Heather Ruth, Valerie Leach, Peter Kemper, and Rebecca Maynard carried heavy burdens with skill and grace and made the work of all of us both easier and more enjoyable. David Kershaw was, as with so many policy research efforts, a prime motivator and tireless co-worker.

determine, in both quantitative and qualitative terms, what the effects of the Supported Work experience were on the participants.

This chapter describes the research design developed for the evaluation of Supported Work. It is organized on an historical basis. First, the origin of the demonstration is discussed; then the research design and its rationale are presented. Issues involved in the implementation of this design are discussed in the third section, while the research findings are summarized and interpreted in the fourth section. The chapter concludes with a few observations, based on the Supported Work experience, on the role of random assignment in program evaluation.

The Origins and Character of the Demonstration

The Supported Work Demonstration had an immediate precedent in the Wildcat program developed by the Vera Institute of New York City in 1972, sponsored by the Ford Foundation and the U.S. Department of Labor. The Wildcat program was designed to provide employment for ex-addicts and was accompanied by a careful research design. The results of the research on the first year of operation of the program were sufficiently positive to encourage the sponsors to seek to broaden its application by extending it to other cities and to other disadvantaged groups.

Guided by an advisory group of eminent social policy specialists, the demonstration planners began by searching out a large group of experienced program operators from cities across the United States who they thought might potentially run Supported Work program sites. They brought these operators together in a conference of 175 persons including, in addition to the operators, representatives of funding agencies and of state and local governments. A subset of this group submitted detailed program proposals for Supported Work-type projects in their cities (based roughly on the Wildcat pilot program structure with which they had been familiarized). While there was a common theme, the proposals differed considerably in concept and detail. Of the 40 detailed proposals, 13 were finally selected as sites for the demonstration. The diversity in the proposals continued to be reflected in the mode of operation of the selected sites throughout the demonstration. The original 13 sites began operation between March and July 1975, and two more sites were added during 1976. In table 2.1 the 15 sites are identified and the character of the agency running them is briefly described.

TABLE 2.1
Supported Work Demonstration Sites

Location	Operating Agency
Atlanta, Georgia*	PREP (Preparation for Employment Program), a unit of the Atlanta Urban League
Chicago, Illinois*	Options, Inc., a nonprofit agency set up to operate Supported Work
Detroit, Michigan	Supported Work Corporation, a nonprofit agency set up to operate Supported Work
Hartford, Connecticut*	The Maverick Corporation, a nonprofit agency set up to operate Supported Work
Jersey City, New Jersey*	Community Help Corporation, a nonprofit agency set up to operate Supported Work
Massachusetts	Transitional Employment Enterprises, a nonprofit agency set up to operate Supported Work
Newark, New Jersey*	Newark Service Corporation, a nonprofit agency set up to operate Supported Work
New York, New York*	Wildcat Service Corporation, a nonprofit agency established by the Vera Institute of Justice to operate Supported Work
Oakland, California* (Alameda County)	Peralta Service Corporation, a nonprofit agency established by the Spanish Speaking Unity Council to operate Supported Work
Philadelphia, Pennsylvania*	Impact Service Corporation, a nonprofit agency set up to operate Supported Work
St. Louis, Missouri	A unit of the St. Louis Housing Authority
San Francisco, California*	The San Francisco Phoenix Corporation, a nonprofit agency set up to operate Supported Work
Washington State	Pivot, a nonprofit agency set up to operate Supported Work
West Virginia (Five counties in the northwest area of the state)	A unit of the Human Resources Development Foundation, Inc., a subsidiary of the West Virginia Labor Federation, AFL–CIO
Wisconsin* (Fond du Lac and Winnebago counties)	A unit of Advocap, Inc., a community action agency

Source: Manpower Demonstration Research Corporation (1980).
* Denotes a research site.

Toward the latter stages of the planning for the demonstration, it was decided that research would be conducted at a number of the sites, using at least part of an experimental methodology that, most important, required random assignment of enrollees to a program participation group (hereafter often referred to as "experimentals") or to a comparison group (hereafter usually referred to as the "control group") and periodic follow-up and interviews with both groups to gather data on key measures of their economic and social status. Ten sites were selected for inclusion in this more rigorous, quantitative research design. (These sites are indicated by an asterisk in table 2.1.) The other five sites continued in the demonstration, but there was no random assignment nor periodic interviewing of participants at these sites (though data on the programs in these sites were gathered systematically as part of the Supported Work Management Information System and accounting and financial records). It is important to be aware that Supported Work was originally conceived of as a demonstration. The experimental aspect of the research design was brought in toward the later stages of planning. This meant that the balance between the more restrictive requirements of a systematic, quantitative research design and the freer, more exploratory and operations-oriented nature of a demonstration were often a matter of conflict and, necessarily, compromise. Aspects of these compromises will be illustrated in the discussion below.

Other important features of the Supported Work Demonstration derived from the character of the funding of the programs. The funding of Supported Work had three major layers: funds from the national level, funds from state and local agencies, and funds obtained by the site programs themselves through the sale of goods and services produced by the participants. At the national level the funding was even more complex: six federal agencies participated in the planning and funding at some stage (the Employment and Training Administration of the Department of Labor; the Law Enforcement Assistance Administration of the Department of Justice; the National Institute on Drug Abuse and the Office of the Assistant Secretary for Planning and Evaluation of the Department of Health, Education, and Welfare; the Office of Policy Research and Development of the Department of Housing and Urban Development; and the Economic Development Administration of the Department of Commerce), and the Ford Foundation played a very important initiating, planning, and funding role.

It was evident from the funding complexity alone that some single agency was necessary to coordinate the demonstration. It was also clear that such an agency should serve to help enforce at least minimal conformity to program design across the multiplicity of local sites and to provide technical assistance to them when necessary. The Manpower Demonstration Research Corporation (MDRC) was formed, as a nonprofit organization, to serve these functions under the guidance of a Board of Directors, which was made up of persons with extensive experience in policy related social research and administration.

MDRC, as a nongovernmental agency intermediating between federal agencies and local program operators, is an innovation which deserves evaluation in its own right, but here we are concerned primarily with the effects of its existence on the nature of the research related to the demonstration. There are many such effects; a few stand out. First, the major quantitative research was carried out under a subcontract from MDRC. Partly as a result of this and partly because of the nature of the demonstration, the researchers had less direct control over the "treatment" given to the experimentals than has been the case in other major social experiments (the Income Maintenance, Health Insurance, and most of the Housing Allowance experiments). Because of the diversity of the program experiences of the experimentals, the research segment of Supported Work should be thought of as more of a quasi-experiment: a control group created by random assignment, but only loosely standardized "treatments" for experimentals. Second, MDRC mediated all contacts between researchers and the federal funding agencies and all contacts with local program operators. Third, since MDRC controlled the flow of national funds to the local operators, it could set requirements for operators and (to some degree) enforce procedures which were necessary to maintain the integrity of the research design. The management and financial data which MDRC gathered from the sites could also be shaped to some degree to assist research objectives and could, in any case, be used to supplement the interview data gathered directly by the research subcontractors.

In addition to leading to the creation and role of MDRC, the funding structure had important implications for the way the Supported Work programs operated in each of the sites. Since on average, over the four years of operation of the demonstration, about 50 percent of the funds came from sources other than the national funding agencies, local operators were under continuing pressure to raise the local share of resources for the demonstration. As might be expected, the level and nature of funds available for such purposes varied considerably from site to site, and this tended to reinforce the initial diversity in program content and procedures. Some sites sought to emphasize work activities that would result in more readily marketable products as a source of funds to meet their local share requirements. Others sought to develop special relationships with key local agencies that could supply funds, and this sometimes created pressures to shape operations in particular ways.

One final feature of the structure of the demonstration which should be mentioned is the requirement that the program be a transitional employment program. After considerable discussion in the planning stage, it was decided that the Supported Work employment opportunity should have a fixed term for any participant; explicitly, it would be a program that would provide a bridge to regular employment elsewhere—in either the private or public sector—rather than one that allowed for very long-term participation, as had been envisioned for some types of public employment programs. For reasons explained below, the fixed term at some sites was 12 months and at others it was 18 months. This requirement, of course, added to the stress faced by program operators in two ways. First, even when particular participants had become clearly stabilized in productive employment, had acquired some limited skills, and, in a few cases, had demonstrated ability to supervise others at work, they had to leave the program when their fixed terms ended. Thus, the "workforce of the enterprise" had to be continually renewed, restructured, and retrained. Moreover, the program operators not only had to find work activities for the participants while they were in the program, but also had to develop the means to assist the participants in making the transition into regular employment—to find jobs.

The researchers were continually awed by the tremendous pressures that were placed upon the program operators: dealing with the most difficult types of participants, finding work opportunities—not just digging ditches and filling them again—which were the substance of the program, meeting the requirements of raising funds for the local share of financing, and trying to place those who had completed their Supported Work experience in good jobs. It does not take sophisticated research to conclude that creating and running these programs in 15 cities, dealing with more than 10,000 participants over four years, was in itself a great accomplishment.

The Research Design

The research design was developed in detail by the research subcontractors selected by MDRC: Mathematica Policy Research, and the Institute for Research on Poverty. It was subjected to revisions and approval by the MDRC staff and Board of Directors as well as by representatives of the federal funding agencies and the Ford Foundation.

Several aspects of the conditions under which the research design was developed are worthy of note. First, the general outlining of the experimental component of the research design was developed during the later stages of the planning of the demonstration, but the detailed work on design came only after the research subcontract was awarded in July and August 1974, by which time commitment had already been made to begin site operations as early as January 1975. On the one hand, the Vera Institute's Wildcat pilot program provided an extremely valuable prior experience that could serve as something of a model for the program. On the other hand, there was really no tightly defined, a priori theoretical model around which an employment program for highly disadvantaged populations could be constructed. Since Supported Work was developed first as a demonstration, the decision had already been made that the site operators were obligated to raise resources locally and, concomitantly, that they would have considerable freedom to adapt the character of their work programs to local circumstances, with regard to both funding availability and labor market conditions. The research design was thus constrained by time, the lack of clearly defined a priori models, and the extent to which procedures of the site operators could be controlled to meet the requirements of any research design.

Design of the "Treatment" and Selection of Target Groups

Drawing heavily on the Vera experience and, to a lesser extent, on the literature on employment programs, the researchers, along with MDRC, defined certain characteristics which were to constitute the key elements of Supported Work. First, as already noted, it was to be a transitional (that is, fixed term) direct employment experience. The emphasis on employment was meant to contrast with other programs whose primary content was either training or counseling. Second, the work experience was to be carried out in a context of peer group support. It was felt that the transitional work experience would be better accomplished in a setting in which persons with similar previous problems were working and could provide support through both understanding and demonstration. This is what was called "peer group support." Third, close supervision was to be provided by persons familiar both with the kinds of work to be undertaken and with the kinds of problems members of these disadvantaged groups experienced. Fourth, graduated stress was to be designed into the work experience so that a participant, when first adjusting to the new experience, would be subject to rather lenient performance standards, but over time the standards would be raised so that the participant became increasingly ready to meet performance standards that regular employers would be likely to impose.

While such characteristics could be said to define in general terms the "treatment" to which experimentals were to be subject, these terms obviously were open to a variety of interpretations when they were embodied in a program process. This reality, and the already noted degree of site diversity in conditions and proposals, led MDRC to work out with the researchers a set of rules of operation with which all of the 10 sites selected for inclusion in the rigorous research design had to comply. While there was considerable detail in the operating rules, the key features were:

1. Enrollees for the program must be from the designated target groups as defined by detailed eligibility requirements. These eligibility requirements are summarized in table 2.2 and will be discussed further below.
2. A wage and bonus structure, as spelled out by MDRC, had to be utilized. The wage structure was designed to take into account differences among sites in local wage structures; it had periodic increases over the participation period and yielded a maximum wage that would provide earnings slightly below what was estimated to be the prevailing market opportunity wage for low-skilled workers in that city. In no case was the starting wage to be below the federal minimum wage. The bonus structure was to be defined so that bonuses were related to performance measures that became increasingly difficult to achieve during the course of participation. This sort of bonus structure was meant to reflect gradually increasing work requirements.

TABLE 2.2
Supported Work Eligibility Criteria, by Target Group

Target Group	Eligibility Criteria[a]
AFDC	Women on AFDC currently and for 30 out of the preceding 36 months; youngest child 6 years old or older.
Ex-addict	Age 18 years or older; enrolled in a drug-treatment program currently or within the preceding 6 months.
Ex-offender	Age 18 years or older; incarcerated within the last 6 months as a result of a conviction.
Youth	Age 17 to 20 years; no high school or equivalency degree; not in school in the last 6 months; delinquency record, conviction, court appearance, or similar (for at least 50% of the youth).
All groups	Currently unemployed;[b] spent no more than 3 months in a job during the past 6 months.

a Supported Work eligibility criteria refer to conditions prevailing at the time of application to the Supported Work program. If a person in Supported Work voluntarily or involuntarily left the program and subsequently reapplied for a Supported Work job, he or she was not to be reviewed again for acceptance under the eligibility criteria.
b Worked no more than 10 hours a week during the last 4 weeks.

3. A fixed maximum term of program participation was established—
   usually 12 months, but in a few sites, for reasons outlined below,
   18 months. At the end of that period, participants had to leave the
   program and move on to other employment, if they could. Of course,
   participants could leave the program voluntarily at any time and,
   in addition, they could be fired, for reason, by the operators prior
   to completion of their full term of participation.
4. Implementation of the key program elements of peer support, close
   supervision, and graduated stress was required. As already noted,
   these were subject to several interpretations, but MDRC had to
   approve any particular technique chosen.

The researchers proposed that, in addition to the rules of operation
that defined common features for all sites, several features of program
structure be varied systematically across research cities. This suggestion was motivated by a desire to see whether, using the experimental
framework, variations in several key parameters of the program treatment would have discernible effects on the quantitative measures of
program impacts. Here the balance between research and operational
concerns fell to the side of the operational, for of the several proposed
variations, only the variation in the length of maximum program participation—18 versus 12 months—was accepted and implemented. Most
important, the proposal that wage levels vary systematically was rejected. MDRC and the funding agency representatives felt that the
restraints on operators which would be required if such systematic
variations were imposed might prove damaging to effective management and, also, that the research sample might not be sufficiently large
to provide a reasonable chance of detecting any effects of variation at
a statistically significant level. They thought that the demonstration
was in danger of becoming too diverted by and cluttered with research
requirements.

A few comments are in order about the selection of the target groups
and the choice of eligibility criteria. From the beginning of the planning, it was felt that Supported Work should be targeted on the most
disadvantaged segments of the working-age population. The Wildcat
pilot program had already singled out ex-addicts as a target population.
Given the high incidence of crime among addicts and the high incidence of addiction among prison populations, the extension of the
program to ex-offenders was obvious. The other two target groups
selected were high school dropouts and women who had been receiving
Aid to Families with Dependent Children for long periods of time.

There was some question among the planners about whether Supported Work was really the relevant concept to be applied to deal with the employment problems of these latter two groups. However, the 1970s had shown a significant rise in teenage unemployment rates, and there was a concern at the national level that existing training and employment programs for youth were not very effective. Youths recently leaving, and often disgusted with, school seemed put off by formal training and employment programs, which seldom offered more than part-time or short-term summer work. Both researchers and operators were doubtful about whether the employment problems of youth were the sort which Supported Work was designed to address. However, since it was a direct employment rather than a training program and was designed as a transition or bridge into the regular job market, it was decided that it was worthwhile to include youth as one of the target groups.

The strong national concern about bringing women on welfare into the employed labor force was reflected in the series of major program initiatives which were generally referred to as the WIN program—started in 1967 and periodically reformed thereafter. At the time of the planning of the Supported Work Demonstration, the few existing evaluations of the effectiveness of WIN and similar programs were not very encouraging. Researchers felt that Supported Work might not be effective for AFDC women because the net gain in income for them would be small, given that these women's expected wages are relatively low and the reduction in their welfare grants would offset a large portion of any wage gains. However, WIN and similar programs had been largely of the training and placement type with no direct and immediate employment, and it was felt that this aspect of Supported Work might make it more effective. After some debate, an attempt was made to define eligibility criteria for AFDC women more narrowly: those selected for Supported Work had to have been out of the labor force for a long period. The thinking was that such a subgroup of AFDC women would be those most in need of the sort of transitional work experience provided by Supported Work (as opposed to just the placement assistance that WIN provided) and would have very few young children—and, therefore, would be more willing and able to leave home for long periods during the day, as required for regular employment.

Random Assignment

What most distinguished the research on the Supported Work Demonstration from that on previous employment and training programs was the use of random assignment of enrollees to participant status or to the control group. The Vera Institute had also used random assignment to create a control group for its research on the effects of Wildcat, but there were questions in the minds of some as to whether such a procedure could be expanded to cover the scope of a demonstration as large and as geographically and administratively dispersed as Supported Work was to be. The experience of the other major social experiments that had been carried out on a large scale and across several cities encouraged the planners sufficiently that they decided that random assignment could be successfully executed.

However, in Supported Work, there were additional pressures put on the random assignment process. These arose, first, because, for the most part, potential enrollees were to be referred to the Supported Work program in a given city by a referral group such as a welfare agency, a drug rehabilitation agency, or a prisoners' assistance society. These groups would have to be convinced to cooperate to the extent of providing twice as many candidates as there were positions in the program. The second major pressure arose from the fact that the research sample would have to be enrolled over a relatively long period of time. Since the programs at any given site would be small to begin with and would grow only slightly over time, it would take a long time for enough positions to be opened up—through increasing program size and through filling of slots vacated by previous experimental subjects who dropped out or completed their terms—to meet the requirements for a sample of research subjects large enough to provide sufficient statistical power to evaluate the impact of the program. (In fact, the random assignment procedure began in March 1975 and was not completed until July 1977.)

Another question that was raised about the value of random assignment had to do with the likely experience of the control group members and how this might affect their value as a comparison group. Many operators felt that there were already "a whole host of programs out there" for which target group members were potentially eligible and which would impinge upon those outcomes which Supported Work was designed to affect. How valuable would the control group be, they asked, if a large percentage of them were enrolled in other work and training programs? It was decided that while this was a possible risk, it was not a highly probable one and that careful monitoring of the extent of such activities among the control group would provide sufficient warning, if this were occurring on a large scale, so that the research design could be altered (for example, by gathering sufficient information on alternative programs to allow comparisons between Supported Work effects and those of the other programs).

Sample Size and Interview Design

In any major social research involving primary data gathering, the point of decision on sample size and interview design is inevitably the one of greatest controversy and pain. The sample size will not only determine, in large part, the financial costs of the study, but it will also affect the magnitude of administrative and human relations problems. Since interview time and frequency are limited, priorities among topics to be researched must be determined. Differences in perceptions about what are the most significant likely effects of a program and what are the significant features that produce those effects can remain divergent and unexpressed most of the time during the operation of a program, but they must be reconciled or compromised in the process of determining priorities for data gathering.

The sample size and design problems in Supported Work were in some respects simpler than those in previous major social experiments because systematic variations in the parameters of the "treatment" (the program attributes) had been almost completely ruled out. This meant that the problem of how to make allocations of the sample among alternative treatments did not arise; no allocation model, a source of controversy in past experiments, was necessary.

In other particulars, however, the sample design problem was more difficult. First, as already mentioned, there were constraints imposed by limitations on the ability of the sites to build up job slots quickly and by the judgment that it was administratively infeasible for individual sites to reach a size in excess of a few hundred job slots. This meant that sample enrollment had to take place over a long period of time and introduced all sorts of complications in the research, as will become apparent throughout the discussion elsewhere in this volume.

Second there was the problem of four different target groups and, eventually, 15 different sites. Would each target group have to be treated as a separate experimental group, or would it be feasible to pool them to increase statistical power? More seriously, would it be feasible to pool the data from all or most of the sites together? As stated several times above, site diversity in operations was evident from the outset of planning, and this was likely to be compounded by diversity in labor market conditions across sites. If the program experiences and labor market conditions of each target group differed from site to site, the sample size requirements for precise estimates would be enormous. The budgetary constraints, of course, precluded taking the step for absolute protection against this contingency by attempting to enroll such an enormous sample.

In addition to the usual problems of estimating a priori the expected variance in outcome measures, determining the magnitude of the impact of the program and of attrition, and choosing the level of the power criterion, there was the problem of estimating the likely rate of turnover in the program. The rate of turnover would have two effects on sample size: by definition, turnover would determine the length of exposure of sample members to program experience, and one would expect that the magnitude of the program effect would be related to length of exposure. It would also determine how fast the sample size would develop, given the constraints on the number of job slots. Fortunately, the Vera pilot program research provided some basis for making a priori estimates of many of these magnitudes.

The final critical issue that affected sample size was the stage at which random assignment would occur. An enrollee reached the door of a Supported Work program through a process of referral which could be long and complex. At each stage of the referral process, there was the potential for selections to be made that could have affected the character of enrollees relative to that of the universe of members of that target group. For example, were AFDC applicants first screened for their potential in WIN placement programs? Did agencies which referred youth perceive Supported Work as appropriate for last-resort cases or for those whose work prospects were pretty good? Random assignment assured that experimentals and controls were equivalent in the degree of selection applied, but that did nothing to control or record the degree and character of selection prior to random assignment. The farther back in the referral process one reaches in setting the point of drawing the sample and performing random assignment, the greater the degree of generalizability of the results to a wider universe. However, to make such inferences one must attempt to follow up *all* those drawn for the sample at the starting point, no matter where they drop out along the chain of referral. Therefore, the farther back in the chain of referral one draws the sample, the smaller the ratio of ultimate program participants to nonprogram controls, and the greater the costs of interviewing. Thus, the sample design required a compromise between the breadth of the generalizability of the results to the population universe and the costs of follow-up interviewing.

The necessity of enrolling the sample over a long period of time presented opportunities to monitor and redesign the sample in light of information feedback from early interviews and program data. (It also, of course, created problems for administration and, as will be discussed below, for analysis). It was decided at the outset that sample redesign should continue as the demonstration progressed. Information on key values such as the variance of outcome measures (earnings, arrests, drug use), rates of movement through the program, attrition from the interview sample, and the costs of interviewing was gathered periodically and the statistical power likely to be yielded by various subsamples reestimated.

There are many technical details about the initial sample design and its revision that may be of interest to some readers.[1] However, only a few will be discussed here.

The sample design was developed so as to maximize, subject to a budget constraint, the statistical power of estimates of program effects (on earnings or recidivism rates for crime or drug use) in a pooled time series–cross-section regression model. The original sample design called for baseline interviews with 5,400 research subjects (experimentals plus controls). This sample of 5,400 would build up over time as the program operators at the sites increased the number of positions and, eventually, as vacancies in the positions (due to firings, quits, or completions) were filled. This build-up stage of the research sample is referred to as the enrollment period. All 5,400 subjects enrolled were to be given a second, follow-up interview 12 months later. A subset of 2,722 of these individuals were to be interviewed a third time 18 months after the baseline, and a further subset of 1,633 would be interviewed again (a fourth interview) 24 months after the baseline. The two subsets for the longer interview periods were to be *randomly* selected.

The rate at which program positions were increased and filled at the sites was obviously a principal determinant of how fast the research sample could be built up. Slower increase meant that the period of enrollment would be longer, ultimate research results would be delayed, and higher costs would be incurred. The early experience at several sites showed that, in fact, the build-up would be slower than was originally projected. In light of this, two decisions were made. First, two additional research sites were added to the eight originally selected, permitting both a faster build-up of the research sample and an increase in the total samples of AFDC women and youth which had been, perhaps, precariously small in the original design. Second, in one site more controls than experimentals (three control subjects for every two experimental subjects) were enrolled,[2] thus permitting the research sample at this site to grow somewhat faster than the number of positions in the Supported Work program.

The greatest change in the design resulted from a decision to drop the requirement that the subset of those chosen to have the longer follow-up (three or four interviews rather than just two) should be chosen randomly. The key to this decision was the realization that the fixed costs of interviewing (having an office at the site and a basic support staff for the interviewers) were far larger and more important than the marginal costs associated with doing an additional interview. In the original design, those in the subset to have the 24-month interviews were equally likely to be drawn from among those enrolled at the end of the enrollment period as from those enrolled at the beginning. This would have required that the site interviewing offices be kept open for as long as 24 months after the end of the enrollment period in order to interview a relatively small number of subjects. It became clear that this was not an efficient use of resources and that it would be more efficient to try to keep the site interview offices open for as short a period as possible but to interview as many subjects as possible, regardless of when enrolled, while a site office was open. A formalized treatment of this insight showed that, for the same budget costs as in the old design, a new design would reduce the standard errors of the estimate of the program impacts substantially (where the impact is estimated as the experimental-control differential at 18 months, the standard errors would be 30 percent smaller). In addition, a portion of the sample could be interviewed a fifth time.

The only cost of the altered design was that the length of the follow-up (the number of postbaseline interviews) would be correlated with the time the subject was enrolled; those enrolled at the start-up of the program would have the longest follow-up period. It was realized at the time that this correlation could ultimately cause problems in the analysis—and, in fact, as will be seen in the discussion below, it subsequently did cause problems. Nevertheless, it could be shown that the revised design was unequivocally better since it produced larger sample sizes for each length of follow-up.[3]

A final design change resulted from the decision to shift to follow-up interviews at 9-month intervals after the baseline. This meant a shorter interval between the baseline interview and the first follow-up (which it was hoped would reduce attrition) and more regularity in the follow-up intervals, making analysis somewhat easier.

Subsequent to the primary evaluation, it was decided to obtain further follow-up data for the AFDC and youth target groups; the design of the AFDC follow-up strategy is discussed in the chapter by Hollister and Maynard on findings for the AFDC target group (chapter 4); the design of the youth follow-up strategy is discussed in the chapter by Maynard on findings for that target group (chapter 7).

In addition to deciding on the number and frequency of the interviews, it was necessary to determine their content. It was clear from the outset that the interviews would provide the major measurements of employment, transfer payment receipt, criminal behavior, and drug use. These subjects were dictated by the employment emphasis of Supported Work and by the special problem areas of the selected target groups, and the major issues were those of the method of measurement. No serious problems were anticipated in the employment area. The primary innovation was the development of a continuous timeline approach to measuring work and other activity covering the entire period between interviews. For crime and drug use, however, there were significant problems because the reliability of the interviewees' self-reports of criminal and drug activity was naturally open to some question. Ultimately it proved feasible to sample official records to check on the reliability of self-reported arrest data[4] and to correct, roughly, for inaccuracies. For drug use, however, sole reliance had to be placed on self-reports, as careful investigation indicated that there simply were no superior alternatives.

Beyond these primary measurement areas, there was some debate as to the priorities for other subjects of investigation. It was decided that minimal measurements would be made in the areas of education, family structure, health, and housing and that no measurements would be made of political participation or "softer" sociological and psychological dimensions.

The consequence of the interviewing and sample size decisions was a rather complex design. Table 2.3 provides the details of the final design of the interview sample by target group and by the number and timing of the follow-up interviews. As that table illustrates, the critical decision was made to maximize the number of persons observed and interviewed by varying the length of the follow-up for various segments of the sample. Those who entered the program at the outset were given a baseline interview at the point of random assignment and four more interviews at 9-month intervals, providing a total of 36 months of follow-up data. Only about a sixth of the total sample was scheduled

TABLE 2.3
Number of Scheduled Interviews, by Target Group

Interview Type	AFDC	Ex-addict	Ex-offender	Youth	Total
Baseline	1620	1433	2305	1252	6610
9-month	1620	1433	2305	1252	6610
18-month	1620	1433	2305	1252	6610
27-month	783	1221	1582	719	4305
36-month	0	472	505	202	1179

to receive this complete set of interviews. Those enrolled at the end of the random assignment procedure were given a baseline, a 9-month, and an 18-month interview. Except for the ex-addicts, this group is larger than the one being interviewed over the 36-month period, one reason being that its members were enrolled during a period when the sites had reached their maximum sizes in terms of job slots and could take on a larger number in any given time period. Those enrolled in the middle period were given baseline, 9-, 18-, and 27-month interviews. Thus, the amount of follow-up ranges from 36 months for a small group to 18 months for a much larger group. The extent of the follow-up differs across target groups primarily because those sites that were chosen to concentrate on ex-addicts and ex-offenders were, for a variety of reasons, able to get started earliest following the planning period, whereas those taking AFDC women were much slower in getting under way.

It was realized at the outset that in choosing this design researchers were going to create a data set in which length of follow-up, stage of program development and its size, and labor market conditions would be confounded and that this could cause headaches at the analysis stage. But alternative designs would simply have thrown away information (about the experience of the early enrollees in months 27–36) for no gain in sample design efficiency. Readers are urged to consider carefully this issue of differential length of follow-up since, as will be seen in the chapters that follow, the anticipated headaches materialized to some degree.

Benefit-Cost

The interviews, supplemented by some official records, were to be the major source of measurement of the effects of Supported Work on the opportunities and behavior of the participants compared to the control group. Whatever the effects on behavior, however, there were further measurements and analysis that would have to be made in order to evaluate the program's effectiveness. Most of these measures and analysis come together in the framework created for a benefit-cost analysis.

Benefit-cost analysis represents an attempt to bring together in a consistent form an accounting of the resources used in a program and the economic and social effects generated by that program. The concept of such an accounting is seductive because of the implied promise of consistency and completeness and, perhaps, a summary simplifying conclusion. On reflection, however, it becomes apparent that if benefits are to be summed in order to balance them against costs, the benefits must be quantified in comparable units, and some important benefits are not susceptible to such quantification. For example, suppose the program had the effect of substantially reducing heroin addiction among participants. How should this be quantified? Is the value of such a change to be measured by the cost of a stay in an addiction treatment center? Most people would argue, I believe, that society would value a change in heroin addiction at more than that cost, but how much more? And what about the reduced stress on the family of an addict?

From the outset, the planners—and particularly the members of the Board of Directors of MDRC—were acutely aware of the dangers that a benefit-cost analysis could become reductive and misleading rather than complete and illuminating. However, realizing that such an analysis was an essential part of the research, MDRC helped the researchers to assure that the range of data required for the analysis was covered as completely as possible, and they carefully reviewed the procedures adopted.

The range of required data was, in fact, quite extensive. Table 2.4 summarizes the accounting framework of the benefit-cost study and indicates the data sources utilized. It also indicates those aspects of benefits and costs that could not be quantified. On the basis of this table, a few comments are in order about the structure of the benefit-cost analysis.

As can be seen from the table, the participant interviews were the primary sources of the data on benefits. The accounting system of the Supported Work Demonstration provided most of the cost data (aside from costs due to the participants' forgone earnings, which were estimated from the control group's earnings recorded in the interviews). But each of these major sources had to be supplemented by special studies, the most important and difficult of which arose from the necessity to value the benefits derived from the output of goods and services produced by the participants while they were working at the Supported Work sites.

On the surface it may appear that in order to value the output produced by Supported Work participants, one need simply look at the volume of the product produced and multiply by the market price for that product. In fact, in almost all cases the valuation was far more difficult. The following are just a few of the considerations which complicate the process:

Few of the products produced were readily standardized— landscaping, painting a house, cleaning and sealing abandoned houses, assisting in food services; all are relatively nonhomogeneous in units and can have varying

TABLE 2.4

Expected Effects of Benefit-Cost Analysis Components, by Accounting Perspective

	Accounting Perspective			Data Source[a]
	Social	Participant	Nonparticipant	
Benefits				
Produced by participants				
Value of in-program output	+	0	+	S
Increased postprogram output	+	+	0	I,P
Preference for work over welfare	+	+	+	U
Increased tax payments	0	−	+	I
Reduced dependence on transfer				
programs				
Reduced transfer payments	0	−	+	I,P
Reduced administrative costs	+	0	+	I,P
Reduced criminal activity				
Reduced property damage and				
personal injury	+	0	+	I,P,S
Reduced stolen property	+	−	+	I,P,S
Reduced justice system costs	+	0	+	I,P,S
Reduced psychological costs	+	+	+	U
Reduced drug and alcohol use				
Reduced treatment costs	+	0	+	I,P
Psychological benefits	+	+	+	U
Reduced use of alternative education,				
training, and employment services				
Reduced education and employ-				
ment costs	+	0	+	I,P
Reduced training allowances	0	−	+	I,P
Other benefits				
Improved participant health status	+	+	+	U
Income redistribution	+	+	+	U
Costs				
Program operating cost				
Overhead cost	−	0	−	A,S
Project cost	−	0	−	A,S
Central administrative cost	−	0	−	S
Participant labor cost				
In-program earnings plus fringes	0	+	−	I,S,A
Forgone earnings plus fringes	−	−	0	I,P
Forgone nonmarket activities	−	−	0	U
Increased work-related cost				
Child care	−	−	−	I,P
Other	−	−	0	U

Note: The components have been listed under "benefits" or "costs" according to whether they were expected to lead to benefits or costs from a social perspective. The contrasts between the expected effects from the social perspective and those from the participant and nonparticipant perspectives are shown by indicating, for each component, whether the net impact is to be a net benefit (+), a net cost (−), or neither (0).

a The codes used for data sources are: S—special study, I—interview data, P—published data source, A—Supported Work accounting system data, U—item not measured.

levels of quality. Although it is sometimes useful to talk about a single market price, for almost any product or service at a point in time there is in fact a range of prices quoted by different providers. For example, janitorial services can be provided by large firms with a lot of equipment on a contract basis or by a couple of individuals with mops and buckets, and the price range can be quite large—and, of course, the quality varies. Since what is really sought is a measure of value added, it is necessary to have a good accounting and valuation of inputs. In something like housing rehabilitation, the problem of valuing the property prior to rehabilitation and after rehabilitation is quite difficult. Some inputs may be supplied below the usual market price because Supported Work is a project considered worthy of charity. One might think that where the output has been purchased, the revenue would be a measure of value. However, revenue may over- or undervalue the output because the operators may have misjudged the market for the product or, again, special commitments may have been made to buy goods or services at above market prices because of the nature of the program.

Once again, the Vera Wildcat program research pointed the way in terms of methods for dealing with the problems of valuing output, but the scale and range of output to be valued posed far greater problems for Supported Work. The valuation of a given type of output was necessarily time-consuming and relatively expensive, and the valuation of a given product or service could and did vary considerably among the sites. Thus, it was not possible to value all of the output produced in the research sites; rather, a sample of site activities had to be selected, intensively studied and valued, and then generalized to the output of the research sites as a whole.[5] That this intensive research effort was worthwhile can be judged perhaps by the fact that, as will be described in the chapter on benefit-cost analysis by Kemper, Long, and Thornton, the value of output produced was equal to more than 50 percent of the per-participant costs.

Returning to table 2.4, I would like to comment briefly on the headings of the columns entitled Accounting Perspective. Most economists doing benefit-cost analysis have found that they have had difficulty getting people to understand the concept of "social net benefits" (that is, a concept of benefits and costs that excludes transfers) and, even when understood, to accept that perspective as the "best" one to be taken. This was again the case in Supported Work. A perspective that precludes counting among the benefits the reduction in welfare payments is, in general, unacceptable among noneconomists and particularly among those close to the political arena, as are representatives of the funding agencies.

The researchers dealing with the Supported Work benefit-cost analysis carefully defined three accounting perspectives. The first, and most easily understood, was that of the participant. From the participant's viewpoint, it was clear that a reduction in a welfare benefit caused by increased earnings was a loss, that an unemployment insurance payment was a gain, and that taxes paid on earnings were a loss.

The second perspective defined was that of nonparticipants, presumably the rest of society. For them, a reduction in welfare payments to participants and an increase in taxes participants pay were clearly gains, but unemployment insurance benefits paid to participants were a loss. The label "taxpayer's perspective," which has been popular in some quarters, was carefully avoided both because of its divisive social connotations and because, in fact, a large number of participants in Supported Work were themselves taxpayers.

The division into participant and nonparticipant perspectives was made carefully in such a way that transfers between these two groups are clearly gains for one and losses for the others. Therefore, when the benefit and cost entries for the two groups are summed, the net benefits and net costs are equivalent to the usual economist's concepts of social costs and social benefits—and this is the third accounting perspective presented.

In table 2.4, each of the entries is either a plus, a minus, or a zero, indicating whether from that accounting perspective the benefit (or cost) would be positive, negative, or not counted. One can see by following across a given row that when transfers are involved, the plus and minus from participant and nonparticipant cancel out and the entry is zero from the social perspective—for example, reduced transfer payments. But where real resource costs or benefits are involved, the net of the two perspectives yields a plus (for example, for reduced administrative costs of transfers) or a minus (for example, forgone earnings of participants). Great care was taken in the research design and implementation to assure that the benefit-cost analysis data could be presented from all three perspectives.

There are two final aspects of the benefit-cost analysis to which I would like to draw attention. Both have to do with the importance of making as clear as possible the points at which critical *assumptions* enter into the benefit-cost analysis. The first is that the researchers have taken unusual pains to clarify exactly the point at which the analysis is based on actually observed behavior of participants—as well as on the costs side, the observed behavior of operators—and where it begins to depend on assumptions about extrapolating that behavior into an unobserved future or into an unobserved universe of potential participants (or operators). Thus, benefits and costs are broken down and reported according to the period of observation in which they were measured, that is, months 1–9 after enrollment, months 10–18, or months 19–27, etc. This makes it clear that, for a program like Supported Work, to complete a benefit-cost analysis one *must* make some *assumptions* about the future unobserved benefits and costs—the behavior of experimentals in the period beyond and further costs which can upset the benefit-cost balance as it stands at the end of the obervation period (though, of course, the discount rate tends to reduce the impact of contingencies very remote in time).

Second, researchers have taken pains to conduct and to present an unusually large amount of sensitivity analysis. All the major, and several minor, assumptions have been varied within a reasonable range and their impact on benefits and costs assessed, making it much easier for the reader to see where benefits or costs and their balance shift sharply as a result of alternative assumptions. The danger mentioned above, that the analysis is reductive or misleading, is reduced when such extensive sensitivity tests are undertaken and reported.

The MIS System and Process Analysis

To help fulfill its role as the agency coordinating the demonstration, it was decided that MDRC should have a fairly complex Management Information System (MIS) through which the various sites reported similar information regarding their program processes. It was realized that the data generated by such a system could also prove to be quite useful for certain aspects of the research. The researchers were invited to participate in the design of the system so that it could be shaped to facilitate research functions wherever possible without unduly distorting the management objectives of the system or imposing excessive costs. The feature that was key to the research uses of the system was that data were reported and preserved at the micro level so that it was possible to track participants through the program processes, identifying not only when they entered the program and when they left and for what reasons, but also the work activities in which they participated and their rate of attendance. Data were also reported on the character of the work projects.

The availability of data from the MIS greatly enhanced the benefit-cost analysis. It was the existence of these data that permitted calculations of lengths of stay in the program and hours devoted to various types of work programs (which was necessary for the value-of-output calculations and allocation of costs).

It was also on the basis of the MIS data that a quantitative analysis of the processes in Supported Work and how they affected outcomes was possible. The process analysis, which is described in detail elsewhere,[6] was a multivariate analysis which related the character of the participants' Supported Work experience to such outcome variables as attendance and length of stay in Supported Work and the type of termination (whether the participant left to a job, was fired, or withdrew for other reasons such as health), and to postprogram outcomes such as hours of work and earnings. Variables which reflected the participants' work experience were developed for the type of work, the work environment (size of the crew, characteristics of other crew members), the type of supervision, and whether the work was for private or public sector clients.

The attempt to link the internal components of an employment program to outcome measures in a quantitative framework was, as far as I know, unique. It should be noted, of course, that in this process analysis it was necessary to use nonexperimental methods, as there was no random assignment of participants to types of work or supervision and, thus, the question of selection bias in any effects found remained difficult to deal with. It was realized from the outset that it was far from certain that the process analysis would yield major results. After all, if the sample size was deemed to be just sufficient to detect effects of the program as a whole on experimentals in a given target group, how could it be expected to yield statistically significant coefficients for type of work experience to which only a subsample of participants had been exposed? However, given the potential provided by the micro data from the Management Information System and the ability to combine those data with the interview data, it was decided that an exploratory effort was worth trying.

Documentation

In addition to the primarily quantitative research effort represented by the analysis of the interview data, the benefit-cost analysis, and the process analysis, a more qualitative effort to assess the program processes was carried out under the title of "documentation." This effort was based primarily on observations and reports by the staff of MDRC, supplemented by consultant reports. The objective was to document and explain the variations among the sites in style of management, types of jobs created, placement efforts, funding strategies, and the general political, economic, and institutional context in which the program operated. This effort was directed by Joseph Ball of the MDRC staff, and the findings are summarized in the following chapter on program implementation.

Implementation of the Research

The main focus of this volume is to be the results of the research, and I have already been overlong in reviewing the background of the demonstration and the design of the research. However, I would like to make a few comments about aspects of the implementation of the research which I think are of interest and which are difficult to work into the necessarily compact discussion of the results.

Random Assignment

The central experimental aspect of the research, random assignment of enrollees to experimental (participant) or control groups, was carried to completion without any technical disruption. It is important to note that operators were permitted to interview all those referred *prior* to random assignment and to eliminate any persons they felt would be too disruptive to their programs. Once they had screened referrals, those *remaining* were randomly assigned to program participation or to the control group. Although there were no technical problems with this process, the whole procedure was greatly resented by most of the operators, whose negative views were strongly reinforced by the agencies that referred potential enrollees to a site program. These hostile attitudes to random assignment were deeply embedded and yielded not at all to any sort of rational argument. For example, it did no good to point out that there were, in any case, a limited number of positions because, as with any program, there were limited funds or that in most cases of referral to training or employment programs, agencies were rarely able to place anywhere near 100 percent of those referred. My own suspicion is that even though, in reality, there was no loss of control, since the operators and the agencies had the opportunity to screen referrals, the random assignment requirement reinforced both their *feelings* that they had lost control as well as their resentment of the process. It was only because of MDRC's adamant refusal to concede on this issue, and its insistence on making it a prerequisite for continued funding at research sites, that the process was carried out successfully over such a long period of time. As far as the research organization could discern, there was very little resentment of the random assignment process on the part of the enrollees themselves. Perhaps it will be easier to apply this method in future studies of employment programs since it will be possible to point to the successful implementation of it, on a large scale, in the Supported Work Demonstration.

The random assignment had to be carried out during the enrollment period for the research sample, which stretched from March 1975 to

July 1977, and during those months the site operators continually inquired about how much longer the process had to continue. Their reaction to the notification of the termination of enrollment and random assignment apparently was one of joy and relief.

The final number of interviews completed and of sufficient quality to be used in the analysis are reported in table 2.5.[7] As can be seen, the completion rates (number of usable interviews/numbers of interviews assigned in the final design), which are reported in parentheses for each target group and each period, range from a high of 83 percent for AFDC at 18 months to a low of 57 percent for ex-offenders at 36 months. When compared to other follow-up surveys for groups even roughly similar to the Supported Work targets, these completion rates are quite good. Still, one might wonder about the degree to which attrition from the sample may have biased the estimates of the effects of the demonstration: Were those who failed to respond to follow-up interviews significantly better or worse than those who did respond, and were they differentially represented among experimentals and controls? Fortunately it was possible to utilize methods recently developed to estimate selection bias in order to investigate the extent to which attrition may have biased the estimated effects of the program on employment, arrests, and drug use. The analyst, Randall Brown, concluded:

TABLE 2.5

Maximum Sample Size for Analysis, by Follow-up Period, Target Group, and Site

| | Follow-up Period (months after enrollment) | | | | | | | | | | |
| | AFDC | | Ex-addict | | | Ex-offender | | | Youth | | |
	1–18	19–27	1–18	19–27	28–36	1–18	19–27	28–36	1–18	19–27	28–36
Total	1351	616	974	885	311	1479	1003	287	861	513	153
Completion rate (%)	(83)	(79)	(68)	(73)	(66)	(65)	(64)	(57)	(69)	(71)	(76)
Site											
Atlanta	148	74	—	—	—	—	—	—	83	15	0
Chicago	234	133	226	172	64	224	145	45	—	—	—
Hartford	109	52	—	—	—	172	135	17	384	232	20
Jersey City	—	—	385	347	117	148	136	63	192	170	85
Newark	242	161	—	—	—	275	135	13	—	—	—
New York	463	136	—	—	—	—	—	—	135	18	0
Oakland	129	38	89	57	4	348	186	31	—	—	—
Philadelphia	—	—	274	309	126	137	136	71	67	78	48
San Francisco	—	—	—	—	—	175	130	47	—	—	—
Wisconsin	26	22	—	—	—	—	—	—	—	—	—

We find very little evidence that interview nonresponse tends to bias our conclusions. Of the large or statistically significant findings, only the estimate of Supported Work's impact on hours worked by youth in the 10 to 18 month period is altered much (from $+13$ hours significant at the 3% level to $+16$ hours significant at the 1% level) by the adjustment for potential nonresponse bias. Small and insignificant estimates remain so, generally exhibiting inconsequential changes in absolute magnitude.[8]

The Role of Preliminary Findings

The results of preliminary analyses of research data were reported very rapidly; for example, the analysis of a partial sample of interviews given nine months after enrollment was reported in early 1977, just a few months after the last of the interviews of this sample had been administered. This early analysis helped in making subsequent decisions on the final sample design or on redesign of interview questions, and the speeding-up of the analysts' familiarity with data types helped to reduce the time lag between the final research interviews and the final reports. Nevertheless, a major failure of the research, in my view, was the inability to provide feedback to the operators about the effects of their particular programs or about those aspects of program design—types of jobs, types of supervisors, etc.—which were most or least effective. The causes were threefold. First, as already noted, the sample size could be built up only slowly so that the samples for individual sites were inadequate to yield significant quantitative results until rather late in the project. Second, the quantitative process analysis was innovative and, as such, time was required for the formulation of variables, extraction of appropriate data from the Management Information System, and writing of programs to create the complex variables from these data. This experience with these problems could contribute to a considerable reduction in time lags in the future. Third, MDRC stood as an intermediary between the operators and the researchers and, as mentioned above, concerns about the balance between demonstration objectives and research objectives caused them to try to avoid "excessive" contacts between operators and researchers.

Changes in the External Environment

A final aspect that deserves some special mention is the way the context of the demonstration and research changed over time. There were dramatic shifts in labor conditions during the demonstration period. Not surprisingly, the planners had not anticipated that the demonstration would get under way while the United States was in the deepest recession it had experienced since the 1930s. The recession not only made it more difficult than expected to create jobs in which the participants could work while in the program, but it also made postprogram placement quite problematical. The job market improved steadily as the demonstration progressed, making life somewhat easier for the participants, the operators, and the members of the control group, but it also complicated, as will be seen repeatedly in the chapters which follow, the analysis of the research results.

Most concretely, the recession led to the creation at the national level of the Special Unemployment Assistance (SUA) program, which paid benefits to unemployed workers who had been previously employed but not covered by the regular unemployment insurance program. With the exception of one site, New York, where it was required by state law, the Supported Work program did not pay the unemployment insurance tax and, therefore, participants were not eligible for regular unemployment insurance payments. However, in some of the sites, participants were able to persuade the local unemployment insurance offices that their time spent in Supported Work should qualify them for benefits under SUA. The ability to obtain SUA benefits was very uneven across sites, target groups, and time. The control group did not have the Supported Work employment period as a basis to argue for SUA eligibility. To the extent that receipt of such benefits discouraged workers from taking jobs, this could obviously have an impact on the measured experimental-control employment differentials. The fact that more experimentals than controls received SUA benefits presented an unanticipated challenge to the research analysts.

Partly as a result of the recession and partly because of other trends in social programs at the national level, over time the availability of alternative employment and training programs for some of the target groups increased. Most particularly, the Comprehensive Employment and Training Act (CETA) program increased the number of positions it funded in several of the cities in which the demonstration operated, and toward the end of the demonstration period there was a sharp rise in funds assigned to youth employment and training programs. These developments had the potential of affecting experimental-control differentials in either direction. On the one hand, the control group might have had increasing access to programs whose general objectives were similar to those of Supported Work, thereby reducing experimental-control employment differences as well as the apparent postprogram effects of Supported Work. On the other hand, through Supported Work, participants could have made contacts which would have increased the probability that they would have greater access than did the controls to such opportunities, and this could have widened the experimental-control difference.

One other dimension of the changing context added complications to the research. It appears that during the course of the demonstration there was a shift in "the drug scene," with a rather substantial decline in the availability and use of heroin and an increase in the availability and use of cocaine. When early analysis showed a comparatively sharp drop in self-reported heroin use among both experimentals and controls, there were concerns that the research subjects might be becoming increasingly leery about, or weary of, reporting their drug use. However, on the basis of careful analyses of interviews on the same calendar date but at different lengths of time after enrollment, as well as of external reports of drug availability "on the street," it was possible for the researchers to attribute these changes to shifts in the general availability of drugs rather than to defects of the data collection.

The Research Findings

The chapters that follow describe and discuss the details of the implementation of the demonstration programs and of the research findings for each of the four target groups. Below, therefore, I simply wish to identify a few common threads which run through the analyses, cover a few points which fall outside the range of the particular target group discussions, and emphasize certain points which I feel deserve special attention.

The Cohort Phenomenon

It was noted earlier in the sample-size discussions that the total research sample must be subdivided not only by target group but also by the length of the follow-up within each target group. It was also noted in the section on implementation that the context in which the program operated was shifting in certain key respects over time. This meant that correlations developed in the sample data between the length of follow-up and the conditions that participants experienced. As shown in table 2.5, the groups with 36 months of follow-up are quite small: none for AFDC, about 300 for ex-addicts and ex-offenders, and only about 150 for youths. These individuals were enrolled when unemployment rates in the labor markets were highest, when the Supported Work programs at their sites were small, and when operators were relatively inexperienced. Those with shorter follow-up periods were enrolled at times when labor markets were improving, the Supported Work programs were larger, and operators were more experienced. Some of those with 27 months of follow-up were enrolled during the period when the Supported Work program at their site was attempting to expand very rapidly. All of these factors could have influenced the way in which the program affected experimentals as well as the opportunities and experiences of the controls. It is particularly important for readers to be aware of these underlying correlations when examining the data on the outcome measures. For example, if one looks at a data series showing hours of work differences between experimentals and controls as a function of the number of months since enrollment, one should be aware that the composition of the sample shifts at 19 months and at 28 months. In terms of research analysis, it becomes necessary to address the question: To what extent are the data covering months 28–36 generated by the sample with 36 months of follow-up likely to be good predictors of what the experience would be during a similar period after enrollment for those who were followed for only 27 months or for 18 months? Therefore, the researchers began to think in terms of "cohorts" defined by the length of follow-up and to carry out analyses in that light.

Though the sample sizes in these 36-month cohorts are relatively small, the researchers found it difficult to resist giving a great deal of attention to the information they provided. For example, when hours worked or crime rates showed a rise or a drop during months 28–36, did this represent the fading out or a pick-up of the effects of the Supported Work program, or did it reflect differences between the 36-month cohort and groups that were enrolled later? To a large degree it was possible to control statistically for any differences among cohorts due to differences in measured characteristics, and it was possible to test for homogeneity of the two "cohort" samples during months 1–18 following enrollment. In most cases these statistical measures indicated that the "cohort phenomenon" was not significant, but a few major questions remained unresolved regarding what could be inferred from the long-term follow-up group about the likely experience over the longer term of those with short-term follow-ups. This issue is complicated. The reader should be alert to the possibilities of such "cohort problems" in the findings reported but, at the same time, to the danger of reading into the data such problems where they do not exist (at least to the degree that they can be ruled out by normal criteria of statistical inference). As will be discussed below, aspects of the benefit-cost analysis are particularly helpful in indicating when "cohort phenomena" pose serious problems and when they do not.

Role of the Control Group

The control group data provided the most important tool in the research analysis. Consider figure 2.1, which gives the hours worked for the experimentals in each of the four target groups, and concentrate

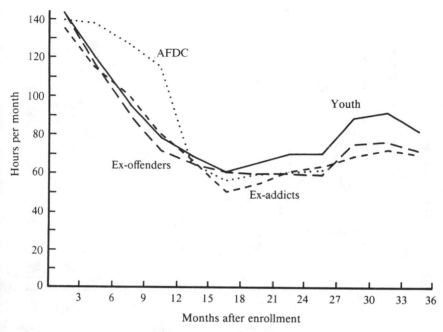

Fig. 2.1. Average Hours Worked per Month: Experimentals

on the postprogram period—from approximately month 15 onward. If one were to reach a conclusion on the basis of these data alone, it would appear that Supported Work had been most effective for the youth group, followed by ex-offenders, then ex-addicts, and lastly the AFDC women. However, when one subtracts off the controls' hours of work for each group and gets the experimental-control difference in hours, as shown in figure 2.2, the judgment about relative program effectiveness is completely reversed: the program appears to be most effective for AFDC and least effective for youth.

Now, it is easy to say that no one would be so foolish as simply to compare the relative hours of work of those who had been in the program without reference to some sort of comparison group, but if Supported Work had been carried out as only a demonstration, without the added research dimension that included control groups, this sort of comparison would have been the major basis for judgments about the groups for which Supported Work was relatively most successful. Furthermore, it seems reasonable to question whether any "comparison group" constructed without recourse to random assignment really would have captured the subtleties of these trends. The problems of

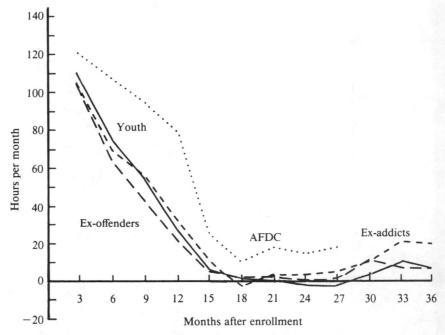

Fig. 2.2. Experimental-Control Differences in Hours Worked per Month

the "cohort phenomenon" add weight, in my view, to the doubt that methods other than random assignment would have been nearly as precise and powerful.

It is important also, however, to use the control group data not merely to convert trends for the experimentals into differences between experimentals and controls. The data should be examined in their own right, for they provide insights as to the possible sources of relative success and failure among groups. From figure 2.3—trends in hours worked for the control groups alone—we can see the sharp increase in the hours worked among the youth control group, which helps us to see that the "failure" of Supported Work with the experimental group can be attributed primarily to this control group trend, over time from enrollment. If the "failure" of Supported Work here had resulted because both experimentals and controls had had no increase over time in hours of work, we might have drawn quite different conclusions than in the case where both groups showed rather sharp rises—the experimentals no faster than the controls.

Two sorts of comparisons can be made with regard to the Supported Work youth controls. First, as already noted, when compared to other

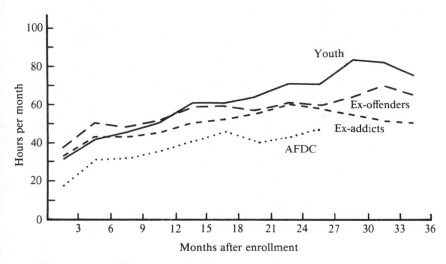

Fig. 2.3. Hours Worked by Control Group Members

Supported Work controls, the sharp relative upward trend in hours suggests that the youths had a less serious job-access problem than did the other groups. Second, when youth controls are compared to other youth groups, it is clear that, despite the upward trend in hours, they had continuously poorer work experience than did other youth groups. From these two comparisons, it appears that, while the Supported Work youth group was more disadvantaged than most other youths, their problems were not those which Supported Work was most effective in overcoming. It may be that for these youths, access to jobs is less of a problem than job stability, but it is not immediately evident how Supported Work might be redesigned so as to enhance the job-retention rates for such youths.

Some Major Themes in the Findings

An overview of the results yields certain broad, qualitative conclusions. From the viewpoint of society as a whole, Supported Work can be judged to have been successful for the AFDC and ex-addict target groups in terms of increasing opportunities and reducing dependency and social costs. For the youth group, Supported Work did not significantly alter opportunities or behaviors from what they would have been in the absence of Supported Work experience. For the ex-offender group, no firm conclusion can be drawn; some aspects suggest positive net effects, others negative net effects.

The source of success or failure varies from group to group. For AFDC, success comes primarily from the increase in postprogram employment above the relatively low employment levels the control group experienced. For the ex-addicts, while there is an effect of sizable magnitude on postprogram employment among those who enrolled during periods of high unemployment, it is the benefit from reduced crime both during and after the program which is central to the judgment that the program is successful. For youths, the strong upward trends in employment among the control group has already been discussed. Supported Work seems not to have been a sharp enough intervention to alter either the behavior—in employment, drugs, or criminal behavior—or the opportunities for this group of youths. For ex-offenders, the research does not yield a firm qualitative conclusion. The uncertainty arises because substantial significant effects in terms of reduced crime, and to a much lesser extent in terms of employment, appear in months 28–36 after enrollment. This is an example of the "cohort phenomenon" which creates uncertainties that simply cannot be dispelled by analysis.

In drawing these broad, perhaps overly facile, conclusions, I have made extensive use of the benefit-cost analyses. At the outset I noted the danger that benefit-cost analyses may be reductive and misleading. In the case of Supported Work, however, these analyses have been particularly helpful in putting together the mosaic of research results for each target group, indicating where technical problems and their related uncertainties are trivial when weighed in the general conclusions and where they are so significant as to preclude any overall conclusion. In this regard, the extensive sensitivity analyses undertaken were of particular importance. They showed that while the dollar magnitude of benefits minus costs (in the various perspectives) varied as assumptions were altered, the qualitative conclusions about the relative success or failure of Supported Work were not sensitive to variations in assumptions over a reasonable range; in fact, they were amazingly robust under alternative assumptions. One should be clear that this is not a necessary result of the methodology utilized; the results for any of the target groups *could have been* within a range such that they could have shifted from net benefits which are positive to net benefits which are negative under variations in key assumptions. The results for the ex-offenders illustrate that this was a very real possibility with any of the groups.

Readers will find a rich variety of research findings in the chapters focusing on individual target groups. However, beyond conclusions that are specific to a target group, there are a few other broad themes that I would like to identify.

It seems a safe generalization that the Supported Work experience has its greatest effect with those participants who were "worst off," where that term is defined by the values that are most extreme from a social point of view—for example, lowest employment or earnings, the higher crime or drug-use rates. This generalization clearly holds for the employment findings for the target groups: AFDC had the lowest values for control group employment; youths had, over the long term, the highest. But, more important, this phenomenon appeared repeatedly when analysis was done within each target group to determine among which subgroups the program effects were strongest. For example, among AFDC women, those who had no prior work experience had the lowest number of hours of work among the controls and the largest differential in hours worked between experimentals and controls. As part of this generalization, it was also observed that for those who entered the program early, when unemployment rates in the labor markets were generally high and employment rates among the controls were low, the effect of Supported Work in raising experimentals' hours of work above those of controls was generally greater than for later "cohorts" when the hours of work of controls were higher, due, apparently, to better labor market conditions.

It was noted earlier, at several places, that there was considerable diversity among the sites in content and style of program operation, and, therefore, there was concern among the researchers that the sample might have to be further fragmented across sites because of these differences in Supported Work experience. Though there were differences in the various outcome measures across sites, they did not show any coherent pattern and, in general, site differences were insignificant under standard statistical tests.

The single systematic variation in program structure—the difference across sites in the maximum length of stay permitted (12 versus 18 months)—yielded no significant effects primarily because there were no significant differences in the *observed* length of stay between the two structures. (Average length of stay at the 12-month sites ranged from 5.5 to 9.7 months; at 18-month sites the range was from 5.3 to 7.4 months.) What happened with this aspect of the demonstration, I believe, was that a firm commitment to the planned variation was lacking. Although the site planners, or the operators, who first committed themselves to this variation expressed the belief that an important aspect of the program should be the discretion of allowing persons to stay in the demonstration for more than 12 months, in practice, as their programs developed, the views of the operating managements about the importance of this aspect either shifted or diminished; in sum, the systematic variation in length of stay was never operational.

Beyond the overall effects of Supported Work, one might wonder whether the length of time experimentals stayed in a Supported Work program had an effect on their postprogram outcomes: Do those who stay longer in a program have better employment, less drug use, fewer arrests than do those who stay only a short time? Analysis of this issue must be done with some care because selection factors affecting length of stay may also affect outcomes. For example, workers who stay longer in the program may be inherently better motivated and able to adjust to work discipline. If this is the case, the longer program exposure may appear to generate better outcomes when what is really happening is that it simply labels the better motivated among the experimentals. (The selection could work in the reverse fashion if the more able among the experimentals leave the program early to take non-Supported Work jobs and the less able stay on, having no better opportunity.) Selection bias techniques were used to analyze the selection effects, and the results showed that when selection bias corrections were made, the length of stay had no effect on outcomes except for the AFDC group. For this group, after correction for selection bias, a longer time in the program was associated with somewhat higher postprogram outcomes.[9]

Process analysis was another technique adopted to try to determine which dimensions of the Supported Work experience had the greatest impact for which groups. The results are not reviewed in this volume. The views as to the success of the process analysis range from strongly negative to mildly positive. MDRC's staff and Board concluded that "this effort was not very successful and contributed little to an understanding of the usefulness of the components of supported work."[10] As noted earlier, the feedback from this analysis came too late and on too limited a basis to prove useful to the operators. However, I believe that enough was learned from the study to warrant undertaking similar studies of future programs. Perhaps the strongest findings were negative. Some features of the program structure that some operators and observers had believed to be important could be shown to have no statistically significant effects on outcomes. For example, it was widely believed that work in large crews yielded less effective experience, but the analysis showed that crew size had no significant effects on attendance, type of termination, or postprogram earnings. The results did show that different characteristics of supervisors and types of work projects had significantly different effects, but that mixing members from different target groups in a single crew did not have the negative effects that some feared it might.

In addition to the analysis of the impact of Supported Work on employment, crime, and drugs, each considered individually, there was some attempt to examine how effects were interrelated across the various outcome measures; that is, how were effects in employment related to those in crime, or how were crime and drug outcomes related? Unfortunately, there are only a few suggestive hints that can be drawn from these data at this time. First, in all three target groups for which crime and drug data were collected (ex-offenders, ex-addicts, and youth), there was no clear relationship between employment status and drug use; for both experimentals and controls, the rate of drug use among the employed was not very different from that among the unemployed. This evidence is consistent with a hypothesis that drug use is not so disabling that it interferes with work. Second, among those who use drugs, experimentals were somewhat less likely than controls to be arrested. This appears to be consistent with the hypothesis that Supported Work reduced the economic motivation among drug users to commit crimes.

It should be recognized, however, that these sorts of simultaneous, cross-outcome relationships are very difficult to analyze; one is trying to examine two or more simultaneous outcomes, differentiated by experimental and control status, over different periods of time and across three target groups. In addition, where the impacts of the program on a single area were weak—for example, employment for ex-offenders— it would be difficult to establish links between that area and the other outcomes—for example, drug use and crime. It must be admitted frankly that in the body of work reported here, not enough time or resources were devoted to the analysis of these complicated relationships. The Supported Work data provide an unusually rich opportunity to investigate the interrelationships of employment, crime, and drug use. It is hoped that this opportunity will be more fully exploited in the near future.

Research Methodology

In closing this chapter, I would like to make a few observations about research methodology based on the experience of the Supported Work Demonstration. There are many aspects of the research methodology used in Supported Work which are of interest but cannot be discussed here. One central issue, however, is the continuing controversy over experimental versus nonexperimental research methods. The Supported Work experience shows, I believe, that with large social programs such as Supported Work, it cannot be a question of using just one or the other of the methodologies. I have tried to point out above the ways in which the existence of control groups created by random assignment was critical to a proper evaluation of the relative effects of the program on different groups. However, I have also noted many instances of the difficulties in implementing a strictly experimental design. Most important, the "cohort phenomenon," which created problems for the analysis of the Supported Work results, is simply a special case of a more general problem. Any such program will take place in a social and economic context which is changing over time; there will be changes in labor markets, additions and removals of closely related programs (Special Unemployment Assistance, CETA), and evolution and change in the management of the "treatment" program itself. All these will preclude attainment of the neatness which is expected in a classic experimental design. Furthermore, research subjects cannot be followed for a lifetime to get unequivocal results; as is so clearly laid out in the benefit-cost analysis, assumptions must be made and nonexperimental analysis must be done in order to extrapolate results. All of this means that the quantitative analysis of experimentally generated data inevitably will require resort to nonexperimental methods of inference.

I think it is reasonable to conclude that, in spite of a sometimes uneasy balance, both the demonstration and the research fulfilled their distinct objectives. The demonstration showed that a major direct employment program could be mounted, and the participants put in a productive employment setting and, to some degree, moved on from the program to regular employment.

Through the research it was possible to determine that for certain of the participant groups the Supported Work experience had significant effects on their behavior and opportunities. It was also possible to determine where these effects were likely to be great enough to justify the sizable resources required to provide a Supported Work experience. For other groups of participants, the message provided by the research was that the Supported Work effort, however admirably executed, did not affect their opportunities and behavior sufficiently to justify the social costs. It was a strong commitment to detect, at the early stages of a major program's development, the negative as well as the positive outcomes that led the funders and planners of Supported Work to initiate and support this sizable research effort.

Notes

1 See Ruth et al. (1980) for a fuller discussion.
2 Researchers had earlier suggested that such an "unbalanced design"—more controls than experimentals—would be more cost-efficient when viewed in terms of the overall demonstration budget. This suggestion was rejected, primarily on the grounds of difficulties which operators at the sites would face in convincing the agencies they depended on to refer potential participants to go along with random assignment; it was hard enough to get them to send two candidates for each assured job opening, and it was feared that getting them to send more than two for each opening would raise the apparent "rejection rate" to unacceptable levels.
3 The details of the sample redesign and the argument for it are presented in Metcalf and Behrens (1975).
4 See Schore et al. (1979) for an analysis of official compared to self-reported arrest data.
5 After starting with an evaluation of a small number of activities selected judgmentally, the researchers shifted to picking activities on a random basis.
6 See Hollister et al. (1979).
7 For a full description of the interviewing procedures and results, see Jackson et al. (1979).
8 See Brown (1979).
9 See Brown (1980), Brown and Mozer (1981a, b), and Brown and Maynard (1981).
10 See MDRC (1980, 41).

3 *Joseph Ball*

Implementation of the Supported Work Program Model

Supported Work was both experiment and demonstration. A central purpose, at the core of the demonstration design, was the evaluation of its impact on employment-related behavior and its value as a social investment. Program applicants, whose criteria for program eligibility were standardized for four categories of participants, were assigned randomly to treatment or control groups, and the principal elements of a treatment model were specified. The findings of the experiment are the primary topics addressed in this volume. However, Supported Work was also a demonstration, the purposes of which included assessing questions of feasibility and replicability in implementing the program treatment model.

The design considerations in shaping an experiment and a demonstration are convergent but not identical. Whereas experimental research findings are easier to interpret to the extent that variation can be minimized or controlled, demonstration purposes are better met by allowing some natural variation: innovation by local program managers, adapting a program model to their own skills and to local circumstances. Demonstration planners sought to strike a balance between these two purposes.

This chapter will address the process of implementing the Supported Work Demonstration at the 13 sites which started in mid-1975, all but one of which operated throughout the demonstration period that ended in December 1978.[1] Particular attention will be given to the diversity in program strategies which emerged within the rules that defined the experimental treatment model. The worksites developed by local op-

50

erators, the job-search and transitional assistance provided to participants, and the patterns of funding which financed program operations
will be described. In addition, the operating dynamic of local Supported Work programs, the factors which shaped the program treatment locally, and the viability of different program operating strategies
will be assessed. Finally, the during-program performance of participants will be documented.

The discussion is designed to address questions of program replicability and to provide some context for the findings on program impacts which are presented in the succeeding chapters. The analysis will
draw upon extensive qualitative interviewing and field observation by
research and operating staff and consultants to the Manpower Demonstration Research Corporation (MDRC), the nonprofit organization
which designed and oversaw program operation and research.

Background: Inception of the Program Model

The great expansion of employment and training interventions directed at disadvantaged populations in the 1960s was generally not
accompanied by high quality research. In addition, many work experience programs were often criticized for being insufficiently structured and thereby for being more akin to income transfer than to the
experience of productive work. This criticism, under rubrics such as
"leaf raking," has been leveled at government public employment programs since the New Deal.[2]

With these considerations foremost, a coalition of policy-interested
actors from the federal government, the academic community, and
the Ford Foundation saw promise in the replication of a highly structured work experience program for ex-drug addicts that had been
launched by the Vera Institute of Justice in 1972.[3] The program represented a distillation of what many regarded as best practice from
employment programs in the 1960s that were targeted to the severely
disadvantaged. The primary emphasis was on developing realistic work
settings, in which productive output was a major component, carefully
balanced by supports and incentives to assist participants in making
the transition to the requirements of unsubsidized regular employment. This was accomplished through well-structured crew-work projects, closely supervised. The goal of Vera's Wildcat program was not
skill-specific occupational training so much as it was the development
of productive work habits and general work coping skills.

In formulating a plan to replicate Supported Work in other communities, within a demonstration setting, program designers and fund-

ing agencies concluded that the Supported Work vehicle might well be tested with other hard-to-employ groups. Ex-offenders, women who had been long-term recipients of AFDC welfare, and young school dropouts, including delinquents, were added to the ex-addict group.

During 1974 program planners solicited the interest of groups and individuals who by reputation and experience were believed capable of implementing the Supported Work concept. Nineteen were awarded planning grants to develop program proposals, and 13 were selected to begin operation in mid-1975.

The local jurisdictions selected proposed two types of structures for the management of Supported Work. Some created new nonprofit organizations with the sole purpose of operating a Supported Work program. Others delegated the development and management of Supported Work projects to existing agencies with experience in operating employment programs, such as an Urban League chapter in Atlanta, an AFL–CIO Human Resources Development Institute affiliate in West Virginia, a Community Action Agency in Wisconsin, a Community Development Corporation in Oakland, and a local public housing agency in St. Louis. Program guidelines required, however, that existing agencies establish a separate staff unit to operate the program. In most instances these staff units were separately incorporated or located apart from the larger agency, and thus could focus on the specialized demands of operating Supported Work, yet still benefit from the administrative, political, and operating experience of the larger agency.[4]

Planners were concerned that local demonstration projects should not be constrained by overly determined program design guidelines. There was a strong sense that social program success is enhanced when innovative and skillful leadership can be attracted to manage the program and can adapt the program to local conditions. Concurrently, however, demonstration research planners specified certain basic conditions for participant eligibility and program treatment, to permit a rigorous experimental evaluation of program impacts.

The basic demonstration guidelines within which these operators were to plan and implement Supported Work are discussed in further detail below. In addition, the principal tasks which they had to face, to interpret and implement the program treatment model, are set forth briefly. Each of these tasks is discussed in greater detail in succeeding sections.

The Standardization of Eligibility and Treatment Criteria

As discussed in the preceding chapter, negotiations among program designers and the research contractor, Mathematica Policy Research, led to agreement on certain program features which would ensure uniformity. These included eligibility criteria for the ex-addict, ex-of-fender, AFDC, and youth target groups; those criteria were summarized in chapter 2. In addition, program designers specified wage and bonus criteria; maximum periods for participation in Supported Work; rules for random assignment of applicants to experimental and control groups at the sites to be surveyed for program impacts; and a standardized information system for reporting programmatic and fiscal data. Of these standardized program features, perhaps the two that most affected program implementation at the local sites were (1) the eligibility criteria, which required site operators to serve exceptionally disadvantaged workers, and (2) the limits on the maximum length of participation (12 months at some sites, 18 at others), which meant that operators would be employing a workforce that was continually changing.

Parameters of the Program Treatment Model

Program designers concluded that guidelines should set forth a description of the program model, but should not attempt to standardize unduly the services that participants would receive. Primary emphasis was given to developing productive work projects—projects that would be suitable to the general skill levels of participants, that would emphasize tangible output or community service, and that would be amenable to close, didactic supervision.

First, the working pace and demands on participants were to be patterned with sensitivity to the relatively unstructured and episodic working habits which participants brought into the program. Over time as participants worked out these dysfunctional habits, the demands of the work project were to increase toward general standards of industry. This process, called graduated stress, was implemented in a variety of ways: by increasing productivity demands and attendance and punctuality requirements; by assigning workers to increasingly complex work assignments; by gradually decreasing the intensity of supervision; and, not least, by placing on probation or firing participants who were recalcitrant.

Second, reflecting in part the progenitor Wildcat supported work model, program guidelines emphasized work in crews so that participants could share the experience of developing more effective work skills with others from similar backgrounds. Through peer support, it was believed, participants could empathize with and help one another to work through unproductive work patterns.

Program concept papers and guidelines emphasized that Supported Work was to be designed as a transitional program, a developmental bridge from preprogram status to regular work in unsubsidized jobs. Program operators were mandated to develop support services, such as job-search training and job-placement assistance, and were allowed to develop other work-related supportive services as they deemed necessary. The principal constraint specified for support services, apart from their restriction to being directly related to work need, was that participants could spend no more than 25 percent of their paid 40 hours per week participating in these ancillary services.

To provide an incentive for transition, and to provide uniformity for the impact research, MDRC specified that wage rates for participants be standardized at roughly three-fourths of the "market opportunity wage" for the target populations in each program community, but no less than the federal minimum wage. All participants were to be considered employees of the local program and were carried on the program's payroll.

Job-Creation Mandate

A central element in the demonstration was the mandate for local directors to solicit possible work projects within their communities that could serve as effective vehicles for implementing these principal treatment elements. While there were discussions between program design staff and the several organizations that competed for Supported Work operating grants in 1974, local planners were expected to develop their own repertoire of worksites. The set of worksites proposed was one element in selecting the 13 organizations that became Supported Work operators.

Although the programs selected generally had the support of local or state government agencies, the program organizations were, with one exception, independent nonprofit organizations with their own boards of directors. It was expected that nonprofit status would enhance the ability of the local directors to locate work projects, establish a working relationship with a variety of "customers," and manage work projects with the flexibility required to balance the dual emphasis on productive output and program support. Guidelines set forth a few parameters for the kinds of work or customers which local directors could develop, such as the avoidance of "dirty and dangerous" work, and consultation with local unions to elicit support and minimize conflict. Apart from these, programs could develop projects in a wide range of industries and offer to work for government, nonprofit agencies, local businesses, or individuals.

Local Revenue-Raising Mandate

One of the purposes of the demonstration was to test the feasibility and local viability of Supported Work operations as delivery mechanisms. The year during which the Supported Work Demonstration was being designed, 1974, marked the beginning of a decentralized block grant mechanism for federal employment and training funds, established under the Comprehensive Employment and Training Act (CETA). Because of the expected trend toward granting state and local governments greater programmatic discretion, program designers planned for the local Supported Work programs to raise an increasing share of their operating funds over time from local sources. It was expected that local programs would raise 25 percent of their operating revenue from local sources in the first operating year, 1975–1976, with MDRC contributing the 75 percent balance in discretionary national funds from the Ford Foundation and four federal agencies under Department of Labor lead.[5] The objectives for second and third years were to move toward 50/50, then 25/75 national/local funding. One distinction in the funding strategy for Supported Work, compared with many nationally funded demonstrations and employment training programs more generally, was the authorization for local directors to raise revenue on a fee-for-output basis from local customers. Local programs were expected to offset public subsidy costs by charging customers a significant share of a project's total production costs.

Several of the demonstration objectives, particularly the job-creation and local revenue mandates, were drawn sufficiently broadly that local directors could develop their own strategies and draw upon their own skills and local contacts.

The implementation of Supported Work locally was a complex playing out of these several demonstration mandates, some trading off against each other. The sections that follow will describe the implementation of Supported Work locally with respect to the following issues: (1) the factors that contributed to the choices of program worksites by the local programs; (2) the program strategy that emerged from the interplay of operational and program considerations; (3) program job-search assistance and placement; (4) financing local program operations; and (5) the implications of the operating experience for replication of Supported Work under other conditions, in particular the levels of program complexity that may be feasible and the role of a central managing agency. In the final section the program outcomes over the short term for participants in each of the four major target groups will be discussed.

Factors Affecting Worksite Development at Local Programs

The process of searching out local targets of opportunity and developing projects for Supported Workers was partly strategy, partly a function of the local networks in which program directors operated, and partly accident. The results were a great diversity of different worksites across the demonstration. Since program worksites are the central treatment setting, the factors that contributed to the choices of worksites at different programs are worth consideration.[6]

Agreement Reached by the Coalitions Which Sponsored
Local Program Applications

Not surprisingly, work projects developed at several of the 13 original programs reflected in many cases the ties with governments and agencies that had supported the applications for program operation in 1974. For example:

The City of Atlanta supported the program application of the local Urban League. Several work projects involved placement of crews in affiliate government agencies, including the city vehicle garage and the Atlanta airport. These projects lasted the course of the demonstration. Later work projects, for local hospitals and colleges, reflected both city sponsorship and Urban League contacts in the black community.

The Washington state program had initial support from the state Department of Social and Human Services. A major initial project involved a contract to microfilm state records, which then led to microfilm contracts with local and county government agencies. Demolition work on the grounds of a state prison also reflected these initial contacts.

The Wisconsin program was sponsored by a two-county community action agency. Most of the projects developed by the program involved provision of services to the CAP agency's clientele and included light home repair and insulation, furniture repair, and home services for the disadvantaged elderly.

Background and Orientation of the Local Program Directors

The predilections and connections of the local program directors shaped their project search strategies in some instances:

The first director of the Newark program came from several years as a professional in the state health and human services bureaucracy.

Initial commitments of public agency projects from the Newark city government floundered as a result of the city's fiscal crisis. The director arranged with a recently completed state medical services complex in Newark to assign over 75 Supported Workers to work in maintenance, repair, and other shops within the medical complex. These projects became the mainstay of the program throughout the demonstration.

The first director of the Hartford program was a retired industrialist. He set about refurbishing an old factory and established several manufacturing projects within the factory, including furniture construction, concrete molding, tire recapping, upholstery, and printing. His successor, who also had a background in the private sector, continued these projects and developed other manufacturing endeavors.

The Mix of Target Groups

During the planning period in 1974, the sites were able to specify which of the four major target groups, or other disadvantaged groups, they wished to serve in their program. The demonstration managing agent, MDRC, maintained the power to determine the overall allocation of program enrollment by target group, as part of its responsibility to ensure that the research samples had sufficient numbers for statistical analysis of experimental-control group differences.

Program operators generally did not find that the mix of target groups had a major shaping effect upon their worksite development strategies, but there were a few exceptions. The most notable was the development of work that was agreeable to the AFDC target group. The great majority of ex-offenders, ex-addicts, and youths were men, and not all AFDC women found suitable some of the construction and manufacturing worksites to which the others were often assigned. The AFDC women generally enrolled later than the other groups, since MDRC limited enrollments of AFDC participants until welfare waivers had been negotiated (see below).

Some of the sites where AFDC enrollments were high made efforts to develop worksites in human and clerical services for them. The Chicago program, notable for its emphasis on assignment of crews to manufacturing firms and projects, started a major effort to develop clerical worksites in local YMCAs and other nonprofit and public agencies. The Oakland project staff included the growth of AFDC enrollments in its calculations as it developed subcontracting arrangements with local manufacturers to package products. The Atlanta and Newark programs developed subcontract work with local businesses for the sewing and packaging of products such as shop towels and clothing accessories. Atlanta also developed an on-the-job training arrangement with the Visiting Nurses Association for its AFDC participants.

Opportunities and Constraints Presented by Local Markets

Although local programs enjoyed substantial flexibility in seeking out subsidized work projects for participants, the local market clearly made certain kinds of work projects more feasible in some communities than in others. The Chicago program, for example, took advantage of the manufacturing base in the Chicago labor market. A continuing customer of the program was a national manufacturer of automotive waxes, and the Chicago site negotiated packaging subcontracts with many other firms over the course of the demonstration. The Hartford program's worksites in office furniture manufacturing and tire recapping owed something to the mixed service and manufacturing economy in the area.

At the other extreme, the rural West Virginia program found that the shortage of potential customers for Supported Work output had a major influence on that program's development strategy. The program served participants from a five-county area in the northern part of the state, where some areas were very isolated. Program staff found that they had to approach nearly every feasible public agency to sponsor their ex-offender, youth, or AFDC Supported Workers. It proved especially difficult to develop program-supervised crew-work projects, given the relative weakness in demand and the geographical problems of moving crews to places of work. Efforts to develop revenue-producing projects, such as machinery to clean mining equipment and mobile homes, tied up capital and supervisors and, at best, provided episodic work for small crews.

Generally speaking, the size of Supported Work programs relative to the opportunities available in local communities (with a modal program size of 100 workers in a community of over 250,000) left substantial room for operator inventiveness. Even though programs were not likely to capture a large share of the market by their worksites, operators nevertheless had to be sensitive to the perceptions of private sector actors. While there might be substantial opportunity for light construction and painting work in the community, for example, apprehension by local construction trades that a subsidized work program threatened the jobs of their members could create a political constraint to developing these projects. Similarly, local entrepreneurs in the fur-

niture business might oppose the subsidized competition of Supported
Work crews manufacturing and selling furniture, particularly if they
perceived that the output would be sold at below market prices.

These essentially "diplomatic" constraints required careful touching
of bases by local operators in the development phases of new projects.
Program operators were, however, rarely dissuaded from developing
projects, and very few were effectively vetoed by union or business
opposition once they had reached final planning or actual implementation.[7] A few guiding rules of thumb were developed within which
programs could usually gain union and business acceptance. Construction work that was small in scale, such as light housing rehabilitation,
particularly if it was in disadvantaged neighborhoods, generally aroused
little opposition from building trades representatives. Where possible,
Supported Work directors would offer to hire out-of-work union journeymen as supervisors of Supported Work construction crews albeit
at annual wages below what fully employed journeymen could usually
earn. With respect to service and retail businesses, program operators
sought to assure local trade associations that their work would involve
relatively small production and, therefore, relatively little pressure on
the market share which local businesses enjoyed. Supported Work
operators took care to explain to businesses that they would not sell
output below market rates. Some directors asked local businesses for
technical assistance, to improve productivity of the proposed worksites
and also to avoid potentially unfair pricing practices. The practice by
most Supported Work programs of appointing local union leaders and
businessmen to program boards of directors helped allay concern by
providing a point of access for those groups.

Worksites Developed by Site and Target Group

The job-creation initiatives of the local programs produced a great
diversity of worksites. The array of work projects is displayed in tables
3.1 and 3.2, with table 3.1 describing the principal projects on which
program crews worked, and table 3.2 showing the percent distribution
by industrial category (at the one-digit level, Standard Industrial Code)
of project time by site and principal target group. As both tables indicate, service projects were the largest single category of worksites,
divided between business services (particularly clerical, building maintenance, and food services) and educational, health, and other human
services. The AFDC target group worked primarily in service projects.
Construction projects involved primarily the other, more predomi-

TABLE 3.1

Target Groups Served and Principal Work Projects Operated by 13 Supported Work
Programs during the National Demonstration

Site	Target Group	Work Project
Atlanta	AFDC Youth	Crews assigned to clerical and health services in public agencies, painting, manufacturing subcontracts
Chicago	AFDC Ex-addict Ex-offender	Manufacturing subcontracts and crews assigned to manufacturers' plants, clerical services, painting
Hartford	AFDC Ex-offender Youth	Manufacturing projects, rehabilitation and construction of several houses, gasoline service station operation
Jersey City	Ex-addict Ex-offender Youth	Light and heavy construction, painting, and food service
Massachusetts	AFDC Ex-offender Youth	Lead paint removal, crews assigned to clerical services in public and private agencies, printing
Newark	AFDC Ex-offender	Crews assigned to clerical and building maintenance services in a public hospital, manufacturing subcontracts
Oakland	AFDC Ex-offender	Painting, grounds maintenance, manufacturing subcontracts, construction and operation of day-care center, gasoline service station operation
Philadelphia	Ex-addict Ex-offender Youth	Demolition and sealing abandoned buildings, grounds maintenance, painting
St. Louis	AFDC	Human and health services, crews assigned to food service
San Francisco	Ex-addict Ex-offender	Painting, building maintenance, grounds maintenance
Washington State	Ex-offender	Microfilming services, furniture manufacturing, demolition
West Virginia	AFDC Ex-offender Youth	Crews and individual participants assigned to clerical, building maintenance, and other services with public and nonprofit agencies, building renovation
Wisconsin	AFDC Youth Other	Light construction and insulation, clerical services, services to the elderly

nantly male target groups, although the ex-offenders, ex-addicts, and youths divided their time fairly equally with service projects as well. In general, all four target groups spent similar amounts of their work time in manufacturing projects, ranging from 6 to 12 percent.

TABLE 3.2

Percentage Distribution of Project Days during the Supported Work Demonstration, by Industry and Target Group within Site

Site and Target Group	Industry						Total
	Agriculture, Forestry, Fishing	Construction	Manufacturing	Transportation, Communication	Wholesale/ Retail Trade	Services	
Atlanta							
AFDC	0.0	5.6	9.2	0.0	0.1	85.1	100.0
Youth	0.0	25.6	7.0	0.0	1.1	65.4	100.0
All groups[a]	1.7	15.0	7.8	0.0	0.7	74.8	100.0
Chicago							
AFDC	0.0	10.4	12.6	14.8	0.0	62.2	100.0
Ex-addict	0.4	50.4	8.1	13.0	0.0	28.1	100.0
Ex-offender	0.2	57.2	10.2	12.3	0.0	20.1	100.0
All groups[a]	0.2	35.5	10.5	13.6	0.0	40.1	100.0
Detroit							
Ex-addict	5.8	63.0	1.0	0.0	0.0	30.2	100.0
Ex-offender	3.6	56.4	12.7	1.5	0.8	25.0	100.0
All groups[a]	3.6	51.5	9.6	1.1	2.3	31.9	100.0
Hartford							
AFDC	4.8	5.9	21.5	1.8	0.0	66.0	100.0
Ex-addict	6.5	41.4	0.0	0.0	0.0	52.1	100.0
Youth	3.8	38.1	14.6	5.4	2.4	35.7	100.0
All groups	4.7	25.6	18.6	4.6	3.5	43.0	100.0
Jersey City							
Ex-addict	0.0	37.6	5.8	12.1	13.6	30.9	100.0
Ex-offender	0.0	42.5	2.0	10.9	11.7	32.9	100.0
Youth	0.0	41.9	5.2	11.3	10.5	31.0	100.0
All groups[a]	0.0	39.8	5.5	7.9	12.9	33.9	100.0

(Continued on following pages)

TABLE 3.2 (Continued)

Percentage Distribution of Project Days during the Supported Work Demonstration, by Industry and Target Group within Site

Site and Target Group	Industry						
	Agriculture, Forestry, Fishing	Construction	Manufacturing	Transportation, Communication	Wholesale/ Retail Trade	Services	Total
Massachusetts							
AFDC	0.0	25.0	14.0	0.0	0.0	61.0	100.0
Ex-offender	0.0	74.2	19.9	0.0	0.0	5.9	100.0
Youth	0.0	70.2	17.6	0.0	6.5	5.6	100.0
All groups[a]	0.0	57.8	17.2	0.0	1.5	23.5	100.0
New York[b]							
AFDC	0.0	0.4	0.0	0.2	0.5	98.9	100.0
Youth	1.5	4.6	0.0	0.0	0.5	93.4	100.0
All groups[a]	0.2	2.1	0.0	0.2	0.5	97.0	100.0
Newark							
AFDC	0.0	0.0	8.0	0.0	5.4	86.6	100.0
Ex-offender	1.5	15.1	11.5	0.4	0.3	71.1	100.0
All groups	0.7	7.3	8.3	0.2	3.0	80.5	100.0
Oakland							
AFDC	0.8	7.1	13.3	21.9	20.2	36.7	100.0
Ex-addict	16.2	61.6	0.0	0.9	7.1	14.2	100.0
Ex-offender	21.1	54.6	0.2	1.4	10.1	12.6	100.0
All groups	19.9	44.3	4.2	7.4	12.9	11.3	100.0
Philadelphia							
Ex-addict	16.5	55.5	0.7	0.2	0.6	26.5	100.0
Ex-offender	19.7	59.7	1.0	0.0	0.1	19.5	100.0
Youth	6.6	78.2	0.0	0.0	5.2	10.0	100.0
All groups[a]	15.3	60.0	0.9	0.1	0.1	22.7	100.0

St. Louis							
AFDC	2.0	6.4	0.0	2.9	20.8	67.9	100.0
All groups[a]	2.0	6.4	0.0	2.9	20.7	68.0	100.0
San Francisco[c]							
Ex-offender	8.2	34.5	2.8	3.6	5.4	45.5	100.0
All groups[a]	6.5	26.7	2.2	5.0	4.2	55.4	100.0
Washington State							
Ex-offender	1.5	17.2	30.3	0.1	0.0	50.9	100.0
Youth	0.0	68.5	17.1	0.0	0.0	14.4	100.0
All groups[a]	1.3	19.5	32.9	0.1	0.0	46.2	100.0
West Virginia							
AFDC	1.1	0.6	2.1	8.1	0.6	87.5	100.0
Ex-offender	3.6	25.6	2.1	6.2	0.2	62.4	100.0
Youth	9.9	21.7	3.0	4.7	0.3	60.4	100.0
All groups[a]	5.6	16.3	2.6	6.3	0.3	69.0	100.0
Wisconsin[d]							
AFDC	0.0	12.2	3.2	0.3	0.2	84.1	100.0
Youth	0.0	34.5	0.0	1.3	16.0	48.2	100.0
All groups[a]	0.3	41.7	1.0	1.6	1.0	54.3	100.0
All sites							
AFDC	0.7	5.4	7.5	4.6	5.0	76.8	100.0
Ex-addict	5.4	47.4	7.5	8.1	6.6	28.0	100.0
Ex-offender	6.1	38.1	11.0	3.8	3.9	37.2	100.0
Youth	2.7	35.6	7.6	3.7	4.8	45.6	100.0
All groups[a]	3.8	29.3	8.2	4.1	4.4	50.2	100.0
Total project days	30,980	241,128	67,888	33,949	35,976	412,974	822,895

Source: Supported Work Management Information System.

Note: Percentages may not add to 100.0 because of rounding.

a Figures for "All groups" include other target groups.

b Figures for New York do not include 1976 or 1977.

c San Francisco closed in 1977. Figures include 1975–1977.

d Figures for Wisconsin do not include 1976.

Managing Supported Worksites:
Maintenance and Adaptation of the Program Model

The requirements of providing a relatively uniform treatment across programs, with specified target group eligibility criteria, wage levels, and an emphasis on full-time work, still permitted program operators a wide range of discretion in creating and managing work projects, as the preceding discussion has indicated. The experience of implementing a variety of work strategies, which MDRC encouraged, offers some lessons about the conditions under which the treatment emphases of close supervision, graduated stress, and peer support are facilitated and constrained. Additionally, the worksite management experience may give some indication of the range of operational complexity within which local nonprofit program operators can function. In particular, the program management experience revealed the inherent tensions in operating a program which seeks to emphasize realistic and productive work while also providing a supportive bridge to the conditions of working in the competitive, unsubsidized labor market.

The variety of worksites that programs launched (with most programs operating eight to ten different projects at any one time) had consequences for the way that program staff were able to manage the Supported Work treatment. In the process, some elements of the Supported Work model of structure, graduated stress, and peer support were affected, or at least more clearly defined than at the outset of the demonstration.

The challenge of operating several projects for program crews, combined with the participation pattern of program enrollees, led local programs to abandon at least one variant of the peer support idea: constituting crews confined to one target group. With participants leaving on their own due to a job, being fired, or for some other reason, and with most participants not serving even the 12 months that they were permitted, the business of assigning participants to crews became a fairly complex one. Generally speaking, programs abandoned the notion of categorically segregated crews, with the exception of the AFDC target group at several sites. In Newark, Chicago, Atlanta, and Oakland, women tended to be assigned to clerical or other services at outside agencies or to assembly and packaging subcontracts managed directly by the program.

Some operators noted that mixing target groups together created a somewhat more realistic work setting, and observed that some participants, particularly youths, benefited from being assigned with others.

Older participants could help stabilize the behavior of youths on crews, although many participants reported in informal interviews some impatience with the behavior and attitudes of many youths. Other program operators noted that peer support could have negative as well as positive implications. Programs had to watch for a bad-apple syndrome, or the revival of hostility among participants who formerly had been inmates together. Several former participants also noted the possibility that ex-addict-dominated crews could become a marketplace for diverse substances on payday.

The turnover of participants and the demands of production made it difficult for operators to implement the graduation of stress through a staged progression of work projects, whereby participants could be promoted from less challenging to more demanding worksites. As an example, the Jersey City program developed a variety of worksites in food services during its first and second years. Program staff proposed to move participants from less demanding kitchen jobs in the program-operated restaurant to waiter and chef's assistant jobs at a historical local restaurant which the program renovated and put into operation. The logistics of production and assignment, compounded by the inability of the program to develop a high quality operation at its renovated restaurant, made the plan for staged progression infeasible. Most programs tried to maintain some projects, however, which operated on or near the program's facility, to which new or "problem" participants could be assigned before going out with a crew that had more direct contact with customers or the public.

Since the flow of participants, and the consequent flux of crew membership, made it difficult to establish formal and structured progressions of tasks for individual participants, the responsibility for interpreting and applying the concept of graduated stress fell primarily upon the crew supervisor, a member of the local program staff. This supervisor had to gauge the progress of each crew member and make an effort to increase the participant's scope of responsibility, task complexity, or level of output. The most effective supervisors appeared to be those who could combine skills in the substantive work of the crew with sensitivity to the behavior of participants, a balance that was particularly difficult to reach in supervising other than AFDC participants. Many of the youths, ex-addicts, and ex-offenders displayed hostile attitudes toward authority and pronounced aggressive or passive behavior which had marred their previous work records. Imposing and supervising such a structure was hardly reducible to any simple set of rules or guidelines.

While the translation of the graduated stress concept into day-to-day application within a crew setting was a challenge, two important, more formal mechanisms were implemented by local programs. First, participants could be fired. While a blunt instrument, and one that had to be applied judiciously with participants who often provoked supervisor frustration, the reality that there was an outer limit to poor attendance and worksite behavior was an important last resort. Over the course of the demonstration, 30 percent of all program departures resulted from firing. Second, as a positive incentive, local programs established bonus policies, whereby excellent attendance could be rewarded by periodic bonuses, which became increasingly difficult to earn over the course of a participant's tenure. In addition, some programs also provided a graduation "nest egg," with the amount based on length of program tenure that was triggered by evidence of the participant's 60 to 90 days' retention on a postprogram job.

Another constraint to implementing structured supervision and feedback to participants arose from the practice at several sites of assigning participants (especially from the AFDC target group) to host-agency worksites. Programs in Hartford, Philadelphia, Oakland, Jersey City, and Washington state argued strongly that the intensive program treatment could be implemented only at worksites under the direct controls of program staff supervisors. Program-supervised worksites were simply not feasible at the rural West Virginia program, however, and the directors at Atlanta, Newark, and Chicago did not hold as strongly to the importance of program-supervised crews.

Host-agency settings reduced the ability of program staff to supervise participants on a day-to-day basis; in addition, many of these placements were for single Supported Workers, thus negating the possibility of peer support on the worksite.[8] Program staff sought to compensate by acting as liaisons with participants and their host-agency supervisors. In instances where enough participants were assigned to a single agency to justify the cost, a full-time supervisor was assigned to the agency worksite. In other cases, a roving supervisor would visit several worksites over the course of a few days. Where their role as members of the Supported Work program was not clearly communicated, participants sometimes expressed some confusion about whom they worked for and to whom they were accountable. On the other hand, some Supported Workers commented that the program held them to higher standards and performance than were displayed by regular workers at host agencies.

Some program directors with host-agency worksites argued that there were countervailing advantages to the arrangement. First, while peer interaction might be less frequent and peer support less intense, participants could benefit from the sense of working alongside unsubsidized workers. Another benefit cited by these directors was the ease of transition to a regular job at the host agency for those who had participated to some degree in the agency's internal labor market. A condition of the agreements between host agencies and Supported Work programs was commitment by the agency to make a good-faith effort to hire capable Supported Workers when openings became available. The process was not straightforward, since typically a Supported Worker would not "roll over" to the same position he or she had held as a participant, and liaison supervisors would have to make some job-placement inquiries within the host agency. Furthermore, since host agencies were primarily in the public sector, agency fiscal constraints frequently reduced the likelihood of available job openings.

In terms of implementing the program treatment at worksites, then, program staffs discovered that the two most critical choices to make were the selection of worksites that were appropriate to Supported Worker skills and the selection of supervisors who were sensitive to the need for balancing stress and support. When the programs shared day-to-day supervision with host agencies, the choice of liaison roving supervisors who could act as effective intermediaries with participants and host agencies was especially important. The ability to develop more formal mechanisms for increasing stress over time within the work setting itself, apart from progressively stringent attendance requirements to earn bonuses, was constrained by the exigencies of participant flow.

The selection of appropriate worksites had implications not only for the ability to implement an effective treatment, but for the ability of program staff to manage work output. Worksites ranged widely in terms of the complexities of the production process and the ability of the program to adjust production demands to Supported Workers. Interacting with the choice of worksites as well was the expectation that programs would seek to offset public subsidy funds to some extent by charging customers for part of the cost of product or service provided by the Supported Work crews.

Work projects varied in their technical complexity and in the degree to which the Supported Work program assumed responsibility for managing the production process from beginning to end. At the extreme were construction and manufacturing projects where the programs assembled all the factors of production and managed them through to a completed product. Operating these projects was akin to running a small business. For example, short-term and repetitive proj-

ects such as sealing abandoned houses, lead paint removal, light housing rehabilitation, or painting demanded careful scheduling and a con-
tinual search for new jobs to keep the crews working every day.
Manufacturing projects required setting up a sequential assembly process, where the interdependency of workers in the sequence, timely
flow of raw materials or subassemblies, and the maintenance of machinery had to be carefully attended, to minimize disruption and downtime in the work process. Where there was not a contract customer,
markets for finished products had to be nurtured. Similarly, where
heavy construction was involved, as with the housing renovation and
construction in Jersey City and Hartford, or the building of a day care
center in Oakland, there were fairly complex logistics to sequencing
the different stages of the project to ensure, for example, that plumbing
work was completed before the walls were finished off.

Experience with construction and manufacturing projects where the
program directed the entire production process revealed, on the one
hand, that it was possible for crews of relatively unskilled and inexperienced Supported Workers to produce tangible output beyond what
might have been expected. On the other hand, such projects were much
more likely than simpler labor-intensive projects to experience problems in production quality and downtime, where programs did not
have the skills to orchestrate such complex production or the ability
to locate customers for output. With effective management and direct
supervision, however, these complex projects were particularly ap-
pealing, in permitting the program to develop progressions of tasks
within a project and giving participants exposure to a wider range of
skills.

With another kind of worksite arrangement, subcontracts for manufacturing and packaging, program operators were able to strike a different balance in terms of program responsibility for managing the
production process. In some of the more typical arrangements, such
as typewriter repair in Jersey City, packaging in Oakland, or partial
assembly and sewing in Atlanta, the programs were able to carve out
one part of the manufacturing process for their management. The business with whom the program contracted would often help the program
set up the operation within the program's facility, would supply the
materials for production, and would receive the finished or repaired
products. The program could not only have more control over the
treatment setting, but could share the burden of management and
technical production with a private business.

The host-agency projects, discussed above, where the program was
responsible primarily for referring Supported Workers to a sponsoring

agency or business and for providing liaison support to the agency and participants, imposed the least management burden on program operators. The trade-off in most cases was loss of a discrete treatment setting for a Supported Work crew, in return for the work sponsor's production expertise and organization of the workplace. Certain host-agency projects provided a middle ground, particularly the vendor payment review projects for the state welfare department and the local Blue Cross–Blue Shield agency at the Massachusetts program. In those cases, a discrete set of tasks was established for a Supported Work crew, under a host-agency direct supervisor, with on-site program liaison staff. There was a distinct treatment setting which, being separate from the host agency's regular work flow, could be more readily paced to meet the productivity of the Supported Work crew and which permitted crew members to work alongside one another.

Another feature of Supported Work implementation, the expectation that program operators should seek to offset workplace operating costs from public subsidies by charging customers for the output, also could affect the program treatment. As will be discussed further below, the degree of subsidy offset varied and did not recoup total production costs, but many program operators believed that the existence of a cash nexus gave the customers a greater stake in the productive output of Supported Workers. Were participants were assigned to host agencies, the agencies' reimbursement of part of the hourly participant wage costs to the program may have given the host agency more incentive to supervise participants closely and to emphasize the importance of their performance as workers. Where a program contracted to provide specific output to a customer, there was even clearer pressure on the workers to perform effectively.

Program operators believed that if the customer took Supported Work output more seriously, then the production process itself would be lent a greater sense of realism and urgency. The revenue nexus created an additional increment of program accountability to the customer, and in effect led program staff and customer to share in the responsibility for a more realistic working environment for participants. Where program staff did not have sufficient production management experience to gauge the productivity of Supported Work crews, however, some programs negotiated unrealistically high output agreements with customers, in terms of volume and scheduling. This, in turn, placed undue demands on program crews and limited a worksite supervisor's flexibility to pace production and to graduate stress. In addition, in some instances quality control problems were exacerbated by such overcommitments, leaving customers dissatisfied. These problems were especially prevalent in the Chicago program, which went through a large number of manufacturing customers because of poorly managed assembly and packaging subcontracts. As programs gained experience with these revenue-producing projects, however, most learned to gauge Supported Worker productivity better.

In summary, depending on the worksite chosen, managing Supported Work projects involved some combination of technical and entrepreneurial skills with a sensitivity to the need to provide a work environment that balanced the urgency of producing output for customers against the supports conducive to improving work habits gradually. During the first year or more of program implementation at most sites, substantial program management attention was dedicated to developing worksites and learning their limits of operational feasibility. Relatively less attention was paid in the early period to the other major aspect of the program model, supports and assistance to participants in making the transition to competitive employment in the regular, unsubsidized labor market. As early enrollees began to reach their maximum 12 (or 18) months of program eligibility, and as MDRC began to urge program operators to place greater emphasis on job-readiness training and job-placement assistance, programs developed more concerted transition strategies. These are discussed in the following section.

Job-Search Assistance and Other Ancillary Supports

As stated previously, program guidelines authorized local programs to pay participants up to 25 percent of their time for receiving services ancillary to their primary work activity. The emphasis of all ancillary supports, whether in job-search assistance, counseling, training to obtain a driver's license, or other activities, was upon the work-related needs of participants. More broadly focused, therapeutic counseling was to be handled by referring participants to other community services, including those that had referred participants to Supported Work originally. Local programs did not come close to utilizing the maximum 25 percent authorized ancillary service time, however, reflecting the general priority on work in the treatment model. Across the demonstration, ancillary services comprised only 8 percent of all paid participant time. The largest share of this time was in "job-readiness" classes to prepare participants for job search and retention in competitive employment. In addition, nearly all programs hired staff job developers to assist participants in finding job openings. Many of the sites authorized participants to spend paid ancillary service time in going to job interviews. The degree of program emphasis on job-readiness classes and program job-placement assistance varied considerably.

Job-readiness training involved periodic classes, usually directed by program counselors or job developers, that offered participants the following basic curriculum: how to fill out a job application properly, how to present oneself for an interview, how to answer difficult questions during the interview (including previous incarceration for many ex-offenders, ex-addicts, and youths), how to use newspaper want ads, how to inquire over the telephone about job openings, and how to make the most of personal contacts with friends and relatives in locating available jobs.

Four of the 13 programs that began operations in 1975, Philadelphia, Washington state, Massachusetts, and St. Louis, did not operate regular job-readiness classes during the demonstration period, either because of problems with staff turnover or because program directors believed that their job developers could readily enough place participants in jobs from fairly skill-specific training projects (St. Louis) or host-agency placements that could "roll over" to regular employment (Massachusetts). The Washington state program took the position that Supported Work offered its participants a job, and that participants must be sufficiently resourceful to find the next job on their own. Other programs offered fairly minimal job-readiness preparation, including the Hartford program, which provided a two-hour session every month or two, and Newark, which held a class for participants once a month.

Several programs offered more intensive job-preparation training. For example, the job developer at the Oakland program led weekly job-readiness classes for participants who had attained a high program attendance rate. His training went well beyond the basic information about using want ads and tips on how to prepare resumes, to fairly intensive exploration of life goals and self-awareness. With somewhat less frequent meetings, but with a similarly intensive counseling approach, the Atlanta program had participants play roles of employer and applicant in mock job interviews and provided other activities directed at self-understanding and overcoming self-defeating behavior.

With the exception of Washington state and Philadelphia, all programs utilized program job developers to line up job openings for participants. As with job-readiness classes, the intensity and structure of job-placement activity varied widely across programs. The most impressively organized job-placement efforts were at two of the programs, Oakland and Hartford. Job developers systematically contacted employers, particularly manufacturers, and nurtured those contacts through regular call-backs and referrals. The Newark program, one that had a high proportion of host-agency worksites, was able to develop a fair proportion of placements for their participants by actively working within the internal labor market at the medical center complex, where more than one-third of the participants were assigned to work projects. The Massachusetts program had similar good fortune with host-agency placements for its AFDC target group.

One measure of the intensity of program job-development efforts and of the target groups that most depended on program assistance is the proportion of all job placements which the programs actively developed, compared to the proportion of jobs that participants found on their own. Table 3.3 distributes program placements by program and target group. Two observations emerge. First, the programs with host-agency placements and those with active job developers tended to place half or more of their participants with program assistance. Second, participants in the AFDC target group were less likely than the others to find jobs on their own. Compared with the ex-offender, ex-addict, and youth groups, where half or more of the participants found their own jobs, three-fourths of the AFDC participants benefited from program job-placement assistance. The AFDC enrollees, as will be discussed further below, tended to participate in the program longer and were less likely to strike out on their own, in either of the two senses of the term; they were less likely to search actively for a job by themselves and less likely to be fired from Supported Work. As a result, they were more "available" for program assistance and more willing to accept it.

The increased emphasis on job placement after the first year appears to have had some effect. Over the course of the demonstration, programs and their participants increased their rates of positive placements as a percent of all participant departures. In each of the four contract years, 1975–1978, job-placement rates increased from 20.9 percent, to 25.3 percent, to 29.7 percent, to 33.8 percent, for a four-year average placement rate of 28.9 percent. The final transition rates, when compared to those in CETA public service employment programs (Titles II and VI) are quite similar, even though each serves a somewhat different population.[9]

Financing Local Program Operations

As previously described, the initial MDRC guidelines required local operators to raise a share of the funds needed to cover operating expenses from local sources. The purpose was twofold: to use national

TABLE 3.3

Volume and Percentage Distribution of Job Placements from 15 Supported Work Programs, by Target Group within Site

Site and Target Group	Number of Placements	Distribution by Placement Process			
		Job-Developed[a]	Self-Placed[b]	Other[c]	Total
Atlanta					
AFDC	48	77.1	22.9	0.0	100.0
Youth	47	46.8	48.9	4.3	100.0
Total	95	62.1	35.8	2.1	100.0
Chicago					
AFDC	68	51.5	48.5	0.0	100.0
Ex-addict	55	38.2	61.8	0.0	100.0
Ex-offender	80	35.0	62.5	2.5	100.0
Total	203	41.4	57.6	1.0	100.0
Detroit					
Ex-addict	11	18.2	81.8	0.0	100.0
Ex-offender	52	28.8	71.2	0.0	100.0
Total	63	27.0	73.0	0.0	100.0
Hartford					
AFDC	46	93.5	4.3	2.2	100.0
Ex-addict	111	76.6	19.8	3.6	100.0
Youth	150	79.3	16.0	4.7	100.0
Total[d]	307	80.5	15.6	3.9	100.0
Jersey City					
Ex-addict	102	49.0	48.0	2.9	100.0
Ex-offender	48	33.3	64.6	2.1	100.0
Youth	58	20.7	72.4	6.9	100.0
Total[d]	208	35.4	61.3	3.3	100.0
Massachusetts					
AFDC	58	70.7	24.1	5.2	100.0
Ex-offender	86	50.0	47.7	2.3	100.0
Youth	66	60.6	39.4	0.0	100.0
Total[d]	210	59.2	38.0	2.9	100.0
New York					
AFDC	97	76.3	22.7	1.0	100.0
Youth	36	38.9	55.6	5.5	100.0
Total	133	66.2	31.6	2.3	100.0
Newark					
AFDC	100	83.0	17.0	0.0	100.0
Ex-offender	166	46.4	52.4	1.2	100.0
Total	266	60.2	39.1	0.8	100.0
Oakland					
AFDC	33	69.7	24.2	6.0	100.0
Ex-addict	28	53.6	39.3	7.1	100.0
Ex-offender	127	43.3	51.2	5.5	100.0
Total	188	49.5	44.7	5.9	100.0
Philadelphia					
Ex-addict	56	46.4	50.0	3.6	100.0
Ex-offender	35	28.6	71.4	0.0	100.0
Youth	13	15.4	76.9	7.7	100.0
Total	104	36.3	58.4	5.3	100.0

(Continued on following page)

TABLE 3.3 (Continued)
Volume and Percentage Distribution of Job Placements from 15 Supported Work
Programs, by Target Group within Site

Site and Target Group	Number of Placements	Distribution by Placement Process			
		Job-Developed[a]	Self-Placed[b]	Other[c]	Total
St. Louis					
AFDC	63	73.0	25.4	1.6	100.0
Total	63	73.0	25.4	1.6	100.0
San Francisco					
Ex-offender	71	56.3	40.8	2.8	100.0
Total	71	56.3	40.8	2.8	100.0
Washington State					
Ex-offender	170	11.8	84.7	3.5	100.0
Youth	21	19.0	71.4	9.5	100.0
Total	191	12.6	83.2	4.2	100.0
West Virginia					
AFDC	30	83.3	16.7	0.0	100.0
Ex-offender	65	49.2	50.8	0.0	100.0
Youth	55	36.4	60.0	3.6	100.0
Total	150	51.3	47.3	1.3	100.0
Wisconsin					
AFDC	7	42.9	57.1	0.0	100.0
Youth	48	31.3	60.4	8.3	100.0
Mentally disabled	111	47.7	40.5	11.7	100.0
Total	166	42.4	47.6	10.0	100.0
All sites					
AFDC	550	74.2	24.4	1.3	100.0
Ex-addict	363	46.1	51.2	2.7	100.0
Ex-offender	900	41.6	55.8	2.6	100.0
Youth	494	50.2	44.9	4.9	100.0
Mentally disabled	111	47.7	40.5	11.7	100.0
Total[d]	2418	51.2	45.5	3.2	100.0

Source: Tabulations of status activity in the Supported Work Management Information System.

Notes: The data include all participants leaving Supported Work for permanent employment from March 31, 1975, through December 31, 1978. Percentage distributions may not add exactly to 100.0 because of rounding.

a Job-developed placements are those which result from interviews arranged by the Supported Work program's or some outside agency's job-placement efforts.

b Self-placed placements are those which result from the efforts of the Supported Work participants.

c "Other" placements include promotion to a Supported Work program staff position, and enlistment in the military services.

d Percentage distributions of total placements by placement process for all sites include 80 participants from other target groups, primarily ex-alcoholics in Jersey City and Massachusetts.

resources as leverage to develop sufficiently large and viable local operations, and to develop a local base of support that could become the main source of funding for these programs when national demonstration funding was terminated. This funding mandate, while increasing the complexity of the local managers' tasks beyond simply getting an operation in place, also created the incentive for operators to reach out to their communities. In addition, as has been discussed, the authorization for programs to raise nongrant revenues from customers had indirect effects upon the worksite development and management strategies of the local programs.

The local operating cost of the demonstration was $66.4 million (see table 3.4). By the end of the fourth and final years of the demonstration, local programs covered 58 percent of their costs from local revenues, below the target of 75 percent that had been established at the outset, but a substantial proportion nonetheless. Initial expectations had been that local funding sources would parallel national funding sources in their diversity (the latter including not only CETA/manpower training funds, but criminal justice, drug-abuse treatment, and housing subsidy monies). This degree of diversity did not materialize at the local level, where local funding sources tended to view Supported Work as another employment program, with the local CETA agency expected to be the

TABLE 3.4

Summary of Supported Work Demonstration Site Operations Expenditures, by Funding Source and Contract Year

Source of Funds for Site Operations[a]	Year 1	Year 2	Year 3	Year 4	Total
Income from sale of goods and services	13%	16%	16%	17%	16%
Other local funding					
CETA	19	16	27	29	23
Other[b]	10	11	10	12	11
National funding (MDRC)	59	56	47	42	50
Total	100%	100%	100%	100%	100%
Total site operations expenditures ($000)	8,937	19,433	23,389	14,659	66,418

Source: Manpower Demonstration Research Corporation (1980, Table 2-40).

Notes: The data for each of the first three contract years cover totals from a 12-month period of each program's operation, with a few isolated exceptions. The Year 1 period ranged from 6 to 12 months, depending on the site. Percentage distribution may not add exactly to totals because of rounding.

a Includes all expenses related to the operation of the local Supported Work programs.

b Includes other forms of grants or contracts and funds received through welfare diversion procedures.

principal supporter. Most local Supported Work directors were not familiar with non-manpower training agencies and thus did not have the experience to pursue funds as successfully from those sources.

As table 3.4 indicates, the local CETA prime sponsors provided the largest single source of local grant subsidies, generally exceeding the proportion of all other grant sources by a factor of two or three each year. Table 3.4 also shows the CETA contribution rising in the third program year, partly as a result of 1976 CETA amendments that encouraged more targeting of funds to welfare recipients and the long-term unemployed and specified more emphasis on discrete work projects instead of the simple allocation of public service employment slots to public agencies. In addition, the local CETA share of Supported Work costs increased as a result of a major increase in public service employment funds in 1977.

Supported Work could offer local CETA prime sponsors well-structured work experience for particularly disadvantaged groups, and thus assist the prime sponsors to target their funds to meet national priorities. Interviews with local CETA officials, however, indicated that the most important factors influencing their decision to fund Supported Work were the reputation of the program director or the program's parent organization and the ability of the program to spend funds promptly and with fiscal integrity. By the end of the fourth program year, every Supported Work program had local CETA funds, which on average amounted to nearly three-tenths of local operating costs.

The second largest source of local revenue was from billing customers for Supported Work labor, goods, and services.[10] By the fourth year these revenues covered 17 percent of program expenses. Most sites shifted toward increased revenue generation during the second year when it became apparent that the expected variety of local grant sources would not materialize and that local CETA agencies, because of local competiton for CETA funds, and in spite of increased CETA allocations nationally, would not be sufficient to provide the resources required.

The shift toward more direct project revenue was something of a mixed blessing. Most programs vastly underestimated the difficulties of making money. It often took 12–18 months for a revenue-gathering project to cover the extra expenses that the project incurred, particularly where capital investment was involved. MDRC provided assistance in planning, financial forecasting, production, and marketing for such worksites. By the conclusion of the demonstration, more than 75 percent of all workdays were partially financed by customer contracts that included such arrangements as percentage of total cost, cost plus fee, Supported Worker wages only, competitive bidding, and retail sales. Most of these revenue-generating projects were able by the last year of the demonstration to cover direct project expenses (supervision, equipment, materials, and supplies) and some portion of Supported Worker wages. Although some program operators began the demonstration with the optimistic belief that they could develop self-sustaining work projects through sales revenues, it became apparent during the course of the demonstration that such revenues can generally not cover more than one-third of operating expenses, and this only after a project has become well organized and stable in its operation.

While direct project revenue provided a relatively modest return with respect to recouping total project costs, its contribution to Supported Work operation can also be considered in light of the expanded range of work activities which it allowed Supported Work programs to develop, yet still remain within public subsidy parameters that were comparable to other intensive manpower programs. Since the more capital-intensive work projects involved outlays for materials and equipment, total costs per year of participant service would rise accordingly. Charging Supported Work customers reduced the public subsidy costs. Thus, in the third and fourth years of the demonstration, project revenues averaged $2,082 per year of participant service,[11] bringing the net public subsidy cost down to $10,281. This public cost is quite close to the public participant/year cost of a comparable program, the Job Corps.

Issues in Replication of Supported Work

Local Supported Work programs were mixed-purpose organizations that combined the features of small businesses with the supports of employment and training programs, reaching out to agencies, businesses, and individuals in the community to provide productive work opportunities for participants. The implementation of Supported Work demonstrated that it is possible for such local nonprofit organizations to launch a managerially complex work experience program for highly disadvantaged populations and to operate technically complex, relatively capital-intensive work projects as well as more straightforward labor-intensive activities. The ability of programs to demonstrate this range of operational possibilities did not proceed without central direction from MDRC, however, and the role of the managing agency deserves some discussion before exploring the range of feasibility within which Supported Work might be replicable under other conditions.

MDRC provided national discretionary funds to the programs, and while the proportion of these national funds declined over time, the role of MDRC did not diminish accordingly. Throughout the demonstration, all program operators had to conduct their programs under the terms of an agreement negotiated annually with MDRC and within uniform operating guidelines established by MDRC. As the demonstration progressed, MDRC placed increasing emphasis on program performance indicators during the annual review. By the third and fourth years, each annual contract set forth the program's expected performance in terms of total participants and breakdown by target group; total budget and unit cost indicators; worksites to be developed; attendance, placement, and other program performance goals—both general and specific to each site.

To oversee these contracts and guidelines, the MDRC staff performed frequent on-site monitoring, provided technical assistance, and participated in major staffing and operating decisions. During the demonstration five changes in program leadership were in part attributable to MDRC intervention. This active oversight role by MDRC was designed to assure both the implementation of basic Supported Work principles and consistent standards for evaluating performance. MDRC closely monitored enrollment levels by target groups across the demonstration and adjusted local program enrollment where necessary to ensure that sufficiently large samples for each target group could be evaluated with statistical confidence.[12]

MDRC also assumed a role of "risk reviewer" with respect to the worksite and local funding strategies of the programs. Beginning in the second year, MDRC issued a guideline requiring local directors to seek approval from MDRC for new worksite ventures. Several attempts at developing projects were vetoed because they required more technical complexity than a program was likely to master, or involved relationships with customers whose reliability might not live up to the occasionally naive trust of some program directors. Since all but one or two of the local directors did not have business management backgrounds, their ability to make sound business judgments and to estimate market demand appeared to require some oversight from a central agent. The review power over worksite proposals was not exercised formally on many occasions, but the dialogue that it produced between local directors and MDRC appeared to help sites avoid costly mistakes with respect to more ambitious manufacturing and construction projects.

MDRC was able to assume the role of banker for local programs, advancing national discretionary funds to help cushion sites against the vagaries of federal grant appropriations, local CETA prime sponsor decision-making, and local customer demand for Supported Work output. In addition, in the annual review of program performance and budget requests for national funds, MDRC sought to encourage sites to increase their local funding share, to develop local project revenues to offset subsidy costs, and to improve their performance with respect to job-placement rates for participants. This effort appeared to contribute to the reduction of public subsidy costs and national share of program revenues over the course of time, and contributed to improved program job-placement rates.

One of the dilemmas of launching demonstrations is the conflicting pull between allowing local programs to succeed or flounder according to local conditions and intervening to ensure a reasonable opportunity for success by helping programs avoid fatal mistakes. In Supported Work, the imperative to ensure sufficiently large sample sizes for the random assignment experiment underscored this dilemma, since allowing a program to fail when some central intervention might have prevented failure would risk a critical loss of statistical power.

It would appear that replication of Supported Work, with the levels of financial and technical risk that were entailed in some program strategies, would require a role for some central managing organization to act as risk buffer or market surrogate. The great majority of program worksites did not entail high risks, however, so that a more modest version of Supported Work might succeed with a more limited central technical assistance and review role.

The most technical and capital-intensive work projects, such as new housing construction and manufacturing, entailed several kinds of risks. If local program operators did not have technical skills or the good managerial sense to purchase them from experts, such projects could run up substantial sink costs and cause occasional disruption that would reduce their value as a program work setting. Unskilled marketing and contracting with suppliers could affect scheduling and distribution. In addition, these projects were more likely to engage Supported Work programs in local markets where political problems with unions and businesses could affect a program's community viability.

It would seem that some central review authority, with the leverage to veto or modify program initiatives on these kinds of complex projects, may be necessary to protect programs from the operational and financial risks of poor strategic choices. The diplomatic problems of assuring the support or quiescence of the local private sector could generally be dealt with by local operators if they made sure that representative business and labor members were included on their boards of directors and that they were consulted before such projects were launched.

Many other projects in light construction, such as painting and light rehabilitation, were generally within the range of competence of Supported Work operators. Subcontract manufacturing was also less risky, technically, if the local program could solicit the assistance of the prime manufacturer in setting up the program worksite. The financial risk of exploitative pricing by the manufacturer might require some central review by a national managing agent, however, to ensure that the subsidy to the manufacturer did not exceed the value of the training opportunity for Supported Workers. In general, however, the less complex projects would not appear to require as much intensive central review as the high-risk ventures, nor would host-agency projects where programs referred participants to work under the agency's direct supervision.

Another buffer role that MDRC played for Supported Work programs, that of banker, would appear to be necessary if the program were to be replicated under the local cost-sharing arrangement that obtained during the demonstration. CETA prime sponsors provided the largest single source of local grants for the programs. Supported Work programs were at the end of a public pipeline that had been characterized since the inception of CETA by stop-start executive and congressional policy emphases, compounded by delays in the congressional appropriations process and in the issuance of program allocations and regulations, and exacerbated by shifts and delays in local prime sponsor decisions. Many Supported Work programs would have been forced to lay off participants, then enroll them in undigestibly large numbers, several times during the 1975–1978 demonstration period, had the central managing agency not had the national funding flexibility to smooth out cash-flow disruptions.

So long as a decentralized employment and training system characterizes the major source of local funding for a program like Supported Work, such risks would continue. One of the hallmarks of the Supported Work treatment model is the emphasis on a stable setting wherein program staff can work with participants to help them acclimate themselves to stable work patterns. Erratic and fluctuating funding levels would threaten to disrupt the treatment that program operators could provide.

Apart from buffering programs against risks and instability in local funding environments, it is worth considering whether a central managing agent may not also play an important role in ensuring that the program adheres to a relatively well-structured treatment model. MDRC played this role during the demonstration, primarily to ensure that program impacts could be evaluated with confidence, and so that samples could be pooled across sites. It does not appear that the MDRC contribution was effective in this regard solely from writing program guidelines and periodically monitoring local programs for adherence. Close monitoring, with attention to program problems in adapting the treatment model to various local conditions and with continuing substantive interaction between operators and MDRC and among local operators themselves, appeared to enhance attention to the content of the program model, not simply its adherence to a form set forth in guidelines. Replication of Supported Work in the absence of some central managing agent would require more modest local job-creation strategies and would probably produce greater variability among program treatments, in both intensity and structure.

The Experience of Participants in Supported Work

The discussion in this chapter has been directed primarily to the operational issues and trade-offs involved in implementing Supported Work locally. The vantage points have been those of program operators and the central managing agent. To provide additional context for the analyses presented in subsequent chapters, this final section addresses briefly the performance of participants in Supported Work and provides some illustrative comments from observers and participants themselves. These latter, apart from reminding the reader that individual people were participants in the "treatment," may give some indication of why Supported Work may work for those whose lives it changed.

While it is difficult to characterize the during-program performance of the four target groups with a few summary statistical indicators, table 3.5 indicates differences among sites and target groups with respect to length of stay in Supported Work and selected positive, negative, and neutral reasons for departure. The table also summarizes program attendance rates by site and by target group across all sites. Two principal factors appear to account for the higher than average attendance rates in Atlanta, Chicago, New York, Newark, Oakland, and St. Louis. All these sites except Oakland had AFDC participants assigned in higher than average proportions. In Oakland, program philosophy emphasized good attendance in two ways. Participation in job-preparation classes was permitted on the basis of attendance, and the crew with the best average attendance each month received a free dinner.

TABLE 3.5
Selected Indicators of Participant Performance in Program, by Site and Target Group

Site and Target Group	Attendance Rate[a]	Performance Indicator				Average Length of Stay (months)
		Percent of Departures				
		To a Job	Fired	Neutral Reasons[b]		
				Mandatory Graduation	Other	
Atlanta						
AFDC		36.0	5.3	27.1	21.9	10.0
Youth		28.5	30.3	18.8	15.7	8.2
All groups	88.1	31.9	19.4	22.5	19.5	9.1
Chicago						
AFDC		31.2	9.6	36.7	13.9	9.5
Ex-addict		22.0	37.6	14.0	10.3	7.0
Ex-offender		28.6	32.6	6.5	13.2	5.4
All groups	87.9	27.2	27.5	17.8	13.0	7.2
Detroit						
Ex-addict		24.5	37.8	4.4	15.9	5.3
Ex-offender		29.0	28.5	6.7	13.3	5.4
All groups	77.1	28.1	30.4	6.3	14.8	5.4
Hartford						
AFDC		40.7	6.2	16.8	26.2	9.4
Ex-offender		30.5	36.3	4.1	5.1	5.8
Youth		26.9	33.5	5.2	9.4	6.2
All groups	69.1	29.7	31.5	6.1	10.4	6.4
Jersey City						
Ex-addict		26.4	28.2	18.4	16.7	8.3
Ex-offender		23.0	31.7	11.1	19.2	8.0
Youth		29.6	34.2	11.7	11.7	8.2
All groups[c]	83.1	26.5	30.9	15.1	16.9	8.2
Massachusetts						
AFDC		53.7	11.1	3.7	19.5	8.5
Ex-offender		27.2	36.1	1.6	13.1	4.3
Youth		18.8	52.8	0.6	8.9	3.9
All groups[c]	84.2	27.5	39.1	1.3	13.5	4.9
New York						
AFDC		30.1	11.5	33.5	23.9	9.8
Youth		21.6	43.7	2.4	29.9	9.0
All groups	87.8	27.2	22.5	22.9	26.0	9.5
Newark						
AFDC		36.4	9.5	26.5	19.9	9.9
Ex-offender		33.0	29.2	6.0	10.2	5.7
All groups	88.8	34.2	20.7	13.2	15.4	7.3
Oakland						
AFDC		31.1	17.0	16.0	25.3	7.7
Ex-addict		26.6	39.0	2.9	11.2	5.3
Ex-offender		29.3	35.8	2.5	13.8	5.0
All groups	90.0	29.1	32.9	4.8	15.9	5.5

(Continued on following page)

TABLE 3.5 (Continued)
Selected Indicators of Participant Performance in Program, by Site and Target Group

Site and Target Group	Attendance Rate[a]	Performance Indicator				Average Length of Stay (months)
		Percent of Departures				
		To a Job	Fired	Neutral Reasons[b]		
				Mandatory Graduation	Other	
Philadelphia						
Ex-addict		18.1	48.2	2.6	6.4	5.5
Ex-offender		20.2	47.4	3.5	5.6	5.2
Youth		13.3	52.0	2.0	4.9	4.4
All groups[c]	78.6	18.6	48.3	3.0	6.5	5.1
St. Louis						
AFDC		30.3	15.4	26.4	15.9	8.6
All groups[c]	90.9	30.3	15.4	26.4	15.9	8.6
San Francisco						
Ex-offender		25.7	37.9	1.1	13.1	5.3
All groups	83.5	25.7	37.9	1.1	13.1	5.3
Washington State						
Ex-offender		28.8	24.9	2.4	16.6	3.7
All groups[c]	82.6	29.2	24.3	2.3	17.9	3.8
West Virginia						
AFDC		30.3	12.1	4.0	42.4	11.5
Ex-offender		37.8	33.1	2.9	10.0	6.8
Youth		29.7	35.1	2.7	15.6	7.5
All groups	78.8	32.8	29.4	3.1	19.2	8.2
Wisconsin						
AFDC		41.2	11.8	5.9	41.2	9.1
Youth		37.0	17.2	3.1	22.3	7.3
All groups[c]	85.8	37.7	17.7	5.8	21.8	8.0
All sites						
AFDC	89.8	34.6	10.9	24.8	20.8	9.5
Ex-addict	83.9	23.1	37.3	10.7	12.3	6.8
Ex-offender	80.3	28.9	32.5	4.1	12.2	5.2
Youth	75.8	25.8	37.2	5.3	12.6	7.6
All groups[c]	83.0	28.9	29.6	9.3	14.0	6.7

Source: Supported Work Management Information System.

a Attendance rates were calculated by dividing total attendance time (paid and unpaid) by total participant days minus scheduled absence days and inactivations. Attendance rate data are not available by target group within each site.

b Mandatory graduations are departures that occur when Supported Workers reach the maximum allowable length of stay in the program without having found postprogram employment. Other neutral departures include such things as death and resignations for reasons of personal or family health problems.

c Figures for "All groups" include other target groups.

The higher attendance rates of the AFDC group are consonant with some of the other indicators of performance, which together form a pattern of longer than average length of program stay, higher than average rates of departure to a job, and much lower than average firing rates—10.9 percent compared with 30 to 40 percent for the other groups. Another notable difference was the much higher than average "mandatory graduation" departure rate for the AFDC women. Nearly one-quarter of AFDC departures resulted from participants remaining in the program for the full 12-month maximum and being required to leave without an unsubsidized job in hand. Other neutral terminations for AFDC women, which were also much higher than average, were usually for health or child-care reasons. The greater than average mandatory graduations for the AFDC group accentuate the importance of program assistance in job placement for these participants.

The performance of the other target groups are more similar to each other, with departure rates to jobs averaging from 23 to 29 percent, firing rates from 33 to 38 percent, and lengths of stay ranging from over five to seven months. Notably, the group with the lowest firing rate of the three also had the shortest length of stay. Ex-offenders were more likely than others to leave Supported Work on their own. This group had the second highest job-placement rate as well.

Ex-addicts had the second highest rate of departures for reasons of mandatory graduation. The Jersey City program, developed initially for ex-addicts, was particularly notable for the greater than average length of stay for all its target groups and probably reflects a supervisory philosophy with more emphasis on empathy than on structure and discipline. The slightly lower than average firing rates in Jersey City appear to support this observation as well. At the other extreme, the Philadelphia program had the shortest lengths of stay and the highest firing rates in general. This program was frequently noted by interviewers as a particularly tough program with respect to discipline.

While it is possible to find some relationship between the general philosophy at different sites and the termination patterns and length of stay or attendance rates, it is more difficult to find clear relationships between job-search assistance strategies and departure rates across sites. Program sites noted for their particularly strong job-preparation classes and job-placement assistance, such as Oakland and, to a lesser extent, Hartford, do not have notably higher job-departure rates than programs with consistently disorganized or relatively weaker job-search components, such as Washington, Massachusetts, and Newark.

In general, with respect to all program indicators, efforts to explain site effects upon participant performance, and especially to differentiate site strategies and the performance of particular target groups, do not produce many consistent patterns. Despite particularly rich and detailed data sources, the several analyses of the Supported Work Demonstration have not advanced very much further the ability to model a "production function" for social services. Impact analyses reported in subsequent chapters find few consistent site effects upon target groups. Both a statistical process analysis and the less rigorous descriptive examination set forth here do not reveal strong patterns that might be attributed to different program strategies. Some of this is due undoubtedly to the failure of analysts to specify variables which might better explain site effects and relate them to participant characteristics. Much, however, probably lies in relatively unmeasurable characteristics of individuals and in the interactions between participants and staff that lie in the realm of psychological factors. A few comments from the consultants who interviewed over 100 former Supported Workers from the four principal target groups, and the words of some of those participants, give a necessarily unsystematic but often revealing sense of what some of those factors might be.[13]

In a report to MDRC, one of the interviewers observed:

Virtually everyone who comes to supported work shares a common heritage, and that is one of a life without the social and economic security that comes to most Americans who hold regular jobs. In nearly every instance, supported workers are trying to make the leap from being either dependent on society or dropouts from it, to being independent and autonomous within it. Thus supported work is more than just a job or an entry to the job market; it is a substantial change in the lives of the participants and in their attitudes toward others. If there is one word that can summarize what got these participants who are now working through the program and into the work force, it is "responsibility." Dozens of people interviewed echoed what a young man in Newark said: "If you want to work, the program is there for you. But you've got to want to do it yourself."[14]

Local Supported Work programs became part of the life streams of the individuals who enrolled in them. The consultants found that the great majority of the former participants they interviewed valued the steady work the program provided and the opportunity to make steady work a part of their life. Not all were ready to make that change, nor, as the experimental findings indicate, did all participants need Supported Work to improve their short-term employment prospects.

Supported Work appeared to the consultants to be a necessary, although not always sufficient, agent of change for many participants. Of the AFDC women, it was observed that

[t]he stultifying impact of years at home with the children and out of the labor market cannot be overlooked. It is crucial to understand that the psychological readiness to work could not alone resurrect—or indeed initiate— stable working lives for these women. Subtle but indispensable supported work offerings were necessary to counteract the paralysis that set in as the women began their supported work year. . . . Many spoke of how shy and fearful they were as they took the plunge into supported work where they would be judged in a new way—not as mothers, but as workers.[15]

An ex-addict who had participated in the Oakland program, and had been incarcerated for two years on a drug charge before enrolling in Supported Work, commented that the structure of showing up at the workplace everyday had been important to him, if not particularly easy to adapt to. Before prison and the Oakland program, he had never held a job for as long as a year, but

[i]t didn't take long to get into the swing of the program, though. I needed a place of my own and I knew I had to go every day. Plus, I'd get a pat on the back every Friday with a paycheck. I've got a theory about money: fast money gets spent fast. Work for it and you hold onto it a little bit longer.[16]

Another ex-addict, interviewed in Philadelphia, had not succeeded as well. Fired from the Philadelphia program, he went back on welfare. Looking back on his experience, he commented:

You know, I kinda liked that job. I like my hard hat, my little yellow hard hat. When I left in the mornings I put my other stuff in a bag, but I always carried my hard hat so the neighbors could see. . . . If I can get my head together . . . I've got to be determined. I liked coming home with mud on my boots.[17]

Interviews with members of the youth target group revealed many who, while realizing the limitations which dropping out of school had placed on their opportunities, had quite clear ideas of what kinds of work they wanted, and most expressed strong opinions against hard labor or menial or boring work. Many of those interviewed said that they would not accept a job at less than four or five dollars an hour. Many seemed unready to accept the responsibility of working within the range of their present skills in order to obtain greater skills and experience. In light of the difficulties which Supported Work staff experienced working with the youth target group and the absence of net program effects revealed in the impact analysis, the Supported Work model has been modified for youths, permitting them to remain enrolled longer than 12 months and providing more educational remediation and counseling.[18]

The informal interviews from which these comments have been excerpted do not in any way resemble a randomly drawn sample of former Supported Work participants. Interviewers consistently observed, however, that a year's intervention in a participant's life that has been hard-pressed and seriously limited often wins his or her efforts at self-help. It is difficult to target a program so that participants will be drawn primarily from among those who will continue to help themselves effectively once they are given some initial assisted work experience. On balance, the AFDC participants appear to be one group for whom the categorical targeting captured a larger share of individuals at that state of readiness. Their steadier performance in Supported Work appears related to the net employment and welfare impacts for them. The supportive setting and job-placement assistance of Supported Work appear to be particularly well adapted to their needs.

That state of readiness is apparently more difficult to reach for the other target groups. With a deeper tangle of criminal behavior and association or with circumstances that led to dropping out of school or drug-dependency, it is a harder road to travel. That Supported Work appears to have worked, on balance, for ex-addicts is fairly remarkable. Perhaps the support-with-structure is more suitable for former drug abusers, many of whom present a more passive face to the world, and perhaps the structure of paid work experience, while not supportive of a large drug habit, has the appeal of a more stable life pattern. For the analyst, the knowledge that an intervention like Supported Work is successful for some groups but not for others, for reasons we have yet to understand, brings at one and the same time both satisfaction and humility.

Notes

1 Experimental research was conducted at nine of those sites and at a tenth which was added later. In this chapter some statistical data will be provided on the fourteenth and fifteenth local programs which were added to the demonstration after 1975, New York and Detroit. Discussion of program implementation strategies, however, will be confined to the initial 13 programs in the demonstration.

2 Kesselman (1978).

3 See Brecher (1978) for a history of the early formulation of the demonstration.

4 See MDRC (1976, 1978, 1980) for further discussion of program management structures.

5 The federal agencies contributing funds for demonstration operations and research were the Employment and Training Administration, U.S. De-

partment of Labor; the Law Enforcement Assistance Administration, U.S. Department of Justice; Office of Planning and Evaluation and National Institute on Drug Abuse, U.S. Department of Health, Education, and Welfare; Office of Policy Research and Development, U.S. Department of Housing and Urban Development; Office of Community Action, U.S. Community Services Administration; and the Economic Development Administration, U.S. Department of Commerce. Funding support was also provided by the Ford Foundation.

6 See Ball (1977) for further discussion of job-creation strategies during the first program year.

7 Over the course of the demonstration, 11 percent of all participant job-hours were spent working for private business customers, 11 percent for private individuals, 46 percent for public agencies, and 32 percent for nonprofit organizations.

8 During the first two years of the demonstration, through May 1977, 19 percent of participants had been in single person assignments, 29 percent in crews of two or three, and 51 percent in crews of four to ten (MDRC 1978).

9 See MDRC (1978, 131ff.).

10 Another important, although smaller, component of funding was the use of welfare payments diverted to the program. MDRC obtained federal and state agreements to an arrangement under which any reduction in an individual's AFDC welfare payment as a result of employment in a Supported Work program could be applied to cover a portion of that person's wage. These funds covered only 2 percent of the demonstration's total operating costs, but they became an important part of a local budget wherever a program employed a significant number of AFDC participants. See Shapiro (1978) for a discussion of the process of establishing welfare waivers. Also, see Shapiro (1979) for a discussion of local grant revenues.

11 Source: MDRC fiscal and management information system.

12 The cost per participant/year of service of MDRC central oversight by the third year (1977–1978), less the costs imposed as part of the MDRC research management role, was $365. This compared to central administrative costs for the Job Corps of $623 per year of service and $164 per year of service for CETA public service employment in fiscal year 1977. This latter is almost certainly a lower bound estimate of CETA/PSE central costs since more of the administrative functions of CETA are performed by local prime sponsors (Kemper et al. 1981).

13 Former participants at Philadelphia, Newark, Oakland, and Jersey City were interviewed. Participants were selected primarily from those who had either stayed in the program as long as possible or had left early to take a job. See Danziger (1981) for further discussion based upon the interviews with the AFDC group in Oakland and Newark; Ritter and Danziger (1983) for more detailed discussion of the AFDC interviews; and Lax (1980) for further detail on interviews with all target groups.

14 Lax (1980, 4).

15 Ritter and Danziger (1983, 23).
16 Quoted from Lax (1980, 16).
17 Ibid, 21, 22.
18 Preliminary findings from this redesigned program are reported in Semo Scharfman (1981).

4 *Robinson G. Hollister, Jr., and Rebecca A. Maynard*

The Impacts of Supported Work on AFDC Recipients

Introduction

From the outset of the Supported Work Demonstration design, it was expected that the program would be *least* effective in improving employment and increasing economic independence among the AFDC (Aid to Families with Dependent Children) target group. This expectation was based, in part, on the general observation that women tend to have greater difficulty finding employment than do men and that those who do find employment often are paid lower wages than are their male counterparts. The pessimism was also attributable to the fact that work incentives are lowered as a result of the availability of the welfare support through AFDC.

The results from this demonstration evaluation lend support for the a priori expectations regarding the adverse labor market experience of members of this target group in the absence of intervention. For example, as seen in figure 4.1, randomly selected members of the AFDC target group not offered Supported Work jobs (the control group) exhibited low levels of employment relative to the other main Supported Work target groups—ex-addicts, ex-offenders, and youths—as well as relative to the population at large. Although the data demonstrate that employment and earnings among this group would have improved in the absence of the Supported Work intervention (primarily due to improving labor markets), they would not have been expected to rise to levels commensurate with economic independence nor even com-

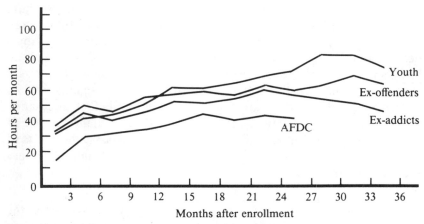

Fig. 4.1. Trend in Hours Worked by Control Group Members

parable to the other Supported Work target groups. Nonetheless, contrary to expectations, the Supported Work program did prove to be effective in improving somewhat the employment outlook for this group. Furthermore, the program was more successful in terms of both its employment impacts and its overall benefit-cost ratio for the AFDC target group than for any of the other three target groups.

Below, we review briefly the historical origins of the AFDC program as it existed during the demonstration period and empirical findings concerning both the employment effects of the AFDC program and the likely impacts of employment or training interventions. This provides a necessary context for the discussions in subsequent sections of the chapter, which focus on the Supported Work program experience and its results for AFDC recipients.

The Relationship between AFDC and Work

The AFDC program was enacted as part of the Social Security Act of 1935 as a program of assistance to families with a single parent. Initially, it was expected that enrollment in the AFDC program would decline over time as coverage under the Unemployment and Social Security programs broadened. However, despite both the expansion of these other programs and major legislative efforts aimed more directly at increasing the economic independence of AFDC adults, the caseload has tended to increase steadily in size. This increase in the caseload was most dramatic between 1968 and 1972, during which time the number of recipients nearly doubled and payments increased from 3 to 7 billion dollars per year.[1]

The persistently high numbers of participants in the AFDC program, together with shifting attitudes toward the roles of women in the work force, contributed to the increased public concern with and political debate about welfare reform during the 1960s and 1970s. The result has been a series of legislative changes designed to increase work incentives, to enhance the employability of AFDC recipients, and to minimize administrative errors and costs; a number of alternative program and demonstration initiatives aimed at reducing the size of the welfare dependent population; and research to assess the effects of the AFDC program parameters and of alternative and complementary programs or services.

Major Legislative Changes in the AFDC Program   Over time, the emphasis of the AFDC program has tended to shift from providing income support to women who were not expected to participate in the work force, to a program designed to meet the income support needs of individuals in and out of the labor force. This shift in emphasis began as early as 1961 with the establishment of the AFDC-UP program, which extended AFDC assistance in participating states to two-parent families with unemployed fathers. In 1967, the emphasis of increasing employment among AFDC recipients and on reducing overall caseloads was underscored by two congressional actions: the implementation of the "thirty-and-a-third rule" and the establishment of the work incentive (WIN) program for AFDC recipients. The "thirty-and-a-third" rule increased the monetary incentives for working by permitting AFDC recipients to retain the first $30 of earnings and one-third of additional earnings. (Prior to this change the rules called for a reduction in benefits exactly offsetting any earnings.) The WIN program also provided child care, other supportive services, employment counseling, and training to employable AFDC recipients. The final major change in the AFDC program resulted from the passage of the "Talmadge Amendments" to the Social Security Act. These amendments shifted WIN priorities to policies designed mainly to increase short-run employment. These policies included placing greater emphasis on on-the-job training, public service employment, direct placement into unsubsidized jobs, and the enforcement of work requirements.[2]

These changes in the AFDC program did not result in the containment of the AFDC caseloads. However, they do seem to have had some positive impact on the employment of AFDC recipients (see, for example, Bolland 1973; Rence and Wiseman 1978; Ehrenberg and Hewlett 1976).

Program and Demonstration Initiatives Concurrent with the several major legislative efforts to increase the economic independence of AFDC adults, including the inception and redirection of the WIN program, numerous evaluations of programs that served the AFDC client population were conducted. However, in general, these evaluations conducted in the 1960s and early 1970s yielded little in the way of specific knowledge as to effective means to reduce the caseloads or to increase the economic independence of clients. These studies include evaluations of programs sponsored under the Manpower Development and Training Act (MDTA) (Perry et al. 1975; Borus 1972; Prescott et al. 1971; Ashenfelter 1974), the Community Work and Training Program and the Work Experience and Training Program (Lowenthal 1971), Job Opportunities in the Business Sector (JOBS) (Farber 1971), and the Work Incentive Program (Auerbach Associates 1973; Reid and Smith 1972; Schiller et al. 1976; Smith 1975; U.S. Department of Labor, ETA 1977). These studies yielded results that suggest the programs may have increased employment of AFDC recipients who participated, but these estimates were statistically unreliable and they failed to provide guidelines regarding programmatic design features or targeting strategies that would be effective.

The rise in the AFDC caseload, combined with the limited knowledge of effective policy options for increasing the employment of the AFDC population, led to the funding in the latter half of the 1970s of a number of demonstrations and evaluations aimed at defining solutions to the problem. Some of these studies, which have been undertaken concurrently with the Supported Work Demonstration, provide evidence to corroborate or to complement the findings from this evaluation. For example, one such group of studies provides evidence that training and work experience programs tend to increase postprogram employment of participants (Ketron, Inc. 1979a,b; U.S. Department of Health, Education, and Welfare 1978; Utah Department of Social Services 1977). Another suggests that existing work requirements and the provision of regular job-search assistance services, such as are provided by the employment service and private employment agencies, themselves will not significantly increase employment (Ohls and Carcagno 1978; Schiller et al. 1976), but that special job-search assistance services may increase employment (Azrin 1978; Goldman 1981). Other studies have simply established a linkage between work requirements

and/or work experience and reductions in welfare dependence (Aje-
main et al. 1981; Ketron, Inc. 1979a).

Organization of the Chapter

The objective of this chapter is to summarize the findings from what
is perhaps the major demonstration undertaken to identify means to
increase long-term employment and economic well-being of AFDC
recipients. In the next section, we describe the Supported Work AFDC
sample and the data used to conduct the evaluation. The third section
outlines the analytic methodology used. The fourth section discusses
estimates of program impacts based on findings from the main evaluation effort and from a special follow-up study. Finally, the results
from this evaluation are discussed in the context of their policy significance.

The Sample and Data

Characteristics of the AFDC Research Sample

Eligibility for Supported Work as members of the AFDC target group
was limited to women who were receiving AFDC and who had received
AFDC payments for 30 out of the preceding 36 months. The youngest
child of such women had to be six years of age or older; they had to
be currently unemployed and to have worked no more than three
months on a regular job during the previous six months.[3]

In order to assess the impact of Supported Work on AFDC recipients, eligible applicants for AFDC target group slots in seven of the
demonstration sites—Atlanta, Chicago, Hartford, Newark, New York,
Oakland, and Wisconsin—were randomly assigned to an experimental
or control group.[4] The first AFDC recipient was randomly assigned in
Newark in February 1976. Random assignment continued through
July 1977, by which time 1,620 persons had been enrolled in the AFDC
target group.

Data Collection Design   The primary source of data for this analysis
is interviews with sample members at the time of program entry (baseline interviews) and at subsequent 9-month intervals for up to 27
months after enrollment. Subsequent to the completion of the main
evaluation's data collection effort, however, an additional follow-up
interview was administered to the AFDC target group, which collected
information for a period of up to 43 months after enrollment.

Table 4.1 presents the sample sizes available for analysis of impacts
for varying periods of time after program enrollment.[5] All members

TABLE 4.1
Number and Percent of AFDC Sample Members Completing
Scheduled Follow-up Interviews

	9- and 18-Month Interviews		27-Month Interview		Subsequent Follow-up	
	Number	Percent[a]	Number	Percent[a]	Number	Percent[a]
Site						
Atlanta	148	11.0	74	12.0	146	12.2
Chicago	234	17.3	133	21.6	185	15.4
Hartford	109	8.1	52	8.4	122	10.2
Newark	242	17.9	161	26.1	225	18.8
New York	463	34.3	136	22.1	384	32.1
Oakland	129	9.5	38	6.2	108	9.0
Wisconsin	26	1.9	22	3.6	28	2.3
Cohort[b]						
18-month	764	56.6	n.a.	n.a.	c	c
27-month	587	43.4	616	100.0	c	c
Total	1351	100.0	616	100.0	1198	100.0

Note: These figures include only sample members who completed a baseline interview, since most of the evaluation results are based on multivariate analysis that controls for preenrollment characteristics of experimental and control group members.

a These are percentages of the AFDC analysis sample in the appropriate reference periods.

b The 18-month cohort consists of sample members who enrolled in 1977 and so were not scheduled to receive a 27-month interview. The 27-month cohort consists of sample members who enrolled prior to 1977 and so were scheduled to receive this third follow-up interview.

c These figures are not available.

n.a. Not applicable.

of both the experimental and control groups were scheduled to be interviewed at the time of their application for Supported Work to determine their demographic characteristics, employment history, and welfare dependence. They were then scheduled to be reinterviewed 9 and 18 months later to collect postenrollment data on items such as employment and welfare dependence. Of the total sample, 1,351 sample members completed both of these interviews. The main demonstration evaluation interviewing effort continued through March 1979, by which time 48 percent of the sample (those enrolled prior to 1977) had been scheduled to receive a 27-month interview, which 616 sample members completed. An additional wave of interviews was conducted in November and December of 1979 with all sample members who could be located (74 percent of the total sample).

Characteristics of the Sample As seen in table 4.1, the majority of the AFDC sample resided in large cities. One-third of the sample lived in New York City, 20 percent lived in Newark, and 16 percent lived in Chicago. Enrollments in the other sites constituted between 2 (in Wisconsin) and 11 (in Atlanta) percent of all AFDC sample enrollments.

Most of the sample was referred to Supported Work by the WIN program. However, a few individuals were referred by state employment services or applied to Supported Work on their own. Regardless of the referral source, as already noted, participation was always voluntary.

As can be seen from the data in table 4.2, the typical person in the AFDC sample was 34 years old, was a black with 10 years of schooling, had two dependents, and had a youngest child between the ages of 6 and 12. The average welfare (AFDC) payment was $282 per month, in addition to which food stamps, with an average bonus value of $72, were also received. Welfare had been received, on average, for almost nine years, and the average woman's last regular job, if she had one, was four years ago.

The characteristics of those whose latest scheduled interview were 18 and 27 months after enrollment—the 18- and 27-month cohorts, respectively—were quite similar, with two exceptions. First, a relatively high proportion of the 27-month cohort, as compared with the 18-month cohort, is from Atlanta, Chicago, or Newark. Second, those in the 27-month cohort had had regular jobs lasting substantially longer, on average, than did the jobs of members of the 18-month cohort.

Based on data from the 1975 AFDC survey, it has been estimated that 17 percent of all AFDC recipients met the Supported Work eligibility criteria. However, as can be seen from table 4.3, those AFDC recipients meeting the Supported Work eligibility criteria differed considerably from the full AFDC population. In addition to differences resulting directly from the eligibility criteria, the eligible sample included a lower percentage of individuals who are young, white, and high school graduates. While those eligible for Supported Work appear to be more disadvantaged than the overall AFDC population, those AFDC recipients participating in the WIN program appear to be less disadvantaged than the average AFDC recipient. For example, the WIN participants are younger, better educated, and less likely to be members of minority groups.

The main difference between the total AFDC population meeting the Supported Work eligibility criteria and the actual Supported Work sample is the higher percentage of minority group members in the

TABLE 4.2
Percentage Distribution of the AFDC Sample, by Characteristics at Enrollment

	Total Sample[a]	Sample with Only 18 Months of Follow-up Data	Sample with 27 Months of Follow-up Data
Site			
Atlanta	10.7	9.8	12.4
Chicago	16.4	13.2	22.7
Hartford	8.8	8.2	7.8
Newark	19.7	13.0	24.4
New York	33.2	42.8	23.1
Oakland	9.2	12.3	6.0
Wisconsin	2.0	0.7	3.6
Years of age			
< 26	12.9	12.9	12.3
26–35	52.5	54.1	48.2
36–44	25.5	25.9	27.4
> 44	9.1	7.2	12.1
(Average)	(33.5)	(33.0)	(34.4)
Race/ethnicity			
Hispanic	12.2	13.9	9.9
White, non-Hispanic	5.0	3.5	6.0
Black and other[b]	82.7	82.6	84.1
Years of education			
0–8	15.7	14.0	18.1
9–11	53.7	53.2	54.6
12	27.3	29.6	23.9
≥ 13	3.2	3.1	3.4
(Average)	(10.3)	(10.4)	(10.1)
Number of dependents			
0–2[c]	63.6	65.4	61.5
3–4	29.9	28.1	31.3
≥ 5	6.4	6.6	7.2
(Average)	(2.2)	(2.2)	(2.3)
(Average household size)	(3.7)	(3.7)	(3.8)
Married	3.2	2.9	3.2
Total years ever receiving welfare			
0–3	6.5	6.4	6.9
4–5	13.7	13.5	12.5
6–7	23.5	23.3	22.7
≥ 8	56.3	56.6	57.9
(Average)	(8.6)	(8.5)	(8.7)
Age of youngest child (years)			
< 6[d]	2.4	2.5	2.2
6–12	78.3	79.3	77.3
13–18	17.9	16.8	18.8
> 18, or no child	1.4	1.4	1.7

(Continued on following pages)

TABLE 4.2 (Continued)
Percentage Distribution of the AFDC Sample, by Characteristics at Enrollment

	Total Sample[a]	Sample with Only 18 Months of Follow-up Data	Sample with 27 Months of Follow-up Data
Job training			
Some in past year	9.4	11.4	7.0
(Average number of weeks in job training)	(1.5)	(1.7)	(1.4)
Months since last regular job			
No regular job	14.1	13.2	15.5
Now working or < 2	3.2	2.2	4.9
2–6	5.2	6.6	3.8
7–12	6.6	6.6	6.3
13–24	11.3	10.9	10.1
25–48	12.8	12.4	14.3
49–144	35.1	37.5	31.5
> 144	11.6	10.6	13.6
(Average years since last employed for those with job)	(4.0)	(3.8)	(4.2)
(Average months in longest regular job ever for those who had a job)	(28.1)	(22.99)	(33.70)
(Average monthly earnings last 12 months [dollars])	(19.39)	(22.25)	(17.01)
Monthly AFDC income[e] (dollars)			
0–200	21.1	24.0	17.9
200–400	65.6	60.9	70.4
> 400	13.3	15.1	11.7
(Average)	(282.01)	(281.59)	(281.24)
Monthly total welfare income[ef] (dollars)			
0–200	20.9	23.9	17.8
200–400	65.6	60.8	70.5
> 400	13.4	15.4	11.7
(Average)	(283.36)	(283.04)	(282.72)
Food stamp bonuses[g]			
Received benefits	92.7	92.4	93.6
(Average monthly bonus value [dollars])	(71.76)	(68.48)	(76.08)
Living in public housing	35.7	34.3	40.5
Having own Medicaid card	94.3	96.0	92.7
Rent home			
(Average monthly rent paid by renters [dollars])	(128.34)	(132.19)	(118.71)
Number in sample	1602	764	587

(Continued on following page)

TABLE 4.2 (Continued)
Percentage Distribution of the AFDC Sample, by Characteristics at Enrollment

Note: Unless otherwise indicated, all averages include zero values.

a For all AFDC this is the number of people who completed baseline interviews—98.8 percent of those enrolled in the sample. The sample sizes in the second and third columns are those completing baseline, 9-, and 18-month interviews with no 27-month interview and those completing baseline, 9-, 18-, and 27-month interviews, respectively.

b Other races constitute 0.3 percent of the total sample.

c No dependents were reported by 2 percent of the sample, indicating either reporting or eligibility determination errors.

d There should not have been any sample member with a youngest child less than 6 years old. Consequently these figures represent either reporting or eligibility determination errors.

e This pertains to the month prior to enrollment.

f This includes General Assistance, Supplemental Security Income, and unspecified welfare, as well as AFDC.

g The bonus value is the face value minus the purchase price.

latter group, a difference probably resulting from the nature of the demonstration sites. These differences, together with other factors discussed below, limit somewhat the extent to which the findings from this demonstration can be generalized to the total population of AFDC recipients meeting the Supported Work eligibility criteria.[6]

Program Experiences of the Experimental Group   The members of the randomly assigned AFDC experimental group, sometimes referred to as "participants," had the opportunity to take a position in the Supported Work program in their local area. As described in chapter 2, there were attempts to standardize key features of the Supported Work program across the different local sites, in particular, the maximum duration of the program treatment and the wage scale. Nonetheless, the programs were run somewhat differently in various cities, partly because the differing labor market conditions dictated such adjustments and partly because the local operators chose organizational strategies of varying types.

As can be seen in table 4.4, which summarizes key program characteristics, all sites enrolling AFDC participants also enrolled at least one other target group. The overall size of the programs varied substantially across sites and over time within a given site. Overall, the size of the work crews tended to average between three and five. How-

TABLE 4.3

Percentage Distributions of the AFDC and WIN Participant Populations and of the Supported Work AFDC Sample, by Demographic Characteristics

	Adults on AFDC 1975[a]	AFDC Recipients Meeting Supported Work Eligibility Criteria, 1975[a]	WIN Participants 1974[b]	Supported Work AFDC Sample[c]
Sex				
Male	12.1[d]	0.0	30.0	0.0
Female	87.9	100.0	70.0	100.0
Age				
Under 25	31.3	2.1	43.5	8.3
25 and over	68.7	97.9	56.5	91.7
Race				
White	41.4	33.4	51.1	5.0
Minority	58.7	66.6	48.9	95.0
Education				
< 12th grade	62.8	74.4	55.2	69.4
≥ 12th grade	37.2	25.6	44.8	30.6
Family size				
≤ 2	21.9	20.5	27.6	25.7
3–4	43.3	42.7	47.0	47.9
≥ 5	34.8	36.8	25.5	26.4
Months on welfare				
1–6	11.2	0.0	50.3	0.4[e]
7–12	10.9	0.0	9.4	0.3[e]
13–24	15.9	0.0	12.7	1.7[e]
≥ 25	62.0	100.0	27.6	97.6
Months since last full-time job				
Now working or < 2	17.6	0.0	7.7	3.2[f]
2–6	3.9	4.2	31.9	5.2
7–12	5.8	4.6	12.8	6.6
13–24	6.2	5.7	11.1	11.3
≥ 25 (or never worked)	66.5	85.5	36.4	73.6
Number of persons	2,977,768	494,501[g]	n.a.	1,602

a These figures are based on data from a survey of 26,617 AFDC recipients conducted by the Department of Health, Education, and Welfare in 1975. Analysis of these data was conducted by the Mathematica Policy Research programming staff.

b These data are reported in Schiller et al. (1976) and are based on a random sample of WIN registrants in 78 sites drawn for the longitudinal evaluation of the Work Incentive (WIN) program.

c These data are from the Supported Work baseline interview.

d If present, males are assumed to be the AFDC recipients.

(Continued on following page)

TABLE 4.3 (Continued)
Percentage Distributions of the AFDC and WIN Participant Populations and of the
Supported Work AFDC Sample, by Demographic Characteristics

e The fact that some persons in the AFDC sample were on welfare less than 30 months
   means that they were technically not eligible to participate in Supported Work or that
   there were reporting errors.
f A full-time job is defined as any job that was 20 hours a week or more and lasted at
   least 2 weeks. (This definition is not consistent with that used to determine eligibility.)
g This figure is based on the assumption that the 123,945 recipients whose eligibility
   status could not be determined because of missing data are represented among the
   eligible and noneligible subsamples in the same proportions as those whose eligibility
   status could be determined.
n.a. Not available.

ever, Hartford was an exception, with an average crew size of over
seven.

The types of jobs on which AFDC participants worked while in the
program and the nature of the supervision provided varied considerably from site to site. For example, in Chicago and Newark, over
70 percent of hours were spent in business (primarily clerical) services,
whereas in Oakland, only 16 percent of hours were spent in such jobs.
In Hartford, Oakland, and Wisconsin most of the supervision was done
by persons hired by the program, while in Atlanta, Chicago, and Newark most of the supervisors were provided by the host agencies.

One of the most important features of the Supported Work experience of the AFDC experimental group is the length of time individuals stayed in the program. As can be seen in table 4.5, AFDC experimentals, on average, stayed in Supported Work nine months, which
is two to three months longer than members of the other Supported
Work target groups stayed in the program. There was considerable
variance across sites in the length of the AFDC groups' program participation, with those in Atlanta, Newark, and New York staying about
9.5 months and those in Oakland and Wisconsin staying fewer than
seven months, on average. However, there was no difference between
those sites that had a 12-month limit on program participation and
those that had an 18-month limit. On the other hand, those with 27
months of follow-up data—the 27-month cohort—stayed in Supported
Work an average of one-half month longer than did those enrollees
for whom the final interview, conducted as part of the initial evaluation
effort, was 18 months after enrollment—the 18-month cohort.

TABLE 4.4
Selected Characteristics of Programs Enrolling AFDC Target Group Members, by Site

	Atlanta	Chicago	Hartford	Newark	New York	Oakland	Wisconsin
Average number of program job slots[a]	90	184	221	163	284	109	115
Range of program hourly wage rate[b]	$2.30–2.60	$2.60–3.00	$2.50–2.88	$2.70–3.11	$2.38–2.88	$2.63–3.02	$2.30–2.60
Average hourly wage rate of employed controls[c]	$2.83	$2.75	$2.80	$2.59	$3.14	$2.89	$1.48
Average crew size[d]	3.1	4.9	7.4	4.3	n.a.	4.2	3.6
Percentage AFDC project hours, by industry[d]							
Services	94.5	79.8	66.3	93.3	n.a.	16.2	81.7
Business	49.1	71.8	10.0	80.1	n.a.	16.2	57.0
Other	45.4	8.0	56.3	13.2	n.a.	0.0	24.7
Construction	3.7	13.9	0.0	0.0	n.a.	16.9	11.4
Other	1.8	6.3	33.7	6.7	n.a.	66.9	6.9
Percentage distribution of AFDC project hours, by type of job supervision[d]							
Program	7.0	16.9	66.8	8.3	n.a.	90.0	83.0
Customer or customer plus program	92.0	83.0	2.5	85.7	n.a.	0.0	17.0
Unknown	1.0	0.1	30.7	6.1	n.a.	10.0	0.0
Maximum allowable months in Supported Work	12	12	18	18	12	12	18

a *Source*: Manpower Demonstration Research Corporation (1978, Table II-1). Data refer to program size as of June 1977.
b *Source*: Manpower Demonstration Research Corporation (1978, Table VI-11).
c These data were calculated from interview data covering the first 9 months after enrollment in the demonstration. The Wisconsin figure is based on a very small sample.
d These data are from a special Supported Work MIS Report and cover the second contract year.
n.a.　Not available.

TABLE 4.5

Average Length of Stay in Supported Work and Percentage Distribution, by Reason for Termination—AFDC Sample

A. BY SITE

	Atlanta	Chicago	Hartford	Newark	New York	Oakland	Wisconsin	Total Sample
Average number of months in Supported Work[a]	9.4	9.1	8.0	9.5	9.5	6.7	6.9	9.0
Percentage who left because of:								
Exhausting allowable time in program	42.4	41.8	0.0	1.9	39.5	17.2	0.0	28.2
Taking another job or enrolling in school or job training	15.2	14.3	22.5	14.6	13.9	25.9	25.0	16.1
Poor performance[b]	9.1	5.5	15.0	10.7	8.5	25.9	37.5	11.0
Other[c]	33.3	38.5	62.5	72.8	38.1	31.0	37.5	44.7

B. BY LENGTH OF POSTENROLLMENT FOLLOW-UP

	18 Months Only	27 Months	Total Sample
Average number of months in Supported Work[a]	8.8	9.3	9.0
Percentage who left because of:			
Exhausting allowable time in program	26.7	30.2	28.2
Taking another job or enrolling in school or job training	17.4	14.5	16.1
Poor performance[b]	12.6	9.0	11.0
Other[c]	43.4	46.3	44.7

Note: Samples are defined as specified in table 4.1. The 27-month sample had completed all scheduled interviews. Atlanta, Chicago, New York, and Oakland permit only 12 months of program participation. Length of maximum participation made no difference to average length of stay. All data came from interviews with sample members.

a The average length of stay differs from the month of the first Supported Work termination for two reasons: some individuals did not begin their Supported Work job immediately upon enrolling in the demonstration sample and some reenrolled after a period of inactivation.

b Poor performance includes problems with absenteeism, punctuality, and productivity.

c "Other" reasons include problems of health, transportation, and child care, as well as disliking the program experience.

Only a small portion, 28 percent, of the participants stayed in Supported Work for the maximum allowable time. Sixteen percent left Supported Work to take a job, go to school, or enter a training program; and 11 percent left because of poor performance.[7]

Data Used in the Analysis

As was noted previously, the primary data for analysis of program impacts were those obtained as part of the main evaluation effort through interviews conducted with experimental and control group members at the time of their enrollment and at subsequent 9-month intervals for 18 or 27 months. In addition, welfare and Social Security agency data were collected for use in special studies aimed at assessing the quality of the interview data used in the main evaluation. Finally, an additional wave of follow-up interviews was conducted late in 1979 to extend the period of follow-up for all sample members to between 27 and 43 months after enrollment.

Interviews Conducted in Conjunction with the Main Evaluation   The evaluation design included use of multivariate analytic methods, which controlled statistically for pre-enrollment characteristics of the experimental and control group members. Thus, the analysis samples included only respondents to the baseline interviews—98 percent of all enrollees. Additional sample restrictions based on the availability of follow-up data were necessarily imposed. In balancing the objectives of maximizing the precision of point estimates of program impacts and of containing computation costs, the basic analysis was conducted using two different subsets of the sample: (1) those who completed both 9- and 18-month interviews (the 18-month analysis sample); and (2) those who completed a 27-month interview, regardless of whether they also completed 9- and 18-month interviews (the 27-month analysis sample). However, because the characteristics of those who completed a 27-month interview differed somewhat from the characteristics of the overall sample (see above and table 4.2), some results were estimated separately for two cohorts of sample members—those enrolled prior to 1977 (the 27-month cohort) and those enrolled in 1977 (the 18-month cohort).[8]

Special Data and Methodological Studies   The evaluation based on the interview data described above could result in biased estimates of program impacts either because of differential interview nonresponse or because of reporting errors. Thus, special studies were conducted to determine whether estimates based on the sample of interview responders were unbiased and to assess the extent of possible response bias in self-reported data on earnings and AFDC receipt. The overall conclusions from these studies were that neither interview nonresponse nor response error affected substantively the overall conclusions presented here.[9]

Follow-up Interviews The additional follow-up study of the AFDC target group was prompted by two factors: indications from preliminary analyses that Supported Work had positive impacts on the AFDC recipients and the relatively short duration of follow-up for this group in the main evaluation. Both to extend the period of follow-up and to increase the number in the overall sample for whom a minimum of 27 months of follow-up was available, the full AFDC sample was scheduled to receive an additional interview in November and December 1979, which was between 27 and 43 months after enrollment.

In all, 1,198 (74 percent) completed this follow-up interview, which unquestionably provides the best information on long-term impacts and change in these effects for individuals over time. However, because of the deviation from the 9-month interviewing schedule adopted in the main evaluation, the analytic model used with the follow-up data also differed, making simultaneous presentation of results from the two studies awkward. Thus, below, we first discuss results from the main evaluation and then discuss those from the follow-up.

Analytic Approach

Before commencing our discussion of the outcomes of the demonstration, we will describe in general terms the analytic methods used in estimating program effects, as well as some of the recognized weaknesses from which these estimating procedures may suffer. Since these procedures have been used for all target groups (see chapters 5–7), the discussion is rather extensive here, but is omitted in subsequent chapters.

Most of the formal evaluation of Supported Work impacts on participants has been conducted using multiple regression analysis. Since random assignment to the experimental and control group was strictly adhered to,[10] a simple comparison of experimental and control group means would provide unbiased estimates of program effects. However, the use of regression analysis has two advantages. First, to the extent that measurable factors exogenous to the program treatment itself influence the outcome measures, regression analysis permits us to obtain estimates of program effects that have a higher degree of precision than those obtained through a simple comparison of means approach. Second, regression analysis permits us to investigate easily whether program effects vary significantly among subgroups of the sample or among people enrolled in different sites. Formally, the impact of program participation is estimated through regression models of the form:

$$Y = a_0 + a_1X_1 + a_2X_2 + \ldots + a_MX_M + bS + u$$

where Y is the observed outcome measure; X_m ($m = 1, \ldots, M$) is a set of variables indicating the Supported Work site and the characteristics of the individual; S is a binary variable indicating whether the individual was assigned to the experimental group; and u is a random error term. The symbol a_m measures the impact of X_m on Y; and b is a measure of the overall impact of the program whose statistical significance level is measured by a t-test. (Appendix table A.1 identifies the control variables used in the analysis and their means.)

The extension of this basic model to estimate effects for subgroups of the sample is quite straightforward. The types of models estimated can be expressed formally as:

$$Y = a_0 + a_1X_1 + a_2X_2 + \ldots + a_MX_M + b_0S + b_1SX_1 + \ldots + b_KSX_K + u$$

where X_k ($k = 1, \ldots, K$) is a subset of X_m. In this model, the program effect for a particular subgroup is measured by a linear combination of the b's. For example, if X is a set of binary variables to designate all but one of the Supported Work sites, then b_0 is the program effect for the omitted site and $b_0 + b_k$ is the program effect at site k. The statistical significance of the various subgroup effects can be measured by an F-test, as can tests of whether effects vary among the subgroups (that is, $b_1 = b_2 = \ldots = b_K = 0$).[11]

We should point out that these simple linear regression models may not yield estimates of program effects with desirable statistical properties in cases where the outcome measure is truncated (for example, hours worked) or in cases where it is dichotomous (for example, employed or not). Maximum likelihood techniques have been developed to account for these properties of the outcome measures, but are prohibitively costly for routine use in a project the magnitude of this one. Thus, since the standard regression techniques have repeatedly been shown to yield quite accurate estimates in most applications, we have tended to rely on this procedure and to selectively reestimate a few of the results using the maximum likelihood techniques—probit (for dichotomous outcomes) and tobit (for bounded outcome measures)—to test whether the basic conclusions are sensitive to this analytic constraint.[12]

Regardless of the analytic technique employed (linear regression, maximum likelihood, or comparison of means), the discussion in subsequent chapters focuses on experimental-control group differences in the various outcome measures. Since those differences are based on estimates of sample means, which are subject to sampling variability, we must consider the likelihood that the estimated difference between experimentals and controls is due to a true program effect as opposed to the random sampling variability. The statistical concepts that relate to this likelihood are the confidence interval and the statistical significance of the estimated differentials.[13] In this report, we have adopted the standard procedure of indicating those estimated program effects that are significant at the 10 and 5 percent levels. Since we are using a two-tailed test, this means that when a positive differential is statistically significant at the 5 percent level, for example, there is less than a 2.5 percent chance that there was no positive program effect.

While we have adopted these standards for denoting "significant effects," there are two counterbalancing considerations which we also consider in interpreting the results. The first is the small probability that a large statistically significant differential may have been observed, even though the true effect is in fact zero. Consequently, one must expect the occurrence of occasional significant differentials, even in the absence of real program effects. The second is that failure to observe significant experimental-control differences does not necessarily mean they do not exist. It may simply mean there is so much sampling variability relative to the true effects that we cannot accurately estimate the size of the true effects. In light of these considerations, in addition to adopting the standard criteria for denoting statistical significance, we have exercised some judgment in deciding which results or patterns of results are particularly worth noting in the discussion and interpretation of the findings. Yet another consideration in interpreting the results is that, in some cases, estimated program effects may meet the criteria of statistical significance but may be so small in magnitude that they are of little policy relevance or, in other cases, results that do not meet standard criteria of statistical significance may be so large that a policymaker may want to act on the basis of the findings.

Despite the advantage of the Supported Work Demonstration's evaluation design, which includes relatively large samples, random assignment to experimental or control groups, and a sizable follow-up period, there are several potentially important qualifications of the study's findings that should be kept in mind. For example, control group members have access to WIN services and some may find employment in subsidized jobs sponsored by WIN, CETA, or other government programs. Thus, the experimental-control comparisons indicate the effects of Supported Work in an environment that includes existing alternative programs and services rather than an environment free of other programs.

Another limitation of the study is that the follow-up period for the main evaluation, while long relative to that available for most program evaluations, includes only nine postprogram months for about half of the sample (those enrolled in 1977). Thus, the subsequent longer-term follow-up study of the full sample is an important complement to the main evaluation (Masters and McDonald 1981). A third type of limitation of the study is that it is not possible to determine the extent to which a program such as Supported Work affects employment opportunities of nonparticipants.[14] The extent to which these limitations are important depends, in part, on the findings of the evaluation. Thus, we shall consider these issues further in the context of the evaluation findings.

Program Impacts

In assessing the impact of Supported Work, one is most interested in how the employment experiences and welfare dependence of those who had the opportunity to participate in the program differed from what they would have been in the absence of such an opportunity. As noted previously, the employment and public assistance experiences of the randomly assigned control group provide excellent information on what the experiences of Supported Work participants would have been in the absence of the program. As figure 4.1 above indicates, that experience with respect to employment would have been quite dismal. Although employment among the controls improved over time as the economy recovered from severe recession, the average hours worked per month never exceeded 50 during any 3-month period, and barely more than one-third of the controls were employed. Their welfare dependence was correspondingly high, with over 85 percent receiving AFDC or General Assistance throughout the follow-up period.

In this section, we present a detailed examination of the employment-related experiences and welfare dependence of experimentals and controls. Although we report on differences during the period in which experimentals could participate in Supported Work, the primary focus is on the postprogram period and on determining whether the program had detectable effects which persisted after individuals had left their Supported Work jobs.

The simple conclusion from this analysis is that the program did lead to significant improvements in the employment experiences of AFDC recipients, both during the period when individuals were eligible to participate in the program and during the postprogram period. In every period of observation, a significantly higher percentage of experimentals than controls were employed, and experimentals worked more hours and earned higher incomes than did their control group counterparts. Furthermore, both during the period of program participation and subsequently, dependence on public transfer programs decreased significantly among experimentals relative to controls. These simple conclusions stand out clearly, despite several potentially confounding issues which arise when the details of interpretation are pursued, as will be explained below.

In this section, we first discuss overall findings related to employment and earnings, based on the main evaluation effort. Subsequently, results for welfare dependence and child-care utilization are discussed, and finally, results from the follow-up survey are presented.

Employment and Earnings Results from the Main Evaluation
The primary focus of the initial evaluation effort was on estimating the impacts of Supported Work on employment and earnings, since these outcomes are viewed as the key to simultaneously increasing economic well-being and reducing welfare dependence among this target group. The overall results of the demonstration can be summarized by figure 4.2A, which shows experimental-control differences in hours worked during the 27-month period covered by the main evaluation. More detailed data on findings for employment rates, hours of work, and earnings are summarized in table 4.6. As can be seen from these results, a higher percentage of experimentals than controls were employed, and experimentals worked more hours and earned higher incomes over the entire 27-month period following enrollment than did their control group counterparts.

The fact that experimentals' employment and earnings exceeded those of the controls during the early months after enrollment is not at all surprising, since the experimental participant was offered a full-time job paying at least the minimum wage, whereas the controls had to search for positions in the low-wage labor market just as they always had. As the experimentals began to leave their Supported Work jobs— some to take other jobs; some because they were fired; and many because of health, child care, or other problems—the experimental-control differential declined, as was expected. By months 16–18, when nearly all of the experimentals had left their Supported Work jobs, the

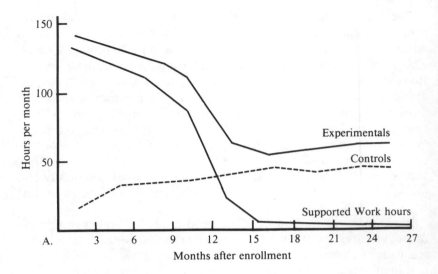

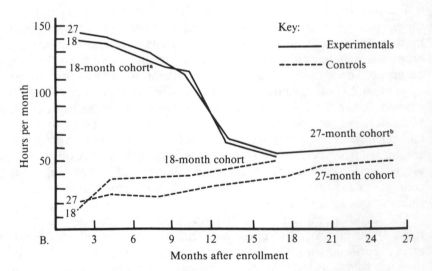

Fig. 4.2. Trend in Hours Worked per Month. *A*, Total AFDC Sample; *B*, By Cohort.
Note: These data are not regression-adjusted.
a The average length of stay in Supported Work was 9.3 months.
b The average length of stay in Supported Work was 8.8 months.

TABLE 4.6

Estimated Program Impacts and Control Group Means for Employment, Hours of Work, and Earnings—AFDC Sample

	Percentage Employed		Average Hours Worked per Month		Average Earnings per Month		Percentage of Experimentals in Supported Work
Months	Experimental-Control Differential	Control Group Mean	Experimental-Control Differential	Control Group Mean	Experimental-Control Differential	Control Group Mean	
1–3	75.8**	19.4	122.5**	17.8	360.16**	49.28	93.6[a]
4–6	63.0**	26.0	107.9**	30.7	321.46**	90.84	85.4
7–9	54.2**	28.2	94.4**	33.1	287.92**	99.28	75.2
10–12	46.0**	27.5	78.9**	35.1	253.40**	117.85	59.0
13–15	26.7**	31.7	24.9**	40.6	96.99**	140.12	32.9
16–18	5.3**	35.1	10.1**	46.0	53.97**	159.33	4.3
19–21	8.1**	33.3	16.5**	42.9	69.13**	161.79	2.9
22–24	7.4*	34.9	15.2**	46.0	78.10**	166.54	1.3
25–27	7.1*	34.9	15.9**	45.9	80.61**	167.86	0.0

Note: Averages include zero values. See table 4.1 for the sample definitions and sizes.

a The 6.4 percent not working for Supported Work participated for less than 2 weeks.

* Statistically significant at the 10 percent level.

** Statistically significant at the 5 percent level.

111

experimental-control differential had fallen to its lowest point—an average of 10 hours and $54 per month. Thereafter, for the remainder of the 27-month follow-up period, statistically significant differentials between experimentals and controls persisted: employment rate differentials ranged from 7 to 8 percentage points; average monthly hours of employment differed by 15 to 17; and average monthly earnings differences ranged from $69 to $81 per month.

After the first postenrollment year, earnings differentials were proportionately larger than were the hours differentials, implying that the average wage rate of the experimentals exceeded that of the controls. In fact, of course, the overall earnings effect is the result of effects in three dimensions: the rate of employment, the hours worked for those employed, and the hourly wage rates. In months 25–27, Supported Work led to differences in employment rates of 20 percent (42 versus 35 percent), in hours worked of 35 percent (62 versus 46 hours), and in earnings of 48 percent ($248 versus $168). This upward trend from employment, to hours, to earnings suggests that the program had the effect of not only increasing the "postprogram" employment, but also of resulting in steadier jobs (more hours) and better-paying jobs (higher wages).

These results for employment and earnings are striking in their persistence over time. However, it is important to keep them in perspective. Although the program had sizable and significant effects on the employment and earnings of AFDC recipients, even when the *postprogram* effects were at their greatest, only 42 percent of the former Supported Work participants were employed and the average earnings of participants exceeded the average for controls by only $81 per month. Nonetheless, these differences are sufficiently large so that, in combination with other benefits, they more than justify the social costs of the program (see chapter 8 on the benefit-cost analysis of the program). However, the program is far from being a complete antidote for all the economic problems faced by AFDC recipients.

Differential Impacts for Selected Sample Subgroups   With the overall employment and earnings results as background, we now consider employment and earnings results for subgroups of the AFDC sample. In this section, we discuss disaggregations of program impacts according to (1) cohorts of enrollees, (2) site, (3) characteristics at the time of enrollment, and (4) length of program participation.

Differential impacts among cohorts. As described in chapter 2, the design of the Supported Work evaluation was such that the research sample was enrolled over an extended period of calendar time, thus creating the possibility of "cohort" effects—the possibility that the effects of Supported Work on those who enrolled over one period of time might differ systematically from its effects on those enrolled during another period. As is shown in chapter 8, the issue of "cohort effects" does not affect the overall conclusions regarding whether Supported Work programs aimed at AFDC recipients represent a sound use of public funds. Nonetheless, it still may affect our understanding of circumstances under which the program is a relatively more attractive investment option.

As can be seen from table 4.7 and figure 4.2B, the experimental-control differentials for the 27-month cohort were significantly larger than those for the 18-month cohort throughout the first 18 months after enrollment. However, it is noteworthy that the differentials between the two cohorts tend to be fully accounted for by differences in the levels of the control group earnings. Furthermore, among both cohorts, the average earnings of the controls were increasing over time, reflecting the generally observed phenomenon of improvements over

TABLE 4.7

Hours Employed per Month, by Cohort and by Site—AFDC Sample

	Months 1–9		Months 10–18		Months 19–27	
	Experimental-Control Differential	Control Group Mean	Experimental-Control Differential	Control Group Mean	Experimental-Control Differential	Control Group Mean
All AFDC	108.7**	26.8	39.2**	40.3	15.6**	44.9
Cohort	#		#			
18-month	103.8**	31.0	33.1**	46.2	n.a.	n.a.
27-month	113.3**	23.5	46.0**	33.6	n.a.	n.a.
Site	#		#			
Atlanta	98.2**	38.6	34.3**	57.8	26.9	51.0
Chicago	112.6**	34.9	40.4**	45.8	7.2	55.5
Hartford	117.7**	29.1	36.8**	40.6	−22.1	58.9
Newark	129.1**	15.0	66.5**	25.3	33.2**	42.2
New York	105.7**	25.1	29.8**	41.7	7.2	31.9
Oakland	92.3**	19.0	35.5**	30.2	29.2	41.5
Wisconsin	40.2**a	57.7	−4.3a	57.0	19.8a	35.1

Note: All averages include zero values. See table 4.1 for sample definitions and sizes.
a Sample size for months 1–9 and 10–18 is 26; that for months 19–27 is 22.
n.a. Not available.
Experimental-control differentials for this time period differ significantly from one another.
** Statistically significant at the 5 percent level. None of the other experimental-control differentials is statistically significant at the 5 or 10 percent level.

calendar time in employment among all target groups. The real significance of these differences lies, however, in whether they persist into the postprogram period, and in fact, this was one of the main questions which provided the rationale for conducting the follow-up survey (see below).

Differential impacts among sites. Another important issue is whether results vary significantly across sites, in which case it might be possible to identify program characteristics, labor market conditions, or other factors that explain these differential impacts. As can be seen in table 4.7, there are statistically significant variations in estimates of program impacts among the sites during the early period when a large portion of experimentals held Supported Work jobs. Although in months 19–27 the variation is not statistically significant, there are still sizable differences in effects across sites.

Because of its relatively decentralized structure, Supported Work can be viewed as a collection of distinct, though closely related, programs, and, thus, it is useful to consider alternative explanations for these differential impacts across sites. During months 1–18, the variation in results across sites is due primarily to differences in length of stay in the program and the employment experiences of the control group. For example, the relatively large effect for Newark mainly reflects the lower than average hours worked by controls and the above average number of hours worked by the experimentals. In contrast, the small effect at Oakland (especially in months 1–9) reflects low hours among both controls and experimentals, who stayed in the program for a relatively short period of time (6.7 months).

From a policy point of view, the most important site differences are those for the postprogram period. During months 19–27, rather sizable positive effects were observed among experimentals in Newark, Oakland, Atlanta, and Wisconsin. Small effects were estimated for New York and Chicago, and a sizable (though nonsignificant) negative effect was estimated for Hartford.

As will be discussed below, the differentials between experimentals and controls in the rate of receipt of unemployment compensation benefits are in part responsible for some of these differentials among sites. Similarly, a part of the differential can be explained by differences in the use of "roll-over" jobs and placement into public sector jobs by Supported Work programs. These too will be discussed further below. Because of the limited data for the postprogram period (months 19–27), however, the most solid evidence for explaining differentials in postprogram effects is based on the follow-up data (see below).

Differential impacts among sample subgroups. Table 4.8 presents regression-adjusted estimates of experimental-control differences in hours worked for various subgroups differentiated by characteristics at the time of enrollment.[15] If only statistically significant differences across subgroup disaggregations are considered (indicated by #), there are no striking results. However, there are some noteworthy patterns of results.

During the first 18 months, experimental-control differentials were reasonably large and statistically significant for all sample subgroups shown. However, by months 19–27, the largest impacts tended to be among those who were between the ages of 36 and 44 when they enrolled, had completed 9–11 years of school, had been on welfare for exceptionally long periods of time, received relatively large food stamp allotments, and had no prior work experience. In general, these larger than average differentials between experimentals and controls were evident as early as months 1–9 and were associated with relatively low levels of employment among control group members and average to above average employment levels among experimentals.

The larger than average differential among the portion of the sample who had never held a regular job is particularly noteworthy,[16] because this finding is consistent with those of evaluations of WIN II, which suggest that the program has had a much greater impact for those with little or no prior work experience (Ketron, Inc. 1978). If the costs of the program do not differ appreciably for those with little previous work experience and if the presence of others with more work experience is not a key ingredient in the program's success for those without such experience, then it appears sensible, on both efficiency and equity grounds, to target the program more particularly on those with little employment history. At a minimum, the results imply that the program should continue to try to serve the more disadvantaged and less experienced individuals, who are less likely than average to find employment on their own.

Differential impacts by length of program participation. The overall results clearly demonstrate that the program had a significant positive impact on employment and earnings for members of the AFDC group. An interesting subsidiary question is whether a longer length of participation increased the size of the impact.

Attempts were made in the initial design of the Supported Work evaluation to extend the experimental framework to vary systematically the maximum allowable length of stay across sites. As was noted in chapter 2 above, some sites permitted participants to stay for up to 18 months, while others limited stay to 12 months. However, in prac-

TABLE 4.8
Hours Employed per Month, by Individual Demographic and Background
Characteristics—AFDC Sample

	Months 1–9		Months 10–18		Months 19–27	
	Experimental- Control Differential	Control Group Mean	Experimental- Control Differential	Control Group Mean	Experimental- Control Differential	Control Group Mean
All AFDC	108.7**	26.6	39.1**	40.3	15.7**	45.2
Years of age					#	
< 26	100.8**	28.7	34.6**	37.8	13.4	39.1
26–35	104.7**	28.7	36.6**	43.9	7.1	49.9
36–44	120.0**	21.6	46.0**	36.8	50.4**	30.1
> 44	108.9**	26.7	40.0**	34.4	−28.1	68.0
Race/ethnicity	#					
White, non-Hispanic	76.8**	41.5	30.4*	52.8	22.2	65.9
Black, non-Hispanic	113.4**	24.1	41.4**	38.3	14.8**	42.0
Hispanic	88.2**	38.8	27.0**	49.3	19.4	60.6
Years of education	#					
≤ 8 or less	102.5**	26.8	32.8**	42.4	13.8	34.9
9–11	114.0**	22.5	44.5**	33.4	20.2**	36.1
≥ 12	102.6**	33.9	33.0**	51.5	8.0	70.3
Age of youngest child (years)						
≤ 12	106.0**	28.6	37.5**	40.8	16.2**	42.7
> 12	120.1**	18.4	46.1**	38.4	14.0	55.0
Years on welfare						
< 4	104.9**	18.6	38.9**	39.6	7.9	47.6
4–7	106.3**	25.3	35.9**	42.5	8.6	48.9
> 7	110.6**	28.3	41.3**	39.0	21.1**	42.7
Welfare and food stamp bonus value received[a]						
$200 per month	108.7**	27.0	40.9**	39.0	26.2**	44.7
$100 per month	108.7**	26.5	38.6**	40.7	13.2**	45.4
Months in longest job						
0	108.4**	23.9	50.5**	34.4	30.1**	33.8
1–12	111.9**	24.7	39.9**	30.8	3.5	52.4
> 12	107.1**	28.5	35.3**	47.2	17.4**	45.2
Weeks worked in year prior to enrollment[a]						
0	109.9**	24.7	40.2**	37.9	15.6**	44.2
5	108.1**	27.6	38.6**	41.5	15.8**	45.7
10	106.3**	30.4	37.0**	45.0	15.9**	47.1

(Continued on following page)

TABLE 4.8 (Continued)
Hours Employed per Month, by Individual Demographic and Background
Characteristics—AFDC Sample

	Months 1–9		Months 10–18		Months 19–27	
	Experimental-Control Differential	Control Group Mean	Experimental-Control Differential	Control Group Mean	Experimental-Control Differential	Control Group Mean
Weeks of job training in year prior to enrollment						
< 8	109.9**	24.6	40.7**	38.5	17.4**	43.1
≥ 8	95.2**	50.1	21.8*	60.8	−16.0	84.9

Note: All averages include zero values. See table 4.1 for sample definitions and sizes. The overall results differ slightly from those in table 4.6, since the results in that table are from a regression with no interaction terms.

a While other subgroup results were estimated using binary variables for the various sample characteristics, these estimates are based on a linear specification of the subgroup characteristics, evaluated at the specified points.

\# Experimental-control differentials within this subgrouping differ significantly from one another for this time period.

* Statistically significant at the 10 percent level.

** Statistically significant at the 5 percent level.

tice, this design failed, in that the average length of stay did *not* vary systematically with the maximum allowable length of stay (see table 4.5 above). Since this experimental variation failed, some attempt was made to use statistical methods to estimate differential effects associated with varying lengths of program participation.

The approach employed to estimate such effects was an instrumental variables approach designed to control statistically for selectivity bias which arises from the fact that length of program participation is probably correlated with both the outcome of interest and unobserved characteristics of the individuals.[17] The estimates resulting from the use of this instrumental estimation technique are reported in table 4.9.

As can be seen from these estimates, it does appear that a longer stay in Supported Work did result in substantially greater impacts on hours of work and earnings among the AFDC target group members. An additional month in the program is estimated to result in a net increase in employment of one to two hours per month and a gain in earnings of between $6 and $9 per month. These results are, of course, subject to the qualifications inherent in the statistical technique used to control for selection bias. However, they are perhaps more convincing when one considers that the results of the applications of sim-

TABLE 4.9

Instrumental Variables Estimates of the Effects of an Additional Month
in Supported Work on Experimental-Control Differentials
in Hours Worked and Earnings—AFDC Sample

	Outcome Measure	
Time Period	Average Hours Worked per Month[a]	Average Earnings per Month[b]
Months 16–18	1.13**	5.73**
Months 19–27	1.92**	9.29**

Note: These sample sizes and thus experimental-control differences differ slightly from those in table 4.6, since only observations with data on all of the dependent variables are used. (There were 1,347 cases in the regressions for 16–18 month outcomes and 585 in the regressions for 19–27 month outcomes.)

   a Ordinary least squares estimates of the differential associated with an additional month of program experience are 1.69 and 2.19 for months 16–18 and months 19–27, respectively.

   b Ordinary least squares estimates of the differential associated with an additional month of program experience are 6.94 and 9.55 for months 16–18 and months 19–27, respectively.

** Statistically significant at the 5 percent level.

ilar techniques to data for the other three target groups showed *no* differentials in the impact estimates that could be related to length of stay, even though in several cases estimates not controlling for selection bias had shown sizable and statistically significant differential impacts.

Special considerations in the interpreting of the employment results. The overall findings of positive and significant postprogram impacts of Supported Work on the employment and earnings of AFDC participants are quite clear and robust. However, two issues arose during the course of the analysis which deserve special discussion. The first relates to the effect of unemployment compensation on the overall results, and the second issue is the implications of subsidized employment and roll-over jobs for the program findings.

THE IMPACT OF UNEMPLOYMENT COMPENSATION PROGRAMS. The overall experimental-control differences for AFDC were undoubtedly affected to some degree by the availability in some of the sites of unemployment compensation benefits to experimental group members upon their termination from Supported Work. Only the New York program was required under law to participate in the State Unemployment Compensation (UC) program. However, with the establishment of the federal Special Unemployment Assistance (SUA) program in 1975, participants in any site *might* be judged eligible for UC benefits on the basis of their Supported Work experience. Whether they were judged eligible was largely a matter of interpretation by the local UC office upon specific application by individuals, and thus, as might be expected, the result was a very uneven pattern of receipt of UC benefits among experimentals subsequent to leaving the program.

Both because the SUA program was temporary (all claims were terminated on July 1, 1978) and because a national Supported Work program would undoubtedly have a uniform policy vis-à-vis participation in state UC programs, the estimated impacts of Supported Work based on the current sample may not be generalizable to future experience. In months 10–18, significantly higher percentages of experimentals than controls in New York, Atlanta, and Newark received UC benefits.[18] Thus, the estimates for these sites are almost certainly underestimates of the effects that would have occurred in the absence of UC receipt, since an individual who received UC benefits undoubtedly had less incentive to find alternative employment in the short run and, perhaps, used this period to search longer for a more desirable job.[19]

An attempt was made to assess the impacts of Supported Work under alternative scenarios of UC coverage and, in particular, to determine the extent to which the estimates of early postprogram impacts may understate effects that would have been observed in the absence of any UC coverage.[20] Rigorous analysis of the issue was precluded by the fact that, among the AFDC sample, most of the variance in receipt of benefits was across rather than within sites. (For example, 70 percent of the experimentals who received benefits in months 16–18 were enrolled in the New York program.) However, estimates based on observed experimental-control differentials among non-UC recipients suggest that, had UC not been available, the overall experimental-control differential during months 10–18 would have tapered off more gradually than was observed. In months 16–18, for example, when an overall differential of 10 hours per month was observed (table 4.6), the differential among experimentals not receiving UC and controls was about twice as large.[21] Over the 19- to 27-month period, as differential UC receipt rates decreased, so did the estimated impact on hours.

FINDINGS BY SECTOR OF EMPLOYMENT. It is of interest to examine the experimental-control differences as they relate to the sector of employment—private sector jobs, CETA and WIN jobs, and other public sector jobs—in order to explore issues related to the way in which program effects on postprogram employment may have been generated and how such gains should be valued from the societal point of view. At one level, some feel that earnings in the public sector are less likely to reflect true social marginal products than do earnings in the private sector. If this is so and Supported Work tends to increase, disproportionately, employment in the public sector, the observed earnings gains may overstate the overall social benefits of the program.

At another level, there are questions of how the gains in employment were actually generated. First, Supported Work may have enhanced employment of experimentals by providing higher than normal access to public sector jobs—access resulting mainly from "connections" or other special efforts of program operators. If the number of such jobs is limited, then the placement of Supported Workers through "connections" would displace other low-income workers who would have gotten the jobs in the absence of the Supported Work program, and the earnings gains to participants relative to controls should be discounted in computing the social benefits of the program.

A second question is whether Supported Work mainly provided a "screening" function for employers. Since a high proportion of Supported Work in-program jobs were in the public sector, public sector employers may have had a disproportionate opportunity to observe and screen Supported Work participants, with the expected result being a higher percentage of employment by experimentals in this sector. Finally, the third question relates to the issue of whether the postprogram impacts can be attributed in part to increased productivity of the workers.

We should emphasize that what we have just stated is a set of questions and concerns. Many of the suppositions upon which they are based can be countered and questioned.[22] We present them simply as issues which have been raised.

Unfortunately, for most of the questions, the research data from the demonstration do not provide unequivocal answers, since the demonstration and research simply were not designed—and with respect to some issues could not have been designed—in such a way as to accomplish this. Nonetheless, we feel that some speculation on these issues, clearly labeled as such and separated distinctly from conclusions that are well-founded in the research design, is useful.

The postprogram results from the main evaluation effort indicate that, in large part, the employment and earnings impacts of the program do reflect success in placing participants in public sector jobs. For example, in months 19–27, over 70 percent of experimentals' gains in average monthly earnings is attributable to higher levels of earnings from public sector jobs other than those sponsored by CETA or WIN (see Masters and Maynard 1981, Table III.5). However, there is nothing in the data to permit us to ascertain the cause of this effect. Because of its potential importance in the overall policy conclusions from the study, this issue is discussed further in the context of findings from the follow-up survey.

Welfare Impacts and Other Results from the Main Evaluation

Impacts on Welfare and Other Income Sources By increasing the employment and earnings of the experimental group, particularly during the early months after enrollment when most participants held Supported Work jobs, it is expected that the program will also have significant impacts on the overall economic well-being and on the share of total income that comes from public assistance programs. Such effects are of particular concern for the AFDC target group.

As can be seen in table 4.10, concomitantly with the increased earnings of experimentals relative to controls, the welfare and food stamps benefits of experimentals fell relative to those of controls. However, largely because, as a result of the AFDC work incentive provisions, the decline in welfare benefits was less than the earnings gains, total income from all sources increased in all time periods. For example, in months 10–18 the total income differential was about 50 percent of the earnings differential; and in months 19–27 the total income differential had fallen to 35 percent of the earnings differential—a difference that is not statistically significant.

Part of the explanation for the decline in the proportion of the earnings gains that is reflected in total income changes relates to the receipt of unemployment compensation. According to the AFDC benefit structure, receipt of UC benefits should be completely offset by reductions in AFDC benefits. Thus, the fact that receipt of UC benefits differed between experimentals and controls, contributes to the relatively modest income gains in comparison with the earnings gains. Yet, one still observes that the experimental-control differences in welfare benefits are greater than can be explained by gains in UC receipt and earnings alone.

There are indications that welfare benefits received by experimentals may be *less* than those of equivalent controls (vis-à-vis earnings and UC benefits). This is most clearly indicated by the data which present results separately for employed and unemployed sample members. We found that, among those employed in both groups, a smaller percentage of experimentals received welfare benefits. More important, among those not employed, 7 percent *fewer* experimentals than controls received welfare benefits. The lower receipt of welfare benefits among experimentals could be voluntary or involuntary: as experimentals left

TABLE 4.10
Income from Various Sources—AFDC Sample

	Months 1–9		Months 10–18		Months 19–27	
	Experimental-Control Differential	Control Group Mean	Experimental-Control Differential	Control Group Mean	Experimental-Control Differential	Control Group Mean
A. Percentage Receiving Income						
Earnings	59.8**	36.5	37.1**	39.4	8.5**	40.6
Unearned income						
Unemployment						
compensation	−1.0	2.0	20.1**	3.0	7.2**	2.0
Welfare[a]	−3.9**	97.7	−7.7**	90.1	−13.7**	85.1
Food stamps	−8.5**	94.6	−12.4**	85.9	−15.1**	82.3
Other[b]	−7.0**	15.7	−3.0*	11.4	−1.4	12.2
B. Average Monthly Income Received (dollars)						
All sources	192.96**	435.10	70.03**	454.44	27.36	470.14
Earnings	322.16**	78.28	142.98**	131.08	77.01**	165.88
Unearned income						
Unemployment						
compensation	−1.77**	2.20	27.39**	3.67	9.44**	2.91
Welfare[a]	−108.08**	277.90	−82.32**	246.60	−51.94**	224.00
Bonus value of						
food stamps[c]	−18.63**	63.46	−15.87**	58.02	−13.11**	60.25
Other[b]	−2.08	14.04	−4.05	16.05	3.58	18.30
Welfare benefits,						
recipients only[d]	−103.40	284.44	−74.33	273.70	−22.25	263.27

Note: Earnings data reported in this table vary somewhat from those reported in tables 4.6–4.9, because of slight differences in the sample used; only individuals who have valid data for all income sources listed in this table were included in the analysis reported here. The sample for months 1–9 and 10–18 is all those with baseline, 9-, and 18-month interviews and with no missing data in any of the dependent variables, a sample of size 1,252. The sample for months 19–27 is all those with a baseline and 27-month interviews and no missing data, a sample of size 609. All figures include zero values except for welfare benefits, recipients only.

  a Welfare includes AFDC, General Assistance, Supplemental Security Income, and other unspecified welfare income. For this target group, almost all welfare payments are for AFDC.

  b Other unearned income includes Social Security, pensions, alimony, child support, and job training income.

  c The bonus value of food stamps is the face value minus the purchase price.

  d Significance tests were not performed on these data.

  * Statistically significant at the 10 percent level.

** Statistically significant at the 5 percent level.

Supported Work and their earnings declined, the level of their welfare benefits may have failed to rise either because they decided not to apply to receive welfare benefits again or because there was a lag in the administrative response to their declining earnings.

These findings lead to the expectation that, in the longer run, receipt of welfare benefits among the experimentals would rise to a level more commensurate with their employment and earnings status, and, therefore, the experimental-control differences in welfare benefits would decline somewhat relative to what they were in months 19–27. Clearly, the data from the follow-up survey, discussed below, provide an opportunity to test this prediction.

In relation to AFDC benefits, it seems natural to inquire whether, given the structure of AFDC, there were sufficient incentives for experimental members of the AFDC target group to grasp whatever added work opportunities the Supported Work experience provided. In fact, it has been estimated that the total income of the employed is substantially higher than that of those not employed, with those who were employed having increases in their total incomes of at least 55 percent of the amount of their earnings.[23]

Impacts on Child-Care Utilization and Barriers to Employment Another area of impacts to consider is the use of and expenditures on child care. All members of the AFDC target group had child-care responsibilities, although none had a child younger than six. Thus, it is natural to inquire how their employment circumstances may have affected, or been affected by, their child-care needs.

As noted just above, the structure of the AFDC program is such that increased employment yields a gain in net income that is less than the gain in earnings. Under AFDC, however, the costs of employment-related child care are an allowable work-related expense. This feature ameliorates the degree to which child care may be an impediment to increased employment among this target group. Nevertheless, child-care responsibilities may still be an important factor in the employment decisions of many women who are on AFDC—especially for those mothers who do not believe that other people should play a major role in bringing up their children. One may also be interested in the effects of Supported Work on child care because the costs to society of providing such care outside the home may be considerable; of course, the costs of providing no care may also be considerable, if lack of care has adverse effects on the children.

At the time of enrollment, about 80 percent of the AFDC sample had a youngest child between the ages of 6 and 12, for whom care was needed at least after school and during school vacations. Yet, only about 10 percent of the control group reported using child-care services during any 9-month interval, although about 30 percent reported employment. In addition, 30 percent of the controls reported having child-care problems that prevented their employment, at least during certain months. In contrast, reports of experimentals suggest that child-care problems may not be so serious once a job is actually in hand: during the in-Supported-Work-program period, only 10 percent of the experimentals reported that child-care problems kept them from working at any time.[24]

Since Supported Work led to increased employment of experimentals, it is not surprising that it also increased their utilization of child-care services. The increase was largest (35 percentage points) in months 1–9, but persisted through the 19- to 27-month period, when 11 percent of experimentals as compared with 7 percent of controls reported using services.[25]

During all time periods, a significantly higher percentage of experimentals than controls received subsidized care, particularly during months 1–9 (17 versus 4 percent) and months 10–18 (7 versus 2 percent) when experimentals participated in Supported Work jobs. Correspondingly, during the first 18 months after enrollment, experimentals paid significantly more per month for child care, even after reimbursement ($16 versus $3), which is a small differential in relation to the earnings differential during this period (over $300 per month). Costs of care relative to earnings gains were similarly small over subsequent periods as well.

Results from the Follow-up Survey

As originally designed, the research on the effects of Supported Work was based on interviews completed by March of 1979, and the findings reported thus far in this chapter have been derived from that set of data. In this section, we summarize key findings from the special follow-up survey conducted in the fall of 1979, in which respondents were asked about experiences for the 12 months preceding the interview.[26] As was noted previously, when these data are combined with those from the main evaluation, we have data for between 26 and 43 months after enrollment for each follow-up sample member, with the average length of the follow-up period being 32.8 months.

These added data permitted an analysis which deepens our understanding of the effects of Supported Work for the AFDC target group. Although, in general, the follow-up analysis reaffirms the conclusions of the original research described above, in some cases the follow-up permitted clarification of issues where uncertainty persisted in the main evaluation.

One of the principal features of the follow-up analysis is that it permits a more comprehensive examination of the long-term program impacts. Most notably, it provides data for the 16- to 26-month period after enrollment for *all* sample members,[27] and thereby avoids questions as to whether the long-term effects observed for the 27-month cohort can be generalized to the full sample.

The approach taken in conducting this follow-up study was to concentrate on the 16- to 39-month period after enrollment, which hereafter is referred to as the "postprogram period," and to focus both on the overall magnitude of the experimental-control differentials during this period and on time-trends in the differentials over this period.

Further Evidence on Employment-Related Impacts The primary results from this follow-up study are summarized in table 4.11. The experimental-control differentials in hours worked and earnings are relatively large and statistically significant, amounting to 8 hours and $59 per month or 15 and 28 percent of the control group means, respectively.[28] These results strongly sustain the conclusion from the main evaluation that the Supported Work program had the effect of

TABLE 4.11
Key Findings from the Follow-up Study of the AFDC Target Group

	Average Results 16–39 Months after Enrollment		Estimated Change in Experimental-Control Differential per Year
	Experimental-Control Differential	Control Group Mean	
Percentage employed	3.8	41.6	−2.0
Average hours worked per month	8.4**	57.7	−2.6
Average earnings per month—all jobs	59.23**	212.99	−2.79
Average earnings per month—CETA/WIN jobs	0.28	35.65	3.22
Average earnings per month—other subsidized jobs	33.80**	26.01	−8.22
Average earnings per month—unsubsidized jobs	18.81	139.80	12.91
Total income per month	$26.87**	$495.12	7.00
Unearned Income per Month			
Welfare	−31.70**	204.93	40.82
Food stamps	−9.73**	63.13	5.57**
Unemployment compensation	11.30**	5.17	−27.28**

Note: These data are from Masters and McDonald (1981, Tables III.1–III.4, III.7, IV.1, F.5 and F.6). All data are regression-adjusted. Averages include zero values.
** Statistically significant at the 5 percent level. None of the other experimental-control differentials is statistically significant at the 5 or 10 percent level.

TABLE 4.12
Average Monthly Earnings in the 9 Months prior to Follow-up Interview—
AFDC Sample

	Experimental-Control Differential	Sample Size
Full sample	$56.70	1,151
Cohorts:		
Months since enrollment at follow-up		
22–24	100.94	202
25–27	21.63	283
28–30	77.25	273
31–33	14.90	219
34–36	43.65	128
37–39	200.13	46

Note: These data are from Masters and McDonald (1981, Table B.2). All data are regression-adjusted. Tests of statistical significance were not computed.

substantially increasing the postprogram earnings of AFDC participants above what they would have been in the absence of the program experience. Furthermore, the subgroup results supported the findings from the initial evaluation, which suggested that the greatest impacts were observed for those with the fewest alternative opportunities.

Differential results among cohorts. The structure of the follow-up study allowed direct examination of the long-run implications of the cohort differences observed in the first 18 months following enrollment. Since in the follow-up study all interviewees were asked about their experiences during the 12 calendar months preceding the interview, it was possible to examine all cohorts of enrollees during a single period in calendar time, where labor market conditions are constant, to determine whether there are major differences in results. The relevant data on earnings are presented in table 4.12. As can be seen from these data, there is no evidence that the long-run results differ systematically among sample subgroups divided according to enrollment period (months since enrollment at the time of the follow-up).[29] Furthermore, it is noteworthy that the fit of the regressions including the cohort variables was not significantly better than that of the simpler model.

Differential impacts among sites. In the main evaluation results discussed above, we found there were differences in impacts among sites. Again, the significance of these differences can be pursued further with the follow-up data.

The site-specific–earnings results from the follow-up analysis are presented in table 4.13. As can be seen from these results, there are,

TABLE 4.13

Estimated Experimental-Control Differentials in Average Monthly Earnings
16–39 Months after Enrollment, by Sector of Employment and Site—AFDC Sample

Site	All Jobs	Sector of Employment		
		CETA/WIN Jobs	Other Public Sector Jobs	Nonpublic Sector Jobs
Atlanta	53.81	54.14**	29.99	−33.47
Chicago	84.66**	10.25	5.77	71.33**
Hartford	−7.59	−7.24	−6.16	−9.33
Newark	121.48**	12.37	115.07**	−12.60
New York	10.03	−32.69**	21.26	16.31
Oakland	100.48*	−10.18	−4.94	99.28**
Wisconsin	89.78	11.76	6.99	47.48
Total	59.23**	0.28	33.80**	18.81

Note: These data are from Masters and McDonald (1981, Tables III.1–III.4). All data are regression-adjusted.

* Statistically significant at the 10 percent level.
** Statistically significant at the 5 percent level.

indeed, considerable differences across sites in the estimated postprogram effects on earnings. Chicago, Newark, and Oakland stand out as clearly most successful for AFDC participants and Hartford and New York as apparently less successful. It is noteworthy that the impacts in Chicago and Newark tended to increase over time, while those in Oakland decreased. Although these differences across sites are not statistically significant, when one groups together the three sites with the highest experimental-control differential (Chicago, Newark, and Oakland) and compares statistically their combined average with the average for the other four sites, the difference is significant at the 5 percent level.[30]

Having apparently identified Chicago, Newark, and Oakland as more "successful" sites, one might be tempted to try to isolate features which these sites have in common and which might account for their apparently greater success.[31] One site characteristic which could be investigated further was the extent of postprogram employment in public versus private sector jobs.

Earnings differences by sector of employment. The data in table 4.13 include earnings results broken down by sector of employment: CETA/WIN; other public sector; and private sector. Several observations are worth noting. First, although there is no significant overall differential between experimentals' and controls' earnings from CETA/WIN jobs, experimentals in Atlanta had significantly higher CETA/WIN earnings and those in New York significantly lower CETA/WIN earnings than did their control group counterparts.[32] Second, the experimentals did have significantly higher earnings from other public sector jobs than did controls. These differences, however, were mainly due to large differences ($115 per month) between experimentals and controls in Newark. In the other two "successful" sites, Chicago and Oakland, public sector employment does not appear to have played a noteworthy role in the success of the programs. Third, overall experimental-control differences in earnings from nonpublic sector (private and nonprofit sector) jobs were positive, though not statistically significant. However, with respect to differences among sites, the results are opposite from those for the public sector earnings: the experimental-control differentials were negative in Newark and positive (and statistically significant) in Chicago and Oakland.

In considering the overall magnitude of experimental-control differentials in earnings from public and from private sector jobs, it was found that the importance of each in the overall program impact tended to converge over time. On average, the differential is $34 for public sector jobs and $19 for private sector jobs (see table 4.13). However, the public sector earnings differential *decreased* an average of $8 per year while the private sector differential *increased* by nearly $13 per year (see Masters and McDonald 1981).

One could speculate that this pattern is due to the fact that there was a tendency to place experimentals primarily in public sector jobs, but for them to find their way gradually into private sector jobs.

At the site level, the contrasts between Newark, on the one hand, and Chicago and Oakland on the other are worthy of noting. Rather than finding a common feature among sites, there is a contrast which *may* suggest that *there is more than one way for a Supported Work program to succeed*. Newark found that focusing on public sector jobs which provided a chance for participants to "roll over" after graduation into regular, unsubsidized employment with the same agency was an effective strategy. Chicago and Oakland found that vigorous efforts to establish performance records of their Supported Workers in private sector activities encouraged private sector employers to take on their graduates at higher than normal rates.[33] This diversity of positive results is encouraging in that it suggests that the success of Supported Work was not based on a simple, narrowly defined strategy but on the broad nature of the effort to assist the participants in finding a way into the regular labor market.

Further Evidence on Welfare Related Impacts   As was noted above, one of the chief issues raised by the main evaluation regarding the program's impacts on total income and welfare dependence was that there was a lag in the adjustment of experimentals' AFDC payments in response to earnings changes. The result was a smaller experimental-control differential in total income than would have been expected on the basis of the observed differential in earnings. This led to the expectation that, in the longer run, the estimated impacts on welfare receipt would be lower and the impacts on total income would be larger as a percentage of the earnings differential.

As can be seen in table 4.11 above, results from the follow-up data confirm this expectation. Over this postprogram period (months 16–39), the estimated impact on total income ($26.87) is 45 percent of the impact on earnings. In contrast, over months 19–27, the impact on total income ($27.36) was only 36 percent as large as the impact on earnings ($77.01) (see table 4.10 above). Furthermore, as is shown in table 4.11, the follow-up data indicated that the total income differential was increasing slightly ($7.00 per year) even though the earnings differential was decreasing slightly (−$3.00 per year). The experimental-control differential in welfare income was increasing by an estimated $40.82 per year. Part of this was due to welfare income replacing diminishing unemployment compensation, but a substantial part was due to a catch-up of welfare income which seemed to lag in earlier periods.[34]

The follow-up data also permitted a more direct estimate of the effect of earnings on welfare income and the lags in adjustment. Using a model to estimate welfare receipt, food stamp bonus values, and total income during each of the four 3-month periods preceding the follow-up interview, it was possible to estimate the lagged effect of earnings in previous periods on welfare, food stamps, and total income in a given period. The results show that a $1 increase in earnings caused welfare income to fall by $0.29 over a 1-year period, with about 40 percent of the effect occurring in the first 3-month period. Similarly a $1 increase in earnings yielded an increase in total income of $0.64 over the following year. Thus, these results suggest that there is a substantial work incentive, in spite of reductions in welfare and food stamp income.[35]

Conclusion

The Supported Work program has a significant and sustained effect on the hours of work and earnings of members of the AFDC target group. The ability to draw this unequivocal conclusion is based on the opportunity, created by the experimental design, to compare AFDC

recipients who participated in Supported Work with a randomly selected control group.

The success of the program with the AFDC target group stands out
even more clearly when compared with the results for the other three
target groups which exhibited more mixed patterns of (or null) impacts.
The postprogram success of the AFDC target group was affected by
the fact that, on average, their length of stay in Supported Work was
noticeably longer than that for other target groups. Further, a nonexperimental analysis suggests that, within the AFDC group itself, those
participants who stayed in Supported Work longer did better in terms
of postprogram employment and earnings gains (whereas longer stays
were *not* correlated with better postprogram results within the other
target groups).

There is a national interest in focusing most closely on postprogram
employment and earnings and on addressing the question of not only
whether postprogram impacts occurred but also to what degree they
were sustained, declined, or increased over time. The ability to draw
strong conclusions in this regard was enhanced by a special follow-up
survey of the AFDC target group that extended the period of follow-
up from between 18 and 27 months to between 26 and 43 months.
The postprogram observations (months 16–39) indicate that the earnings of the AFDC Supported Work participants were, on average, $59
per month higher than that of their control group counterparts,
amounting to a 28 percent increase. Furthermore, the evidence suggests
that this differential was sustained over time.

The analysis of subgroups within the AFDC target group provides
weak indications that the program tended to have greater impacts
among older (36–44) participants, those who had been on welfare for
exceptionally long periods of time, and those who had no prior work
experience. It was among these subgroups that the controls had especially low levels of employment and earnings. This is consistent with
the findings for other target groups, which suggest that Supported Work
is most effective among the most disadvantaged within each group.

The analysis of differences in impacts across sites is more equivocal.
A strict statistical test of differences in the postprogram period across
all sites fails. However, examination of the point estimates suggests
that Chicago, Newark, and Oakland were particularly successful with
the AFDC group, and that significantly different average impacts were
observed in these three sites as compared with the rest of the sites.

Limited attempts to determine analytically whether there was some
common feature which differentiates the successful from the unsuccessful sites yielded no simple answer; the features of the "successful"

sites differed considerably, suggesting perhaps that there is more than one mechanism through which Supported Work may enhance employment among AFDC recipients.

The sustained postprogram increase in earnings of the AFDC group naturally had the effect of creating postprogram reductions in welfare income. Because of the lower level of welfare and food stamps benefits, the differential in average total income between experimentals and controls was only 45 percent of the differential in earnings (that total income differential was $27 per month in the postprogram period).

While the Supported Work program was successful in raising the employment and earnings of the participants from the AFDC target group, it should be clearly understood that it is far from a total solution to the employment barriers this group faces and to their economic difficulties. This is seen most clearly when it is noted that the average monthly earnings of the experimental group, while significantly higher than that of the controls, were considerably below the average earnings for the *controls* in the other three target groups during comparable time periods. Even among the AFDC experimental group, only 45 percent were employed during the postprogram period.

The success of Supported Work in increasing employment and income among AFDC recipients is clearly established. Two substantial questions remain from the wider societal view. The first is: overall, did the benefits from Supported Work to AFDC participants exceed the costs of the program? This issue is examined in detail in chapter 8. As explained there, from the point of view of participants and society as a whole, the benefits of Supported Work clearly and substantially exceeded its costs for the AFDC sample. The benefits to nonparticipants are also positive during the short run. However, one key finding from the follow-up survey was that benefits to nonparticipants decreased sharply as the reference period increased, because of the lagged impacts on transfer income.

The second question is: how applicable are the results of this Supported Work Demonstration and the research based on it to the broader AFDC population? If we interpret these results by the strictest standards, we estimate that the target group criteria limit the direct translation to about 17 percent of the total AFDC population. For this proportion of the AFDC population (subject always to necessary reservations concerning time and place), the results of the Supported Work Demonstration establish the potential for enhancement of employment and income. As to the effectiveness of Supported Work for wider segments of the AFDC population, one can only speculate. However, Supported Work results establish a rebuttable presumption that employers have undervalued the earnings potential of members of the AFDC population.

Notes

1 There are a number of reasons for the growth in AFDC caseloads, including increased benefit levels, court decisions which liberalized eligibility rules, and increased numbers of female-headed families. However, most of the increase in caseloads arose from higher participation rates of women who were eligible for benefits but previously had not claimed them. In 1967 only 67 percent of eligibles claimed benefits; by 1971 the participation rate had increased to 94 percent (Bolland 1973). The failure of the WIN program to reduce caseloads substantially is due largely to the program's inability to provide jobs to large portions of the eligible population, but also to the incentive components of the program, namely the earnings "disregards" and the tax rate which result in large numbers of individuals eligible for benefits even when they are employed.

2 The 1971 amendments also required WIN registration for all AFDC recipients 16 years of age or older, unless exempt for reasons of health, incapacity, home responsibilities, advanced age, school status, or remoteness from a WIN project.

3 Supported Work programs obtained waivers of the WIN mandatory work requirements, thereby making participation voluntary.

4 In all sites except Hartford, 50 percent of the applicants were assigned to the experimental group and 50 percent to the control group. In order to increase the research sample beyond that which would be generated by a 50–50 assignment to given funded program slots, 40 percent of the Hartford applicants were assigned to the experimental group and 60 percent were assigned to the control group.

5 The difference between the 1620 sample members enrolled and the figures reported in table 4.1 is due to interview nonresponse (this is discussed further in this chapter).

6 The major problem in generalizing the findings from this study may relate to selectivity issues. However, because Supported Work is a voluntary program, the sample included in this evaluation may still be representative of that group of eligibles who would participate given the opportunity. For further discussion of the selection problem see Masters and Maynard (1981).

7 Among the other three target groups, over 40 percent left because of poor performance (see chapters 5–7).

8 Although the analytic methods used to estimate program impacts controlled statistically for observable differences, unobservable differences may exist or the models, which did not fully interact participant characteristics with program treatment status, may not fully account for such differences.

9 One study applied recently developed econometric techniques to assess the extent of bias due to interview nonresponse (Brown 1979). A second study

(Masters 1979) compared interview data on earnings with Social Security data on SSA-covered earnings (for both responders and nonresponders to follow-up interviews), and a third study (Kerachsky et al. 1979) compared interview data on welfare receipt for sample members in one site (Newark) with welfare agency data on welfare payments to assess the degree of response error.

10 For evidence of the success of the random assignment procedure, see Jackson et al. (1978).

11 In subsequent tables, statistical significance of experimental-control differences for both total samples and sample subgroups is denoted by asterisks. Statistically significant differences in the magnitude of program impacts among subgroups (that is, whether the hypothesis that the program impacts are similar for all subgroups can be rejected) are denoted by the symbol #.

12 Results of maximum likelihood estimates are available from the authors upon request.

13 The confidence interval, which is uniquely defined at various levels (the most common being the 95 percent level), is the range of values which has 95 percent probability of containing the true value. That is, if repeated samples were drawn, and estimates and confidence intervals constructed for each, 95 percent of these intervals would contain the true value of the impact. If both ends of the confidence interval are greater or less than zero, an experimental-control differential is referred to as statistically significant (at the designated confidence level). For example, if we observe a differential whose 95 percent confidence interval is between $100 and $400 per month, there is only a .05 probability that the true differential is less than $100 or greater than $400.

14 This issue is referred to in the economics literature as displacement and is discussed at considerably greater length in chapter 8, which presents findings from the benefit-cost analysis. For further discussion of this issue, see Johnson (1979) and Bishop (1979).

15 There are a very large number of statistical tests represented in table 4.8, and, therefore, we should expect to see a certain number of indications of statistically significant differences appearing by chance even if there were, in fact, no underlying differences. On the other hand, some subgroups are so small that estimates of program impacts will have high sampling variability and, therefore, not be statistically significant even though the estimated experimental-control differential is large and follows a consistent pattern (for example, across time periods). Therefore, some judgment must be exercised in interpreting this complex set of results.

16 This group constitutes roughly 15 percent of the sample.

17 See Brown and Maynard (1981) for a discussion of the statistical problems and the attempted solutions.

18 See Masters and Maynard (1981, Table IV.1).

19 Classen (1977), Ehrenberg and Oaxaca (1976), Solon (1979), and others provide evidence of the general work disincentive effects of unemployment

compensation. However, there are no reliable estimates of the magnitude of these effects, especially for populations such as those in the Supported Work Demonstration.

20 Among the methods considered to address these issues were (1) obtaining a predicted value of employment for UC recipients, based on an employment equation estimated for nonrecipients; and (2) estimating experimental-control differences for recipients and nonrecipients using selection-bias correction methods (for example, see Heckman 1976).

21 These estimates are, of course, subject to selection bias of unknown direction.

22 For example, Kemper (1980) discusses these issues and presents a set of equally plausible counterpropositions—labor replacement without displacement—under which the experimental-control differentials *underestimate* the social benefits.

23 To estimate the full effect of increased earnings on the economic well-being of the AFDC sample members, it is necessary to take into account any reductions in in-kind benefits, such as subsidized medical care and public housing, as well as federal, state, and local taxes which were paid. For the benefit-cost analysis, described in chapter 8, all of these elements were estimated. Details about the impact of Supported Work on various in-kind benefits are also reported in Masters and Maynard (1981, 117–119).

24 The fact that there is virtually no difference between experimentals and controls in absences from work leads us to speculate that the differences between experimentals' and controls' reports of the difficulty of making adequate child-care arrangements result mainly from women discovering that they *can* make satisfactory arrangements once the job search problem is solved.

25 In general, less than 10 percent of those using child-care services (either experimentals or controls) used day-care centers, but, instead, most used care in either their own or other people's homes.

26 The full description of the follow-up survey and the results of analysis are reported in Masters and McDonald (1981) and Masters (1981).

27 At the sixteenth month only about 5 percent of the experimentals were still participating in Supported Work.

28 In the original research for months 19–27, the differential in earnings was $77 or 47 percent of the control group mean (see table 4.6 above). The differences between the earlier result and the follow-up is largely due to cohort differences, a subject discussed further in "Differential results among cohorts."

29 The largest differences are observed for the earliest and latest quarters. However, it must also be noted that these data do not control for time since having left the program and so decay effects may be confounded with cohort differences.

30 There is, however, some question as to whether such regrouping of observations on the basis of outcomes ("successes") and then testing for significance of difference in the new group averages of that same outcome

is an appropriate statistical procedure. This leaves us with some uncertainty regarding the statistical significance of site differences.

31 However, there are serious potential pitfalls and biases in trying to proceed in this fashion *after* having labeled "successes" to characterize them in terms of common features which might explain their success. (One part of the research on Supported Work, the process analysis, did attempt to relate characteristics of programs defined *prior* to the outcome analysis to post-program results. See chapter 2 for a brief description.) There is no way to test whether features thus identified do in fact generate success, unless one runs another experiment specifically designed to do so.

32 It should be noted that the classification of jobs as to whether CETA/WIN, other public sector, or private was done by the respondents, and there is some evidence to suggest that they had difficulty distinguishing CETA/WIN sponsored jobs from other public sector jobs (see chapter 7).

33 See chapter 3 for further discussion of these site tendencies.

34 Similar conclusions hold for receipt of food stamp bonuses.

35 Masters and McDonald (1981, 67–73) further concluded that the long-term effect of Supported Work on total income of AFDC experimentals will be somewhat larger than the $27 differential observed over the follow-up period as further lagged adjustments work themselves out.

5 *Felicity Skidmore*

The Impacts of Supported Work on Former Drug Addicts

One of the populations suffering generally from severe labor market difficulties is the estimated 200,000 persons in the United States receiving treatment for drug abuse. In addition to the poor employment records and extensive involvement with drugs of this group, something like three out of four have spent time in jail by the time they get into treatment programs. High recidivism rates of drug use (over 70 percent) and crime (nearly 50 percent) and persistent employment problems also characterize the experience of ex-addicts after leaving drug treatment (U.S. Department of Health, Education and Welfare 1978; Simpson et al. 1976).

Providing the former drug user with a job is frequently mentioned in the drug-use literature as an important step in reducing recidivism. This chapter discusses the design and findings from an evaluation of the Supported Work Demonstration's effectiveness in achieving the multiple goals of increasing employment, reducing drug-use recidivism, and decreasing criminal activity among former drug users. The first section discusses the nature of the Supported Work intervention and its expected effects for ex-addicts. Then, the characteristics of the sample are outlined. The third section discusses issues related to the context in which the demonstration was conducted. The fourth describes the program experience of experimentals, and the fifth presents the findings regarding the impacts of those program experiences. Fi-

This chapter was abridged by Felicity Skidmore from Katherine Dickinson and Rebecca Maynard, *The Impact of Supported Work on Ex-Addicts*, Volume 4 of the Final Report on the Supported Work Evaluation, New York: MDRC, 1981.

nally, the general policy implications of the findings of the study are outlined.

Supported Work and Its Expected Effects
on the Ex-addict Group

The primary purpose of Supported Work is to improve earnings and employment (see chapter 2). It is also hoped that by increasing their employment options, Supported Work will make it easier for ex-addicts to resist pressures to return to drug use. If the program does increase employability and/or reduce drug use, then it may also reduce participants' involvement in criminal activity.

With respect to employment and earnings, human capital theory argues that Supported Work will increase both of them by increasing the productivity (and thus the wage rates and possibly hours worked) of participants. If Supported Work does indeed improve productivity, it may be particularly appropriate for ex-addicts. Not only do ex-addicts tend to have low levels of education and training, their extensive involvement with drugs may have fostered the poor work habits that Supported Work is designed to improve. Segmented labor market theory also predicts increased earnings because the work experience record compiled by Supported Work participants will make them more attractive to the employers in the primary labor market. This will lead not only to higher paying jobs but also to fewer spells of unemployment.

With respect to drug use, the net expected effect of Supported Work is not predictable from theory alone. On the one hand, Supported Work is hypothesized to reduce drug use through several mechanisms. To the extent that work performance is affected by drug use, increasing the ex-addict's employment opportunities makes it more expensive to use drugs; it may change the person's self-image from addict to worker; and may counterbalance the influence of a subculture in which work is devalued. The additional income from the program may also reduce deprivation distress to which drugs may have become a generalized response. On the other hand, Supported Work may tend to increase drug use to the extent that participants may spend some of their additional income on drugs.

With respect to crime, although the association between criminal activity and drug use is well established, the causal link is greatly debated (Greenberg and Adler 1974; Platt and Labate 1976; Preble and Casey 1969). The view that drug use leads to crime is based on economic considerations: drug users generally earn little through legal

employment and thus may turn to crime as a means of economic
support. The main alternative view is that there is no causal relationship between crime and drug use, but that both behaviors are manifestations of deviant lifestyles. Supported Work is hypothesized to
reduce economically motivated criminal activity by increasing participants' wage rates and income. And, to the extent that crime and drug
use manifest the same deviance, the program is hypothesized to reduce
drug use.

Although training programs and sheltered workshops are frequently
recommended as useful tools in the rehabilitation of addicts, little
empirical work exists on the effects of such programs on former drug
users.[1] Several follow-up studies of people who were in drug treatment
have found that those who are employed after treatment are less likely
to return to drug use or to engage in crime.[2] However, the direction
of causation is unclear. It may be that those who want to reduce both
drug use and crime are more likely to obtain employment.

Two experimental evaluations of employment programs for ex-addicts—Wildcat (the prototype for the national Supported Work Demonstration) and TREAT—provide limited evidence in support of employment and training programs as remedial strategies. The Wildcat
program included graduated stress and peer support for ex-addict
workers but differed from the national demonstration in that there was
no mandatory graduation. Based on a comparison of 197 experimentals and 207 controls in the third year of the program, experimentals
worked an average of 26 weeks and earned an average of $3,596, while
controls worked an average of 17 weeks and earned an average of
$1,951 (Friedman 1978).[3] There was also a significant reduction in
arrests among the experimentals in the first program year, but no significant difference between experimentals and controls by the third
year. No significant effects on drug use were observed for any period.
The TREAT program provided employment and training for six to
nine months for a sample of ex-addicts in Washington, D.C. The reported employment and earnings results, which include experience
while in the program, indicate significant short-run gains in employment rates and hours of work although, surprisingly, not in earnings.
There were also significant reductions in drug use among participants
but no significant effects on arrests. Longer-term effects have not been
assessed.[4]

The Supported Work Ex-addict Sample

Characteristics of the Sample

By design, the Supported Work sample of ex-addicts is not representative of all former drug users. Since the program was intended for
those with severe labor market difficulties, eligibility standards were

established to *exclude* those expected to have a reasonably good chance of finding employment on their own. The employment history criteria, which were imposed on all target groups, specified that a person had to be currently unemployed and had to have spent no more than three months in one regular job during the preceding six months (see chapter 2). In addition, to qualify for the ex-addict sample a person had to be 18 years of age or older and in a drug treatment program within the last six months.[5]

Tables 5.1 and 5.2 present selected characteristics of the Supported Work ex-addict sample. The sample was predominantly between the ages of 21 and 35, male, and black. Only 40 percent of the sample had the equivalent of a high school education. The typical Supported Work ex-addict exhibited a poor work history and an extensive criminal record.

The drug-use histories of the Supported Work ex-addicts are also extensive (see table 5.2). Virtually all had had experience with opiates and nearly half had used heroin for more than five years. Three-quarters had used other types of drugs in addition to opiates. These data also show a pronounced pattern of recidivism to heroin use.

To examine how the Supported Work sample compares to a more general sample of ex-addicts, data from the Drug Abuse Reporting Program (DARP)—a representative sample of 27,500 people who were enrolled in federally funded drug treatment programs between 1969 and 1972—are also presented in tables 5.1 and 5.2.[6] The Supported Work sample is similar to the DARP sample in terms of work history and educational background. However, it underrepresents both younger and older treatment clients, as well as Hispanics and whites. The Supported Work sample also exhibits more extensive criminal records than does the DARP sample.

The Distribution of the Sample

Eligible applicants for the ex-addict target group slots were randomly assigned to either an experimental or a control group. Members of the experimental group were offered a Supported Work job for up to 12 or 18 months, depending on the site; members of the control group were not. The random assignment process was successful in terms of its generating experimental and control groups with similar characteristics.

All members of both the experimental and control groups were scheduled to be interviewed at the time of their application for Supported Work to determine their demographic characteristics, their employment history, welfare dependence, drug use, and criminal justice

TABLE 5.1

Percentage Distribution of the Ex-addict and DARP Samples, by Demographic, Employment, and Criminal Characteristics

	Supported Work Ex-addict Sample[a]	DARP Sample[b]
Years of age		
< 21	7	30
21–25	39	33
26–35	42	16
> 35	12	21
(Average age)	(27.7)	n.a.
Sex		
Male	83	75
Female	17	25
Ethnicity		
Black (or other)	77[c]	46
Hispanic	9	18
White	14	35
Education		
High school diploma or equivalent	40	37
Years of education		
≤ 8	14	n.a.
9–11	58	n.a.
≥ 12	28	n.a.
(Average number of years)	(10.5)	n.a.
Marital status		
Married	23	24
Other	77	76
At least one dependent	38	32
Employment experience		
Worked in past year	51	42
(Average weeks worked in past year)	(10.1)	n.a.
Length of longest job ever held		
No job	5	10
1–12 months	40	45
> 12 months	55	45
(Average dollar earnings in last 2 months for those who worked)	(589)	(612)
Received welfare last month[d]	40	n.a.
(Average dollar amount of welfare)	(78)	n.a.
Criminal history		
Number of arrests		
0	10	22
1	11	16
2–10	53	48
> 10	26	14
(Average number of arrests)	(8.6)	n.a.

(Continued on following page)

TABLE 5.1 (Continued)
Percentage Distribution of the Ex-addict and DARP Samples, by Demographic,
Employment, and Criminal Characteristics

	Supported Work Ex-addict Sample[a]	DARP Sample[b]
At least one conviction	76	55
(Average number of convictions)	(2.9)	n.a.
(Average number of weeks incarcerated)	(134)	n.a.
Number in sample	1,154	27,460

Note: Unless otherwise specified, these data refer to the full sample. Numbers in parentheses are averages rather than percentages.

a The sample includes all individuals who are included in any of the analysis samples and the data come from enrollment interviews conducted by Mathematica Policy Research staff.

b DARP is a representative sample of ex-addicts entering federally funded treatment programs. These data are from Simpson et al. (1976).

c Three sample members are from "other" ethnic/racial groups.

d Welfare includes AFDC, General Assistance, Supplemental Security Income, and other welfare.

n.a. Not available.

experiences. They were then scheduled to be reinterviewed 9 and 18 months later to collect postenrollment data on items such as employment, welfare dependence, drug use, and criminal activities. Because all interviewing was terminated in March 1979, only 85 percent of the sample (those enrolled prior to 1977) were scheduled to be interviewed again 27 months after their enrollment, and 33 percent (those enrolled prior to April 1976) were scheduled to be interviewed both 27 and 36 months after their enrollment. Table 5.3 shows the enrollment of the ex-addict sample by site and over calendar time.

Because of the differential length of follow-up among sample members and interview nonresponse, analysis of impacts for the various postprogram periods have been based on different subgroups of enrollees: analysis of outcomes during the first 18 months following enrollment have been based on those who completed an enrollment, a 9-month, and an 18-month interview; analysis of impacts for the 19- to 27-month period is based on data for those who completed an enrollment interview plus a 27-month interview, regardless of whether or not they completed the assigned 9- and 18-month interviews; and the analysis of 28- to 36-month outcomes relies on data for those who completed an enrollment and a 36-month interview.[7] In addition, particularly for analysis aimed at measuring program impacts on criminal recidivism, some analysis has been based on cumulative results over

TABLE 5.2
Percentage Distribution of the Ex-addict and DARP Samples, by Drug Use History

	Supported Work Ex-addict Sample[a]	DARP Sample[b]
Most recent treatment		
Methadone maintenance	53[c]	40
Drug free	25	21
Other	22	38
Number of treatment programs ever enrolled in		
0	6[d]	0
1	53	55
2	23	24
≥ 3	18	21
(Average number of treatment programs)	(1.7)	n.a.
In treatment at time of enrollment	76	n.a.
Types of drugs ever used		
Heroin	94	n.a.
Other opiates	28	n.a.
Cocaine	67	n.a.
Barbiturates	37	n.a.
Amphetamines	32	n.a.
Psychedelics	26	n.a.
Marijuana	91	n.a.
Opiates only	20	n.a.
Other drugs only	3	n.a.
Both opiates and other drugs	75	n.a.
Length of time used heroin		
Never used (or used less than a few times a month)	9	n.a.
< 1 year	11	n.a.
1–5 years	39	n.a.
> 5 years	46	n.a.
(Average years of heroin use)	(6.3)	n.a.
Number of times previously stopped using heroin (for those who ever used)		
0	11	n.a.
1–2	23	n.a.
3–4	20	n.a.
≥ 5	46	n.a.
(Average for those who used)	(6)	n.a.
Number in sample	1,154	27,460

Note: Unless otherwise specified, these data refer to the full sample. Numbers in parentheses are averages rather than percentages.

a The sample includes all individuals who are included in any of the analysis samples and the data come from enrollment interviews conducted by Mathematica Policy Research staff.

b DARP is a representative sample of ex-addicts entering federally funded treatment programs. These data are from Simpson et al. (1976).

(Continued on following page)

TABLE 5.2 (Continued)
Percentage Distribution of the Ex-addict and DARP Samples, by Drug Use History

c The data for the Supported Work sample pertain only to those in treatment within
   the 6 months prior to enrolling in the demonstration. Twelve percent were not in
   treatment during this period.
d Prior enrollment in treatment was an eligibility requirement for ex-addicts. That some
   individuals reported never having been enrolled in drug treatment is due to some
   ineligible persons having been enrolled in the program or to reporting errors.
n.a. Not available.

18-, 27-, and 36-month periods. For these cumulative analyses, the
samples used consist of only those individuals who completed *all*
scheduled interviews within the cumulative time periods. Thus, the
samples used to estimate cumulative results over the 1- to 27- and the
1- to 36-month periods are somewhat smaller than the samples used
to analyze results for the 19- to 27- and the 28- to 36-month periods.

An implication of the analysis samples is that those used for analysis
of various postenrollment periods are distinguished from one another
by the date an individual enrolled: only the earliest enrollees received
the longer-term follow-up interviews. We refer to these subsamples
followed for varying periods of time as the 18-, the 27-, and the 36-
month cohorts. Thus, to the extent that individuals' characteristics,
local labor market conditions, and program characteristics varied across
these enrollment periods, the estimates of longer-term results based
on these particular subsamples may not be representative of those that
actually occurred for the full sample. Because of this, care has been
taken to discuss the extent to which the results vary among the sample
cohorts.[8]

TABLE 5.3
Enrollment by Site and Time Period—Ex-addict Sample

	Site				All Sites	
	Chicago	Jersey City	Oakland	Philadelphia	Number	Percentage
Enrollment period						
March–December 1975	51	86	0	78	215	15.4
January–June 1976	65	183	72	176	496	35.2
July–December 1976	103	169	44	170	486	34.6
January–July 1977	80	61	28	41	210	14.9
Total						
Number	299	499	144	465	1407	100.0
Percentage	21.3	35.5	10.2	33.0	100.0	

Note: These figures are only for ex-addicts who completed an enrollment (baseline) interview, including 13 persons
who completed a substitute baseline interview at the time of a scheduled follow-up survey. This includes all but 26
of those subjected to random assignment.

Local Labor Market Conditions and Employment, Drug Use, and Crime Experiences of the Control Group

One of the most significant aspects of the research design of Supported Work is that the control group provides directly comparable information on what the experience of participants would have been had they not joined the Supported Work program. It is useful, then, to look first at the experience of the control group, which provides the context in which the Supported Work program was operating. However, by way of background, it is useful to first outline the nature of local labor market conditions prevailing during the course of the demonstration. In subsequent sections, the employment experiences of controls will be contrasted with the experience of the experimentals during the same period in order to determine the magnitude of program impacts.

Local Labor Market Conditions

The Supported Work Demonstration was conducted within an environment that could not be controlled by the research design, but yet had potentially important impacts on the results. Among the most important environmental factors are local labor market conditions.

During the period of this study, for example, national economic conditions improved substantially. The national unemployment rate declined from 9.3 to 5.7 percent. Local unemployment rates for the various Supported Work sites enrolling ex-addicts also declined: in Chicago, from 7.0 to 5.1 percent; in Jersey City, from 13.0 to 12.1 percent; in Oakland, from 10.7 to 5.7 percent; and in Philadelphia, from 8.1 to 7.5 percent.[9] It is not clear what effects these enhanced economic conditions may have had on experimental-control differentials since the possibility of finding a job in the regular labor market increased for both groups.

Another change in the environment that occurred during the course of the interviewing period was the introduction of the Special Unemployment Assistance (SUA) program. As initially designed, participation in Supported Work would not have qualified workers for regular unemployment compensation benefits. However, depending on how local officials viewed Supported Work, workers could become eligible for the SUA benefits. As a result, many of the ex-addict participants (primarily in Jersey City) did receive this form of assistance immediately after leaving the program, thereby lowering their incentives to become reemployed quickly, although possibly improving their long-run prospects to the extent that the time was used for a more thorough job search. Alternatively, if the experimentals remained out of the labor force for prolonged periods, the benefits from the Supported Work experience may have been lost.

The estimated impact of Supported Work should be interpreted as taking place under these relatively poor but improving labor market conditions, with an inconsistent pattern across sites in unemployment compensation coverage. Because of the unplanned and uncontrolled nature of these variations in local factors that may affect the program's outcomes, it is not possible to estimate Supported Work's impacts under alternative situations. Nonetheless, subsequent discussion will relate program results to the prevailing conditions during a given time period or at a given site where a particular set of conditions prevailed, in order to provide as much insight as possible into the influence of those conditions on the observed results.

Employment among Controls

Over the period covered by the study, employment among controls tended to increase, and both drug use and arrests—indicators of involvement in crime—tended to decrease. During the first six months after random assignment, employment among controls rose from 0 to 47 hours per month, and it continued to increase, although at a slower rate, throughout the first two years. For those followed for three years subsequent to their enrollment, their employment rates tended to stabilize, but at a lower level than the average for the full sample during the preceding nine months.

The initial rise in the employment level of the controls was due to two factors. Particularly during the first 6-month period, a large portion of the increase was attributable to individuals who, because of program eligibility criteria, were unemployed at the time they were enrolled in the sample. They then gradually reached their "typical" employment level—a phenomenon known as regression to the mean. The second factor was the improving labor market during the period of the study. Estimates are that roughly 20 percent of the total change in hours was attributable to this improvement in the labor market and 80 percent to the regression to the mean.

Drug Use and Criminal Activity among Controls

Drug use among controls was prevalent; during the first 9-month period, 38 percent of the controls reported the use of some drug other than alcohol or marijuana, and 22 percent reported the continued or renewed use of heroin. Over the subsequent 9-month time periods the percentage reporting use of any drug declined quite steadily, with only about 21 percent reporting any use during months 28–36. Two factors contribute to this change. First, there was a decline nationally in drug use during the calendar year 1978, the period when this lower use was reported; and second, the later enrollees in the Supported Work program reported a higher incidence of drug use than did the early ones.

The incidence of arrests among the ex-addict controls was also high. About 19 percent of the control group members reported having been arrested during each of the first three 9-month periods, and 14 percent were arrested during months 28–36. (As with the employment and drug-use results, at least a partial explanation for this trend in arrest rates is the changing sample.) Because these data include multiple arrests of the same individuals, it is also useful to examine the number of members of the control group arrested over the full period of the study. Cumulatively, during the first 18 months after enrollment, 34 percent of the controls had been arrested at least once and, among those followed for the full 36-month period, over half reported having been arrested during the three years since their enrollment. Between 20 and 25 percent of those arrested reported having been charged with a robbery, and a similar proportion reported having been charged with a drug offense.

The Supported Work Program Experience

As a result of there having been much local flexibility to meet local needs and circumstances and to conform with philosophies of the local program directors, the program experiences of experimentals varied by site. Table 5.4 highlights key characteristics of the programs in which ex-addicts were enrolled.

Most programs attempted to create jobs for participants that were labor-intensive and relatively low-skilled (MDRC 1978), much of it for public or private nonprofit agencies. Consistent with the nature of the jobs, the initial wage rates paid to ex-addicts in Supported Work were set equal to approximately 78 percent of the wage rate that participants might be expected to earn on a regular job and always above the minimum wage. Longevity and cost-of-living adjustments were made, although the extent of adjustments varied among sites.

In all sites except Philadelphia, the maximum length of program participation was 12 months; in Philadelphia it was 18 months. In fact, the ex-addict subsample on average stayed in Supported Work only 6.7 months, over one month less than has been estimated for participation in CETA public service employment (MDRC 1978). The length of stay in the program tended to decrease with calendar time, as evidenced by the fact that members of the 36-month cohort stayed

TABLE 5.4
Selected Characteristics of Programs Enrolling Ex-addicts

	Program Location			
	Chicago	Jersey City	Oakland	Philadelphia
Program hourly wage rate as of January 1977[a]	$2.60–3.00	$2.68–2.83	$2.63–3.02	$2.30–2.65
Other main target groups served	AFDC, Ex-offender	Ex-offender, Youth	AFDC, Ex-offender	Ex-offender, Youth
Program size[b] (number of slots)	184	303	109	99
Average crew size[c]	4.9	6.7	4.2	7.2
Percentage of ex-addicts in various types of jobs[d]				
Construction	63	45	57	62
Business services	27	24	8	19
Other	10	31	35	19
Maximum length of program participation	12 months	12 months	12 months	18 months

a *Source:* Manpower Demonstration Research Corporation (1978, Table VI-11). Program wages were always above the prevailing minimum wage.
b *Source:* Manpower Demonstration Research Corporation (1978, Table II-1). The program size figures are for June 1977.
c *Source:* Manpower Demonstration Research Corporation (1978, Table IV-2).
d These averages are for the second contract year. They represent the percentage of project hours in these industries. Source: Special MIS Report, July 1977.

7.8 months, on average; the 27-month cohort stayed 6.4 months, on average; and the 18-month cohort stayed only 6.2 months, on average. Four factors are associated with relatively early termination from Supported Work: being white, having recent employment experience, receiving welfare at enrollment, and residing in Oakland or Philadelphia. A common characteristic of short-term participants is that they were likely to have better employment alternatives or have more sources of nonlabor income than other ex-addicts.

Estimates of Program Impacts

In assessing the impacts of the Supported Work experience, multiple regression analysis was employed.[10] The basic data source, as already mentioned, is a series of interviews with experimentals and controls.[11]

Employment-Related Outcomes

Employment and Earnings Table 5.5 shows experimental-control differences, for each 3-month period covered by the data, for three employment-related outcomes: percentage employed, hours worked

TABLE 5.5
Employment-Related Outcomes—Ex-addict Sample

Months	Percentage Employed			Hours Worked per Month			Average Gross Earnings per Month		
	Experimental Group Mean	Control Group Mean	Experimental-Control Differential	Experimental Group Mean	Control Group Mean	Experimental-Control Differential	Experimental Group Mean	Control Group Mean	Experimental-Control Differential
1–3	91.7	30.9	60.8**	138.4	32.4	106.0**	395.31	122.30	273.01**
4–6	76.8	39.0	37.8**	116.7	46.7	70.0**	348.00	184.58	163.42**
7–9	67.2	37.1	30.1**	97.3	42.9	54.4**	306.08	166.99	139.09**
10–12	54.5	36.4	18.1**	80.2	46.7	33.5**	280.71	205.37	75.34**
13–15	50.6	40.4	10.2**	64.9	51.4	13.5**	251.65	211.81	39.84*
16–18	39.4	40.0	–0.6	50.4	52.3	–1.9	215.51	222.22	–6.71
19–21	40.0	40.4	–0.4	55.1	55.4	–0.3	243.78	250.25	–6.47
22–24	43.0	43.4	–0.4	61.6	60.2	1.4	281.02	270.36	10.66
25–27	45.4	43.0	2.4	63.7	58.9	4.8	287.05	259.88	27.17
28–30	42.0	37.8	4.2	66.6	56.3	10.3	304.09	237.45	66.64
31–33	47.2	38.7	8.5	73.1	51.9	21.2**	332.18	221.85	110.33**
34–36	48.8	31.6	17.2**	70.4	50.0	20.4**	318.60	218.76	99.84**

Note: All data are regression-adjusted. The coefficients of the control variables used are given in Dickinson and Maynard (1981, Table 4.1). Means and standard deviations of control variables are presented in Appendix table A.1 of this volume.

* Statistically significant at the 10 percent level.
** Statistically significant at the 5 percent level.

per month, and average gross earnings per month. The basic pattern is the same for all three measures. Experimentals initially did better relative to controls (largely because of their Supported Work jobs), an advantage that diminished as they left their Supported Work jobs. After a period in which experimentals had the same employment and earnings as controls, among those interviewed 36 months after enrollment, experimentals did significantly better than controls during the latest six-month period. Furthermore, the differentials in hours and earnings were not due solely to the differences in employment rates: in these later periods, among those who were employed, experimentals tended to work more hours (and have somewhat higher wage rates, not shown) than did controls.

This pattern of results raises a number of questions, the most important of which is whether the upturn during the last half of the third year is representative of the results that would have been observed had the full sample been followed for as long as 36 months. Moreover, what was the cause of the long delay between participants leaving Supported Work and realizing these longer-term benefits?

As noted previously, the amount of follow-up data available for various sample members depends on the calendar date they enrolled in the demonstration. Thus, the trend in experimentals' and controls' employment and hours reflects changes over time in both employment of individuals and sample composition.

These two components of the overall effect can be seen from figure 5.1, which depicts the average number of hours worked by experimentals and controls in each cohort over time. During the initial months following enrollment, all three cohorts exhibited large experimental-control differentials that decreased over time and became insignificant at varying points: significant positive differentials persisted throughout months 13–15 among the 36- and the 27-month cohorts, and only through months 7–9 among the 18-month cohort. There are two primary reasons for differences in the timing of the decreases in experimental-control differentials. Part of the difference is due to controls' employment increasing more rapidly for the 18- and 27-month cohorts than for the 36-month cohort. Part of the difference is also due to experimentals in the 36-month cohort staying in the program 1.5 months longer than those in the other cohorts.

For the 36-month cohort, no significant employment differentials were observed again until months 25–27, when experimentals increased their employment relative to controls, resulting in a significant differential of 18 hours per month. The differential was somewhat smaller, but persisted, through the 28- to 36-month period. For the

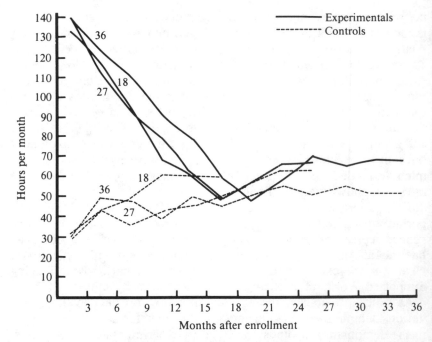

Fig. 5.1. Trend in Hours Worked per Month by Subsamples with Varying Amounts of Follow-up Data—Ex-addict Sample
    Note: These data are not regression-adjusted.
    18 = 18 months of follow-up data.
    27 = 27 months of follow-up data.
    36 = 36 months of follow-up data.

18-month and 27-month cohorts, no significant postprogram effects were observed. Whether such effects occurred beyond the period of observation for these groups is simply not known. If any postprogram benefits did result, they must almost certainly have been smaller than those observed for the 36-month cohort because, in the earlier periods that were observed, the program tended to be less effective for these later cohorts than for the 36-month cohort, and also because controls in the later cohorts exhibited substantially higher employment levels than did controls in the 36-month cohort—a factor which has shown a consistent pattern of being related to less favorable program impacts.

Why these differences? One explanation that comes immediately to mind is the possibility that the programs were most effective during the initial period of operations. In fact, this appears not to be the case, as individuals who enrolled in programs when they had been in operation for longer than a year and a half also exhibited relatively favorable responses to the program. Another possible explanation is that the differences are related to differential impacts across sites. This did turn out to account for part of the difference between the cohorts during the 19- to 27-month period; controlling statistically for differential program impacts among the sites lead to a reduction in the difference between the estimated program impacts for the 27- and 36-month cohorts. However, the site composition of the cohort samples did not account for cohort differences in program impacts during the 10- to 18-month period.

Changes over time in economic conditions probably contribute more to the observed cohort differences. The fact that in months 10–27, controls in the 36-month cohort worked substantially fewer hours than did controls in the 27-month cohort is consistent with this hypothesis. Because of the correlations between calendar time, program time, and cohort, it was not possible to produce more than crude estimates of the extent to which changing labor markets affected program outcomes. However, when we controlled for time since program enrollment, we found that employment increased over calendar time, suggesting that changes in economic conditions may indeed provide a partial explanation for differences in program impacts among the cohorts.

The last obvious possibility for the observed differences in outcomes among the three cohorts is that the type of people applying to Supported Work changed over time. Although there are some differences in the characteristics of the individuals in the various cohorts and although the program, in general, was more effective for some types of individual than for others (see below), differences in *measured* sample characteristics do not appear to account for the cohort differences.

The possibility, of course, remains that those who applied for the program in its initial phases were different from later applicants in ways that are not identified by demographic or background characteristics. For example, in the early phases there might have been a stock of people who had been in drug treatment for whom Supported Work was particularly appropriate whereas, after this stock was depleted, applicants were drawn from the flow of people coming out of treatment who, on average, were less appropriate candidates for Supported Work. It is not possible to test this hypothesis, however, since it postulates the existence of unobserved differences among the cohorts.

In addition to considering the time trend of overall impacts, we also estimated impacts for selected sample subgroups in order to determine whether the diversity among the four Supported Work programs that enrolled ex-addicts and among the types of people who applied for Supported Work affected significantly its success. Table 5.6 presents

TABLE 5.6

Hours Employed per Month, by Site and Site Characteristics—Ex-addict Sample

	Months 1–9		Months 10–18		Months 19–27		Months 28–36	
	Experimental-Control Differential	Control Group Mean	Experimental-Control Differential	Control Group Mean	Experimental-Control Differential	Control Group Mean	Experimental-Control Differential	Control Group Mean
All ex-addicts[a]	78.2**	40.5	16.4**	50.0	1.5	58.6	18.3**	52.6
Site	#							
Chicago	90.8**	30.8	20.5**	31.5	11.7	55.8	39.7**	45.8
Jersey City	87.4**	49.7	16.9**	56.4	-4.9	68.1	6.9	73.8
Oakland	59.1**	41.3	16.0	38.4	-20.4	67.2	[b]	[b]
Philadelphia	61.4**	35.9	12.5	43.9	7.1	47.9	17.4	35.8
Years of site operation at time of enrollment			#					
<1	73.1**	45.8	27.5**	51.1	3.7	55.1	n.a.	n.a.
1–1.5	79.1**	35.0	4.2	46.8	-1.0	60.0	n.a.	n.a.
>1.5	84.2**	41.6	19.9**	54.1	2.3	66.5	n.a.	n.a.

Note: See note to table 5.5.

a These overall sample results were estimated from an equation that did not include variables interacting experimental status with site or years of operation. Thus, the subgroup results may not weight up to these overall sample values.

b There are only four persons in this Oakland sample.

n.a. Not applicable.

Experimental-control differentials for this time period differ significantly from one another.

** Statistically significant at the 5 percent level. None of the other experimental-control differentials is statistically significant at the 5 or 10 percent level.

152

estimated impacts on hours worked by site and by the length of site operation at the time an individual enrolled. For each 9-month period, two numbers are presented for each site. The first is the difference between the average hours worked per month by experimentals and controls in that site; the second is the average hours worked by controls. In the first nine months, the effectiveness of the program did vary significantly by site, largely as a result of differentials in the length of time experimentals in the various sites stayed in Supported Work. In all sites, experimentals worked significantly more than did controls in this period, the difference being largest in Chicago and Jersey City, and smallest in Philadelphia and Oakland. In the later periods, estimated program impacts did not vary significantly among the sites. The differential between experimentals and controls continued to be largest in Chicago, however, and was significant in months 28–36. It is noteworthy that, although the widening experimental-control difference in employment after month 27 was largest in Chicago, it was also evident in the other sites. And, these site-specific postprogram results follow a pattern which is found consistently in other subgroup differences: throughout the 19- to 36-month period, experimental-control differences were most positive in those sites where controls worked fewer hours than average (Philadelphia and Chicago).[12]

Supported Work help in job placement after Supported Work participation may explain some additional part of the differences by site. Reports of assistance were most prevalent among the Chicago sample and least prevalent in Philadelphia. In addition, the experimental-control difference in the proportion of CETA and WIN jobs held, particularly in months 28–36, was highest in Chicago, possibly accounting for another small part of Chicago's superior results.

Table 5.7 shows experimental-control differences for subgroups defined by demographic and background characteristics. Since there are many comparisons, and some are significant in only one period, the discussion focuses on those effects that are sustained and consistent across several periods. The consistent differences again suggest a pattern in which Supported Work is more effective for those subgroups who might be expected to work less than average (as measured by average control hours worked), although no individual difference is so large as to suggest that targeting Supported Work at a specific subgroup of ex-addicts would result in substantially more favorable impacts than observed for the ex-addict sample as a whole.

With respect to demographic characteristics, we found a consistent variation in program effects depending on whether the individual had at least one dependent: those experimentals with dependents tended

TABLE 5.7

Hours Employed per Month, by Individual Demographic and Background Characteristics—Ex-addict Sample

	Months 1-9		Months 10-18		Months 19-27		Months 28-36	
	Experimental-Control Differential	Control Group Mean	Experimental-Control Differential	Control Group Mean	Experimental-Control Differential	Control Group Mean	Experimental-Control Differential	Control Group Mean
All ex-addicts[a]	78.2**	40.5	16.4**	50.0	1.5	58.6	18.3**	52.6
Years of age								
< 21	69.8**	49.9	-5.7	68.4	8.6	69.3	80.9*[b]	0.1[b]
21-25	75.8**	43.2	12.3*	51.0	-6.4	60.5	3.8	57.5
26-35	80.1**	38.7	21.1**	49.0	9.4	58.6	32.8**	44.0
> 35	82.4**	29.7	24.2*	37.5	-6.0	48.2	-15.6	66.0
Sex	#				#			
Male	75.0**	41.4	14.5**	51.0	5.4	60.2	15.7*	55.9
Female	90.5**	34.4	24.0**	44.0	-18.9	52.6	37.0	7.6
Race/ethnicity								
White, non-Hispanic	65.7**	46.2	25.0**	53.4	5.1	79.2	-35.2	95.9
Black, non-Hispanic	83.3**	36.5	15.1**	45.7	2.7	51.8	22.0**	44.9
Hispanic	48.5**	63.8	14.8	80.9	-17.2	90.8	62.1[b]	36.4[b]
Years of education								
≤ 8	84.1**	39.2	25.5**	37.4	8.4	42.3	-4.6	48.9
9-11	78.3**	34.7	16.2**	43.8	5.1	56.9	15.8	49.1
≥ 12	74.7**	51.2	12.4	67.0	-9.3	70.4	35.6**	50.8
Welfare and food stamp receipt in month prior to enrollment[c]	#							
None	86.4**	38.7	15.8**	53.1	-3.9	65.6	28.6**	42.0
Some	69.8**	41.3	17.0**	46.1	6.2	52.6	9.9	55.9

154

Dependents	#		#					
None	72.2**	47.1	9.2*	53.7	−5.3	61.9	17.7	51.4
One or more	87.4**	29.0	27.5**	43.2	12.2	53.9	19.9	46.3
Months in longest job								
0	104.5**	16.5	−9.5	57.1	−5.7	56.0	−12.5[b]	70.8[b]
1–12	72.7**	39.9	14.3**	50.0	2.9	56.6	28.0*	43.9
> 12	79.3**	42.5	20.5**	48.5	0.8	60.8	15.4	51.1
Weeks worked in year prior to enrollment[d]								
0	82.2**	38.6	18.1**	44.3	1.9	54.3	9.0	50.2
5	80.2**	39.3	17.3**	46.9	1.6	56.5	12.6	49.9
10	78.2**	40.0	16.4**	49.5	1.3	58.7	16.3*	49.7
Weeks of job training in year prior to enrollment	#							
< 8	75.2**	41.4	17.0**	48.1	2.5	57.5	19.0**	49.9
≥ 8	106.8**	26.1	9.8	65.0	−9.7	71.7	13.3	45.4
Prior drug use[e]								
Used heroin and cocaine regularly	71.4**	44.2	19.4	55.2	−21.3	85.3	10.2	48.8
Used heroin regularly but not cocaine	82.5**	36.6	19.6**	47.8	1.4	56.3	25.4**	46.8
Did not use heroin regularly	61.7**	53.6	−2.2	53.7	20.6	49.6	−19.1	68.3
Drug treatment in last 6 months			#		#			
Methadone maintenance	80.8**	33.1	24.1**	38.1	14.8**	48.5	28.6**	42.7
Drug-free program	66.1**	55.5	−6.0	71.1	−6.8	75.9	−14.3	83.0
Other type of program	75.1**	47.0	8.3	64.1	−17.0	66.9	43.5*	41.1
Not in treatment	94.4**	28.6	39.2**	34.1	−15.2	59.2	−25.8	38.8

(Continued on following page)

155

TABLE 5.7 (Continued)

Hours Employed per Month, by Individual Demographic and Background Characteristics—Ex-addict Sample

	Months 1–9		Months 10–18		Months 19–27		Months 28–36	
	Experimental-Control Differential	Control Group Mean	Experimental-Control Differential	Control Group Mean	Experimental-Control Differential	Control Group Mean	Experimental-Control Differential	Control Group Mean
Prior arrests[d]								
0	82.1**	37.5	15.9	46.0	# 12.2	49.2	−33.5	86.6
4	76.6**	41.8	14.8**	52.8	−3.4	63.1	20.5*	49.9
9	78.9**	39.2	17.2**	50.5	2.1	59.5	27.2**	43.8
Months since incarceration							#	
Never incarcerated	90.1**	29.3	24.1**	53.0	# 22.2**	52.4	45.6	33.3
≤ 12	77.4**	37.1	20.2**	39.0	11.1	52.9	60.1**	29.7
> 12	71.6**	48.2	9.8	56.1	−17.4	68.0	4.4	54.6

Note: See note to table 5.5.

a These overall sample results were estimated from an equation that included only the standard control variables and an experimental-status variable. Thus, the subgroup results may not always weight up to these overall sample values.

b Sample size is less than 20.

c Welfare includes AFDC, General Assistance, other welfare, and welfare income for which respondents could not identify the source.

d These estimates of subgroup effects and means are based on a linear (or piecewise linear) specification of the sample characteristic, evaluated at specified points.

e Regular use is defined as use on a daily or almost daily basis for 2 months or more.

Experimental-control differentials within this subgrouping for this time period differ significantly from one another.

* Statistically significant at the 10 percent level.

** Statistically significant at the 5 percent level.

to work more hours, relative to comparable controls, than did experimentals without dependents. The tendency is evident in all periods, and the differences between the subgroups are significant in months 1–9 and months 10–18. Also, after the initial 9-month period, effects tended to be more favorable than average among those with some longer-lasting jobs prior to enrollment in Supported Work and among those with little or no recent job training. Another consistent pattern of effects was that the program tended to be less effective for those who, during the six months prior to enrolling in Supported Work, had been in drug-free treatment programs, and to be relatively more effective for those in methadone maintenance programs. Again, a common characteristic of each of the subgroups where effects were largest is that controls tended to work less than the overall average for controls.

Total Income and Its Sources   In the previous section, we found that Supported Work increased the earnings of experimentals both in the periods when a substantial proportion were participating in the program and, for those who enrolled in the demonstration and so were interviewed three years later, in the 28- to 36-month period. At the time that the ex-addicts applied to Supported Work, over 50 percent were receiving welfare and/or food stamps. Undoubtedly these income-conditioned transfers as well as other sources of income were affected by the changes in earnings due to participation in Supported Work. Table 5.8A presents the experimental-control differences in income received from five sources: earnings, unemployment compensation, welfare, the bonus value of food stamps, and other types of unearned income. Table 5.8B presents differences in the average amounts received.

As seen from these tables, in periods when experimentals had higher earnings than controls, they also tended to have higher total incomes. Concurrent with the earnings differences, there were estimated reductions in public assistance income received by experimentals relative to controls. In both the first and second 9-month periods, significantly fewer experimentals than controls received welfare.[13] Experimentals were also significantly less likely than controls to receive food stamps in months 1–9, although not in the later periods.

The picture is different with respect to unemployment compensation. During months 10–18 and months 19–27, a significantly higher percentage of experimentals than controls received unemployment compensation, primarily because some experimentals became eligible for the temporary Special Unemployment Assistance (SUA) program.[14]

TABLE 5.8
Income from Various Sources—Ex-addict Sample

	Months 1–9		Months 10–18		Months 19–27		Months 28–36	
	Experimental-Control Differential	Control Group Mean	Experimental-Control Differential	Control Group Mean	Experimental-Control Differential	Control Group Mean	Experimental-Control Differential	Control Group Mean
A. Percentage Receiving Income								
Earnings[a]	44.8**	50.2	10.8**	53.1	3.5	53.0	10.1*	53.9
Unearned income								
Unemployment compensation	-5.0**	7.4	10.7**	4.3	5.2**	6.0	0.5	7.4
Welfare[b]	-21.7**	50.7	-6.1*	46.7	-0.4	40.2	-3.6	45.1
Food stamps	-10.1**	45.7	-3.5	43.3	1.8	38.8	0.6	42.0
Other[c]	-4.2**	7.1	-2.4*	4.2	-2.1	5.3	2.3	2.2
B. Average Monthly Income Received (dollars)								
All sources	134.09**	295.50	36.00	344.53	23.17	373.98	92.03**	352.40
Earnings[a]	201.44**	159.79	39.20*	220.42	16.42	261.33	101.73**	224.36
Unearned income								
Unemployment compensation	-6.59**	10.86	17.84**	8.42	15.11**	10.31	1.16	16.62
Welfare[b]	-48.49**	92.88	-12.50*	86.99	-3.12	74.70	-9.83	82.84
Food stamp bonus value	-6.01**	20.89	-3.47	22.60	0.37	18.56	0.48	20.90
Other[c]	-4.66	10.24	-2.21	4.61	-3.30	7.86	-0.43	7.14

Note: See note to table 5.5. All data pertain to the full sample, not only to recipients.

a Only individuals who had valid data for all income sources were included in this table.

b Welfare includes AFDC, General Assistance, Supplemental Security Income, and other unspecified welfare income.

c Other unearned income includes Social Security, pensions, alimony, child support, and training income.

* Statistically significant at the 10 percent level.

** Statistically significant at the 5 percent level.

For example, in months 10–18, only 4 percent of the controls compared with 15 percent of the experimentals received income from unemployment compensation, and experimentals received an average of nearly $18 more per month from this source than did controls. It is not clear, of course, what the impact of Supported Work would be on this type of transfer income in the period subsequent to the SUA program.

Effects on Drug Use

The ex-addicts were asked about their use of alcohol and eight other drugs: heroin, other opiates, cocaine, amphetamines, barbiturates, illegal methadone, psychedelics, and marijuana. The outcomes analyzed were chosen on the basis of importance and reliability.[15] On the premise that society's concern with the use of a particular drug is due to the cost it imposes on others, a ranking of drug-use patterns in terms of the seriousness of their social consequences was developed and used to construct an additive index of drug use (Dickinson 1979).

Supported Work did not have a significant influence on the participants' use of drugs, in spite of the substantial experimental-control differences in employment during certain periods (see table 5.9). In months 1–9, about one-fifth of both experimentals and controls reported using heroin. Among both experimentals and controls, a smaller percentage reported using heroin in the later periods, reflecting, in large part, a general decline in its use (the extent of which was similar for both experimentals and controls).[16] Measures of the frequency of heroin use for the full sample are not available for the first 9-month period, but in months 10–18 a lower proportion of experimentals than controls used heroin daily or almost daily. However, this difference is not significant and does not persist into the later periods.

With respect to the other drugs, 5–10 percent of the sample (both experimentals and controls) used opiates other than heroin, and between 12 and 19 percent of the sample used cocaine during each 9-month period.[17] The use of marijuana was widespread, with approximately 65 percent of both experimentals and controls reporting its use in each 9-month period. Experimental-control differences were neither large nor significant. There were also no significant differences between experimentals and controls in the prevalence of enrollment in drug treatment programs as a result of Supported Work nor any persistent differences in the types of treatment used.

These overall results on drug use do, however, mask some important differences by site and by subgroup (Dickinson and Maynard 1981, Tables V.2–V.10). Among the Oakland sample, heroin use by exper-

TABLE 5.9

Percentage Reporting Use of Various Drugs—Ex-addict Sample

	Months 1–9		Months 10–18		Months 19–27		Months 28–36	
	Experimental-Control Differential	Control Group Mean	Experimental-Control Differential	Control Group Mean	Experimental-Control Differential	Control Group Mean	Experimental-Control Differential	Control Group Mean
Any drug (other than marijuana or alcohol)	−2.1	38.2	1.4	32.7	0.5	27.5	2.7	20.7
Heroin								
Any use[a]	−1.3	21.5	−1.0	17.8	1.7	11.7	1.3	8.8
Daily use[b]	n.a.	n.a.	−2.5	7.7	−0.2	4.8	−0.8	4.3
Any use of opiates other than heroin[ac]	−0.7	10.1	1.8	5.5	0.9	5.2	−2.4	7.4
Any use of cocaine[ac]	2.6	16.2	2.6	15.3	1.5	15.2	−1.4	13.7
Any use of amphetamines, barbiturates, psychedelics, or illegal methadone[ac]	0.2	9.2	1.0	9.2	0.3	8.5	−1.7	6.6
Marijuana								
Any use[a]	−0.2	65.4	−0.5	66.3	2.2	62.5	0.8	61.8
Daily use[b]	n.a.	n.a.	−1.4	25.4	−0.2	23.4	2.0	20.7
(Additive index of drug use)[d]	(0.2)	(33.1)	(0.6)	(32.8)	(2.6)	(21.9)	(−0.2)	(18.3)

Notes: See note to table 5.5. None of the experimental-control differentials in table 5.9 is statistically significant at the 5 or 10 percent level.

a Any use is defined as use at any time during the 9-month period.

b Daily use is defined as use on a daily or almost daily basis at any time in the 9-month period.

c Daily use of other opiates, cocaine, amphetamines, barbiturates, and psychedelics was reported by less than 5 percent of the ex-addict sample and so is not included in this table.

d This index weights the use of each drug by its association with arrests. See Dickinson (1979) for a description of the methodology used to develop the index.

n.a. Not available.

160

imentals was significantly less prevalent than among controls in both the first and second 9-month periods. However, between months 10–18 and 19–27, heroin use among Oakland experimentals remained quite stable (27–30 percent of the sample), while the percentage of Oakland controls reporting heroin use fell substantially (from 48 to 25 percent), resulting in a small and not significant differential in the later time period. It should be noted that the overall rate of use among controls was much higher in Oakland than in other sites. This is the same pattern that was found for hours of work: Supported Work tended to be most effective for those who would have done less well on their own.

With respect to background and demographic characteristics of the sample, again it was found that the program was relatively more effective in reducing heroin use among those whose control group counterparts were particularly likely to use the drug. Especially in the early period, the program led to reduced heroin use among those over 35, among whites and Hispanics, and among short-term heroin users; controls in all of these subgroups had high rates of use.[18] In the later periods, among those who enrolled in drug-free treatment programs, experimentals were significantly more likely to use heroin than were controls—and comparable controls had lower than average rates of use. For the ex-addict sample, estimates of program effects on heroin use varied little by the extent of one's criminal history, unlike the ex-offender target group members (see Piliavin and Gartner 1981 and chapter 6).

For cocaine use there were fewer significant subgroup differences in the program effects than for heroin use. Further, for cocaine we do not observe the relationships we observed for heroin use and for employment, namely that the program tended to increase employment and reduce heroin use most for individuals at highest risk. The largest subgroup difference in cocaine use occurred among those who had previously used both heroin and cocaine regularly.[19] In the first nine months, 37 percent of the experimentals with this history used cocaine, while only 19 percent of the comparable controls did so; in months 10–18, there was a similar effect. However, these differences did not persist into the later periods when all the experimentals were out of the program. These results raise the possibility that participants with a history of regular cocaine use will tend to use some of their additional income from the program to purchase drugs.

With respect to alcohol, in months 1–9, significantly fewer experimentals than controls used alcohol daily, with approximately 12 percent of the experimentals and 16 percent of the controls reporting drinking alcohol daily. In the later periods the effect is reversed: a higher percentage of experimentals than controls used alcohol daily, although results for these later periods are not statistically significant. The effect observed in the first nine months is primarily the result of a large difference in Jersey City, where both experimentals and controls had relatively high rates of daily alcohol use, but where use among experimentals was significantly lower.

The increase in daily alcohol use among experimentals after program participation might have been expected if experimentals had altered their drug-use patterns.[20] However, Supported Work did not have an overall impact on the experimentals' drug use. Furthermore, the subgroups for which there were significant decreases in drug use were not, in general, the same subgroups for which there was an increase in daily alcohol use.

Another possible explanation for the increase in alcohol use involves the relationship between alcohol use and employment. It is consistent with other studies that the low initial and only gradually increasing stress of Supported Work may have lessened the daily use of alcohol among participants relative to controls, but that movement into non-program jobs may have produced more stress and increased the alcohol consumption of experimentals as a consequence. There is some evidence for this view. Although among the controls there was no consistent relationship between alcohol use and employment, in every period, employed experimentals were more likely to consume alcohol than were unemployed experimentals and, among the employed, the experimental-control differential in daily alcohol use was somewhat larger in the third and fourth 9-month periods than it had been earlier.

Crime-Related Outcomes

Data were collected on three measures of criminal activity: self-reported crime; self-reported contacts with the criminal justice system, including arrests, convictions, and incarcerations; and officially recorded criminal justice contacts. We placed greatest emphasis on the self-reports of contacts with the criminal justice system, particularly arrests for reasons discussed in chapter 2.[21]

Overall Effects by Time Period Supported Work did substantially reduce the criminal activity of the ex-addicts, as measured by their contacts with the criminal justice system. The results presented in table 5.10 indicate that, in every time period, a lower percentage of experimentals than controls were arrested—a difference that was significant in months 10–18, when 19 percent of the controls were arrested, com-

TABLE 5.10

Arrests, Convictions, and Incarcerations—Ex-addict Sample

	Months 1–9		Months 10–18		Months 19–27		Months 28–36	
	Experimental-Control Differential	Control Group Mean	Experimental-Control Differential	Control Group Mean	Experimental-Control Differential	Control Group Mean	Experimental-Control Differential	Control Group Mean
Percentage with any arrest	−2.5	19.5	−5.9**	18.6	−2.3	18.2	−5.0	13.5
Number of arrests	0.00	0.23	−0.09	0.23	−0.04	0.22	−0.04	0.15
Percentage with robbery arrests[a]	−3.4**	4.5	−2.0**	3.3	0.5	2.2	−0.9	1.9
Number of robbery arrests[a]	−0.04**	0.05	−0.02**	0.03	0.01	0.02	−0.01	0.02
Percentage with drug-related arrests[b]	−1.4	3.6	−3.0**	4.1	−2.4*	4.9	−2.2	3.5
Percentage convicted	−0.2	8.7	−3.4*	9.6	−1.6	8.0	−3.4	6.5
Percentage incarcerated	0.3	10.3	−4.9**	16.2	−2.9	18.6	−5.9	21.2
Number of weeks incarcerated	−0.20	1.81	−1.40**	2.90	−0.66	4.14	−1.20	4.36

Note: See note to table 5.5. All data pertain to the full sample.

a Robbery arrests are defined as those for which robbery was the most serious charge. Only murder and felonious assault are considered to be more serious than robbery.

b Drug-related arrests are defined as those for which narcotics law violation is the most serious charge. More serious charges include murder, felonious assault, robbery, burglary, larceny, motor vehicle theft and other property crimes, and other crimes against persons.

 * Statistically significant at the 10 percent level.

** Statistically significant at the 5 percent level.

pared to 13 percent of the experimentals. The number of arrests for experimentals was also somewhat less than for controls, although this difference was smaller and not significant.

The two types of crime singled out in table 5.10 (drug-related crime and robbery) are particularly salient for the ex-addict group—the former for obvious reasons and the latter because it has a very high social cost and because other studies have found drug users particularly likely to commit crimes of this type. As can be seen from these data, drug-related arrests were significantly reduced for Supported Work participants in months 10–18 and 19–27. Robbery-related arrests were significantly reduced in months 1–9 and months 10–18.

Supported Work also had an effect in reducing the percentage of ex-addicts who were convicted and incarcerated. These results were largest and statistically significant in months 10–18, when 9.6 percent of the controls were convicted, compared to 6.2 percent of the experimentals, and when over 16 percent of the controls spent some time in jail or prison, compared to 11 percent of the experimentals.

Site and Subgroup Differences   In examining the subgroup differences in hours of work and in drug use, a consistent pattern is observed whereby Supported Work was more effective for those who did less well on their own. There is less evidence of this pattern for the subgroup differences in arrests (see Dickinson and Maynard 1981, Tables IV.2–IV.3).

There were some site differences in the effects on criminal activity, but the pattern of results was inconsistent across time periods and generally did not coincide with site differences in employment. The site differences found for heroin use *were* reflected in the site differences for arrests, however. In the first and second 9-month periods, the program in Oakland did result in decreases in heroin use among experimentals relative to controls. The effect on arrests was also largest for Oakland in these two time periods. However, these favorable results with respect to drug use and arrests did not persist into the third 9-month period, when virtually all the participants had left the program.

With respect to individual characteristics, Supported Work had a consistently greater impact on arrests among those who were not receiving welfare at enrollment. Since the program would result in a larger change in income among those who were not receiving welfare than among those who were, these results suggest that the extra income provided by the program may have been an important mechanism in reducing arrests. The program also tended to be more effective for those with at least one dependent. Differential impacts were also associated with age: among those over 35 arrest rates generally were lower than average, and the experimental-control differences in arrests were generally considerably larger than average.

If Supported Work had reduced criminal activity solely because it increased employment, then we would expect that those subgroups with the largest increase in employment would be the subgroups with the largest decrease in arrests. As noted above, this was not the case for the site differences, nor was it the case for other subgroup differences in arrests.[22]

While there is evidence that economic factors were an important mechanism, they do not appear to be the sole mechanism by which Supported Work reduced criminal activity. In general, the subgroup differences in arrests do not coincide with the subgroup differences in employment. Further, the experience of participating in Supported Work may change the relationship between employment and arrests, as evidenced by the fact that experimentals who were employed were less likely to be arrested than were controls who were not employed— suggesting that experimentals' experiences in Supported Work may have strengthened their commitment to conventional behavior.

In examining the experimental-control differences in each 9-month period separately, a potential problem arises for gauging the effects of Supported Work on criminal activity. If an individual is arrested for a serious crime early in the study period, that person may not be free to commit crimes in the later periods. To abstract from this potential difficulty, the cumulative differences in the measures of criminal activity were calculated for the first 18 months, the first 27 months, and the full 36-month period following enrollment (see table 5.11).

The cumulative results provide further support for the finding that Supported Work produced a significant reduction in the experimentals' contacts with the criminal justice system. In all the time periods considered, significantly fewer experimentals were arrested, convicted, or incarcerated. Over the full 36-month period, for example, 53 percent of the controls were arrested at least once, as compared to 35 percent of the experimentals. Over the 3-year period, controls spent an average of nearly 14 weeks in jail or prison, while the experimentals spent an average of less than 7 weeks. This persistence of experimental effects in the cumulative results indicates that, among the experimentals as compared with controls, there was a higher incidence of the same individuals reporting arrests in more than one time period.

Cohort differences once again provide an important part of the explanation. Table 5.12 shows the differences among cohorts with different amounts of follow-up data. The strongest experimental effect is

TABLE 5.11

Cumulative Arrests, Convictions, and Incarcerations—Ex-addict Sample

	Months 1–18		Months 1–27		Months 1–36	
	Experimental-Control Differential	Control Group Mean	Experimental-Control Differential	Control Group Mean	Experimental-Control Differential	Control Group Mean
Percentage with any arrest	−8.2	33.5	−10.9**	43.3	−18.1**	53.1
Number of arrests	−0.08	0.48	−0.19**	0.70	−0.43**	1.01
Months to first arrest among those arrested	−0.9	8.9	1.3	11.5	4.5	12.8
Percentage with robbery arrests[a]	−5.2**	7.5	−6.9**	9.8	−13.2**	13.4
Number of robbery arrests[a]	−0.06**	0.08	−0.08**	0.11	−0.14**	0.15
Percentage with drug-related arrests[b]	−3.8**	7.9	−4.6**	10.5	−7.2	14.0
Percentage convicted	−4.3*	17.8	−5.7*	22.1	−13.6*	32.9
Percentage incarcerated	−4.4*	20.2	−8.1**	28.4	−14.1*	36.6
Number of weeks incarcerated	−1.5*	5.4	−4.0**	9.7	−7.1*	13.8

Note: See note to table 5.5. All data pertain to the full sample. The sample for each period includes individuals who have completed all relevant interviews. The 1–18 month sample includes all individuals who completed at least the baseline, 9-month, and 18-month interviews; the 1–27 month sample includes those who completed at least the baseline, 9-month, 18-month, and 27-month interviews; and the 1–36 month sample includes those who completed the baseline and all four follow-up interviews.

a Robbery arrests are defined as those for which robbery was the most serious charge. Only murder and felonious assault are considered more serious than robbery.

b Drug-related arrests are defined as those for which narcotics law violation is the most serious charge. More serious charges include murder, felonious assault, robbery, burglary, larceny, motor vehicle theft and other property crimes, and other crimes against persons.

* Statistically significant at the 10 percent level.

** Statistically significant at the 5 percent level.

TABLE 5.12

Cumulative Percentage with Any Arrests by Latest Follow-up Interview—Ex-addict Sample

	Months 1–18		Months 1–27		Months 1–36	
	Experimental-Control Differential	Control Group Mean	Experimental-Control Differential	Control Group Mean	Experimental-Control Differential	Control Group Mean
Total sample	−8.2	33.5	−10.9**	43.3	−18.1**	53.1
Latest follow-up interview						
18-month	3.1 #	31.4	n.a.	n.a.	n.a.	n.a.
27-month	−9.5**	32.2	−9.4	42.1	n.a.	n.a.
36-month	−17.3**	38.4	−14.2**	46.1	−18.1**	53.1

Note: See note to table 5.5. The total sample has been partitioned according to the most recent scheduled interview completed. This partitioning of the analysis sample does not yield subgroups that are exactly the same as would the formal definition of cohorts given in the text, in that it is based on interviews completed (as opposed to interviews assigned as determined by the date of enrollment in Supported Work).

Experimental-control differentials within this subgrouping for this time period differ significantly from one another.

** Statistically significant at the 5 percent level. None of the other experimental-control differentials is statistically significant at the 5 or 10 percent level.

167

for the 36-month cohort, among whom the "risk" of arrest is highest, as indicated by the control group's arrest rate.

Conclusion

A major impetus for the conduct of the National Supported Work Demonstration was a belief that providing former drug addicts with work experience in a supportive environment and under conditions of graduated stress—which approaches, over time, conditions in the regular work force—would facilitate their return to a drug free and independent lifestyle. The limited empirical evidence from previous demonstration efforts in support of this view have gained some support from the Supported Work findings. However, these demonstration findings also suggest that Supported Work is far from a panacea.

Most significantly, the demonstration findings indicate that a sizable number of former drug addicts will enroll in a program like Supported Work, and that many will increase their employment and earnings through program participation; on average, they will reduce their involvement in crime (especially robbery and drug-related offenses); and at least some portion of the target population will, under certain program and/or labor market conditions, experience long-run gains in employment and earnings. The net result of these program impacts has been valued in excess of program costs (see chapter 8), indicating that Supported Work programs for ex-addicts are likely to constitute an efficient use of public resources.

Despite this positive overall assessment of the program, it must also be recognized that the important objective of reducing drug use appears not to be met by the program. However, the findings also indicate that, among this group who applied to Supported Work, drug use showed no relationship to labor market behavior. Alternative strategies to mitigate problems of drug abuse must, therefore, be sought.

In all of this analysis, there was a consistent pattern of results suggesting that Supported Work is relatively more effective among those who would have done less well on their own—for example, those whose control group counterparts exhibited low levels of employment and high drug use and arrest rates. This generalization is consistent with the observation that program impacts were largest among the earliest enrollees (that is, the 36-month cohort).

In conclusion, under a variety of reasonable assumptions, Supported Work for ex-addicts appears to be an efficient use of public resources. Thus, public funding of programs of this type should be given serious consideration. However, results from this demonstration also point to the need to target the program carefully in an effort to maximize the return on the public investment and the need to continue the search for alternative means to mitigate the drug abuse problem itself.

Notes

1 See, for example, Jacks (1973), Lamb and Mackota (1973), and Danaceau (1973).
2 See Platt and Labate (1976), Stephens and Cottress (1972), and Duvall et al. (1963).
3 These results undoubtedly overstate program impacts for two reasons. First, experimentals who did not show up for the program and those experimentals who were ineligible according to the program criteria were excluded from the evaluation sample, and second, as a result of there being no mandatory graduation policy, 23 percent of the eligible ex-addicts were still working in Wildcat jobs at the time of the third-year follow-up report on the program.
4 In interpreting these results, it should be noted that although a random control group was chosen, the experimentals who dropped out early were "replaced" and not included in the experimental-control comparisons. Seventeen percent of the experimentals were replaced (see Bass and Woodward 1978).
5 According to interview data, 95 percent of the ex-addict sample met each of the employment criteria, and all the sample members were at least 18 years of age. Although only 88 percent reported having been in drug treatment within the last six months, 95 percent reported having used drugs other than marijuana or alcohol regularly.
6 Unfortunately, there is no information on lifetime drug use from the DARP sample to compare with that of the Supported Work sample. The DARP drug history pertains to the two months before treatment. Supported Work drug data are available on the month prior to assignment, but this period is after or during drug treatment.
7 Analysis samples for the 19- to 27- and 28- to 36-month outcome measures were defined in this manner in order to maximize the number of usable observations, given the smaller sample sizes for the later follow-up periods.
8 Another potentially serious problem for the analysis concerns the attrition of sample members scheduled to be given later interviews. There was a somewhat higher response rate to the 9-month interview for experimentals than controls (80 versus 75 percent). To the extent that respondents were not a randomly selected subset of the full ex-addict sample, the inclusion of only postbaseline experiences of respondents may have biased the results of the evaluation. However, in a detailed analysis of the effects of nonresponse on selected outcome measures in various time periods, no significant biases were found (Brown and Mozer 1981).

9 See various issues of the U.S. Department of Labor publication, *Employment and Earnings*. The data cited apply to the period between April 1975 and February 1979.

10 In cases where the outcome measure is truncated (for example, hours of work) or in cases where it is dichotomous (for example, employed or not), simple linear regression models may not yield estimates of program effects with desirable statistical properties. Since the standard regression techniques have been shown repeatedly to yield quite accurate estimates at substantially lower cost, we chose only to reestimate selected models using the theoretically more appropriate maximum likelihood techniques probit (for dichotomous outcomes) and tobit (for bounded outcome measures) to ensure that the basic conclusions are indeed insensitive to this analytic constraint. Results of these maximum likelihood estimates are available from R. Maynard, Mathematica Policy Research, Inc., on request.

11 The quality of the interview data was assessed by comparing it with data from other sources. A comparison of Social Security records of the ex-addicts with their self-reported earnings data shows that more earnings were reported in the interview than were reported to Social Security (Masters 1979). This may be due either to lack of complete coverage by the Social Security system or to errors in reporting. The Social Security records also showed a substantially smaller experimental-control difference than did the interview data, although the difference in the two estimates was not statistically significant. When data on arrests reported in the interviews were compared with official arrest records for a sample of respondents in California and Connecticut, there was some evidence of underreporting in the interviews but no significant experimental-control difference in the extent of underreporting was found (Schore et al. 1979). No official records data exist for drug use, but some comparisons of reported use for identical periods across interviews were made, which turned up no evidence that reported use during any 9-month period was differentially reported by experimentals and controls.

12 It should be noted that the variation across sites in the area unemployment rate is not reflected in the variation in employment patterns of controls. During the study period the unemployment rate in Jersey City was exceptionally high, ranging from 13 to 17 percent, while the unemployment rate in Chicago was approximately half that. In all periods, however, controls in Jersey City worked more hours than did controls in Chicago, perhaps in part because public sector jobs were much more prevalent in Jersey City.

13 Of those ex-addicts who received welfare, 63–76 percent received General Assistance and 24–35 percent received AFDC.

14 As noted, SUA was a temporary program enacted in 1974 to extend unemployment compensation coverage to individuals who met the standard eligibility criteria but who were employed by businesses not covered by the regular unemployment compensation program.

15 All of the analysis is based on the respondents' self-reported drug use. We did not attempt to verify their responses through chemical testing, since

(1) such procedures would pose administrative problems and (2) the less costly and more easily administered tests tend to be unreliable and detect only current use. Other studies that have validated interview responses concerning drug use with chemical tests have found a high rate of agreement (for example, see O'Donnell 1969).

16 Some of the decline was due to a difference in drug-use patterns of those enrolled at various points in time: use was substantially less prevalent among the earliest enrollees, who have proportionally greater representation in the 19- to 27- and 28- to 36-month results.

17 Unlike for heroin use, there was no sizable decline over time in reported use of cocaine.

18 In the early periods, the recidivism rates among controls over 35 were higher than among those who were younger. Several previous studies have found that those over 30 are less likely to return to drug use after treatment (see, for example, Duvall et al. 1963). As mentioned, the Supported Work sample had substantially fewer people over 35 than the otherwise comparable DARP sample used for comparison in tables 5.1 and 5.2. Those older ex-addicts in the Supported Work sample may have been selected by referral agencies as being at higher risk for recidivism to heroin use.

19 Regular use is defined as use for at least two months on a daily or almost daily basis.

20 Several studies have found that those who remain abstinent from heroin following treatment are more likely to use alcohol (for example, see O'Donnell 1969).

21 While clearly arrests are not perfectly correlated with criminal activity, they are less dependent on the abilities and workload of criminal justice personnel than are convictions and incarcerations. Further, due to delays in the adjudication of arrests, the disposition of some arrests would not have occurred within the period covered by the follow-up interviews.

22 The single exception occurs for those with at least one dependent, among whom the program resulted in a larger than average increase in employment and a larger than average reduction in arrests.

The Impacts of Supported Work on Ex-offenders

In this examination of the program experiences and postprogram outcomes of ex-offenders who participated in the Supported Work Demonstration, we focus mainly on their employment, earnings, and criminal activities. Our examination is complicated by several factors, among the more salient being that the demonstration was implemented in different types of communities, program implementation was not uniform, and sample members varied greatly in terms of personal attributes having potential links to crime and employment. To the extent the data permit, our analysis will attempt to identify which of these site, program, and participant factors in fact condition program response.

This chapter first outlines the theoretical bases for Supported Work as an intervention strategy for ex-offenders. Then, the second section describes the sample and data used in the analysis, and the third outlines the nature of the experimentals' program experiences. The succeeding three sections discuss program impacts on employment and earnings, criminal justice contacts, and drug use, respectively. The final section summarizes the results and discusses their implications for both policy and theory.

Theoretical Bases for the Hypothesized Effects of Supported Work

Supported Work Experience and Increased Employability

Achievement of the employment-enhancing objectives of any job program requires not only that program content will increase participants' employability, but that the training endeavor itself is operated in a manner that permits participants to remain in the program sufficiently long to acquire the required substance. As was discussed in chapter 2, there are three features of Supported Work which, according to a substantial body of psychological theory, are geared to achieving these requisites and which, operating together, distinguish the demonstration from other job programs. The first is its major substantive departure from many of its predecessors through its focus on improving participants' work habits rather than increasing their technical skills. The emphasis on work-habits development reflected program operators' belief that the major immediate job problems of program enrollees involved their lack of disposition toward and inadequate knowledge about getting along in the workplace. The limited attention given to skill development was based, in turn, on the assumption that at minimum this required more discipline than participants could maintain.

Second, in order to better assure that program substance did not become too demanding on enrollees and that participants' motivation did not lag, the demonstration incorporated features that are directly related to principles advocated within learning theory for shaping behavior. These features included use of peer-based work groups, employment of graduated stress,[1] and the awarding of bonuses for outstanding performance. The general utility of these and related techniques in educational and skill development programs has received substantial documentation (Tharp and Wetzel 1969).

Finally, the postprogram employment of Supported Work participants obviously rests not only on their increased capacity to work, but on recognition of this increase by employers. The relatively high visibility of the demonstration and its emphasis on developing good work habits should help confer on "successful" graduates a mark of competence or credential. Elaboration of this theme and its particular relevance for offenders can be found in the extensive literature on labeling theory (Becker 1963; Lemert 1964; Schur 1971; Erickson et al. 1973).

At this point some comment is warranted on the results of prior efforts to increase the employability of offenders. For the most part these results provide little basis for optimism. Vocational training, job placement, and subsidized employment programs have generally been found to have no sustained effects on participants' later employment or criminal activities.[2] Cook (1975) has suggested that the failures of training programs may be due either to participants' inability to locate jobs or to their not having requisite social skills and discipline for sustained employment. Both explanations may also account for the negative findings associated with job-placement programs and most subsidized employment programs. Among the isolated exceptions to this generally bleak picture was a New York-based program called Project Wildcat. Although the early positive results of Wildcat were found to decay over time, the overall results of the program were sufficiently favorable to generate interest in a more broadly based test of the Wildcat idea, thus leading to the National Supported Work Demonstration.

Employment and Criminal Behavior

As noted in chapter 2, the development of the Supported Work Demonstration was not guided explicitly by theory that related experience in employment programs to participants' subsequent legal and illegal activities. Nevertheless, the relevance of the Supported Work approach for apparently unemployable criminals can be derived from theoretical sources in psychology, sociology, and economics. Here we will briefly summarize the more material implications from these theories for the program. A more elaborate discussion can be found in Piliavin and Gartner (1979).

Economic Formulations The development of formal economic models of criminal behavior is of recent origin, and most of the theoretical and empirical work to date has concentrated on tests of the deterrent effects of punishment (Becker 1968; Blumstein et al. 1978; Block and Lind 1975; Sjoquist 1973). Early theoretical formulations suggested a relatively straightforward link between criminal and noncriminal behavior, that link being the individual's subjective evaluation of the costs and rewards associated with illegitimate activities against those associated with alternative legitimate activities. According to Becker (1968) and, later, Ehrlich (1973), increasing probable costs for participation in crime or, conversely, increasing probable rewards for participation in legitimate activities should decrease an individual's inclination to participate in illegal activity. Of course, the influence of marginal changes in the relative returns from legal and illegal activities varies across individuals. Thus, for example, among individuals for whom the psychic rewards associated with illegal activities are greater than those associated with legal work, there would be many who might choose crime over legal work unless there were substantial improvements in their legal opportunities.[3]

Second, for a given expected return, individuals who have a preference for risk may choose crime rather than work in seeking this return. Again, a sufficient increase in the returns from work can be expected to lead to work being preferred to crime among these individuals, but the size of the sufficient return will depend on the individual's risk preference and the returns from crime.

The preceding examples fail to exhaust the various complications that are suggested by economic theory in predicting how the criminal activity of known offenders will be altered by employment opportunities. However, they do suffice to indicate that the success of such programs may easily vary across individuals and that, given the relatively low wages provided by employment-enhancement programs, the success of these programs might be expected to be greatest among individuals who are risk averse and who receive relatively low monetary and psychic rewards from crime.

Sociological Formulations Sociological theories that deal with possible employment effects on individuals' criminal activities are more specific regarding the necessary conditions for employment effects to be observed. Among the more widely known of these theories are those based on the concepts of anomie, labeling, and self-concept.

Anomie theory,[4] as applied to the problem of crime in the United States (Merton 1938; Cloward and Ohlin 1960) argues that illegal behavior, particularly among the poor, results from the disparity between the culturally prescribed and almost universally held material success goals among American citizens and the means available for achieving those goals. For many of the poor, legitimate means to achieve these economic goals are not available. According to the theory, such individuals will be strongly motivated to use illegitimate means (for example, crime) to "get ahead" (Cloward and Ohlin 1960). As just stated, anomie theory appears to parallel economic theory in its explanation of crime. However, one apparent and potentially important difference between the theories concerns their assumptions regarding the motivational significance to individuals of future earnings. Economic theory assumes that, other things equal, the attractiveness of alternative activities is positively related to the financial return that can be obtained from these activities. Considerable emphasis is given to short term financial returns. Expected future returns are subject to a discount rate, first, because current wealth can be invested, at interest, and thus be worth more in the future, and, second, because of the inherent uncertainty of the future, including risks of mortality. In contrast, anomie theorists assume that future returns are exceedingly important to Americans. These analysts refer not only to the "supreme value" placed on success in the United States, but also to the emphasis placed on "social ascent" as a virtue. There is, in brief, within anomie theory the assumption that, even when discounted, the promise of

future increased income—particularly that which represents social advance—has a strong motivational impact. Although anomie theorists
do not explicitly indicate the functional form of the influence, one of
many versions consistent with the theory is that the attractiveness of
future income increases (decreases) as a power function of the relative
advance (reduction) associated with that income. The relevance of
anomie theory for programs like Supported Work is the implication
that for long-term offenders the desirability of conventional employment as an alternative to crime depends heavily on its future income
and career opportunities. The theory suggests that, to the extent that
a Supported Work employment program does not imply such opportunities, it will not only be ineffective, but will have difficulty in re-
taining participants.

The second perspective relevant to a discussion of employment and
crime combines a labeling perspective (Becker 1963) with self-concept
theories, such as those developed by Reckless and Dinitz (1967). Self-
concept theories of deviance view an individual's self-concept as a key
factor in explaining choices among alternative behaviors. In Becker's
formulation, among individuals who have been labeled "criminal" or
"delinquent" by agents of social control (for example, police, judges),
there is an increased likelihood that self-concepts will align with this
public image, contributing ultimately to a continuation of deviant or
criminal behavior (Becker 1963, 31–34). For ex-offenders the prison
experience provides an even more powerful reinforcement for criminal
identification, since it may encourage for each individual the development of "a self-protective posture which rejects those who reject
him" (Sullivan 1971, 5).

Although among the noncriminal population an individual may have
many roles and statuses, his or her occupation often takes on the role
of "master status" (Becker 1963), that is, a central status under which
other roles become subsumed. A change in this status can have substantial impact on the individual's self-concept (Cohn 1978; Dale 1976).
For offenders, the role of criminal often constitutes their occupation
and, therefore, their "master status," increasing the probability of their
returning to crime (Glaser 1964, 490). However, if the offender can
obtain a job, associations with supervisors and co-workers may replace
old relationships, the use of criminal attributions by others may decrease, and the offender's self-concept may also change to accommo-
date the new status. Thus, the linkage between labeling and self-concept
theories can work in two directions, to encourage either deviant or
nondeviant behavior. For ex-offenders, the major intervening variable
in this process is likely to be their employment status.

In sum, the relevance of legal employment opportunities for crime reduction is suggested in more or less complex form by both sociological and economic theories. The central empirical questions concern whether the substance and rewards of Supported Work as implemented in the demonstration represent an attractive enough employment opportunity to affect substantially the participants' criminal activity and long-run legal employment.

Sample and Data

Over a period of 28 months, from March 1975 to July 1977, 2,276 ex-offenders were enrolled in the Supported Work sample at the seven different sites. Selected characteristics of the ex-offender samples analyzed in each time period are presented in table 6.1. Although these attributes vary somewhat across sites, the participants are generally males in their mid-twenties, black, unmarried, and without dependents. Almost 75 percent of the sample did not complete high school; their recent earnings are quite low; and almost two-thirds of them have either never had a regular job or not held one in more than a year. As could be expected, contacts with the criminal justice system are numerous; participants on average have had nine previous arrests and three previous convictions, and they have served an average of four years in jails or prisons. More than one-third of the sample claim regular drug use.

Most ex-offenders learned about the Supported Work program through some type of referral agency; over 80 percent of the sample were referred by criminal justice agencies, manpower programs, and social service agencies. It is possible that variations in source of referral could account for some differences in behavioral outcome, although aggregate site data fail to show strong differences in ex-offenders' baseline characteristics, despite site variation in referral source.

Data for the evaluation are drawn primarily from the interview responses of ex-offender sample members at program entry and at subsequent 9-month intervals, up to 36 months after enrollment. As was discussed in chapter 2, all enrollees were scheduled to be interviewed both 9 and 18 months after enrollment. However, only slightly more than two-thirds of the original sample (1,600 sample members) were scheduled to receive the first three interviews, covering 27 months after enrollment (the 27-month cohort), and only 505 ex-offenders, or about one-fifth of the sample, were assigned to have the full complement of four postbaseline interviews (the 36-month cohort).[5]

TABLE 6.1
Percentage Distribution of Ex-offenders' Characteristics at Enrollment

	Sample		
	1–18 Month Outcomes[a]	19–27 Month Outcomes[b]	28–36 Month Outcomes[c]
Experimental group	49	49	52
Pressured by agency to apply to the program	14	16	22
Complies with formal eligibility criteria	83	82	75
Site			
Chicago	15	15	16
Hartford	12	14	6
Jersey City	10	14	22
Newark	19	13	5
Oakland	24	19	11
Philadelphia	9	14	25
San Francisco	12	13	16
Male	94	95	97
Race/ethnicity			
Black	84	83	86
Hispanic	9	9	8
White	7	8	6
Years of age			
< 21	14	17	16
21–25	42	44	44
26–35	37	32	32
> 36	7	7	8
Years of education			
< 9	12	14	12
9–11	61	61	62
$\geq$ 12	27	25	26
Married	12	14	18
Any dependents	19	19	20
Number of people in household	3.8	3.8	3.9
Welfare or food stamp receipt in month prior to enrollment	32	33	38
Weeks worked, last year	5.6	5.8	8.5
Length of longest job ever held			
No job	12	12	11
$\leq$ 12 months	51	53	55
> 12 months	37	35	34
Use of any drug, other than marijuana	65	62	68
Regular heroin use	32	32	37
In drug treatment last 6 months	12	11	10
Number of arrests, ever	8.9	8.5	8.3
Weeks in jail last two years			
$\leq$ 26 weeks	38	38	44
> 26 weeks	62	62	56

(Continued on following page)

TABLE 6.1 (Continued)
Percentage Distribution of Ex-offenders' Characteristics at Enrollment

	Sample		
	1–18 Month Outcomes[a]	19–27 Month Outcomes[b]	28–36 Month Outcomes[c]
Time since incarcerated			
< 3 months	34	34	44
≥ 3 months	66	66	56
On parole or probation	74	78	77
Number of cases	1458	1003	287

Note: The above percentage distributions were obtained from actual analysis samples, as opposed to potential samples based on interview completions. Variable values may vary from one analysis to another because of slightly different sample sizes for various outcome measures.

a This sample includes all individuals who completed an enrollment, a 9-month, and an 18-month interview.

b This sample includes all individuals who completed an enrollment and a 27-month interview.

c This sample includes all individuals who completed an enrollment and a 36-month interview.

Program Experiences of Experimentals

Program experiences of experimentals varied across sites and over time for several reasons. Flexibility in programming to take account of unique local opportunities and specific competences of program staff was inevitable. In the early stages of the program, several sites experimented with different types of work programs, but over the entire four years most ex-offenders' program time was spent in labor-intensive and relatively low-skilled jobs in the construction and service industries, including building rehabilitation and maintenance, painting, carpentry, and automotive repair.

On average, ex-offenders stayed in the program for much shorter periods than allowed by program guidelines. Approximately 35 percent had terminated by the end of three months, and the average length of stay for all program participants was 5.9 months. Only 8.4 percent exhausted their allowable time in the program. Program departures resulted from several factors, but only 18.5 percent of them were due to opportunities for other jobs or schooling. Almost half of the terminees stated that their program departures were due to their own poor performance. In brief, although the Supported Work experience was intended to develop participants' capacities to operate in the labor market, relatively few participants used the program as a direct stepping stone to employment in the labor market.

Impact of Supported Work on the Employment
and Earnings of Ex-offenders

Our examination of the effects of Supported Work on the employment and earnings of ex-offenders over the last three years following program entry is based on monthly figures on hours worked, percentage employed, earnings, and hourly wage rates. We expected experimentals to work substantially more than controls in the early postrecruitment months because of Supported Work employment, but also to work more and at better wages than controls after program termination.

With respect to employment and earnings, the general results suggest short-term but no long-term benefits from program participation. During the first three months, experimentals worked almost 145 hours per month, compared to an average of 37 hours for controls (table 6.2), and they maintained an employment level of almost 95 percent. In months 4–6 the hours-worked differential favoring experimentals decreased, in part because of an increase in hours worked by controls but, more important, as a result of a 41-hour-per-month average reduction in work among experimentals. This reduction was largely the result of a decrease among those employed by Supported Work. The pattern of results established during months 1–6 continued through month 18, at which time the employment of both experimentals and controls leveled off to about 60 hours per month. Significantly, experimentals who left the demonstration worked, on average, about the same hours per month and had the same employment rate as controls.[6]

Data on average earnings trends of experimentals and controls also fail to suggest significant long-term effects due to Supported Work participation. Experimentals' earnings averaged more than three times those of controls during the first three months of observation, then declined over the next 18 months to virtually the same level as controls (table 6.2). A slight increase in relative earnings was observed among experimentals in the last nine months of follow-up. This reflected an increase in the percentage of those employed and, in the final three months, a 15 percent higher wage rate among experimentals.

We turn now to an examination of possible variation in employment effects for different subgroups of our sample. One potentially significant distinction in this regard is time of sample entry. This possibility is suggested by the observed tendency for experimentals to work more than controls during the last nine months of the 3 year follow-up. Since the data for this comparison pertain only to the early Supported Work enrollees (that is, the 36-month cohort), the possibility is raised that the employment experiences of this group may have been different

TABLE 6.2

Hours Worked, Percentage Employed, and Average Earnings per Month, by Time Periods—Ex-offender Sample

Month	Sample Size	Average Hours Worked per Month		Percentage Employed during Period		Average Earnings per Month		Percentage of Experimentals Enrolled in Supported Work
		Experimental-Control Differential	Control Group Mean	Experimental-Control Differential	Control Group Mean	Experimental-Control Differential	Control Group Mean	
1–3	1497	107.7**	37.1	55.7**	38.0	$308.17**	$138.74	90.7
4–6	1497	62.8**	51.0	35.9**	40.4	200.59**	185.15	63.2
7–9	1497	43.3**	47.5	23.2**	39.2	150.20**	173.74	43.3
10–12	1497	20.9**	52.7	12.1**	39.3	55.19**	221.37	24.7
13–15	1497	4.3	59.4	4.1	44.1	28.73	246.15	11.8
16–18	1497	0.6	59.5	1.4	44.6	19.01	250.10	3.8
19–21	995	1.2	57.9	0.8	41.0	12.81	252.92	2.0
22–24	995	−0.2	60.8	1.5	42.4	8.18	265.63	1.2
25–27	995	0.0	59.8	−0.9	43.6	3.08	263.72	0.6
28–30	302	12.2	63.9	4.2	44.8	67.66	285.48	0.0
31–33	302	7.6	69.9	4.0	47.8	55.78	319.99	0.0
34–36	302	7.2	64.6	5.7	45.2	65.93	295.35	0.0

Source: Interviews conducted between April 1975 and March 1979 with experimentals and controls at seven Supported Work sites.

Notes: The data are regression-adjusted estimates that control for differences of age, sex, race, education, prior work experience, household composition, site, and length of site operation. Averages are calculated for all members of the sample, including those with no employment in the covered period. Mean values of control variables are included in Appendix table A.1.

** Statistically significant at the 5 percent level. None of the other experimental-control differentials is statistically significant at the 5 or 10 percent level.

181

TABLE 6.3
Average Hours Employed per Month, by Cohort—Ex-offender Sample

	All Ex-offenders	Cohort		
		18-Month	27-Month	36-Month
Months 1–9				
Experimental-control differential	71.1**	70.3**	73.9**	67.2**
Control group mean	46.0	50.6	39.8	48.6
Months 10–18				
Experimental-control differential	8.5**	7.6	9.5*	11.1
Control group mean	57.8	63.7	53.5	51.7
Months 19–27				
Experimental-control differential	−0.2	n.a.	−1.4	3.0
Control group mean	60.0	n.a.	59.8	60.7
Months 28–36				
Experimental-control differential	8.3	n.a.	n.a.	8.3
Control group mean	66.8	n.a.	n.a.	66.8

Source: See table 6.2.
Notes: See table 6.2.
n.a.   Not applicable.
 * Statistically significant at the 10 percent level.
** Statistically significant at the 5 percent level.

from those of other cohorts throughout the follow-up period. The time trends by cohort are found in table 6.3. These trends indicate that experimental-control differentials in employment varied little across cohorts through month 27. The conditions leading to the substantial, though not statistically significant, differentials in the last observation period are thus not explained by a simple cohort effect.

Aside from time of sample entry, a large number of program and participant attributes may have influenced offenders' response to Supported Work. Organizational, criminological, and human capital theories in fact suggest the possible relevance to program impact of phenomena whose range is beyond the limits of the data-gathering capacity of the Supported Work evaluation. This analysis of possible mediators of program impact is thus based on a group of program and sample member attributes whose selection was determined by theoretical and policy relevance as well as ease of collection. The findings are presented in table 6.4.

With some exceptions, these attributes were not found to have large or persistently significant mediating influence on the employment im-

TABLE 6.4
Hours Employed per Month, by Demographic and Background Characteristics—Ex-offender Sample

	Months 1–9		Months 10–18		Months 19–27		Months 18–36	
	Experimental-Control Differential	Control Group Mean	Experimental-Control Differential	Control Group Mean	Experimental-Control Differential	Control Group Mean	Experimental-Control Differential	Control Group Mean
All ex-offenders[a]	71.1**	46.0	8.5**	57.8	-0.2	60.0	8.2	66.8
Years of age								
< 21	70.7**	43.6	3.2	58.4	-4.7	53.0	33.2	62.5
21–25	73.2**	46.1	9.2*	56.2	0.8	60.2	-2.4	79.0
26–35[b]	69.7**	44.2	6.5	60.2	0.3	61.7	10.7	50.5
> 35[b]	63.5**	59.7	28.0*	51.7	1.2	65.4	[c]	[c]
Sex								
Male	71.1**	46.1	9.0**	58.2	0.7	60.6	8.8	66.3
Female	67.2**	43.6	0.2	47.0	-19.1	45.7	[c]	[c]
Race/ethnicity								
White, non-Hispanic	63.1**	64.3	9.1	84.6	1.7	78.0	[c]	[c]
Black, non-Hispanic	73.5**	43.5	8.9**	54.1	0.6	56.1	14.5	59.5
Hispanic	53.0**	54.0	3.9	68.2	-9.9	75.9	[c]	[c]
Years of education								
≤ 8	65.7**	39.7	5.0	46.8	9.1	39.6	-23.4	61.8
9–11	70.7**	46.3	7.1	58.6	-6.8	62.8	10.6	66.2
≥ 12[b]	73.7**	48.1	13.3*	60.2	10.0	64.2	14.0	69.1
Welfare and food stamp receipt in month prior to enrollment								
None	65.9**	47.9	#	61.4	#	63.5	-6.8	73.2
Some[b]	81.8**	41.7	25.6**	49.2	13.6	52.1	29.3	55.6
Dependents								
None[b]	72.4**	43.4	8.5**	56.7	1.6	59.4	4.1	69.9
One or more	64.8**	57.1	8.7	61.3	-8.4	61.6	19.2	52.6

(Continued on following pages)

TABLE 6.4 (Continued)

Hours Employed per Month, by Demographic and Background Characteristics—Ex-offender Sample

	Months 1–9		Months 10–18		Months 19–27		Months 18–36	
	Experimental-Control Differential	Control Group Mean	Experimental-Control Differential	Control Group Mean	Experimental-Control Differential	Control Group Mean	Experimental-Control Differential	Control Group Mean
Months in longest job								
0	74.7**	37.1	5.8	46.7	−17.4	51.0	20.7	26.3
1–12	65.9**	45.9	12.0**	49.2	−1.2	58.4	−4.0	79.5
> 12[b]	76.8**	49.0	4.5	73.0	7.2	65.0	20.8	58.6
Reason for applying to Supported Work[d]								
Pressure from drug treatment, law enforcement, or other agency	61.3**	51.8	5.8	57.3	−5.3	73.4	−2.1	84.1
Other[b]	72.7**	45.0	8.9**	57.7	1.2	57.3	12.1	61.2
Weeks worked in year prior to enrollment[c]								
0	68.7	44.0	8.5**	54.6	−2.1	55.2	15.4	54.9
5	70.7**	45.8	8.5**	57.3	−0.6	59.1	10.5	61.7
10[b]	72.7**	47.6	8.5**	59.9	0.9	63.0	5.7	68.5
Weeks in job training in year prior to enrollment								
< 8[b]	73.5**	43.2	9.9**	54.9	2.8	56.7	9.2	70.9
≥ 8	59.8**	57.9	2.4	68.9	−15.0	74.0	−2.7	43.9
Prior drug use								
Used heroin regularly[b]	72.3**	45.3	12.8*	52.2	1.1	45.4	18.5	59.4
Did not use heroin regularly	70.3**	46.3	6.5	60.0	−1.0	66.7	0.5	70.5

184

Drug treatment in last 6 months								
In treatment	65.5**	48.9	-2.1	62.6	-20.0	82.6	3.2	118.4
Not in treatment[b]	71.7**	45.6	10.0**	56.9	2.1	56.9	7.8	58.8
Prior arrests[e]								
4[b]	71.5**	48.5	11.3**	58.8	2.3	61.1	19.4	68.3
9	72.1**	44.1	3.9	55.2	-5.5	52.9	-12.0	62.8
14	71.1**	42.4	3.0	54.9	-6.2	54.3	-14.0	62.7
Weeks incarcerated in year prior to enrollment								
< 27[b]	72.6**	41.0	5.1	54.8	2.3	52.7	14.0	48.7
≥ 27	69.9**	49.0	-10.6**	59.2	-1.9	64.2	1.6	80.9
Months since incarcerated								
< 3[b]	68.4**	46.3	6.7	56.3	1.7	55.9	6.6	72.8
≥ 3	76.0**	44.4	12.1	60.0	-4.2	67.2	7.9	58.4

Source: See table 6.2.

Note: The data are regression-adjusted estimates that control for differences of age, sex, race, education, prior work experience, household composition, site and length of site operation. Averages are calculated for all sample members, including those with no employment in the period.

a These results were estimated from an equation that controlled only the standard control variables and an experimental status variable. Thus, the subgroup results may not always weight up to these overall sample values. Mean values of control variables are included in Appendix table A.1.

b Experimental-control differentials for this subgroup are positive at each observation period.

c These statistics have been omitted since they are based on samples with fewer than 20 observations.

d These subgroup results were estimated in a separate regression which did not simultaneously control for potential differences among other characteristics.

e These estimates of subgroup effects are based on a linear (or piecewise linear) specification of the sample characteristics evaluated at the specific points.

Experimental-control differentials for this time period differ significantly from one another.

* Statistically significant at the 10 percent level, two-tailed test.

** Statistically significant at the 5 percent level, two-tailed test.

pacts of Supported Work. One exception involves sample members' welfare status at the time of their program application. Among ex-offenders who were welfare or food stamp recipients in the month prior to program application, experimentals consistently reported more postenrollment hours worked than did controls. Among nonrecipients, experimentals reported more hours worked than controls only during months 1–9 when virtually all experimentals were active in Supported Work programs. Two other attributes of ex-offenders that seem to mediate program impacts are drug use and age. Experimentals who were regular users of heroin at baseline appear to have responded somewhat more positively to Supported Work than did irregular or nonusers, and older experimentals appear to have responded much more positively than did those who were younger.

Despite these variations, the overall findings concerning employment and earnings outcomes provide little support for the hypothesis that Supported Work participation will improve the employment experiences of ex-offenders. In general, experimental group members, after participating in the program, were no more likely than the controls to report being employed, working more hours, or having higher earnings.

Impact of Supported Work
on the Criminal Justice Contacts of Ex-offenders

Having established that Supported Work does not have long-term employment effects for ex-offenders, it may seem that a crime analysis is superfluous. However, the analysis is warranted for three reasons. First, because employment among experimentals was much greater than among controls during the early months after program enrollment, if crime incidence data favored experimentals during this period, this would be evidence for the employment provision/crime reduction linkage. Second, if experimentals' early employment experiences provided favorable views of the advantages of legitimate jobs, long-term crime reductions could result. Third, certain participants (and controls) were employed at various periods throughout the 36-month observation time, providing the opportunity to investigate the concurrent link between employment and crime.

Our primary criterion to index the criminal activities of sample members is a dummy variable indicating whether an individual was arrested at least once. In addition, for comparison purposes we employ in table 6.5 a variety of other criteria including those pertaining to arrests for robbery and drug offenses.[7] We do not use admitted criminal

TABLE 6.5

Cumulative Arrests and Incarcerations—Ex-offender Sample

	Months 1–18		Months 1–27		Months 1–36	
	Experimental-Control Differential	Control Group Mean	Experimental-Control Differential	Control Group Mean	Experimental-Control Differential	Control Group Mean
Percentage with any arrest	1.0	46.2	0.4	53.3	−8.0	64.8
Number of arrests	0.00	0.81	0.03	1.10	−0.50	1.66
Percentage with robbery arrests[a]	−0.8	8.1	1.5	10.1	−8.2	21.0
Number of robbery arrests	−0.00	0.08	0.03	0.12	−0.11	0.26
Percentage with drug-related arrests[a]	−0.4	5.9	−0.3	7.5	−2.3	7.7
Percentage incarcerated[a]	−1.0	39.1	−1.6	47.0	−13.9	57.5
Number of weeks incarcerated	0.28	10.71	0.97	18.97	−1.03	29.86

Source: Interviews conducted between April 1975 and March 1979 with experimentals and controls at seven Supported Work sites. Cumulative data for months 1–18 are for the sample of 1,497 individuals who completed baseline 9- and 18-month interviews. Cumulative data for months 1–27 are for the sample of 829 individuals who completed baseline 9-, 18-, and 27-month interviews. Cumulative data for months 1–36 are for the sample of 219 individuals who completed baseline 9-, 18-, 27-, and 36-month interviews. These data refer to a sample of individuals different from that in table 6.2.

Notes: The data presented are regression-adjusted estimates that control for differences in age, sex, race, education, prior work experience, household composition, site, and length of site operation. The data in all cases refer to the entire sample. Average numbers thus include zero values. None of the experimental-control differentials is statistically significant at the 10 percent level. Mean values of control variables are included in Appendix table A.1.

a Percentages refer to the entire sample, not just those with any arrest.

187

activities for two reasons. First, admitted crime has recently been found to be a less adequate measure of criminal activity than reported arrests.[8] Second, there are insurmountable problems in deriving equivalent counting procedures for different forms of crime.[9] Our primary reliance on the criterion of arrest rather than other official dispositions (for example, convictions, incarcerations) is based on the assumption that arrests more validly index individuals' criminal activities. Correction and incarceration data depend not only on probable guilt, but also on the abilities, work pressures, and compromises that characterize and are exprienced by criminal justice personnel. While it is true that arrests also involve the actions of criminal justice personnel, namely police, the decisions of these workers, as noted above, have been found to correspond with criminal incidence patterns observed through victimization studies.[10] The percentage with any arrests is used as the preferred criterion on the assumption that sample members' first follow-up arrest is a stronger indication of failure than those that may follow. Finally, the arrest data we employ are those reported by sample members. Since the validity of these self-reports cannot be taken for granted, a study was undertaken to determine the degree of bias in the arrest data provided by 774 ex-offender and ex-addict sample members in San Francisco, Oakland, and Hartford (Schore et al. 1979). These data, when compared to official records maintained by criminal justice agencies in California and Connecticut were found to underreport recorded arrests by about 50 percent. However, no experimental-control differentials in underreporting were observed, thus lending support to the assumed validity of the comparisons on which the analysis is based.[11]

The postbaseline criminal justice experiences of ex-offender sample members are summarized in table 6.5. The table entries pertain to cumulative results over the periods designated in the columns of the table.[12] Entries are included for only those individuals for whom valid data are available for each follow-up interview, up to and including the interview referred to by the end point found in each column heading (for example, 18, 27, or 36 months). The striking characteristic of the data in table 6.5 is the absence of statistical significance for results based on any of the criteria we employ. The substantial, though not statistically reliable, reduction in reported arrest probabilities for the total 36-month follow-up period suggests a delayed effect of Supported Work on crime. However, a more likely possibility is that it reflects the response to Supported Work of early program enrollees. We will return to this issue shortly.

In table 6.6 we examine the possiblity that individual attributes of sample members at the time of enrollment may mediate the effect of

TABLE 6.6

Cumulative Percentage with Any Arrests, by Demographic and Background Characteristics—Ex-offender Sample

	Months 1–18		Months 1–27[a]		Months 1–36[b]	
	Experimental-Control Differential	Control Group Mean	Experimental-Control Differential	Control Group Mean	Experimental-Control Differential	Control Group Mean
All ex-offenders[c]	1.0	46.2	0.4	53.3	−8.0	64.8
Years of age	#		#			
< 21	−10.4	55.7	−8.9	68.8	−10.5	54.3
21–35	8.5**	43.2	11.7**	48.6	−0.3	59.6
26–35	−0.9	46.1	−8.0	55.0	−5.7	72.2
> 35	−7.6	38.5	−14.7	39.4	d	d
Sex	#					
Male	0.3	47.1	−1.4	54.4	−4.1	64.4
Female	8.5	32.0	24.7	34.3	d	d
Race/ethnicity	#					
White, non-Hispanic	−3.4	53.2	−2.4	68.1	d	d
Black, non-Hispanic	3.3	45.1	1.3	51.7	−7.4	61.8
Hispanic	−18.6	50.3	−10.8	55.5	d	d
Years of education						
≤ 8	0.8	52.5	9.3	52.8	12.4	74.6
9–11	−0.3	47.9	−0.6	53.4	−10.6	67.3
≥12	3.3	39.6	−2.8	55.3	5.9	48.8
Welfare and food stamp receipt in month prior to enrollment					#	
None	3.8	43.9	2.5	51.9	18.4	45.4
Some	−5.9	51.3	−4.9	56.0	−31.7**	84.4
Dependents						
None	1.9	45.8	1.5	52.7	−2.3	62.6
One or more	−3.8	47.8	−5.7	55.8	−6.4	61.0
Months in longest job						
0	6.4	54.8	−10.0	67.7	17.6	48.3
1–12	−3.0	47.0	−1.4	53.7	−17.2	69.2
> 12	4.2	42.2	5.7	47.6	10.6	56.5

(Continued on following page)

189

Category							
Weeks worked in year prior to enrollment							
0	#	-1.9	48.6	-3.2	56.1	-10.6	71.0
5		0.6	46.3	-0.3	53.6	-6.0	65.5
10		3.1	44.1	2.6	51.0	-1.4	60.1
Prior drug use							
Used heroin regularly		-1.0	47.6	-2.7	56.3	-13.3	65.2
Did not use heroin regularly		1.6	45.6	1.4	51.9	2.2	60.6
Drug treatment in last 6 months							
In treatment		1.8	47.2	8.9	51.0	# 45.0	38.7
Not in treatment		0.7	46.1	-1.0	53.6	-9.7	65.4
Prior arrests							
4		0.5	42.1	0.9	49.2	-9.6	63.0
9		0.1	53.8	4.3	64.4	5.0	61.6
14		0.7	54.7	1.8	64.5	7.4	61.2
Weeks incarcerated in year prior to enrollment							
< 27		2.5	47.6	0.1	54.0	9.0	60.7
≥ 27		-0.2	45.4	0.0	52.8	-12.6	63.4
Months since incarcerated							
< 3		3.5	46.6	2.6	56.3	-2.3	69.3
≥ 3		-4.8	45.3	-4.7	47.7	-4.6	52.9
Parole or probation at enrollment							
Not on parole or probation	#	-8.0	51.9	-8.2	60.8	-1.3	58.3
On parole or probation		3.9	14.2	2.4	31.2	-3.7	63.3

Source: See table 6.2.

Notes: See table 6.4.

a The sample for this period includes people who completed 9-, 18-, and 27-month interviews.

b The sample for this period includes people who completed 9-, 18-, 27-, and 36-month interviews.

c These results were estimated from an equation that controlled only the standard control variables and an experimental-status variable. Thus the subgroups may not always weight up to these overall sample values.

d These statistics have been omitted since they are based on samples of less than 20 members.

Experimental-control differentials within this subgrouping for this time period differ significantly from one another.

** Statistically significant at the 5 percent level. None of the other experimental-control differentials is statistically significant at the 5 or 10 percent level.

Supported Work in terms of arrests. None of the subgroup contrasts is statistically significant across all time periods. However, persistent and substantial interactive effects appear to be associated with sample members' age, race, welfare recipiency, and prior drug use. Recognizing that generalizations from statistically nonsignificant trends should be approached with caution, we note that several findings are consistent with trends previously observed among the employment results. There were more arrest-free members among those experimentals who were older, who had been regular users of heroin prior to sample entry, and who received welfare at the time of sample entry than among sample controls. Though the differences are often not statistically significant, their persistence and agreement with the employment findings suggest that these attributes may have been important mediators of the impact of Supported Work. This is particularly true with respect to heroin use where the mediating influence is consistent with the overall results for the ex-addict sample.[13]

Chapter 5 discusses the response of ex-addicts to Supported Work and in the last section of this chapter, we address the response of older ex-offenders.[14] Here we wish to examine briefly the influence of prior welfare receipt because its relevance to employment and crime reduction is not immediately apparent. A simple and obvious explanation for this effect is that welfare recipients are heads of families with children and such individuals are more likely than others to take advantage of opportunities provided by employment programs.[15] Additional analyses provided results that tended to be consistent with this argument. That is, having dependent children was associated in the sample with pre-enrollment receipt of welfare and lowered probability of postenrollment arrest. Further, experimental-control differentials favoring experimentals were larger among sample members who had dependent children. Despite these findings, the dependent children variable failed to account fully for the welfare receipt effect. Its residual influence remains unexplained with these data.

In table 6.7, we present estimates of program impacts on criminal justice contact by 9-month time periods. The data permit a comparison of those experiences with the employment results of table 6.2. There is clearly no evidence that the high employment of experimentals relative to controls during months 1–9 led to a relative reduction in criminal justice contacts in the same period. Furthermore, during months 10–18 and extending through months 19–27 when experimental-control employment differentials, though smaller, still favored the experimentals, these individuals were more likely than controls to be arrested. Only in months 28–36 did experimentals work more and

TABLE 6.7

Arrests, by Type of Offense, and Incarcerations—Ex-offender Sample

	Months 1–9		Months 10–18		Months 19–27		Months 28–36	
	Experimental-Control Differential	Control Group Mean	Experimental-Control Differential	Control Group Mean	Experimental-Control Differential	Control Group Mean	Experimental-Control Differential	Control Group Mean
Percentage with any arrest	−2.2	34.2	4.1*	23.3	1.8	20.7	−8.7*	22.8
Number of arrests	−0.03	0.48	0.04	0.32	0.09	0.26	0.11*	0.27
Percentage with robbery arrests[a]	0.0	5.0	−0.4	3.4	1.0	3.3	−3.3	5.0
Number of robbery arrests	0.0	−0.05	−0.01	0.04	0.01	0.03	−0.03	0.05
Percentage with drug-related arrests	0.4	3.0	−0.5	3.1	0.6	2.3	−0.2	1.2
Percentage incarcerated	−1.9	28.7	2.8	27.2	0.2	32.9	−5.1	34.2
Number of weeks incarcerated	−0.39	4.53	0.66	6.19	0.30	8.10	−0.46	8.41

Source: See table 6.5.

Notes: The data presented are regression-adjusted estimates that control for differences of age, sex, race, education, prior work experience, household composition, site, and length of site operation. The data in all cases apply to the entire sample.

a Percentages refer to the entire sample, not just those with any arrest.

* Statistically significant at the 10 percent level. None of the experimental-control differentials is statistically significant at the 5 percent level.

remain more arrest-free than controls. These final 9-month results, together with the cumulative arrest results for months 1–36, suggest that the 36-month ex-offender cohort had a different pattern of criminal justice experiences than did other cohorts.

Analysis of cumulative percentage-arrested data by cohort partially supports this hypothesis. Although the differences are not statistically significant, experimentals in the 36-month cohort reported more arrest-free members than did controls for each cumulative follow-up period.[16] Furthermore, only these experimentals reported more arrest-free members than did controls for any follow-up period. Efforts to explain this "cohort effect" by program and participant attributes have been only partially successful. While one program and several individual characteristics were associated with "success" and early program entry, they accounted for only a small fraction of the positive outcomes associated with the 36-month cohort.

We have noted previously that the data in tables 6.2 and 6.7 fail to demonstrate a clear link between sample members' employment and crime rates. On the assumption that different findings might emerge from a more detailed analysis, the arrest percentages among experimentals and controls for each 9-month follow-up period were compared, holding constant sample members' cohort and work status during the period.[17] The findings, presented in table 6.8, indicate that with one exception employed sample members with a given experimental status were less likely to report an arrest during a given 9-month period than were non-employed sample members with the same experimental status. This suggests some link between employment and crime.

On the other hand, experimentals within the 18- and 27-month cohorts having a given employment status were in fact marginally more likely to report having been arrested than were controls with the same employment status. At best, this suggests that Supported Work for these cohort members failed to reduce the incidence of arrest beyond that of employment in general.[18] An exception to this pattern is found among employed members of the 36-month cohort. Experimentals within this group report somewhat lower arrest percentages than do controls. While this helps specify which members of the 36-month cohort are influenced by Supported Work, it fails to suggest an explanation for this effect.

Impact of Supported Work on Drug Use of Ex-offenders

In this final section on program impacts, we will briefly examine the impact of Supported Work on drug-use patterns of ex-offenders. Table 6.9 presents data on the percentage of experimentals and the experi-

TABLE 6.8

Percentage Arrested, by Employment Status, by Cohort—Ex-offender Sample

	18-Month Cohort		27-Month Cohort			36-Month Cohort			
	Months 1–9	Months 10–18	Months 1–9	Months 10–18	Months 19–27	Months 1–9	Months 10–18	Months 19–27	Months 28–36
Employed									
Experimental-control differential	5.2	7.4*	0.2	1.8	0.4	−9.1	−3.0	−2.0	−9.9
Experimental group mean	31.6	26.8	31.1	21.5	19.6	32.2	17.4	16.2	13.0
Control group mean	26.4	19.4	30.9	19.6	19.2	41.3	20.4	18.2	22.9
Not employed									
Experimental-control differential	[a]	7.2	[a]	3.9	2.5	[a]	5.0	9.6	4.7
Experimental group mean	[a]	33.3	[a]	34.9	28.0	[a]	33.3	31.6	22.9
Control group mean	40.6	36.2	35.3	31.0	25.6	48.8	28.3	22.0	18.2
Total									
Experimental-control differential	0.7	7.1**	−0.8	1.3	1.5	−13.0*	−1.6	1.7	−4.6
Experimental group mean	33.0	29.2	31.0	26.3	23.5	31.8	23.2	21.7	16.4
Control group mean	32.3	22.1	32.4	25.0	22.0	44.8	24.8	20.0	21.0

Source: See table 6.5.

Note: These data are not regression-adjusted.

a These statistics are omitted because there are fewer than 20 observations.

* Statistically significant at the 10 percent level.

** Statistically significant at the 5 percent level.

TABLE 6.9
Reported Drug Use—Ex-offender Sample

	Months 1–9		Months 10–18		Months 19–27		Months 28–36	
	Experimental-Control Differential	Control Group Mean	Experimental-Control Differential	Control Group Mean	Experimental-Control Differential	Control Group Mean	Experimental-Control Differential	Control Group Mean
Any drug (other than marijuana or alcohol)								
Percentage reporting any use[a]	-4.2*	34.2	-3.0	29.0	-1.3	24.1	-11.2**	28.2
Heroin[a]								
Percentage reporting any use	0.2	14.1	-2.3	10.8	0.0	7.5	-3.8	8.4
Opiates, other than heroin[a]								
Percentage reporting any use	-0.5	10.5	-2.4*	9.1	-3.1*	9.3	-2.4	5.9
Cocaine[a]								
Percentage reporting any use	-3.1	21.0	-1.4	18.3	1.3	13.7	-6.6	19.4
Amphetamines, barbiturates, or psychedelics[a]								
Percentage reporting any use	-1.8	9.7	1.4	5.5	-0.5	6.0	-0.8	3.9
Marijuana								
Percentage reporting any use	-0.8	65.5	-2.2	66.0	-5.0	58.1	-6.8	53.7
Percentage reporting daily use	n.a.	n.a.	-4.9**	26.0	-5.7**	25.3	-7.5	25.3
Alcohol								
Percentage reporting daily use	-2.2	14.4	-0.2	15.5	2.9	16.1	1.6	20.5
Drug Use Index[b]	-1.8	28.6	-3.9	26.9	0.1	17.2	-7.0*	19.2

Source: See table 6.5.

Notes: The data presented are regression-adjusted estimates that control for differences of age, sex, race, education, prior work experience, household composition, site, and length of site operation. The data in all cases apply to the entire sample. Mean values of control variables are included in Appendix table A.1.

a Daily use of heroin, other opiates, and amphetamines, barbiturates, or psychedelics was reported by less than 5 percent of the ex-offender sample and so are not included in this table.

b This index weights the use of each drug by its associations with arrests. See Dickinson (1980) for a description of the methodology used to develop the index and for the actual weights used.

n.a. Not available.

* Statistically significant at the 10 percent level.   ** Statistically significant at the 5 percent level.

mental-control differential in the percentage reporting use of a number of different drugs in each 9-month period.

In postenrollment interviews, ex-offenders were asked whether there was any use and, if so, the frequency and duration of use of several categories of drugs. This discussion focuses on two summary measures of ex-offenders' drug use: the use of any drug other than marijuana or alcohol, and a drug-use index, which weights the use of each drug by its social cost, as reflected by its association with criminal activity in the Supported Work sample (see Dickinson 1980 for details). The data in table 6.9 show that for the summary drug measure there was a consistent program effect in all four 9-month observation periods. In months 1–9, 34 percent of the controls reported use of some drug versus 30 percent of the experimentals—a significant differential. In months 10–18 and 19–27 these rates narrow to insignificant differentials, but in months 28–36 the differential widens to 28 percent versus 17 percent—again, a significant differential. The index of drug use shows only a slight experimental effect in the first two 9-month periods; however, as with the "use of any drug" measure there is evidence of a significant program impact in the last 9-month period.

While these overall results indicate that Supported Work participation led to reduced drug use among ex-offenders during the first and last 9-month periods, subsequent analyses suggest that these results were due to effects among specific sample subgroups. Most important, these positive effects seem to have been linked to ex-offenders who enrolled in Supported Work during its early months. For the 36-month cohort, consistently fewer experimentals than controls reported any drug use in all time periods, a difference which is statistically significant in the 28–36-month period. In contrast, for other cohorts, after months 1–9, approximately the same proportion of experimentals and controls report the use of drugs. Further analysis failed to identify the basis for this cohort effect, site factors being at best only a partial explanation.

Two individual attributes of ex-offenders, age and prior welfare receipt, appeared again as persistent mediators of the impact of Supported Work. Among those over age 25, fewer experimentals than controls reported drug use; this was not true for those who were younger. And, among recipients of welfare prior to sample enrollment, a consistently smaller proportion of experimentals than of controls reported any drug use; this was not true for nonrecipients. These results are particularly intriguing. They are consistent with those obtained in our analysis of both crime and employment, and they may reflect the influence of family headship and ex-offender "burnout" on program impact.[19]

Summary and Conclusions

Two fundamental hypotheses were associated with the Supported Work Demonstration: first, that participants would work more and increase their earnings relative to a group of controls, and second, that because of their increased employment and earnings, participants would also be less involved than controls in crime and drug use. The results provide little basis for optimism. Despite early and strong income and employment effects, experimentals' hours of work and earnings decreased over time while controls' employment increased, so that after 12 months of follow-up there was almost no difference between the two groups. The reduction in experimental-control work and earnings differentials was hastened by early termination from Supported Work by experimentals. On average, ex-offender Supported Work participants in 12-month programs spent little more than six months in them; the average participant in 18-month programs dropped out even sooner. The causes of this high rate of early termination are not known. Among other reasons, they could include the low wages of Supported Work, problems encountered by participants in the discipline associated with work, participants' belief that Supported Work site operators would fail to help them locate permanent jobs, or participants' preferences for crime over legitimate work.

In general, experimentals also failed to remain more arrest-free than did controls. If our hypotheses linking employment and crime were valid, this finding would appear to follow from the previously noted employment results. However, even in the period when the vast majority of experimentals were employed (months 1–9), the probability of their remaining arrest-free was not significantly higher than that of controls. Thus, it appears that the causal nexus between employment, earnings, and crime commission is more complex than is implied by the assertion that providing ex-offenders with legitimate employment will lead them to reduce their criminal activities.

Finally, drug-use results indicate an overall experimental effect, with participants in Supported Work showing a reduction in drug usage in the 1–9 and 28–36-month periods. These positive results are qualified somewhat by further analyses which showed them to be limited to early program enrollees.

Within the context of these generally negative findings, there were selected positive results. Essentially, we observed experimental-control differentials favoring experimentals among those sample members who were older, who received welfare or food stamps prior to sample entry, and who were early entrants in the Supported Work sample. It is possible that these selected positive outcomes are due to chance factors. We will, however, suggest some plausible hypotheses for these outcomes and will attempt to incorporate them into our explanations of the overall results.

We first address the results which indicate positive impacts of Supported Work among older ex-offenders, individuals who received public assistance prior to sample entry, and early sample entrants. Then we turn to the less favorable results concerning the overall impact of Supported Work.

Older Ex-offenders and Burnout

One of the trends noted in the crime and drug results was that, among older ex-offenders (especially those over 35 years of age), experimentals were consistently more likely than controls to remain arrest free and to abstain from drug use throughout the three years during which follow-up observations were carried out. Furthermore, among controls, those who were older were more likely to report being arrest free and abstainers from drug use. Our interpretation of these findings is that they suggest that Supported Work provides a particularly important opportunity for a conventional lifestyle to a key group of ex-offenders, namely, those who, with the passage of time, are withdrawing from a long-term pattern of crime.

The apparent withdrawal of older ex-offenders from crime commission has been a long-noted, but not a well-studied, phenomenon. It has been assumed to reflect discouragement and a retreat from a stressful and costly existence rather than retirement from a profitable career. The fact that the older controls in this study were less likely than those who were younger to incur any arrests is consistent with this "burnout" effect. In this context, the fact that among older ex-offenders, experimentals were even more likely to be arrest free than were controls can be interpreted as an indication of individuals, already in the process of change, taking advantage of the opportunities provided by Supported Work to accelerate this change.

While the burnout hypothesis is in accord with our crime and drug-use results, it is not entirely consistent with our employment findings. Presumably, if older ex-offenders wish to give up criminal activity, we should find that, other things equal, they should work more in legal occupations than would the younger ex-offenders. Data not presented here were not consistent with this prediction; that is, older controls failed to uniformly report more employment than younger controls across four 9-month follow-up periods. A possible reason for this is that older ex-offenders are less attractive to potential employers and, thus, have more difficulty locating jobs than do younger ex-offenders.

Two types of data are consistent with this interpretation. First, during the period when experimentals had an opportunity for employment in Supported Work (that is, during the first 18 months of follow-up), those who were over age 35 worked more hours on average than did those who were younger.[20] Second, among sample members who reported being unemployed during a given time period, those who were older reported more job-seeking contacts with potential employers.

Sample Cohort, Welfare Receipt, and Family Responsibility

While the age burnout effect could be rather directly inferred from our basic results, it was not at all clear initially what explained the differential impacts related to cohort and welfare/food stamp receipt. Thus, additional descriptive analysis was conducted to provide some clarification. First, the two phenomena are related in that individuals who received welfare or food stamps in the month preceding sample enrollment were more likely than others to be early entrants to the Supported Work sample.[21] Second, prebaseline receipt of welfare is correlated with having related dependents—spouses and children—and experimental-control differentials favoring experimentals are more likely to be found among individuals having children. Put in these terms, the cohort and welfare receipt results have a plausible interpretation, namely, that Supported Work had positive effects on ex-offenders with families. This in turn suggests that experimentals with families may have been more motivated to give up crime and utilize Supported Work as a vehicle to achieve this end than were those who were unattached.[22] However, even when we controlled for these factors, we still found a persistent cohort effect, which could be the result of unmeasured characteristics that distinguish the initial pool of ex-offenders in our sample from later sample members.

Overall Results: Implications for Theory and Policy

Despite positive results among selected sample members, it is clear that our research findings indicate no positive employment or crime effects of the program for ex-offenders in general. While these findings may seem to imply the invalidity of the various theoretical models we have cited to justify the merits of Supported Work, we believe the failure of the program in relation to ex-offenders can be understood in terms of these theories and can be attributed to problems of implementing employment programs for this type of clientele.

Perhaps the first problem with Supported Work that comes to mind concerns its inability to retain the majority of experimentals for as long as six months. We have suggested earlier that this need not imply that ex-offenders are uninterested in long-term employment, but rather that the net rewards associated with Supported Work participation, and with the jobs to which this participation would eventually lead, were not sufficient to attract long-term commitments from participants. In effect, Supported Work paid weekly wages that brought no more proceeds than could be obtained from about two street muggings a week. Furthermore, for many, the jobs provided by the program were uninteresting, failed to provide learning opportunities, and promised little in the way of improved future employment opportunities. Under these conditions, the absence of long-term commitment to the program on the part of many ex-offenders seems a plausible consequence.

Often when reference is made to the rewards of criminal behavior, these are specified in terms of earnings net of the potential costs of punishment. However, as noted by many students of crime, illegal activities have other payoffs including those associated with excitement, the respect and fear offered by others, and the companionship offered by those who might otherwise be one's exploiters. The rewards from legal jobs that are necessary to compensate for these payoffs may well be substantial and, for some classes of criminals, they may be unattainable. Having said all this, we recognize that while, for some, the rewards of crime may cut across many dimensions, for others they may be limited to but a few. For example, among drug addicts whose concerns are dominated by the need to obtain funds to get a "fix," the crucial payoffs to crime may be essentially monetary. Thus, when these individuals are given access to alternative sources of income, they may be likely to reduce criminal activities. This is a possible explanation for the favorable effects of Supported Work on the criminal activities of the ex-addict sample and the regular users of heroin in this sample. Furthermore, tastes change. When individuals marry and have families, they acquire new responsibilities and perhaps develop different aspirations. And, as they grow older, they often become more sedentary and less daring. For such individuals, the perceived costs associated with crime can increase and the relative attractiveness of legitimate work may increase. This, we have suggested, may account for the success of Supported Work with older ex-offenders and those with families.

However, among the remaining ex-offenders—in fact, the bulk of ex-offenders—the payoffs of Supported Work may not have been enough to wean them away from engaging in crime. But, then, what is enough? We do not have sufficient knowledge to answer this question. However, we suggest that the answer may not be merely an increase of wages above those supplied by Supported Work. Perhaps what is required as well is the opportunity for secure and better employment—in effect, an opportunity to participate in what is called the primary labor market.

Appendix

TABLE 6.10
Income from Various Sources—Ex-offender Sample

	Months 1–9		Months 10–18		Months 19–27		Months 28–36	
	Experimental-Control Differential	Control Group Mean	Experimental-Control Differential	Control Group Mean	Experimental-Control Differential	Control Group Mean	Experimental-Control Differential	Control Group Mean
A. Percentage Receiving Income								
Earnings	37.2**	58.7	6.8**	59.2	3.2	53.3	1.2	57.8
Unemployment compensation	−3.2**	4.8	−3.3*	7.4	0.7	6.3	−0.7	7.2
Welfare[a]	−12.6**	28.1	−7.6**	29.0	0.4	24.0	−3.1	29.2
Food stamps	−4.4	36.0	−2.9	33.4	−1.0	30.0	−5.9	34.2
Other unearned income[b]	−1.9	5.6	−3.1**	5.6	−1.4	4.0	0.3	3.1
B. Average Monthly Income Received (dollars)[d]								
All sources[c]	177.18**	239.00	7.47	341.01	18.17	321.01	78.11	366.56
Earnings	200.36**	178.38	25.16	260.83	14.99	254.18	62.60	304.20
Unemployment compensation	−4.64**	5.57	5.31	11.20	3.06	9.58	5.02	10.63
Welfare[a]	−17.41**	33.54	−16.10**	44.80	2.39	37.38	−1.44	41.02
Food stamp bonus value[e]	−2.68*	15.00	−3.42**	16.10	−0.40	12.50	0.90	12.53
Other unearned income[b]	1.36	6.60	3.55	8.11	−3.38	9.12	−0.21	4.91

Source: See table 6.2.

Notes: All data are regression-adjusted. Earnings data reported vary somewhat from those reported in the section on employment and earnings because of a slight difference in the samples used: only individuals who have valid data for all income sources listed in this table were included in this analysis.

a Welfare includes AFDC, General Assistance, Supplemental Security Income, and other unspecified cash income.

b Other unearned income includes Social Security, pensions, alimony, and child support.

c All sources include earned and unearned income, as itemized in the table, and do not include the value of Medicaid or other in-kind benefits.

d Averages are calculated including individuals with zero benefits.

e Represents the difference between the purchase price of the food stamps and their face value.

* Statistically significant at the 10 percent level. ** Statistically significant at the 5 percent level.

Notes

1 This term refers to the job requisites, increasing over time, which participants had to meet in order to perform acceptably.

2 It should be noted that financial assistance programs have had some success in lowering the arrest rates of participants (California Council on Criminal Justice 1973; Feeley 1974; Mallar and Thornton 1978). Since these programs make no demands in the form of attendance and work, participants may find it easier to remain in the program, obtain benefits, and, by virtue of these, reduce crime. However, a recent study has suggested that the crime-reduction success of financial assistance programs may be much more limited than initially assumed (Rossi et al. 1979).

3 There may, of course, be some individuals for whom there is no monetary equivalence of the psychic rewards from crime. These individuals will obviously be intractable to any incentives from legal employment.

4 Anomie theory was initially formulated by Durkheim (1951) to explain suicide rates across societies. Although Merton (1938) and, later, Cloward and Ohlin (1960) use the theory to analyze patterns of crime in the United States, these analysts examine as well the implications of the theory for crime rates in other countries.

5 A potentially serious problem of interview response bias involves the attrition of sample members scheduled to receive later interviews. Such attrition ranged from 27 percent on the 9-month interview to 40 percent on the 36-month interview. However, detailed analyses of the effects of nonresponse on the distribution of responses found no significant biasing effects (Brown and Schore 1981). Since analyses based on interview data may be subject to considerable uncertainty, efforts also were made to verify the interview data for some of the outcome measures through comparisons with official records. Comparisons of self reported earnings and arrest data with official Social Security and criminal justice records, respectively, provide encouraging evidence for the reliability and validity of the interview data (Masters 1979; Schore et al. 1979).

6 We also examined impacts on income from welfare and unemployment compensation and on the income from food stamps and found a short-term reduction (corresponding to the increase in earnings) but no significant long-term impacts (see table 6.10 in the appendix to this chapter).

7 Our use of the drug offense criterion is based on the admitted high involvement in drug use among members of the Supported Work sample. The robbery arrest criterion is employed because this offense perhaps represents the most serious form of property crime.

8 See Hindelang (1978). Hindelang's study uses victimization survey data as the basis for determining the validity of other measures of criminal activity.

9 Some types of crime are generally measured in terms of incidence (for example, robberies, burglaries, assaults); others are usually measured in terms of duration (for example, drug use, pimping, numbers running).

10 We do employ incarceration data among the entries in table 6.5. The trends in these data are similar to those suggested by reported arrests.

11 While it could have been advantageous to utilize official records for this analysis, access to criminal justice files was not possible in several jurisdictions.

12 While separate time-period analysis (that is 1–9-, 10–18-, 19–27-, and 28–36-month periods) is used for the employment and earnings results, we do not regard this approach as appropriate for criminal activity findings where the concern is with crime deterrence. An appropriate index for this criterion is the probability of remaining arrest-free during the entire course of the postprogram entry observation periods. Thus, our crime analysis is based on findings over the postentry months 1–18, 1–27, and 1–36. Because these cumulative results are not comparable with the results in the employment and earnings section, and because employment results would be meaningless if presented cumulatively, criminal behavior results are also reported by separate time periods to allow comparisons with the employment analysis.

13 See chapter 5. Two other results in table 6.6 should be noted. These suggest that young experimentals (those under 21 years of age) and experimentals who received no drug treatment in a six-month period prior to their Supported Work participation also were more likely to remain arrest-free than their corresponding controls. We do not take up these interactions in detail for the following reasons. The apparent mediating effect of being a young ex-offender is inconsistent with employment results and with results for the school dropout sample, among whom known offenders failed to improve relative to controls. The effect is also diluted somewhat by the high percentage of controls who reported at least one arrest in months 1–18 and 1–27. The latter suggests that experimentals' reduced arrests in these periods may reflect regression to the mean. The drug treatment results are also inconsistent with employment findings as well as with the overall results for the addict target group.

14 In chapter 5 the impact of Supported Work on the criminal activities of addicts is explained partly in terms of risk-preference changes resulting from increased legal income. Thus, accordingly, the need for drugs is viewed as at least part of the basis for drug addicts' criminal activities.

15 We did include a control variable intended to capture family headship. However, this measure was based on the presence of dependent adults as well as children. Thus, the measure may not have been adequate to capture the effect of interest here.

16 Over 18 months, the differential was 5.2 percent; over 27 months it had increased to 10.3 percent, and over 36 months it had decreased slightly to 8.0 percent.

17 The data for this analysis are not regression-adjusted.

18 It is, of course, possible that the causal relationship runs in a direction opposite to that assumed here.

19 An analysis of ex-offenders' income from such sources as welfare, food stamp bonuses, and unemployment compensation which paralleled the employment, crime, and drug-use analyses yielded similar results. Most attributes of sample members failed to have a sustained mediating influence on the income effects of Supported Work, with one exception. Among those who received welfare and food stamps in the month prior to enrollment, experimentals reported less postenrollment welfare than did controls. Details of this analysis can be found in chapter 6 of the initial ex-offender report (Piliavin and Gartner, 1981).

20 During months 1–9, experimentals over age 35 worked 123 hours per month on average; other experimentals worked about 116 hours. During months 10–18, those over 35 worked 80 hours per month; those who were younger worked 64 hours.

21 The percentages of ex-offenders who received welfare in the month preceding sample enrollment were 29.1, 31.5, and 39.1 for the 18-, 27-and 36-month cohorts, respectively.

22 Conceivably this effect might have been the consequence of welfare agencies' attempts to reduce costs associated with the maintenance of cases having male heads of household.

7 *Rebecca A. Maynard*

The Impacts of Supported Work on Youth

Public concern with the persistently high unemployment rates among youth has heightened in recent years, and a variety of program and research strategies aimed at identifying ways of reducing youth unemployment have been implemented. One youth group of particular concern is school dropouts, among whom the unemployment rate during the mid-seventies averaged more than 30 percent.

Many factors are commonly cited as contributing to the persistence of these high unemployment rates. They include the low skill levels and lack of job experience among youth, minimum wage legislation, discrimination on the part of employers, and increases in the labor force participation among youth and among women, who often compete with youth for entry-level, lower skill jobs.[1] The continued search for solutions to these employment problems is prompted by evidence suggesting that youth unemployment may lead to juvenile delinquency and subsequent criminal lifestyles and that it may contribute to employment problems during adulthood. In addition, there has been some speculation about a possible association between youth unemployment and drug use.[2]

One possible approach to the problem is Supported Work, which is designed to mitigate a number of factors thought to be related to the unusually high unemployment rate among young school dropouts and, thereby, to improve their long-run employment prospects, reduce their involvement in crime, and limit their drug abuse. The program provides an employment opportunity with gradually increased standards of performance aimed at permitting youth to develop good work habits

205

and to build up a work history. This employment opportunity is followed by job-readiness training and placement assistance designed to facilitate the transition to regular employment.

This chapter examines Supported Work as both a short- and a long-term solution to youths' employment problems. The first section describes the sample of youths who enrolled in the national Supported Work Demonstration's evaluation sample and the nature of their employment, criminal, and drug-abuse problems. The second section is a discussion of the Supported Work employment experience of sample youths. Findings related to the impacts of this experience are presented in the third and fourth sections. The third section presents findings based on data collected as part of the main demonstration and the fourth presents results based on data from a follow-up survey conducted three to five years after program application. Conclusions and policy recommendations are discussed in the final section.

The Supported Work Youth Sample

The sample for this analysis is a subset of the 1,252 youths who applied to five Supported Work programs serving the youth target group, located in Atlanta, Hartford, Jersey City, New York City, and Philadelphia. Five hundred seventy of these youth applicants were randomly assigned to the experimental group and were offered a Supported Work job; 682 were assigned to a control group.[3] The 861 experimental and control group youths who completed an enrollment interview plus a 9- and 18-month follow-up interview constitute the sample for the in-program and early postprogram analysis. Five hundred thirteen sample members who completed an enrollment and a 27-month interview provide the data for analysis of impacts over the 19–27 month period following enrollment, and 153 persons who completed an enrollment plus a 36-month interview constitute the sample for analysis of longer-term impacts. Finally, 746 youths completed a special follow-up survey of sample youths, which was conducted between July 1979 and January 1980 and which, thus, yielded data for up to five years after enrollment for the earliest sample enrollees.

Table 7.1 presents the sample sizes for analyses of impacts during each of the time periods, broken down by site and by the length of the follow-up period. Most of the reduction in usable sample data between the early and later follow-up periods is due to a sample design feature whereby only 57 percent of the sample were scheduled to receive the 27-month interview (those enrolled prior to January 1977) and 16 percent were scheduled to receive the 36-month interview (those

TABLE 7.1

Maximum Sample Sizes for the Analysis, by Reference Period of the Outcome Measure—Youth Sample

	Months 1–18		Months 19–27		Months 28–36		Months 15–67 (resurvey period)[a]	
	Number	Percent[b]	Number	Percent[b]	Number	Percent[b]	Number	Percent[b]
Site								
Atlanta	83	9.6	15	2.9	0	0.0	63	8.4
Hartford	384	44.6	232	45.2	20	13.1	367	49.2
Jersey City	192	22.3	170	33.1	85	55.6	172	23.1
New York	135	15.7	18	3.5	0	0.0	83	11.1
Philadelphia	67	7.8	78	15.2	43	31.4	61	8.2
Latest follow-up interview[c]								
18 months	442	31.2	n.a.	n.a.	n.a.	n.a.	n.a.	n.a.
27 months	298	34.6	368	71.7	n.a.	n.a.	n.a.	n.a.
36 months	121	14.1	145	28.3	153	100.0	n.a.	n.a.
Total	861	100.0	513	100.0	153	100.0	746	60.0

Note: Actual sample sizes varied somewhat by outcome measure, but generally included 90 to 99 percent of the cases in these totals. Most of the evaluation results are based on multivariate analysis that controls for pre-enrollment characteristics of experimental and control group members. Therefore, all analysis samples include only individuals who completed the enrollment (baseline) interview. Analysis of outcomes during the first 18 months after enrollment has been based only on individuals who, in addition to the enrollment interview, completed both the 9- and 18-month follow-up interview (referred to hereafter as the 18-month analysis sample). Analysis of outcomes during months 19–27 and months 28–36 are based on individuals who completed the 27- and 36-month interviews, respectively.

a For some sample members the resurvey data cover as little of the follow-up period as 15–38 months after enrollment, while for others they cover as long as 44–67 months after enrollment.

b These are percentages of the total youth sample in the appropriate reference period.

c These figures refer to the latest *completed* interview conducted as part of the main evaluation effort. A few sample members were scheduled to receive subsequent interviews but failed to complete them. Also, recall that some individuals in the samples for analysis of 19–27- and 28–36-month outcomes did not complete a previously scheduled follow-up interview. Thus row totals vary.

n.a. Not applicable.

who enrolled prior to April 1976).[4] All sample youths were scheduled to receive the special follow-up survey. However, of particular consequence for the analysis are the facts that date of enrollment is directly related to the length of the follow-up period and that not all sites are represented in the samples available for analysis of the 19–27- and the 28–36-month results.

A program objective was to serve school dropouts with demonstrated employment problems. To ensure appropriate targeting of the program, enrollment in the demonstration's youth sample was limited to those who had the following characteristics: were 17 to 20 years old; had worked no more than 40 hours during the last four weeks; had worked no more than three months in one regular job (a job of 20 or more hours per week) during the last six months; had not previously participated in either Supported Work or in the evaluation control group; and did not have a high school or high school equivalency diploma. In addition, at least 50 percent of the youths enrolled must have had a record of delinquency.

Of those enrolled, about 60 percent were younger than age 19 and more than one-third had completed fewer than 10 years of school. About one-fifth had never held a regular job and, of those who had held such a job, a third had not had one during the past year (see table 7.2). Other noteworthy characteristics include the racial composition of the sample, their reasons for having left school, their family status, and their criminal histories. More than 90 percent of the sample were from minority ethnic groups, among whom the national unemployment rate is about double the national average for youth. Two-thirds of these young people had left school more than a year before they enrolled in the sample, and 29 percent reported having been expelled from school or leaving because of problems with the police. Few were married and supporting dependents; in fact, nearly two thirds were living with their parents. Over half of these youths had been arrested and more than a third had been convicted of a criminal offense.

These characteristics describe not only a group of youths who are expected to have serious labor market disadvantages in relationship to the general population of young people, but also a more disadvantaged group than the typical enrollee in CETA Youth Employment Demonstration Projects Act (YEDPA) programs. For example, a much higher proportion of the Supported Work sample youth belong to black and other minority ethnic groups (92 percent versus 54 percent for YEDPA and 15 percent nationally); virtually none of the Supported Work sample as compared with 12 percent of CETA enrollees and 62 percent of all youth in this age range had completed high school; the

TABLE 7.2
Demographic and Background Characteristics—Youth Sample

	Supported Work Youth Sample (At Enrollment)	YEDPA Enrollees[a] (FY1978)	U.S. Youth Population[b] (1976)
Age			
Percentage younger than 18	29	56	50[c]
Percentage 18 or older	71	44	50[c]
Average age	18	n.a.	n.a.
Sex			
Percentage male	88	52	49
Percentage female	12	48	55
Race/ethnicity			
Percentage Hispanic	19	15	n.a.
Percentage black, non-Hispanic	73	39	13
Percentage white, non-Hispanic	8	46	85
Years of school completed			
Percentage completed fewer than 10	39	} 88[d]	n.a.
Percentage completed 10 or 11	61		n.a.
Percentage completed 12 or more	0	12	62
Average years	10	n.a.	12 (median)
Reason left school			
Percentage expelled or left due to trouble with the police	29	} 21	} 28
Percentage dropped out for other reasons	71		
Job training—percentage with any employment	18	n.a.	7
Percentage unemployed	87	49	29
Percentage who never held a regular job	23	n.a.	n.a.
Percentage whose most recent job was			
Last 6 months	34	} 58	} 70
7 to 12 months ago	18		
More than 12 months ago	25	n.a.	n.a.
Average earnings last year	$821	n.a.	n.a.
Family status			
Percentage married	4	6	3
Percentage living with parents	65	84	n.a.
Percentage supporting dependents	10	n.a.	n.a.
Welfare status			
Percentage who received welfare (AFDC, GA, other) last month	13	} 42	8
Percentage who received food stamps last month	23		5
Average dollar value of welfare, food stamps received last month	$39	n.a.	n.a.

(Continued on following page)

TABLE 7.2 (Continued)
Demographic and Background Characteristics—Youth Sample

	Supported Work Youth Sample (At Enrollment)	YEDPA Enrollees[a] (FY1978)	U.S. Youth Population[b] (1976)
Criminal history			
Percentage arrested	57	5	n.a.
Percentage convicted	38	n.a.	n.a.
Drug use			
Percentage having used heroin	8	n.a.	4[e]
Percentage having used marijuana	61	n.a.	60[e]
Number of cases	1244	239,494	16,822,724[c]

a Youth Employment Demonstration Projects Act enrollees. These data are taken from CETA MIS Rep. No. 54, May 20, 1979.
b Except as noted, U.S. population data were obtained from various Census publications. Age categories and variable definitions were matched as closely as possible with those from the Supported Work sample.
c Includes 16–19-year-olds.
d Sixty-seven percent were enrolled in school at the time they entered the YEDPA program.
e These data are based on interviews with a national survey of 1,500 18–25-year-olds, conducted in 1977 as part of a nationwide survey of persons age 12 and older living in households in the contiguous United States (Abelson et al. 1977). They are similar to those based on in-person interviews with a sample of 290 20-year-olds conducted in 1974 and 1975 as part of a study of nonmedical use of psychoactive drugs by young men in the U.S. (see O'Donnell et al. 1976).
n.a. Not available.

Supported Work sample consists of school dropouts, while roughly two-thirds of the YEDPA participants were still enrolled in school; and less than 5 percent of YEDPA enrollees are reported to have a criminal record, as compared with 57 percent of the Supported Work sample.[5]

Employment Experiences of Youth Controls

The nature of the employment problems faced by the Supported Work youth sample can best be described through an examination of the employment experiences of the control group. As shown in table 7.3, youths who applied to Supported Work and were assigned to the control group tended to have relatively high labor force participation rates, low employment rates, and high unemployment rates during the early months after enrolling in the demonstration, in comparison with both the total youth population and young school dropouts. The relative status of sample youths did improve over time, however, as a

TABLE 7.3
Employment Status of Youth

	All Youths 18–19 Years Old, 1977[a]	Youths Who Dropped Out of School in 1977[b]	Supported Work Control Group, by Month after Enrollment				
			At Enrollment	Ninth	Eighteenth	Twenty-Seventh	Thirty-Sixth
Percentage in the labor force	66.3	67.5	100.0	71.4	76.4	75.8	46.8
Percentage employed	55.6	46.4	12.6	30.4	40.3	42.9	46.8
Unemployment rate	16.2	31.2	87.4	57.6	47.2	43.4	0.0
Total population/sample	8,466,291	466,000	682	523	487	266	76
Average age	18.5	n.a.	18.3	19.1	19.8	20.6	21.3
Reference period	1977	October 1977	September 1977[c]	June 1977[c]	March 1978[c]	August 1978[c]	October 1978[c]

a These data are from U.S. Department of Labor (1979, Tables A-3, A-4, A-5).
b These data are from U.S. Department of Labor (1979, Table B-8). They refer to employment status in October 1977.
c This is the average reference month for sample members.
n.a. Not available.

result of three factors: (1) a natural phenomenon by which some youths (all of whom were unemployed at the start of the period) gained employment through a process termed "regression to the mean"; (2) these youths were getting older; and (3) there was a general improvement in labor market conditions during the period of the study, but particularly in 1978.

These relatively low employment rates mask the fact that, as is typical of youth in general, a high proportion of the youth control group (83 percent) was, in fact, successful in locating some job during the main follow-up period of between 18 and 36 months, but they experienced a high rate of job turnover: on average, sample youths held two jobs during the period, with the first job lasting just over five months. Average wage rates on these jobs were 10–50 percent above the prevailing minimum. Thus, while some sample youths certainly exhibited chronic problems finding employment, instability of employment seemed to be the main problem for a sizable portion of them.[6]

Criminal Experience of Youth Controls

As noted previously, a substantial proportion of the youth sample had criminal records prior to enrollment in the demonstration, and the control group's postenrollment behavior demonstrates that, in the absence of some form of intervention, many of these youths will continue to engage in crime. For example, roughly 15 percent of the sample were arrested during each 9-month period, and among those with at least 27 months of follow-up data, more than a third were arrested and roughly a quarter were convicted and incarcerated at some time subsequent to their enrollment in the demonstration.[7] Both economic and sociological theories have linked this prevalence of a criminal lifestyle among young school dropouts to their employment problems.

Drug Use among Youth Controls

The youth sample did not have an unusually high prevalence of drug use prior to enrolling in the demonstration. The one exception is that 8 percent of the Supported Work sample, compared to 4 percent of the nation's youth, reported ever having used heroin (table 7.2). And with the exception of marijuana, which over half of the control group reported using, drug use during the postenrollment period was not unusually prevalent.[8] Both this lack of a serious drug-abuse problem among sample youths and the ambivalence of sociological and economic theories concerning the relationship between employment and drug use lead to an agnostic view as to whether Supported Work might then be expected to affect significantly the drug use among this sample.

The Supported Work Employment Experience

It is useful to preface the discussion of Supported Work's impact for youths (the following section) with a description of the Supported Work employment experience of those youths in the experimental group. Thus, in this section, we briefly examine the length of time that youths stayed in Supported Work and the nature of their departure from the program.

The design of the Supported Work program was predicated on the belief that an opportunity to work in a supportive environment with gradually increased standards of performance would permit the development of good work habits while simultaneously building up employment credentials necessary for youths' successful competition in the labor force. From the outset it was recognized that there would be considerable variance in both the time it would take a target group member to acquire work skills commensurate with general market standards and the amount of work experience that employers would view as convincing evidence of job readiness. Furthermore, there was a strong commitment to the concept that Supported Work should be a transitional program. Thus, in an effort to balance the objectives of permitting sufficient program experience to be of benefit and of assuring that the programs not take on the character of sheltered workshops, participation in Supported Work was limited to 12 months in Atlanta and Jersey City and to 18 months in Hartford, New York, and Philadelphia.[9]

On average, the youths stayed in Supported work for considerably shorter periods of time than allowed under program guidelines: 29 percent stayed three months or less, and only 25 percent stayed as long as 12 months. The average length of participation was 6.7 months which, while short in comparison with program guidelines, compares favorably with the length of time youths stay in CETA programs, including the Job Corps, and with the length of time control youths stayed in jobs they found during the follow-up period. This average length of program participation did vary considerably across site (although not in a manner that is consistent with the variation in programs' policies on maximum duration of participation) and among those samples of youths followed for varying lengths of time: those in Philadelphia stayed less than four months; those in Jersey City and New York stayed an average of just over eight months; and the earliest enrollees (for whom the follow-up period is longest) stayed nearly one month longer than average.[10] Nineteen percent of the youths left to take another job or to enroll in an education or job-training program; 44 percent left for reasons related to their job performance (such as low productivity, failure to show up on time, conflicts with the boss or crew); and 36 percent reported other reasons for having left (such as low pay, health, and child-care or transportation problems).[11]

In the next section, we assess whether, overall, this target population benefited from its Supported Work experience, regardless of its duration and the variety of reasons for leaving the program. We also allude to an assessment of whether, by identifying means to extend the average period of program participation, Supported Work's effectiveness in mitigating employment problems of youth could be improved.[12]

Program Impacts: Results from the Main Evaluation

Most of the evaluation of Supported Work impacts has been conducted using multiple regression analysis.[13] This analytic technique has the advantages of (1) permitting us to obtain more precise estimates of program impacts than would be possible through a simple comparison of means for experimental and control group members, (2) facilitating investigation of whether program effects vary significantly among subgroups of the sample and among youths enrolled in different sites, and (3) being a relatively inexpensive technique for estimating program impacts on the large numbers of outcome measures considered as part of this evaluation. Although multiple regression estimates of program effects on outcome measures that are truncated or binary do not have desirable statistical properties, the common finding that, in most applications, ordinary least squares techniques yield estimates similar to those based on "more appropriate" techniques was borne out in selective comparisons of the results presented here with estimates based on tobit or probit analyses.[14]

In this section, we present the findings from the initial evaluation effort, which relied on data collected through 9-, 18-, 27-, and 36-month interviews and which is comparable to data available for analysis of impacts for the other three main target groups of the demonstration. Subsequently, findings based on an additional follow-up survey with sample youths are discussed.

Employment-Related Outcomes

Offering youths an opportunity to participate in Supported Work did have short-run beneficial effects on employment rates, employment levels, and earnings.[15] However, the results of this evaluation suggest that those impacts were due entirely to employment in Supported Work. Upon leaving their Supported Work jobs, experimental group members were about as likely as controls to find nonprogram jobs, the two groups averaged about the same number of hours of work per month, and they earned similar amounts in these jobs.

The general trend in outcomes is depicted in figure 7.1. The large employment gains during the first few months declined sharply as experimentals left Supported Work and as controls gradually increased their employment. By the start of the second year, when less than 20 percent of the experimentals were still in the program and by which time more than a third of the controls had found employment, there was essentially no difference in the overall employment levels of the two groups.

As can be seen from the figures in table 7.4, the pattern of results is generally similar for employment rates, hours worked, and earnings. The exception is that over the 19–36-month period there was a shift in the relative wage rates from experimentals earning somewhat more

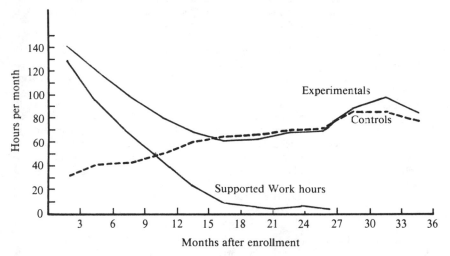

Fig. 7.1. Trend in Hours Worked per Month—Youth Sample.
Note: Data plotted in this figure are regression-adjusted estimates of hours worked by experimentals and controls during each 3-month period following enrollment. Means and standard deviations of control variables are presented in Appendix table A.1. Experimental-control differentials are significant only for the first 12 months following enrollment.

The fact that some Supported Work hours were reported during later months may be attributable either to data errors or to occasional failure on the part of program operators to terminate individuals promptly upon expiration of their eligibility period.

TABLE 7.4
Employment-Related Outcomes—Youth Sample

	Experimental Group Mean[a]	Control Group Mean	Experimental-Control Differential
Percentage with some employment			
Months 1–9	97.6	53.3	44.3**
Months 10–18	68.0	60.2	7.8**
Months 19–27	61.5	61.0	0.5
Months 28–36	74.0	65.9	8.1
Average hours worked per month[b]			
Months 1–9	120.4	39.7	80.7**
Months 10–18	69.9	58.2	11.7**
Months 19–27	68.8	68.2	0.6
Months 28–36	88.6	81.4	7.2
Average earnings per month[c]			
Months 1–9	$338.68	$125.48	$213.20**
Months 10–18	229.63	196.48	33.15*
Months 19–27	263.92	248.48	15.44
Months 28–36	301.94	336.33	−34.39

Note: These data are adjusted using ordinary least squares regression techniques. Means and Standard deviations of control variables used are presented in Appendix table A.1. The samples used are described in the first major subsection of the text, pp. 207-14.

 a These figures include Supported Work employment.

 b When these results were estimated using tobit analysis to take account of the bounded nature of the dependent variable, results were very similar: the estimates of experimental-control differentials are 85, 12, 2, and 12 for each 9-month period, respectively.

 c These figures are not price adjusted. If all earnings data are inflated or deflated to equivalent dollars as of the fourth quarter of 1976, the absolute value of the differential will be about 10 percent smaller during the first nine months, 5 percent smaller during the second, 18 percent smaller during the third, and 11 percent smaller over the fourth. Estimates are that 10–15 percent of gross earnings were paid in state and local income taxes and Social Security taxes.

 * Statistically significant at the 10 percent level, two-tailed test.

** Statistically significant at the 5 percent level, two-tailed test.

per hour than controls to their earning substantially less ($3.93 versus $4.37) in the last quarter of the third year. The result of this shift is that, while point estimates of hours and employment-rate differentials are positive (though not significant) in the later periods, those for earnings are negative (but, also, not significantly different from zero).

Qualifications of the Overall Results The most important consideration in interpreting these results is whether the results for the later time periods are representative of what would have been observed had the full sample (or a random subsample) been followed for 36 months after their enrollment in Supported Work.[16] It is clear from figure 7.2A that program impacts differed substantially among groups with varying amounts of follow-up data,[17] which suggests that the longer-term results estimated from the subsample who were assigned to and completed a 36-month interview may not be generalizable to the entire sample. In part, this pattern of differential impacts can be explained by the overrepresentation of Jersey City in the 36-month sample.[18] However, it is also related to differential employment patterns among controls in the various subgroups. Abstracting from the confounding influence of the Jersey City sample, we observe a pattern of more favorable experimental-control differentials occurring among those youths whose control group counterparts worked relatively little (see figure 7.2B); of particular note is the fact that a similar pattern of results has been observed for each of the other target groups for the Supported Work Demonstration—AFDC recipients, ex-addicts, and ex-offenders.[19]

Several possible explanations for this pattern of differential impacts for the sample subgroups with various amounts of follow-up data were considered, including changing site composition of the sample, extreme values of employment outcome measures, differential nonresponse to interviews, differing local labor market conditions, differential receipt of unemployment compensation benefits, and the availability of CETA employment opportunities. The only factor that was observed to be related to this pattern of program impacts was the availability of CETA employment.[20] The availability of CETA employment does not appear to have influenced program impacts during the early months after enrollment. Yet there is evidence to suggest that it had a substantial impact on the later period results. For example, the differential in earnings from CETA and WIN jobs during the 28–36-month period was sizable and fully accounts for the large negative earnings differential ($34 per month).[21]

Differential Impacts across Sites and among Other Sample Subgroups Estimates of program impacts were found to vary considerably among sites.[22] These differentials in impacts during the first nine months are due almost entirely to variation in the average length of time experimentals spent in Supported Work; impacts were largest in Jersey City, where youths stayed in the program longest, and they were smallest in Philadelphia where youths left the program in less than four months, on average. In the later time periods, when success of experimentals in non-Supported Work jobs was more relevant, the pattern of estimated differentials across sites was quite different. The

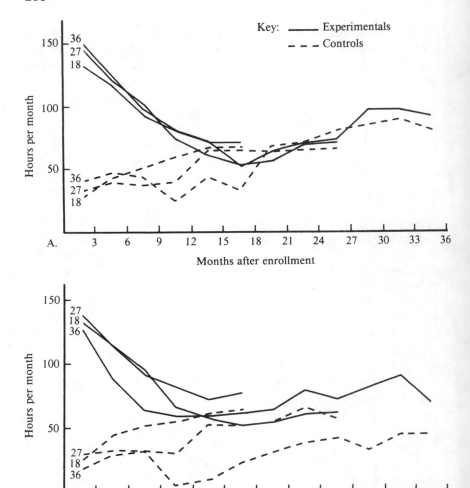

Fig. 7.2. Trends in Average Hours Worked per Month by Subsamples with Varying Amounts of Follow-up Data. *A*, All Sample Youth; *B*, Sample Youth in All Sites except Jersey City.

Note: These data are not regression-adjusted. To ensure that changes in results over program time are due only to changes in experimentals' and controls' behavior and not to changes in sample composition, results pertain only to those individuals for whom continuous data throughout the follow-up period are available.

18 = 18 months of follow-up data (436 cases).
27 = 27 months of follow-up data (298 cases).
36 = 36 months of follow-up data (121 cases).

point estimates of the experimental-control differences are always negative (though not significantly different from zero) for the Jersey City
sample, and they are always positive (though usually not statistically
significant) for the Hartford, New York, and Philadelphia samples.
The differential impacts in these later periods are attributable primarily
to the high variances across sites in the employment levels of controls.
Thus, as in the case of the differential impacts among samples with
different amounts of follow-up data, we observe a more favorable pattern of estimated program impacts for those youths who otherwise
have more limited employment opportunities.

The reason for the relatively low employment among controls in
New York, Philadelphia, and Hartford is not obvious. Trends in area
unemployment rates are not consistent with this pattern, as the unemployment rate tended to be highest in Jersey City and lowest in
Hartford. On the other hand, CETA employment opportunities for
youths were relatively less prevalent in New York and Philadelphia
as compared with those in other sites.[23]

With respect to differential program effects among other subgroups
of youth, the results are no more than suggestive that a program of
this type *may* be more successful if targeted at younger youths, those
raised in intact families, those who have dependents to support, those
who have little or no recent work experience, and those who have used
drugs other than marijuana or alcohol. Each of these subgroups is
characterized by relatively low employment among control group
members, as were the sites where more positive experimental-control
differentials were observed.[24]

Patterns of Non-Supported Work Employment The employment
experiences of experimentals after they left Suported Work were surprisingly similar to those of the control group. A slightly lower percentage of experimentals than controls had some non-Supported Work
job, and experimentals worked only a slightly higher percentage of the
available weeks than did controls. Among both experimentals and
controls, two-thirds to three quarters of the jobs were in the manufacturing, retail trade, and service industries, and they were mainly in
clerical, service, and miscellaneous occupations.

A surprisingly small percentage (less than 20) of the sample reported
that the Supported Work program or the Employment Service had
helped them find their jobs, and less than 3 percent of the experimentals' nonprogram jobs were a continuation of their Supported Work
jobs with a shift to alternative funding and supervision (that is, roll-
over jobs).

Among both experimental and control youths who were employed, nearly all worked at full-time jobs. Average hourly wage rates varied between experimentals and controls by 5 to 10 percent in either direction. Among the 36-month sample, experimentals exhibitied a tendency toward more stable employment than did the controls, with the average length of their first nonprogram jobs being six months as compared to five months for controls.

As noted in the discussion of experimentals' Supported Work experiences, youths tended to stay in Supported Work longer than they stayed in other types of jobs (6.7 months as compared to 5–6 months for nonprogram jobs). Yet, neither for Supported Work jobs nor for nonprogram jobs has longer tenure been found to produce improvements in other dimensions of employment-related outcomes such as employment rates or levels.

Impacts on Job Search, Education, and Training In addition to altering employment opportunities for youths directly, it was expected that Supported Work might increase youths' participation in the labor force and alter the extent and nature of their job-search activity. However, except during the time when many were employed in Supported Work and so not actively engaged in job search, there was little difference between experimentals and controls in either their labor-force status or job-search activity.[25]

Limited education and lack of formal training are often cited as among the main reasons for the employment problems of youth. Results from this demonstration indicate that Supported Work will have no effect on formal investments in human capital. Throughout the study period, education and training by both experimentals and controls were quite limited: 6–16 percent were enrolled in education programs (mainly high school) during any 9-month period, and less than 10 percent were in formal training programs (a third or less of which were sponsored by CETA).

Income and In-Kind Transfers As can be seen from table 7.5, a Supported Work program for youths can be expected to have short-term benefits to participants in the form of substantially higher standards of living, and such changes in income will be accompanied by small benefits to taxpayers in the form of reduced transfer payments. However, after they leave Supported Work, the impacts on both personal incomes and public subsidies will be small at best. Over the first two years following enrollment in Supported Work, the net income gain per participant was almost $2,300, over 80 percent of which was

TABLE 7.5

Income from Various Sources—Youth Sample

	Months 1-9		Months 10-18		Months 19-27		Months 28-36	
	Experimental-Control Differential	Control Group Mean	Experimental-Control Differential	Control Group Mean	Experimental-Control Differential	Control Group Mean	Experimental-Control Differential	Control Group Mean
A. Percentage Receiving Income								
Earnings[a]	45.6**	52.5	6.2*	62.7	0.0	-62.6	8.7	66.2
Unearned income								
Unemployment compensation	-2.0	4.0	6.8**	3.7	3.8*	3.8	-5.6	6.8
Welfare[b]	-6.8**	17.0	-3.5	21.4	-1.3	20.6	-11.4*	25.0
Food stamps	-0.5	32.4	-3.7	30.5	-0.6	29.0	6.6	30.3
Other[c]	-2.0	6.3	-1.1	5.1	0.4	3.1	0.7	1.7
B. Average Monthly Income Received (dollars)								
All sources	215.01**	176.04	21.95	265.44	26.99	311.68	-54.54	408.01
Earnings[a]	226.73**	123.95	30.71	205.25	19.30	248.98	-41.53	342.58
Unearned income								
Unemployment compensation	-2.99	5.63	11.16**	4.71	10.14**	5.80	-8.16	10.25
Welfare[b]	-9.66**	22.85	-12.49**	33.00	-6.20	37.30	-15.75	36.01
Food stamps	0.88	17.52	-3.63*	15.44	-1.42	16.82	5.18	18.78
Other[c]	0.94	5.65	-3.34	6.81	5.91	2.42	5.33	0.58

Note: These data are adjusted using ordinary least squares regression techniques. Means and standard deviations of control variables used are presented in Appendix table A.1. The samples used are described in the first major subsection of the text, pp. 207-14. All data pertain to the full sample, not only to recipients.

a Earnings data reported in this table vary somewhat from those reported in table 7.4 because of a slight difference in the samples used; only individuals who have valid data for all income sources listed in this table were included in the analysis reported here.

b Welfare includes AFDC, General Assistance, Supplemental Security Income, and other welfare income for which respondents were unable to identify the source.

c Other unearned income includes Social Security, pensions, alimony, child support, and job-training income.

* Statistically significant at the 10 percent level, two-tailed test.   ** Statistically significant at the 5 percent level, two-tailed test.

received during the first nine months after enrollment.[26] The net reduction in public assistance benefits (welfare and food stamps) totaled
less than $300, while unemployment compensation benefits (mainly
from the Special Unemployment Assistance program) increased by
about $130. Impacts on other forms of transfer were very small.[27]

Impacts on Criminal Activities

A recurring argument in support of employment programs for youths
pertains to the association between unemployment and criminal
lifestyles. The results from the Supported Work Demonstration indicate, however, that this employment program did not have a significant impact on criminal behavior among the sample youths, either
during the period when individuals were working in their program
jobs or subsequently. As can be seen in table 7.6, during each of the
first two 9-month periods following enrollment in Supported Work,
about 16 percent of both the experimentals and the controls reported
having been arrested and, among those arrested, the average number
of arrests was about 1.5. Between 15 and 20 percent of the arrests were
for robbery and less than 10 percent were for drug related offenses. A
sizable portion of the arrests did lead to conviction and incarceration.
However, again there is no significant difference between experimentals and controls.

The results for months 19–27, while not statistically significant, show
a somewhat more favorable pattern in that a lower percentage of experimentals than of controls reported having been arrested (11 versus
14 percent), a lower percentage were convicted (4 versus 7 percent),
and experimentals spent an average of 30 percent less time in jail than
did controls (2.6 versus 3.7 weeks). However, results for months 28–
36 generally are *not* favorable; a higher percentage of experimentals
than of controls were arrested (23 versus 17 percent) and incarcerated
(20 versus 17 percent). Again these differentials are not significantly
different from zero and, because the sample size for these later period
results is small, the difference in arrest rates is due to a difference of
only four arrests in the total sample.

In an effort to better assess the importance of the 19–27 month
results in particular, cumulative program impacts over the 18-month
and 27-month periods following enrollment were estimated.[28] These
results indicate that over the full 27-month period following enrollment, small differences *had* accumulated to result in significant overall
impacts: only 30 percent of the experimentals as compared with 39
percent of the controls reported having been arrested, and a large share
of this reduction (35 percent) was due to a reduction in experimentals'

TABLE 7.6
Arrests, Convictions, and Incarcerations—Youth Sample

	Months 1–9		Months 10–18		Months 19–27		Months 28–36	
	Experimental-Control Differential	Control Group Mean	Experimental-Control Differential	Control Group Mean	Experimental-Control Differential	Control Group Mean	Experimental-Control Differential	Control Group Mean
Percentage with any arrest	0.3	16.8	1.6	15.2	−3.2	13.6	6.4	16.7
Number of arrests	0.06	0.20	0.03	0.18	−0.05	0.16	0.09	0.18
Percentage with robbery arrests[a]	−0.3	3.4	0.6	2.6	−1.0	3.1	2.2	2.3
Number of robbery arrests[a]	−0.00	0.04	0.00	0.03	−0.01	0.04	0.02	0.02
Percentage of drug-related arrests[b]	1.0	0.9	−0.5	1.2	0.8	0.4	1.6	1.3
Percentage convicted	1.2	9.1	0.0	8.3	−2.3	6.7	−1.8	9.8
Percentage incarcerated	−2.7	11.6	2.0	12.6	3.8	15.5	2.5	17.2
Number of weeks incarcerated	−0.58	1.62	−0.14	2.37	−1.06	3.66	−1.12	3.67

Note: These data are adjusted using ordinary least squares regression techniques. Means and standard deviations of control variables are presented in Appendix table A.1. The samples used are described in the first major subsection of the text, pp. 207-14. None of the experimental-control differentials is statistically significant at the 5 or 10 percent level.
a Robbery arrests are defined as those for which robbery was the most serious charge. Only murder and felonious assault are considered to be more serious than robbery.
b Drug-related arrests are defined as those for which narcotics law violation is the most serious charge. More serious charges include murder, felonious assault, robbery, burglary, larceny, motor vehicle theft, and other property crimes, and other crimes against persons.

arrests for robbery. While not a statistically significant difference, a lower percentage of experimentals than of controls were convicted during this 27-month period (20 versus 24 percent), and a significantly lower percentage of experimentals than of controls were incarcerated (18 versus 28 percent).

One of the first questions that arises when comparing the results in table 7.6 with those for the 1–27-month period is whether the different pattern of results is due in part to varying program responses among those with different amounts of follow-up data. In order to examine this issue, results for the probability of arrest were estimated for subgroups of the samples defined by the length of the interview follow-up period. This analysis showed that, in most time periods, those experimentals with 27 or more months of follow-up data exhibited reductions in arrest rates. This persistent pattern of reductions in arrests results in differences of 8 to 11 percentage points between experimentals and controls over the 1–27-month period. But evidence from the 28–36-month data suggests that the favorable pattern of cumulative results for the 28–36-month subsamples may not persist into later time periods.[29] A partial explanation for this pattern of subsample differences relates to the differential impacts across sites that could not be adequately adjusted for because of the nature of the sample design.

Differential Impacts across Sites and Among Other Sample Subgroups   Program impacts on the likelihood of being arrested were estimated for each of the five sites and for a variety of other subgroups of the youth sample with a view toward possibly identifying a more effective program targeting strategy. These results indicate that there was substantial variation among sites but show weaker indications of differential impacts among other subgroups.

As can be seen in table 7.7, estimates of program impacts are consistently positive for the New York sample and most often negative for the Jersey City and Philadelphia samples.[30] Since Jersey City and Philadelphia are overrepresented in the sample with 27 or more months of follow-up data, much of the differential impact among subgroups with varying amounts of follow-up data can be attributed to the site composition of the sample. However, because the pattern of impacts on arrests is different from the employment and total income results (estimates of program impacts on employment and income are positive for Philadelphia and negative for Jersey City) and because there is no evidence of decreased criminal activity among experimentals during the time they are in Supported Work, it appears that employment and

TABLE 7.7

Percentage Arrested, by Site—Youth Sample

	Months 10-18		Months 1-18		Months 19-27		Months 1-27	
	Experimental-Control Differential	Control Group Mean	Experimental-Control Differential	Control Group Mean	Experimental-Control Differential	Control Group Mean	Experimental-Control Differential	Control Group Mean
All youths	1.6	15.2	-0.3	27.0	-3.2	14.0	-8.8*	39.3
Site								
Atlanta	-1.4	9.9	0.0	15.0	1.5[a]	1.6	-28.5[a]	33.5
Hartford	1.0	7.0	1.0	21.3	-6.6	19.0	-6.8	43.4
Jersey City	3.2	12.2	-4.6	25.8	-4.1	12.0	-10.7	35.8
New York	7.3	25.9	3.4	33.0	29.0*[a]	-4.3[b]	15.9[a]	21.7
Philadelphia	-10.5	21.9	-7.9	31.5	-1.8	12.8	-15.2	42.7

Note: These data are adjusted using ordinary least squares regression techniques. Means and standard deviations of control variables used are presented in Appendix table A.1. The samples used are described in the first major subsection of the text, pp. 207-14.

[a] These data are based on a sample of fewer than 20 persons.

[b] This negative estimate for the control group mean arose because linear regression as opposed to probit analysis was used.

* Statistically significant at the 10 percent level, two-tailed test. None of the experimental-control differentials is statistically significant at the 5 percent level.

225

improved economic status, per se, are not causally related to criminal behavior in this sample.

Results for other sample subgroups suggest that Supported Work may affect differentially the initiation of or recidivism to a delinquent or criminal lifestyle. The program appears to be relatively more effective in reducing involvement in crime among those who exhibit a greater tendency toward criminal behavior: those who are younger, who are male, who have more than eight years of education, and who have prior but not recent employment experience. However, in general, comparing these subgroup results with those for employment-related outcomes leads to equivocal conclusions. Among youths younger than age 19, both employment and crime results are relatively favorable. However, for other subgroups, employment and crime results do not correspond. Particularly, the lack of a significant reduction in experimentals' arrest rates during the first nine months when they participated in Supported Work suggests that the lack of employment opportunity may not be a principal factor in criminal behavior of these young people.

Impacts on Drug Use

As noted previously, drug use among the sample youths was not unusually prevalent, and economic and sociological theories do not yield unambiguous hypotheses as to the expected impact of an employment program like Supported Work. Thus, it is not surprising that, as can be seen in table 7.8, Supported Work appears to have had no effect on the prevalence of drug use among the youth sample.[31] During each 9-month follow-up period, 10–17 percent of the youths reported use of some drug other than marijuana; 1–4 percent reported using heroin; 7–15 percent reported use of marijuana; and 6–11 percent reported use of alcohol daily. The only statistically significant difference in reported use between experimentals and controls was estimated for daily alcohol use during the first nine months after enrollment, when 8 percent of the experimentals, compared with 6 percent of controls, reported such use. (However, when estimated using probit analysis, this estimated differential, while of about the same magnitude, was not statistically significant.) Furthermore, there is little evidence of either a consistent pattern of effects within a site across time or across sites. Similarly, there was no evidence of program effects for subgroups of youth characterized by particular demographic or background characteristics.

TABLE 7.8
Percentage Reporting Use of Drugs, by Type of Drug—Youth Sample

	Months 1–9		Months 10–18		Months 19–27		Months 28–36	
	Experimental-Control Differential	Control Group Mean	Experimental-Control Differential	Control Group Mean	Experimental-Control Differential	Control Group Mean	Experimental-Control Differential	Control Group Mean
Any drug (other than marijuana or alcohol)	-2.9	14.2	0.3	10.2	0.4	10.6	5.8	11.0
Heroin, any use	0.4	3.6	-0.7	2.4	0.6	1.2	0.9	1.0
Cocaine, any use	-1.1	8.2	-1.2	8.2	-1.0	8.4	5.7	9.7
Marijuana								
Any use	4.5	52.4	1.6	51.2	0.3	57.6	0.1	64.1
Daily use	n.a.	n.a.	0.0	22.4	5.4	21.1	-0.3	29.4
Alcohol, daily use	2.6*	5.5	1.9	9.3	0.7	9.9	-1.6	8.9

Note: These data are adjusted using ordinary least squares regression techniques. Means and standard deviations of control variables are presented in Appendix table A.1. The samples are described in the first major subsection of the text, pp. 207-14. Daily use of heroin, cocaine, and any use of other opiates, amphetamines, barbituates, and psychedelics were reported by less than 1 percent of the youth sample, and data for these categories are not included in this table.

n.a.   Not available.

* Statistically significant at the 10 percent level, two-tailed test. None of the experimental-control differentials is statistically significant at the 5 percent level.

Results from a Follow-up Survey

As was noted previously, subsequent to the completion of the main evaluation of the Supported Work Demonstration, sample youths were resurveyed and an analysis was undertaken both to reassess the conclusions of the main study, which relied on limited follow-up data for much of the sample, and to determine whether program performance data could be used to more effectively target program resources. This follow-up study included survey data for 746 sample youths, which covered the two-year period prior to the resurvey—as short a follow-up period as 15–38 months after enrollment for some sample members and as long a follow-up as 44–67 months after enrollment for others. These interview data were supplemented by program attendance and termination data and by data from CETA prime sponsors on records of participation by sample members.

Overall Program Impacts During the Resurvey Period

This follow-up study generally upheld the conclusion of the initial evaluation: on average, Supported Work did not meet its objective of increasing the long-run employment and earnings of school dropouts, nor did it result in significant reductions in welfare dependence, drug use, or criminal activity. Key research findings on which these conclusions are based are summarized in table 7.9.

Employment and Earnings   On average, employment experiences of experimentals and controls were very similar throughout the follow-up period, with both groups increasing their employment and earnings considerably over time. Just over half of the full sample of experimentals and controls were employed during any given quarter of the follow-up period: the youths worked an average of 80 hours per month; and they earned, on average, about $350 per month. There is evidence that participants in the Atlanta and Philadelphia programs significantly increased their earnings as a result of the program. However, these gains faded over time. The common characteristics of these two sites were the relatively small size of their Supported Work programs and particularly low employment levels among control group members.

Transfer Income   Despite the fact that Supported Work had no overall impact on earnings, there is some evidence that it reduced slightly dependence on transfer payments. The probability of receiving AFDC or General Assistance was not affected by Supported Work but, although most results are not statistically significant, it is estimated

TABLE 7.9
Summary of Findings Based on Data from the Youth Follow-up Survey—
Youth Sample

Outcome Measure	Experimental Group Mean	Control Group Mean	Experimental- Control Differential
Percentage employed per quarter[a]	55.29	56.83	−1.54
Average hours worked per month[a]	78.36	80.54	−2.18
Average monthly earnings[a]	$344.42	$348.56	$−4.14
Percentage receiving welfare per quarter[a]	15.72	15.69	0.03
Average monthly welfare benefits[a]	$31.00	$36.64	$−5.64
Percentage receiving food stamps[b]	24.30	31.18	−6.88*
Average monthly bonus value[b]	$15.67	$20.97	$−5.30
Percentage arrested[b]	26.59	21.83	4.76
Average number of arrests[b]	0.40	0.31	0.09*
Percentage who used marijuana only	53.20	53.46	−0.26
Percentage who used drugs other than marijuana[c]	14.64	12.67	1.97

Note: These figures are regression or maximum likelihood estimates. The sample includes 746 youths who responded to the resurvey interview.
a These figures are based on quarterly data for the 24-month period covered by the resurvey. These quarterly observations include a range of postprogram time of 6–22 quarters after enrollment in the research sample (application to Supported Work).
b These data pertain to the 2 years prior to the resurvey.
c These figures pertain to the 6 months prior to the resurvey.
* Statistically significant at the 10 percent level, two-tailed test. None of the experimental-control differentials is statistically significant at the 5 percent level.

that the average benefits paid to former program participants fell slightly (differences range from $2 to $10 per month). It is also estimated that the program reduced significantly the probability of receiving food stamps (from 31 to 24 percent) and, as a result, reduced average monthly benefits from $21 to $16 per month, although the estimated reduction in benefits is not statistically significant.

Criminal Activity On average, participating in Supported Work is estimated to have had no significant impact on the likelihood of being arrested at least once. However, during the two years prior to the resurvey, it is estimated that former participants were arrested an average of .09 more times than they otherwise would have been, suggesting that their criminal activity increased. Of particular importance is the fact that nearly half of this total increase in the number of arrests reflects a higher incidence of arrests for robbery.

Drug Use Supported Work had no overall impact on drug use. Nearly 70 percent of the youths reported using drugs during the six months preceding the resurvey: 54 percent used only marijuana and the remainder used other drugs (primarily cocaine).

Differential Impacts Associated with Short-run Program Performance Measures

The second major objective of this follow-up evaluation was to assess the usefulness of short-run program performance data in judging the relative effectiveness of Supported Work in targeting program resources on those most likely to benefit from them. The results from this study confirm previous findings based on the CETA program experience (Geraci and King 1981 and Gay and Borus 1980) that positive program outcomes are valid indicators of positive program impacts. Table 7.10 shows that Supported Work increased earnings of participants who terminated for positive or neutral reasons above what they would have been had these youths not participated. However, the results also reveal evidence of significant adverse impacts for youths who left the program for negative reasons. Furthermore, the magnitude of the adverse impacts associated with negative terminations is related to length of participation in the program. It is also noteworthy that the adverse program impacts on arrests that were noted above are significantly related to negative terminations.

TABLE 7.10

Estimated Program Impacts over the Resurvey Period Associated with Termination Types and Attendance Rates—Youth Sample

Short-Run Program Performance Measure	Outcome Measure	
	Average Monthly Earnings	Number of Arrests
Termination type		
Nonnegative[a]	$128.77**	−0.11
Short-tenure negative[b]	−72.49	0.13
Long-tenure negative[b]	−200.67**	0.55**
Attendance rate, weeks 1–13		
≥ 80 percent	−7.09	0.12
50–79 percent	113.42	0.07
< 50 percent	−100.71	0.19

Note: These estimates are based on instrumental variables procedures designed to correct for selection bias (see Maynard et al. 1982).

a This category includes positive and neutral terminations.

b Short-tenure negative terminations are those negative terminations occurring in the first 3 months of participation in Supported Work; long-tenure negative terminations are those occurring after more extended participation.

** Statistically significant at the 5 percent level, two-tailed test. None of the other results is statistically significant at the 5 or 10 percent level.

The implications of these results are twofold. First, they suggest that program-monitoring criteria based only on positive terminations may not yield valid indications of the relative effectiveness of programs, since it is necessary to consider both the favorable impacts associated with positive terminations and the adverse ones associated with negative terminations. Second, the results suggest that the performance of individual programs could be improved if short-run performance standards could effectively identify youths who are likely to leave for negative reasons. As part of the study, an investigation was undertaken of the usefulness of attendance rates during the early months of program participation for providing such identification. However, it was found that, although attendance rates did correlate with termination statuses, their relationship to long-run impacts was not sufficiently strong to recommend adopting absolute attendance standards for continued program participation (see Maynard et al. 1982).

Conclusion

The goal of Supported Work is to mitigate a number of factors thought to be related to the unusually high unemployment among a particular segment of the young population—school dropouts with limited or no prior work experience and often with a history of involvement in crime. The evidence from the national demonstration suggests that Supported Work can be expected to have short-run impacts on employment and, consequently, on dependence on public assistance. However, it does not meet its central objective of improving the long-run employment prospects of disadvantaged youth.

Those youths who met the Supported Work eligibility criteria and applied to the program are among those who characteristically have the most serious employment problems. However, based on the post-enrollment employment experiences of the control group, it appears that the employment prospects for those youths who applied to and were enrolled in the demonstration are similar to those of the population of young school dropouts and better than those of the other Supported Work target groups. Employment experiences of youth controls were considerably more favorable for those enrolled later in calendar time, for those in Jersey City and Atlanta compared with those in other sites, for males as compared to females, and for those with more as opposed to less prior work experience. Other characteristics, including age, showed only weak relationships with employment.

During the period when experimentals were employed in Supported Work, their hours of work and earnings, of course, exceeded those of controls by a significant amount. Consequently, their dependence on welfare decreased at the same time that their economic status improved.

Although nearly 40 percent of the experimental youths reported that Supported Work had helped prepare them for unsubsidized employment, the postprogram employment experiences of experimentals do not reflect such improvements in employability: by the start of the second year after enrollment, there was essentially no difference in the overall employment levels of the two groups. Perhaps the most noteworthy fact concerning these employment results is that the majority of both experimentals and controls did find some employment and those employed worked the equivalent of about two thirds time at wage rates averaging between $3.41 and $4.13 per hour.

Among the reasons for public concern with the high rates of youth unemployment is the belief that unemployment contributes to drug abuse and criminal behavior among young people. Yet, results from this study indicate that providing youths with employment opportunities like Supported Work will not reduce either their drug abuse or their criminal behavior. Even during periods when all experimentals could work in a program job, the extent of drug use and involvement in crime was similar between experimentals and controls: roughly 13 percent reported using drugs (other than marijuana or alcohol) and 17 percent were arrested.

In assessing the policy implications of these findings, it is useful to compare them with the results for other programs aimed at a similar target group and with the same program directed at other target groups. In comparison with participants in CETA programs targeted at youth (see table 7.2), Supported Work youths were somewhat more likely to obtain employment shortly after leaving the program (28 percent versus about 22 percent of those in CETA's Youth Employment Demonstration Project (YEDP) slots).[32] On the other hand, the postprogram results for the Supported Work sample indicate that these higher employment rates do not represent a net gain in employment over what these youths would have experienced in the absence of their Supported Work experience.

Supported Work impacts are decidedly less favorable for youth than for other target groups of the demonstration, particularly AFDC recipients and ex-addicts, and less favorable than the impacts of the Job Corps.[33] In comparison with other Supported Work target groups, youth experimentals had employment rates during the 19–36-month period that averaged 9–25 percent higher and they worked between 12 and 25 percent more hours (though at substantially lower average wage rates). Thus, that this group exhibited less employment gain vis-à-vis their control counterparts than did experimentals in other target groups appears to be related to their having a less chronic problem at the time of their enrollment. This conclusion is further supported by the observation that those youths for whom relatively more favorable (though generally not significant) patterns of effect were estimated are those whose control group counterparts had low employment rates and levels.

In contrast to the above cross–target group comparison, Job Corps participants and otherwise comparable nonparticipants exhibited substantially more favorable employment experiences than did Supported Work youths and their control group counterparts, and the net gains from program participation were substantially higher for Job Corps than for Supported Work.[34] For example, 12–18 months after leaving the Job Corps, former Corps members worked an average of 14 hours per month more than comparison group members (94 versus 80 hours), while for a comparable time period Supported Work youths and their control group counterparts both worked an average of only 68 hours per month. This differential in results for the two programs may be due to a combination of differences in the targeting strategies of the two programs and differences in the program treatments themselves: Job Corps provides a more comprehensive package of services than does Supported Work, which stresses work experience and, perhaps most important, Job Corps is a residential program that emphasizes basic skills development and job training.

In designing future employment-related programs for youths, it would seem to be useful to experiment with both the targeting strategy and program content.[35] The Supported Work programs, as implemented in the national demonstration, evoked such limited average program impacts that the estimates of the net social costs of Supported Work for youths are high: costs are estimated to exceed benefits by an average of about $1,500 per participant.[36] Thus, experimentation with programs of lower cost, and perhaps of higher cost but offering a more comprehensive package of services, may prove valuable.[37]

Perhaps, the most noteworthy findings from the evaluation of Supported Work's impacts for youths are those from the resurvey data which suggest that negative termination, especially of long-term participants, seriously weakened the overall impacts of Supported Work for the youth target group. For example, with all else the same, had it been possible to screen out youths who would have had a negative termination, the estimated overall program impact on earnings would have been $114 per month—a difference that is significant at the 5 percent level. The remaining challenge is to translate these findings into useful guidelines for either program evaluations or successful management strategies that will lead to a program that qualifies as an efficient use of public expenditures.

TABLE 7.11

Average Hours Worked per Month by Site—Youth Sample

	Months 1-9		Months 10-18		Months 19-27		Months 28-36	
	Experimental-Control Differential	Control Group Mean	Experimental-Control Differential	Control Group Mean	Experimental-Control Differential	Control Group Mean	Experimental-Control Differential	Control Group Mean
All youths[a]	80.7**#	39.7	11.7**	58.2	0.6	68.2	7.2	81.4
Site								
Atlanta	77.1**	59.1	5.5	79.2	-15.5[b]	127.9[b]	n.a.	n.a.
Hartford	87.2**	35.1	11.9*	49.7	3.9	62.5	9.6[b]	81.1[b]
Jersey City	94.6**	45.1	-0.2	73.1	-11.2	85.8	-10.5	102.7
New York	61.5**	39.9	22.5*	61.8	21.2[b]	32.8[b]	n.a.	n.a.
Philadelphia	46.9**	31.1	30.7*	30.8	14.3	45.3	35.9	44.6

Note: These data are adjusted using ordinary least squares regression techniques. Means and standard deviations of control variables used are presented in Appendix table A.1. The samples used are described in the first major subsection of chapter 7.

a These overall sample results were estimated from an equation that did not include variables interacting experimental status with site. Thus the subgroup results may not weight up to exactly the overall sample results.

b These data are based on sample sizes of 20 or fewer.

n.a. Not applicable.

Experimental-control differentials vary significantly among the sites.

* Statistically significant at the 10 percent level, two-tailed test.

** Statistically significant at the 5 percent level, two-tailed test.

234

Notes

1 For example, see National Commission for Employment Policy (1979), Barton and Fraser (1978), Diamond and Bedrosian (1970), Clark and Summers (1978), Freeman and Wise (1980), Gramlich (1976), and Ragan (1977).

2 For example, see Singell (1967), Mahoney (1979), Funke (1979), and Elliot and Knowles (1978) for discussions of the relationship between youth employment problems and crime; see Osterman (1978), Adams and Mangum (1978), and DiPrete (1978) for discussions of long-run employment consequences; and see O'Donnell et al. (1976) for evidence of a relationship between youth unemployment and drug use.

3 In all sites except Hartford, 50 percent of the sample were assigned to the experimental group; in Hartford, only 40 percent were experimentals.

4 The response rates to scheduled interviews ranged from 99 percent for the enrollment interview to 70 percent for the 27-month interview. An analysis of the impact of nonresponse to scheduled interviews on estimates of program effects indicates that results reported in this chapter are not biased as a result of this factor (see Brown 1980). This analysis used econometric procedures developed by Heckman (1976) to correct for selection bias due to interview nonresponse.

5 The CETA data referenced here are from Westat, Inc. (1979), Tables 4-4 and 5-2 and from CETA MIS Report No. 54, May 20, 1979. It should be noted that, recently, increasing emphasis has been placed on targeting CETA funds toward the most severely disadvantaged. As a result of this change in focus, the characteristics of CETA youths may become more like those of the Supported Work target group in the future (see U.S. Department of Labor 1979).

6 Few characteristics that distinguish those with more versus less postenrollment employment experience were identified. In general, control youths in Jersey City and Atlanta were employed more than were controls in other sites, perhaps as a result of the relatively higher ratio of CETA jobs to the youth population in those sites. Similarly, those youths who enrolled later in calendar time worked substantially more than did the earlier enrollees, perhaps due to increases in employment opportunities. Among personal characteristics, however, only sex and prior work experience seemed to be important: males worked significantly more than did females, and employment was positively and significantly related to prior work experience.

7 Throughout the Supported Work evaluation, arrest rates were used as the primary indicator of criminal activities. The reasons for the emphasis on arrest rates rather than on self-reports of crime are: (1) there is considerable evidence that self-reports of criminal activity are unreliable; and (2) a study of the accuracy of self-reported arrest data, undertaken as part of the Supported Work evaluation, demonstrated that self-reported arrest measures would yield valid conclusions concerning the program's impacts (Schore et al. 1979).

8 Eight to 10 percent reported using cocaine during each 9-month period, 1 to 4 percent reported using heroin, and less than 1 percent reported using

other drugs. Similarly, few of the control youths reported daily use of alcohol.

9 Twelve and 18 months of program participation could, under some circumstances, be spread over 15 and 21 calendar months, respectively.

10 This longer average stay for the 36-month sample is due largely to the fact that over half of this sample is from Jersey City, where experimentals stayed in the program the longest, but it is also due in part to the more relaxed termination policies of programs during the early period of their operation when their job-placement procedures were still in formative stages.

11 Less than 3 percent of the sample reported having left the program because they did not want to work—classified as a neutral reason. Participants' assessments of Supported Work indicate that a majority of them (62 percent) felt that Supported Work did not prepare them to obtain a regular job, a factor which could partially account for the relatively short program tenure.

12 Maynard (1980) presents a more detailed investigation of factors related to length of stay and reasons for termination from Supported Work and of the relationship between this program experience and postprogram impacts.

13 Mean values and standard deviations of control variables used in the regressions are presented in Appendix table A.1.

14 These maximum likelihood results are available from the author upon request.

15 Earnings data from Supported Work interviews were compared with those maintained by the Social Security Administration, primarily to assess the potential usefulness of Social Security data for a long-term follow-up of the sample (see Masters 1979). The results of this comparison show 25 to 45 percent higher earnings reported in interviews, at least partly as a result of some employment not being covered by Social Security. However, estimates of experimental-control differences were similar for the two data sources.

16 Other issues of interpretation that were addressed in the study include the likely effect on the results of both unemployment compensation and CETA employment programs and whether program impacts would improve if youths could be enticed to stay in the program longer. As reported in Maynard (1980), the unemployment compensation program had negligible effects. Results do show some evidence of being sensitive to the availability of CETA and other public employment opportunities, however. Using techniques developed by Maddala and Lee (1976) to correct for selection bias, we found no evidence that longer stay in the program per se led to more favorable results. However, as discussed later, there is some evidence to suggest that a relationship between program impacts and length of stay/ type of termination does exist.

17 For computational ease, subgroups were defined according to the amount of available data rather than the types of interviews scheduled to be completed. The slight differences in sample definitions have been found not to

affect the conclusions. As noted previously, 35 percent of the youth sample were followed for 27 months and 14 percent for 36 months. The remainder of the sample completed only 9- and 18 month follow-up interviews.

18 Because of the sample design, it was not possible to obtain reliable estimates that adjust for these differences in the site representation in the various analysis samples (see table 7.1).

19 See Masters and Maynard (1981), Dickinson and Maynard (1981), and Piliavin and Gartner (1981), respectively.

20 See Maynard (1980) for a discussion of the analysis of these issues.

21 To the extent that youths failed to distinguish between CETA jobs and other government jobs, the above figure understates the importance of subsidized employment, since the differential between experimentals' and controls' earnings from all government jobs, including CETA and WIN, is more than $80 per month. Differentials were particularly large among the Atlanta and Jersey City samples.

22 See table 7.11 in the appendix to this chapter. Site impacts were also estimated using tobit analysis, with similar results except that the 28–36-month differential for the Philadelphia sample is significant at the 10 percent level in the tobit equation.

23 Other factors that affected the net impact of Supported Work in the various sites are the Supported Work programs themselves and the receipt of unemployment compensation by former program participants. These five Supported Work programs varied along so many dimensions that it was not possible to assess the impact of various program characteristics on subsequent employment experiences of experimentals or on net program impacts. Estimates of the effects of unemployment compensation programs suggest that these programs, at most, had small effects on estimated results for the Jersey City and New York samples.

24 The point estimates of experimental-control differentials for these various subgroups tend to be consistently positive and larger than for the overall sample, but they are infrequently significantly different from zero except during the early months after enrollment when Supported Work jobs were prevalent. Furthermore, the variance across subgroups in the point estimates of program impacts is sufficiently large that, generally, they are not significantly different from each other.

25 During the second and third years following enrollment, between half and three-quarters of these youths were in the labor force in a given month and about half of those in the labor force were employed. Those looking for work spent an average of about eight hours per week in search activities, which included an average of five to six contacts with employers. Less than half the youths looking for work reported checking with the State Employment Service and less than 15 percent checked with the CETA office. Most efforts appeared to have involved less formal search methods such as contacting friends, looking in the newspaper, and checking with employers directly.

26 These estimated effects are 4–5 percent smaller if expressed in constant third-quarter 1976 dollars.

27 Furthermore, there was little evidence of significant changes in various other outcomes considered, such as household composition, housing quality, and medical care utilization.

28 There were 809 sample members with data to permit an analysis of cumulative crime impacts over the 1–18-month period and 379 with data for analysis of the impacts over the 1–27-month period. However, only 79 persons had continuous data for the 36 months following enrollment. Thus, results for the 36-month period were not estimated.

29 As noted previously, data for the 1–36-month period are available for too few sample members (79) to permit calculation of reliable estimates of cumulative effects over this period.

30 Tobit estimates of the number of arrests incurred during the various time periods yield results that are similar to those reported in table 7.7.

31 In all instances, the outcome measures are based on self-reports of any use (or daily use) of the drug during the previous nine months. The quality of self-reported data on drug use is, of course, questionable. While there is evidence that such reports will understate the use rates (O'Donnell et al. 1976), there is little reason to expect differential underreporting by experimentals and controls. Equal proportional underreporting by both groups still poses two potential analytic problems, however: one is that the absolute value of any program effect will be biased toward zero, and the other is that tests of the statistical significance of estimated differentials will tend to be conservative.

32 These figures for CETA placements are from U.S. Department of Labor, Report No. 45, Pt. 1, May 20, 1979.

33 The Job Corps program is the only employment-related program for out-of-school youth which has been subjected to a rigorous evaluation.

34 Estimates of Job Corps impacts are presented in Long et al. 1982.

35 There is currently an attempt to experiment with program content (see Semo Scharfman 1981).

36 See chapter 8.

37 The present view among both the Administration and the Congress is that the serious labor market problems faced by particular groups of youth—minority youth, youth from low-income families, and high school dropouts—require a more comprehensive remedial strategy. For example, see National Commission for Employment Policy (1979).

8 *Peter Kemper, David A. Long, and Craig Thornton*

A Benefit-Cost Analysis
of the Supported Work Experiment

This chapter presents the benefit-cost analysis of the demonstration and is divided into five sections. A description of the analytic approach is provided in the first section. Next, the benefit-cost findings for the program are presented along with a detailed explanation of the methodology. The third section contains an analysis of the results disaggregated along two important dimensions, target group and site. Some key theoretical and empirical issues in interpreting the results are discussed in the fourth section. The concluding section summarizes the results and considers the implications of the analysis for evaluation research methodology. For more details regarding the analysis reported in this chapter, see Kemper et al. (1981).

Approach to the Analysis

Supported Work is, in several ways, an excellent candidate for a benefit-cost evaluation. Because the program is promising, yet unproven, an appraisal of some kind is desirable. Benefit-cost techniques in particular are useful as a means of pulling together the program's wide variety of effects and comparing them to program costs. In ad-

This chapter benefited from the comments and efforts of many persons, particularly Lee Friedman, Judy Gueron, Robinson Hollister, Stanley Masters, Rebecca Maynard, Richard Murnane, Robert Solow, and Ernst Stromsdorfer. Additional technical details can be found in Kemper et al. (1981) and other project documents referenced in the chapter. A shorter and slightly different version of this chapter can be found in Haveman and Margolis (1983).

dition, the evaluation of the demonstration included an experimental design with random assignment to experimental and control groups, providing an unusually good basis for measurement of many of the program's benefits and costs.

The program also presents some challenges for benefit-cost evaluation. Supported Work's emphasis on helping disadvantaged workers requires that attention be given not only to its economic efficiency, the usual focus of benefit-cost analysis, but also to its effects on the distribution of income. In addition, many of the program's important effects are not normally valued in dollars and therefore require special estimation efforts.

This benefit-cost analysis builds on analytical techniques that have been developed in previous benefit-cost studies of employment and training programs.[1] The principal departures from this earlier work are the use of a single accounting framework to assess efficiency and distributional issues consistently,[2] and the measurement of a broader range of benefits and costs using a restricted, but consistent, valuation technique.

The "bottom line" of the benefit-cost analysis is an estimate of the net present value of Supported Work, that is, the difference between the present discounted value of benefits and costs.[3] In the accounting framework used here, this estimate is made from each of three perspectives: society, program participants, and nonparticipants. The social perspective values all benefits and costs to society as a whole—ignoring transfers among groups within society. This perspective is the one typically taken in benefit-cost analyses and used to judge whether the program is an efficient use of resources.[4] The perspective of program participants is analyzed because it indicates the extent to which Supported Work redistributes income to participants. The third perspective is that of nonparticipants, sometimes referred to as "taxpayers,"[5] who bear most of the direct costs of Supported Work. This perspective is of interest because it indicates the program's impact on government budget accounts—often of paramount political concern.[6]

Incorporating the three perspectives and all component benefits and costs into a single accounting framework structures the analysis in several useful ways. The framework requires that the values of all benefits and costs and their distributional impact be specified. Imposing the constraint that benefits and costs to participants and nonparticipants add up to those for society as a whole[7] keeps analytical relationships clear. Readers can easily see how a given benefit or cost affects participants, nonparticipants, and society, and simultaneously see which components are most important to the overall results. In short, it forces both analyst and reader to consider carefully how various analytical "pieces" fit into the final results.

In estimating the benefits and costs within this accounting framework, the first step was to measure Supported Work's effects, which was done using the original evaluation data described in chapter 3. (Analysis of the longer follow-up data available for the AFDC group is contained in the appendix to this chapter; as indicated in chapter 7, the results for youth are essentially unchanged when the longer follow-up data are used so those additional data are not analyzed here.) The program effects were measured as experimental-control differences in means of outcome measures such as postprogram earnings or number of arrests.[8] This procedure provides reasonably precise estimates of the effects of Supported Work for the first 27 months after enrollment.[9]

The second step was to value these effects. A shadow price corresponding to each measured program effect was estimated. For example, to estimate part of the benefit from reduced crime, the reduction in the number of arrests (estimated by the difference between the mean number of arrests for experimentals and controls) was multiplied by an estimate of the average criminal justice system cost per arrest (derived from published data). In estimating these shadow prices, an attempt has been made to determine the market cost of supplying the resources or outputs identified as affected by the program. Shadow prices were derived either from published research and federal government data or from special studies done for this evaluation.

This resource cost approach will accurately value program effects if the estimated prices reflect both the marginal costs and marginal benefits of additions of these resources. This need not be the case if the economy is not competitive or is out of equilibrium, if the government does not accurately interpret social demand for public goods, or if the program brings about large enough changes to alter market prices. In these situations, it is possible for the resource cost estimates of value to differ from their demand value. For example, if, because of a failure of the political process, public goods are over- or undersupplied, the resource cost will not represent society's willingness to pay for the additional output of these goods. Another difficulty with the resource cost approach is that market prices may not represent marginal social costs because of indirect effects not reflected in the market prices. This is most problematic in labor markets where jobs obtained by Supported Work participants may simply "displace" other workers—with no net increase in society's output. Alternatively, hiring a worker from a market with excess supply has a zero social cost, despite positive wages for some workers in the market. (Because of their importance, indirect labor market effects are discussed further in a later section.)

Despite these difficulties, the resource cost approach has several important advantages. It is practical—market prices and resource costs can be measured where demand often cannot. It is relatively easy to explain and interpret. It can be used consistently across a wide range of benefits and costs. When demand considerations are important, the supply side estimates give an estimate which serves as a starting point from which qualitative adjustment may be made.[10]

In interpreting the resulting estimates, it is important to recognize that members of the control group in this evaluation were eligible for numerous alternative programs and services. The comparison on which the evaluation is based, therefore, is not Supported Work versus no program, but Supported Work compared to the various other programs and services available to the four target groups. The benefits and costs of these alternative programs are implicitly taken into account in this evaluation, since all program effects—including utilization of other public programs and services—were measured as experimental-control differentials. As a result, the estimates presented here represent the net benefits and costs of the Supported Work Demonstration beyond those of the existing array of social programs.[11]

The analysis assumes that the resources invested in Supported Work (other than participant labor) would have been used efficiently in the absence of the program. It is not possible, therefore, to compare directly an investment in Supported Work with an equivalent investment in a specific alternative program. For example, it is impossible, based on the results reported here, to compare Supported Work to an increase in welfare payments which entails inefficiencies arising from work disincentives. Proper comparison to any specific alternative would require a comparable benefit-cost evaluation of that alternative—a requirement beyond the scope of this analysis.

Finally, this analysis focuses on the benefits and costs of the demonstration as it was fielded. Questions concerning the benefits and costs of variants of the Supported Work concept implemented in different environments can only be addressed by inference and extrapolation. While we present disaggregations of the overall benefit-cost results with such questions in mind, formal extrapolations to alternative program designs or environments, as well as to implementation of the program nationwide, are also beyond the scope of this analysis.

Overall Methodology and Results

This section has the dual purpose of presenting the results for Supported Work as a whole and describing in some detail the methodology used. In presenting the methodology, attention is focused on specific techniques used to make the estimates; discussion of theoretical issues and qualifications is deferred to the fourth section. Readers interested primarily in results may wish to skip to the end of the section where the summary estimates are presented. All results are expressed in fourth quarter 1976 dollars.

Benefits and Costs during the Observation Period

We begin with a discussion of the results for the first 27 months after enrollment, the period for which effects were actually observed for a large sample of participants; the issue of extrapolating benefits and costs into the future is deferred.

Costs and Value of In-Program Output[12]   While participants are enrolled in Supported Work they receive services and use materials, for which the program incurs costs. Participants also produce output on their subsidized jobs. The difference between the costs and the value of the output produced—the "net cost" of participating in Supported Work—can be viewed as the net investment made to achieve increased employability, reduced welfare dependence, reduced crime, and other benefits.

Table 8.1 summarizes the estimates of cost and value of output per year of service—that is, per year of calendar time enrolled in Supported Work. Expenditures by the nonparticipants who pay the bulk of the taxes that fund employment and training programs are about $14,000,[13] of which about $6,000 are offset by the value of the output produced

TABLE 8.1
Summary of Costs and Value of In-program Output per Year of Service,
by Accounting Perspective
(1976 dollars)

	Perspective		
	Social	Participant	Nonparticipant
Project cost	3797	0	3797
Overhead cost	3014	0	3014
Central administrative cost	365	0	365
Participant labor cost	1867	−4916	6783
Increased child-care cost[a]	67	28	38
Total cost	9111	−4888	13999
Value of in-program output	−6018	0	−6018
Net cost	3093	−4888	7981

Source: Kemper and Long (1981).

a Increased cost of child care is measured for the AFDC group only; it is assumed to be zero for the other groups.

on work projects, leaving a net cost to nonparticipants of about $8,000 per year of participant enrollment.

Program operations costs account for about half the cost to non-participants. These costs can be divided into three mutually exclusive categories: (1) project cost, the cost of all Supported Work inputs used directly in the production of goods and services on participants' in-program jobs; (2) overhead costs, the cost of office space, staff salaries, and other management and support services costs; and (3) central administrative cost, the cost at the national level of managing Supported Work grants and monitoring the sites.[14] Project costs averaged about $3,800 per year, indicating the substantial use of materials, supplies, transportation, equipment, and supervision on many work projects. Overhead costs averaged about $3,000 per year, due in large part to the management effort involved in raising funds, creating jobs, recruiting and later placing participants, providing supportive services, and generally managing the program and its work projects. Project and overhead costs together make up the program operating cost (other than participant labor) at the site level. The central administrative costs are small by comparison, averaging $365 per year. All three of these costs were estimated using accounting data from the third year of operations, thereby excluding start-up costs.

The other half of the nonparticipant cost is for participant labor—the wages plus fringe benefits paid to participants by Supported Work. This cost was estimated based on the periodic interviews and accounting data, and averaged about $6,800 per year of service.[15]

Unlike project, overhead, and central administrative costs, which are both nonparticipant and social costs, the Supported Work wages are transfers from nonparticipants to participants and hence are not costs to society. The social cost of participants' labor is rather the forgone output they would have produced had they not enrolled in Supported Work—estimated as the earnings of the control group during the in-program period (marked up for an average 15 percent value of fringe benefits earned in low-wage jobs). That this opportunity cost averaged under $2,000 per year indicates that Supported Work served an extremely disadvantaged group.

The difference between the Supported Work wages and participants' forgone earnings is a benefit to participants (shown in table 8.1 as a negative cost) in the form of increased earned income. It averaged nearly $5,000 per year, demonstrating the substantial increase in earned income resulting from the subsidized Supported Work job.

The final measured cost, increased child-care cost, includes only the monetary cost of care and was measured using interview data on child-care arrangements and out-of-pocket expenses, and published data on the average day-care cost. It was measured for the AFDC group only, because the other target groups were assumed to have minimal child-care needs. The costs even for the AFDC group turned out to be small—$271 per year, of which an estimated $115 were out-of-pocket expenses borne by participants.[16] The cost was low because eligibility criteria required that children be of school age, and because most mothers relied on inexpensive care with family, friends, and babysitters for the limited care they needed.

Offsetting the costs of Supported Work, as we have noted, is an important benefit—the value of the goods and services produced on Supported Work jobs. The jobs are on work projects developed by the Supported Work site staff or by arrangement with a client agency. The work in these projects has involved housing rehabilitation, painting, building and grounds maintenance, clerical services, and a variety of other types of work. Consistent with the resource cost approach described earlier, we have used the amount an alternative supplier would charge for output equivalent to that produced by Supported Work as a measure of the value of in-program output.

Although this alternative supplier's price is theoretically a well-defined concept, its measurement is not always straightforward in practice, and a variety of estimation techniques have been used.[17] When a contract was awarded to a Supported Work site through competitive bidding, the next highest bid provided a direct estimate of the alternative supplier's price. When Supported Work sold its output in regular markets (not through bids), the revenue received provided a basis for estimating the alternative supplier's price.[18] Where output was not actually sold, indirect estimates had to be made—either by professional contractors who estimated what an alternative supplier would charge to produce the same output, or by analysts using production standards found in published estimating guides available for many industries. Finally, some estimates were constructed based on estimates of the productivity of Supported Workers relative to that of regular workers.

These estimation procedures were applied in case studies of a sample of 44 work projects. The average alternative supplier's price per hour worked—around which there was considerable variance—was $4.58 per hour, or $6,018 per year of service. Because an estimated $2.89 per hour in project costs was incurred for supervision, materials, transportation, and equipment used in producing the output, $1.69 per hour is the approximate contribution of program labor.[19] This is about half the actual Supported Work wage rate, indicating that while the value of in-program output is a substantial offset to program operating costs, the Supported Work jobs are nonetheless subsidized.[20]

In summary, budget outlays excluding start-up costs averaged about $14,000 per year of participant service. From the perspective of society as a whole, however, Supported Work's cost is lower—about $9,000 per year—because participants' social opportunity cost is less than their Supported Work wages (by about $5,000 per year). The value of in-program output, estimated at about $6,000 per year, offsets both the social and nonparticipant costs, leaving net nonparticipant and social costs of about $8,000 and $3,000, respectively.

Because the natural units for collecting data on costs and value of output are units of participant enrollment time, these components are all expressed per year of service in Supported Work. For purposes of comparison with other benefits, which are not naturally measured in units of program time, it is necessary to convert them to a per-participant basis. Since participants typically stayed in Supported Work less than a year—the average length of stay was just over seven months—the per-participant cost is less than the annual cost. Net social cost per participant averaged about $1,800; net nonparticipant costs averaged about $4,600 per participant; and participants' earned income (less child-care cost) increased about $2,800 during the average enrollment in Supported Work.

Postprogram Output, Taxes, and Transfers   To estimate the increase in postprogram output produced by participants, it was assumed—as it was assumed in estimating the opportunity cost of participant labor—that the value of a worker's output equals the total compensation (pretax earnings plus employer payroll taxes and fringe benefits) paid by the employer. Interview data were used to estimate experimental-control differentials in postprogram earnings. Increased total compensation was then estimated by multiplying the earnings differential by 1.15 to reflect the average 15 percent value of fringe benefits for low-wage workers. During the 27-month period, postprogram output gains were estimated to be about $300 per participant, suggesting a modest impact on postprogram employability overall.[21]

Because participants' earnings increased from program wages and increases in postprogram employment, their tax payments also increased. The taxes include federal and state income taxes, payroll taxes for social security, sales taxes, and excise taxes.[22] They have been imputed based on each individual's total income, household size, and state of residence; on relevant tax rates and regulations; and on average consumption patterns. Estimated increases in taxes were about $450 per participant for both the in-program and postprogram periods. These taxes are a transfer from participants to nonparticipants.

Increased participant employment also results in reduced dependence on transfer programs. This generates a social (and nonparticipant) benefit because it frees administrative resources, and a distributional benefit to nonparticipants who otherwise would have had to pay for the transfers. Changes in eight types of transfers were assessed: five programs providing direct cash transfers—Aid to Families with Dependent Children (AFDC), general assistance programs, unemployment compensation, social security, and the Supplemental Security Income program—and three programs providing in-kind transfers—food stamps, public housing, and Medicaid.[23] Cash transfers were estimated by multiplying changes in months of receipt by the average benefit per month. The changes in administrative costs were estimated separately for each program by multiplying the estimate of the change in months of transfer program participation by that program's average administrative cost per case month.

During months 1–27, transfers per participant were reduced by about $900 and administrative costs of transfer programs were reduced by $70. Since the earnings gain is largest while participants hold their Supported Work jobs, the largest reductions in transfers (and the largest increase in taxes) occur during the in-program period.

Benefits from Reduced Crime   In addition to increasing employability, reducing crime is an important objective of Supported Work. Measuring that benefit, however, is not a simple matter. While there are undoubtedly many intangible benefits of reduced crime, we have based the estimates on the resource cost savings from reduced crime. Even this, however, requires a fairly complicated set of estimates.[24] The assumptions on which this approach is based are discussed in the fourth section (below), where the results based on alternative assumptions are also presented.

The estimates of the net reduction in crime are based on the control-experimental differential in the average number of arrests.[25] (The implications of sampling variability are also discussed in the fourth section.) These estimates were based on self-reports gathered as part of the periodic interviews. To correct for that fact that respondents tend to underreport their arrests, the estimates were multiplied by 1.7, the ratio of officially recorded to self-reported arrests.[26] The net reduction in arrests was disaggregated into eight categories: murder and felonious assault, robbery, burglary, larceny and motor vehicle theft, drug-law violations, other personal crimes, other miscellaneous crimes, and an unspecified category for those where information on specific charges was not available. This procedure allows changes in both the overall level and the specific types of criminal activity to be valued.

Estimates of the values of crime reductions per arrest were based on the resources saved by the criminal justice system (police, prosecution, courts, and corrections) and the costs of personal injury, property damage, and stolen property. The average criminal justice system costs for each crime category were estimated on the basis of a study of justice system costs by Lettre and Syntax (1976) and the U.S. Department of Justice (1978) data on total expenditures and arrests for the United States. The per-victimization costs of personal injury, property damage, and stolen property were estimated using unpublished data from the National Crime Panel Survey,[27] these per-victimization estimates were multipliied by the appropriate ratio of victimizations to arrests (estimated using national victimization and arrest data) to provide cost estimates on a per-arrest basis.

Reductions in criminal activity affect nonparticipants and participants differently. Nonparticipants will view all the components mentioned above as benefits. Participants, on the other hand, forgo theft income (a cost) and are not affected by decreased criminal justice system, personal injury, and property damage costs.[28] Information on fencing activities suggests their forgone income would be, on average, 35 percent of the stolen goods' market value. The social benefit is the difference between the nonparticipant benefits and participant costs.

Estimates of the resource cost of crime per arrest, in table 8.2, confirm that the cost of crime is indeed high. If robbery could be reduced by an average of one arrest per participant, that would create a social benefit of more than $13,000 per participant. As it turned out, there was little impact on arrests overall during the 27-month period. There was a slight unexpected increase in total arrests among participants—about three more arrests per hundred participants—but because participants generally committed less serious crimes, there was a small net social benefit resulting from the Demonstration. Participants committed fewer robberies and burglaries—crimes with high system costs—and more larcenies. Thus, there is a saving of criminal justice system resources, but an increase in property damage, personal injury costs, and stolen property. The net effect is a small net cost to nonparticipants of $10 per participant and an average net gain of $22 for participants. The resulting social benefit is therefore estimated to be only $12 per participant. As will be seen in the next section, however, this estimate disguises a great deal of variation in program effects across target groups.

TABLE 8.2
Cost of Crime per Arrest
(1976 dollars)

Type of Arrest	Criminal System	Personal Injury and Property Damage[a]	Unrecovered Stolen Property[b]	Total Cost per Arrest by Perspective[c]		
				Social	Participant	Nonparticipant
Murder and felonious assault	4338	7782	0	12120	0	12120
Robbery	12087	569	738	13135	−259	13394
Burglary	5895	537	3564	8749	−1247	9996
Larceny and motor vehicle theft	2618	408	1951	4294	−683	4977
Drug law violations	2590	0	0	2590	0	2590
Other personal crimes	756	94	0	850	0	850
Other miscellaneous crimes	919	0	0	919	0	919
Unspecified crimes[d]	2048	171	536	2567	−188	2755

Source: Thornton and Long (1980).

a The drug-law violations and other miscellaneous crimes categories contain primarily "victimless" crimes. This implies direct losses to victims are small; hence a value of zero is assumed.

b These costs are assumed to be zero for arrests classified as nonproperty.

c Criminals are estimated to net 35 percent of the value of stolen property; social benefits equal the sum of participant and nonparticipant costs.

d The unspecified crimes category contains arrests for which no charge was recorded. Costs for this category are estimated as the weighted average of the costs of the other crime categories.

Reduced Drug and Alcohol Abuse   In general, Supported Work did not have a profound effect on participants' drug and alcohol abuse, and no effort was made to measure society's willingness to pay for such changes as were observed, but the resource cost savings from reductions in drug or alcohol treatment were estimated. Indirect benefits that might have resulted from reduced drug use are captured in other benefit components such as increased earnings or decreased criminal activity.

The changes in utilization of drug and alcohol treatment programs were estimated by multiplying estimates of Supported Work effects on the use of the major types of drug and alcohol treatment programs—methadone maintenance; residential and nonresidential drug-free treatment programs; inpatient and outpatient detoxification programs; and inpatient, outpatient, and intermediate alcohol treatment programs—by the average costs of these treatments. The estimated overall drug treatment benefits during the 27 months after enrollment are negligible. However, eventual reductions in drug and alcohol treatment may not appear in the short run. Even if participants are induced to reduce their use of drugs, the short-run effect could be either a reduction in the need for treatment or an increase in the desire for treatment in order to reduce drug dependence. When this is considered along with the weak effects on drug and alcohol use, it is not surprising that the treatment benefits are small.

Reduced Use of Alternative Programs   Participants' enrollment in Supported Work generally implied a reduction in their use of alternative education, employment, and training programs. These forgone alternative program opportunities represent the treatment participants would have received if they had not entered the demonstration.

To estimate the cost savings resulting from this change in program use, seven types of programs were examined: high school, vocational school, college or university education, WIN training, CETA and other training, CETA public service employment, and unspecified schooling. In each case, the net reduction in cost was estimated by multiplying the differentials in the mean number of weeks experimentals and controls used each program by an estimate of the program's average cost per week obtained from published data.[29] In addition, the net reduction in training allowances from programs other than Supported Work was estimated using interview data.

Participants reduced slightly their use of these programs. None of the differences in average number of weeks enrolled in any of the specific programs considered here was greater than two weeks, and the estimated value of the resources saved because of these reductions was small—$112 per participant for the first 27 postenrollment months. There was almost no change in the average training allowance received by participants.

Forgone benefits from these alternative programs (for example, increased earnings) are reflected in control group behavior and, hence, in the experimental-control differences used to estimate the impact of Supported Work. However, because the observation period is limited and the control group may not complete the alternative programs during this period, observed control group earnings may understate expected future earnings. Experimental-control differences may therefore overstate long-run earnings gains. An offsetting bias could arise if Supported Work motivates participants to obtain additional education and training. In that case, the finite observation period will imply, by analogous reasoning, that the effects on earnings are understated.[30] Any bias is likely to be small, however, because program effects on alternative program use is small.

Summary of Results for the Observation Period Table 8.3 summarizes the results for the first 27 months after enrollment within the social, participant, and nonparticipant accounting framework. Supported Work redistributed income to its participants. The average participant's earnings plus fringe benefits during and after the program increased by about $3,200; these increased earnings were reduced by about $1,400, primarily in increased taxes and lost transfer payments.

This redistribution was purchased at a cost to society—during the 27-month period social benefits fell short of costs by $1,300 per participant. Net social costs of $1,800 per participant ($5,300 cost less $3,500 value of in-program output) produced about $500 in benefits, largely from postprogram earnings gains, reduced welfare administrative costs, and reduced use of alternative programs. From the perspective of nonparticipants, who bear both the program operating costs and the costs of redistribution, measured benefits fell short of costs by about $3,100.

Future Benefits

The results for the observation period indicate that an economic assessment of Supported Work requires a judgment about the magnitude of future benefits and how much to value them. There is little evidence, however, upon which to base quantitative estimates of future benefits. In extrapolating benefits into the future, we have made the simple assumptions that the benefits observed during the last nine

TABLE 8.3

Measured Benefits and Costs per Participant during the 27-Month Observation Period (1976 dollars)

	Perspective		
	Social	Participant	Nonparticipant
Benefits			
Output produced by participants			
Value of in-program output	3517	0	3517
Increased postprogram output	306	306	0
Increased tax payments	0	−452	452
Reduced dependence on transfer programs			
Reduced transfer payments	0	−924	924
Reduced administrative costs	73	0	73
Reduced criminal activity			
Reduced property damage and injury	−72	0	−72
Reduced stolen property	−41	22	−63
Reduced justice system costs	125	0	125
Reduced drug treatment costs	−4	0	−4
Reduced use of alternative services			
Reduced alternative service costs	112	0	112
Reduced training allowances	0	−11	11
Total benefits	4016	−1059	5075
Costs			
Program operating costs			
Project costs	−2214	0	−2214
Overhead costs	−1759	0	−1759
Central administrative costs	−210	0	−210
Participant labor costs			
In-program earnings plus fringes	0	3934	−3934
Forgone earnings plus fringes	−1047	−1047	0
Increased child-care costs	−87	−40	−47
Total costs	−5317	2847	−8164
Net present value (benefits minus costs)	−1301	1788	−3089

months of observation (the "base" period) decay at a constant rate over a time horizon extending through an expected working life. In addition, all benefits and costs were discounted to the initial observation period. Formally, future benefits were estimated by:

$$F = B \int_o^T e^{-(r+d)t}dt,$$

where F = the present discounted value of future benefits, B = the benefit for the base period, T = the time horizon over which benefits extend, r = the discount rate, and d = the decay rate.[31]

In estimating the base to be extrapolated, two options could be considered: (1) use the results for months 28–36, available for a small sample, or (2) use the results for months 19–27, available for the larger sample, and ignore the longer follow-up information. Because both options have disadvantages, a mixed strategy that makes use of the information in both samples was chosen. It averages the 28–36-month results for the smaller cohort that was followed for 36 months with the 19–27-month results for the larger cohort that was followed for only 27 months (weighting the cohorts in proportion to their size).[32]

The time horizon over which benefits were assumed to extend was the expected working life of participants, which was estimated from population tables. Given the average age of participants, this was estimated to be between 27 and 42 years after enrollment, depending on the target group.

The real discount rate (that is, the nominal discount rate minus the rate of inflation) was assumed to be 5 percent per year. While there is no agreed-upon way of choosing a discount rate, this is within the range generally used in benefit-cost analyses.[33]

Because the Supported Work data provide insufficient evidence upon which to estimate a decay rate, we have based decay rate estimates on a study by Ashenfelter (1978) which collected data over a longer follow-up period. Based on this study, which found different decay rates for men and women, a 3 percent annual decay rate was used for the AFDC target group and a 17 percent annual rate was used for the other three (predominantly male) target groups. This and the other extrapolation assumptions are clearly approximations and will be subjected to sensitivity tests below.

Using these assumptions to extrapolate all benefits, estimates of total benefits and costs are shown in table 8.4. Once future benefits and costs are taken into account, net present value is positive from all perspectives. Social benefits exceed costs by about $1,500 per participant, largely because of about $2,400 in estimated future earnings gains. Small future benefits from reduced welfare administrative costs, reduced use of drug treatment programs, reduced crime, and reduced use of alternative services together add about $600 to net present values. Thus, these benchmark estimates indicate that Supported Work is an efficient use of society's resources. In addition, the program redistributes a modest amount of income to participants—about $1,500 under the benchmark assumptions—and the benefits to nonparticipants who pay the bulk of the taxes required to finance the program are about equal to their costs.

TABLE 8.4

Estimates of Total Benefits and Costs (Including Extrapolation) per Participant
(1976 dollars)

	Perspective		
	Social	Participant	Nonparticipant
Benefits			
Output produced by participants			
Value of in-program output	3517	0	3517
Value of postprogram output	2666	2666	0
Increased tax payments	0	−786	786
Reduced dependence on transfer programs			
Reduced transfer payments	0	−3218	3218
Reduced administrative costs	263	0	263
Reduced criminal activity			
Reduced property damage and injury	405	0	405
Reduced stolen property	−155	83	−238
Reduced justice system costs	−162	0	−162
Reduced drug treatment costs	129	0	129
Reduced use of alternative services			
Reduced alternative service costs	289	0	289
Reduced training allowances	0	−13	13
Total benefits	6952	−1268	8220
Costs			
Program operating costs			
Project costs	−2214	0	−2214
Overhead costs	−1759	0	−1759
Central administrative costs	−210	0	−210
Participant labor costs			
In-program earnings plus fringes	0	3934	−3934
Forgone earnings plus fringes	−1047	−1047	0
Increased child-care costs	−179	−82	−97
Total costs	−5409	2805	−8214
Net present value (benefits minus costs)	1543	1537	6

Disaggregations of the Overall Results

The results presented in the preceding section represent estimates for the program as a whole that are based on numerous assumptions and judgments. Taken at face value, they indicate that, in terms of both economic efficiency and distributional effects, Supported Work has been a succcessful program. However, it is important to look beyond the aggregate estimates at the methodological assumptions used to compute them and at several additional aspects of the results. In this section we examine disaggregations of the overall estimates by target group and site to obtain some insight into the determinants of program success.[34] In the next section we consider the confidence that can be placed in the results by (1) testing the sensitivity of the estimates to various assumptions, (2) examining the question of chance sampling variability, and (3) assessing the importance of benefits and costs that were not measured in the analysis. Together, these two sections will help the reader interpret the overall results and assess their implications.

Target Group Differences

In several ways, Supported Work is not a single demonstration program, but many different programs. Because Supported Work has served four separate target groups and operated in 15 different sites, it should be expected that program treatments and effects will vary by the group served and the site providing the service.

Table 8.5, which presents the results by target group for the 27-month observation period, tells a general story of differences among the target groups, with only one result that is always the same as the overall finding: participants' income increased over the 27-month period as a result of Supported Work employment. Increases in income range from $1,500 per participant for ex-addicts to $2,100 for ex-offenders.

Even this similarity masks an important difference, however, between the AFDC group and the other three groups. The earned income (including fringe benefits) of ex-addicts, ex-offenders, and youths increases about $2,500 per participant as a result of increased wages from Supported Work; there is little indication of increased postprogram earnings. For the AFDC group, earned income increases much more—by about $5,000—as a result of three differences: their opportunity cost is lower; their Supported Work earnings are higher because they stay in the program an average of two months longer than the other groups; and postprogram earnings increased an estimated $1,000 during the period. They give up about two-thirds of their increased income, however, in lost welfare payments, increased taxes, and increased child-care costs—leaving them with about the same net increase in income as the other target groups, which lose much less in transfer payments. These results confirm that AFDC mothers face substantial work disincentives. Despite their disincentives, the AFDC group did work—it stayed in Supported Work longest (9.1 months on average), and it was the only group with a substantial increase in postprogram earnings.

Turning to the social perspective, net cost (total cost minus the value of in-program output) ranges from about $1,600 for youths to about $2,100 for AFDC recipients. This relatively small variation in net costs

TABLE 8.5
Measured Benefits and Costs during the 27-Month Observation Period,
by Target Group
(1976 dollars)

	Perspective		
	Social	Participant	Nonparticipant
AFDC			
Increased postprogram output	1028	1028	0
Increased tax payments	0	−565	565
Reduced dependence on transfers	137	−2615	2752
Reduced use of alternative services	133	10	123
Net cost[a]	−2086	3815	−5901
Net present value	−788	1673	−2461
Ex-addict			
Increased postprogram output	−153	−153	0
Increased tax payments	0	−293	293
Reduced dependence on transfers	47	−530	577
Reduced criminal activity	1677	−84	1761
Reduced drug treatment	−3	0	−3
Reduced use of alternative services	72	−13	85
Net cost[a]	−1855	2558	−4413
Net present value	−215	1485	−1700
Ex-offender			
Increased postprogram output	304	304	0
Increased tax payments	0	−553	553
Reduced dependence on transfers	41	−219	260
Reduced criminal activity	−1048	116	−1164
Reduced drug treatment	6	0	6
Reduced use of alternative services	136	−32	168
Net cost[a]	−1664	2489	−4153
Net present value	−2225	2105	−4330
Youth			
Increased postprogram output	−3	−3	0
Increased tax payments	0	−301	301
Reduced dependence on transfers	78	−474	552
Reduced criminal activity	103	−4	107
Reduced drug treatment	−26	0	−26
Reduced use of alternative services	87	4	83
Net cost[a]	−1616	2577	−4193
Net present value	−1377	1799	−3176

Source: Kemper et al. (1981).

Note: Benefits are entered as positive numbers, costs as negative numbers, as appropriate for each perspective. Columns should sum to net present value.

a Net equals overhead, project, central administrative, participant labor, and child-care costs less the value of in-program output.

masks some larger differences across the target groups in its components (which are not shown in the table). Costs total about $5,000 per participant for ex-addicts, ex-offenders, and youths and $6,000 for the AFDC mothers. The AFDC group stayed in Supported Work longer, resulting in higher per-participant cost, and incurred child-care costs.[35] Opportunity costs varied somewhat, the AFDC and youth groups having the bleakest alternative employment opportunities. The value of in-program output was the largest benefit for all groups, offsetting about two-thirds of the social costs. The absolute dollar amount was largest for the AFDC group because of its longer average length of stay.[36]

The AFDC group had a substantial benefit (in addition to in-program output) during the 27-month period: an estimated $1,000 increase in postprogram earnings. Social benefits nonetheless fell short of costs by about $800 per participant during the 27-month period. If the postprogram earnings gain were to persist for an additional year, social net present value would be positive for the AFDC target group.

For the ex-addict group, benefits (other than value of in-program output) total just over $1,600, almost all of them from reduced crime. As discussed in chapter 5, these large benefits arise because of substantial reductions in robbery, burglary, and drug arrests. Overall, measured benefits fall short of costs by only $200. Thus, only minimal unmeasured or future benefits are necessary for Supported Work to be an efficient social investment for ex-addicts.

For the ex-offender and youth groups there are no substantial measured benefits. For ex-offenders there was an unexpected increase in the estimated social cost of crime and an increase in postprogram earnings of about $300. There are problems with both results, however. The confidence interval around the crime results is quite wide, so it is quite possible that the true results could have been no change or even a reduction in arrests. (This issue is discussed in detail in the section below on chance sampling variability.) The increased postprogram earnings estimate, as noted above, required an arbitrary division of control group earnings between inprogram and postprogram periods and hence is subject to uncertainty. As discussed in chapter 6, there is no evidence of an impact on postprogram earnings for ex-offenders, leading us to attach little significance to the $300 estimate. Whether or not these benefits are disregarded, social benefits fall short of costs for ex-offenders. For youth, there were no substantial social benefits other than value of inprogram output during the 27-month period.

From the perspective of nonparticipants, benefits fell well short of costs for all target groups as they did in the overall results. During the

27-month period, the net investment of nonparticipants was about $2,500 for AFDC, $1,700 for ex-addicts, $4,300 for ex-offenders, and $3,200 for youths.

Table 8.6 presents results that include future benefits estimated under the benchmark extrapolation assumptions described above. The results show positive social net present values for the AFDC and ex-addict target groups. Estimated benefits exceed costs by $8,150 for the AFDC group primarily because of the large extrapolated postprogram earnings gains. For ex-addicts, large extrapolated benefits from reduced crime cause benefits to exceed costs by about $4,300 per participant. For ex-offenders and youths, net present value remains negative—indeed, extrapolating some negative crime results actually reduces estimated benefits and net present values for these groups.

From the nonparticipant perspective, the extrapolated reductions in transfer payments for AFDC and crime reductions for ex-addicts create benefits large enough to exceed nonparticipant costs; for ex-offenders and youths, the lack of benefits leaves nonparticipant net present values quite negative.

With extrapolated future earnings, participants' change in income remains positive for all groups except AFDC women. This suggests that AFDC target group members face a financial disincentive against participating in Supported Work. In the long run, as the future income decrease became known to potential participants, they would be unlikely to participate unless they had a strong preference for work for its own sake, or a higher discount rate. However, this AFDC result appears to be an artifact of the extrapolation procedures which are based on a limited observation period. The negative net present value from the perspective of participants is due to the extrapolation of a large reduction in welfare payments during months 19–27 (the base for extrapolation for the AFDC group). We believe the magnitude of this reduction is likely to be temporary as a consequence of lags in the effect of changes in employment on welfare payments. This implies that the long-run reduction in welfare payments is overstated as a consequence of the extrapolation methodology's heavy reliance on the estimated impacts for months 19–27. (As indicated in the appendix to this chapter, the longer AFDC group follow-up data collected subsequent to this analysis confirms that this is indeed an artifact—based on the longer follow-up data, benefits to participants do exceed their costs and consequently, nonparticipant benefits fall short of costs.) Thus, it does appear that Supported Work redistributes a modest amount of income to all of its target groups.

TABLE 8.6
Estimates of Total Benefits and Costs
(Including Extrapolation) per Participant, by Target Group
(1976 dollars)

	Perspective		
	Social	Participant	Nonparticipant
AFDC			
Increased postprogram output	9193	9193	0
Increased tax payments	0	−1722	1722
Reduced dependence on transfers	811	−11863	12674
Reduced use of alternative services	608	−43	651
Net cost[a]	−2462	3642	−6104
Net present value	8150	−793	8943
Ex-addict			
Increased postprogram output	819	819	0
Increased tax payments	0	−453	453
Reduced dependence on transfers	−64	315	−379
Reduced criminal activity	5178	−168	5346
Reduced drug treatment	153	0	153
Reduced use of alternative services	114	6	108
Net cost[a]	−1855	2558	−4413
Net present value	4345	3077	1268
Ex-offender			
Increased postprogram output	642	642	0
Increased tax payments	0	−573	573
Reduced dependence on transfers	96	−308	404
Reduced criminal activity	−2873	461	−3334
Reduced drug treatment	340	0	340
Reduced use of alternative services	275	−124	399
Net cost[a]	−1664	2489	−4153
Net present value	−3184	2587	−5771
Youth			
Increased postprogram output	29	29	0
Increased tax payments	0	−341	341
Reduced dependence on transfers	228	−1361	1589
Reduced criminal activity	−89	−218	129
Reduced drug treatment	−116	0	−116
Reduced use of alternative services	100	205	−105
Net cost[a]	−1616	2577	−4193
Net present value	−1464	891	−2355

Source: Kemper et al. (1981).

Note: Benefits are entered as positive numbers, costs as negative numbers, as appropriate for each perspective. Columns should sum to net present value.

a Net cost equals overhead, project, central administrative, participant labor, and child-care costs less the value of in-program output.

Site Differences

Benefit-cost estimates from the social perspective are disaggregated by site in table 8.7. The estimates provided are: net cost (that is, social cost minus the value of in-program output), increased postprogram output (the estimated difference in earnings plus fringe benefits), reduced crime, other benefits (reduced administrative costs of transfer programs, reduced drug treatment costs, and reduced costs of alternative education and training programs), and the overall net present value after 27 months. The results are not extrapolated beyond the observation period because the site-specific samples are too small to support extrapolation. Indeed, even the estimates for months 1–27 are subject to greater uncertainty from sampling variability than the target group results due to the smaller samples, so that the site-specific estimates must be interpreted cautiously.[37] Estimates were constructed using the same assumptions as above except that site-specific estimates of net cost were used.[38]

There is a striking amount of variation in net present values after 27 months. Three sites achieved a positive net present value during the observation period alone, while the other sites had large negative net present values. The variation is in both net cost and benefits—both range widely across sites. Because some of this variation is undoubtedly random, it is difficult to draw firm conclusions. However, variation as great as this does suggest that although Supported Work was successful overall, the program was not uniformly effective. This leads one to inquire about possible reasons for the site differences.

TABLE 8.7
Social Benefits and Costs, by Site, for the Observation Period
(1976 dollars)

	Net Cost	Increased Postprogram Output	Reduced Crime	Other Benefits	Net Present Value
Atlanta	−1282	1122	202	328	370
Chicago	−1985	839	265	161	−720
Hartford	−2261	713	−30	80	−1498
Jersey City	−2499	−1203	1117	37	−2548
Newark	−465	672	−87	189	309
New York	−2369	671	−895	333	−2260
Oakland	−882	1618	−609	559	686
Philadelphia	−2523	228	944	83	−1268
San Francisco	−4693	567	37	100	−3989

Note: Costs and negative benefits are preceded by a minus sign.

The greatest variation in table 8.7 is in net cost. Although average length of stay, the opportunity cost of participant labor, and overhead cost[39] all affect net cost, differences in value of output and project cost account for much of the variation across sites. Analysis of the relatively small sample (n = 44) of case studies of work projects[40] suggests that value of output net of associated project costs is higher on jobs where the participants were placed in outside agencies under agency supervision, typically in service occupations such as clerical services, building maintenance, and grounds maintenance. While the cause of this difference is not known,[41] three sites—Atlanta, Chicago, and Newark—emphasized agency-supervised projects and had low estimated net cost.[42]

Turning to program benefits, one might conjecture that a larger investment while enrolled in Supported Work would pay off in larger benefits. The data suggest the contrary, however. There is no association between high net cost and large total benefits (other than value of output). Nor is there any evidence of a positive relation between a large investment during the in-program period and large increases in postprogram earnings. One might expect, for example, that low value of in-program output might arise from extra time spent training or from more intensive supervision which would pay off in greater postprogram employability. But the data suggest the contrary—the three sites with the highest net cost are also the three sites with the lowest postprogram earnings gains and the three sites with the largest earnings gains have among the lowest net costs.[43]

One possible explanation of differences in postprogram earnings gains across sites may be differences in the target groups served.[44] Sites serving the AFDC target group (such as Atlanta) tended to have higher postprogram earnings gains, while sites with no AFDC women (Jersey City, Philadelphia, and San Francisco) had the lowest earnings gains. But the target group explanation of site differences is far from perfect—Oakland and Hartford had relatively high postprogram earnings gains, although less than 20 percent of their participants were AFDC women. While the direction of causation cannot be certainly identified, there is suggestive evidence that target group differences are more important than site differences in determining postprogram earnings gains.[45]

Differences in crime benefits are even more difficult to explain. While, as will be discussed further below, they are subject to more sampling variability than are earnings, it appears that the target group composition of the sites is an important explanatory factor—over half the enrollees at the two sites with the largest crime benefits (Jersey City and Philadelphia) were drawn from the ex-addict target group. As with earnings, however, the direction of causation—whether from target site, or vice versa—is not clear, and neither explains all the variation.

In short, the substantial variation of net present value across sites suggests that there may be important differences in site effectiveness. While the evidence is limited, it suggests that two factors are particularly important in determining site effectiveness: the choice of work projects, which affect the cost and value of in-program output, and the target groups served, which affect the benefits. While these factors appear most important, they do not by any means account for all site differences. For example, Oakland had the highest net present value of all sites although serving mainly ex-offenders and managing for itself a diverse group of work projects. Further analysis of the determinants of differences across sites is called for.

Confidence to Be Placed in the Results

The virtue of benefit-cost analysis is that it provides an internally consistent framework for summarizing the effects of a program and weighing their relative importance. But this virtue is purchased at a price: benefit-cost estimates are inevitably subject to uncertainty. Estimates of program effects are subject to sampling variability; not all benefits and costs are measured, and the theoretical assumptions and empirical estimates of shadow prices are required to measure those that are. Examination of these issues in some detail will permit readers to judge how much confidence to place in the summary benefit-cost results presented above.

Sensitivity Tests

The estimates reported in this chapter have incorporated assumptions and shadow prices that we believe are reasonable. Nonetheless, the assumptions and estimates are inherently subject to uncertainty. The estimates presented above are "benchmarks," whose sensitivity to alternative assumptions and shadow prices can be tested. By examining these tests, better judgments can be reached regarding the relative magnitudes of program benefits and costs, the areas of greatest uncertainty, and the confidence that can be placed in the estimates. We have identified several important assumptions that are related to extrapolation, employment, cost and value of output, and crime.

Extrapolation   Table 8.8 presents the tests of the sensitivity of the social net present value estimates to alternative extrapolation assumptions, for the entire sample and the four target groups. The first

TABLE 8.8
Benchmark Estimates of Social Net Present Value and
Changes from It under Alternative Extrapolation Assumptions
(1976 dollars)

	Target Group				All
	AFDC	Ex-addict	Ex-offender	Youth	Groups
Benchmark estimates	8150	4345	−3184	−1464	1543
Changes from the Benchmark Estimates under Alternative Assumptions					
Discount rate = 3%	+1582	+650	−155	−16	+472
Discount rate = 10%	−3511	−1189	+293	+31	−1009
Time horizon = 27 months	−8937	−4559	+960	+88	−2822
Time horizon = 36 months	−8322	−3864	+814	+75	−2575
Decay rate = 3%	0	+6433	−1385	−132	+869
Decay rate = 17%	−5396	0	0	0	−1327
Base = 19–27-month results	0	−4172	−1732	+1215	−1265
Base = 36-month cohort results	−	+5048	+11476	−2653	−

row repeats the social net present value estimates from tables 8.4 and 8.6 above. The remaining rows show the *change* in social net present value when an assumption is altered as indicated (holding all other assumptions constant).

For three of the four target groups and the overall results, the magnitudes of the social net present value estimates are quite sensitive to altering extrapolation assumptions, but the conclusions change only under the extreme assumptions. For the AFDC target groups, using a 10 percent real discount rate (instead of the benchmark's 5 percent) reduces net present value by $3,500, and using a 17 percent decay rate reduces it by $5,400, but it remains positive in both cases. For this group, benefits would have to decline extremely rapidly (that is, go to zero after 36 months) in order to reverse the conclusion that Supported Work is efficient (that is, to change the estimated sign of net present value from positive to negative). For ex-addicts, using a 3 percent decay rate or the 36-month cohort base more than doubles the numerical estimates, but only the extreme assumption of no benefits beyond 27 months alters the conclusion that social benefits exceed costs. For youths, the magnitudes are not substantially changed by alternative extrapolation assumptions, and net present value is negative under all assumptions.

For ex-offenders, however, the conclusion drawn from the analysis depends crucially on which results are used as the base for extrapolation. The results for months 28–36 for the small (n = 262) 36-month cohort were quite favorable—crime benefits exceeded $1,300 for the

9-month period alone. If the 28–36-month results are used as a base for extrapolation, social net present value changes from *negative* $3,200 to *positive* $8,300—a huge swing of $11,500. Given this uncertainty, it is worth examining the ex-offender crime results in more detail, in particular to see whether the large crime benefit in months 28–36 might have occurred by chance, and we will do so in a subsequent section.

Employment We have assumed that, except on Supported Work jobs, wages plus fringe benefits equal the marginal product of labor. This assumption implies that increased postprogram earnings represent the value of the additional output produced by participants after they leave the program, and that the opportunity cost of participant labor equals the earnings plus fringe benefits of the control group. Although standard in benefit-cost analysis, this assumption is a strong one, for it implies that Supported Work has no indirect labor market effects. Two such effects are possible, however, and they are important in interpreting the benefit-cost results.

One possibility is that Supported Work participants displace regular workers. In the extreme, Supported Work might simply shuffle workers among a fixed number of jobs—with no net increase in output. The Supported Work participants would have higher incomes, but at the expense of nonparticipants who are displaced. The measured benefit-cost results would consequently show both postprogram earnings gains and value of in-program output in excess of opportunity cost, but they would overstate Supported Work's net present value from an economy-wide perspective because the estimates ignore the loss of income and output of displaced workers. As indicated by the heated political debate and the volume of professional literature on the subject,[46] displacement is a key issue in assessing employment programs.

The possibility at the other extreme is that Supported Work participants are placed in markets where there is an excess demand for labor, but are drawn from markets with an excess supply of labor so that the opportunity cost of participant labor is zero. In this case there would be no displacement effect. Moreover, withdrawing a worker from a market with an excess supply of labor will not affect employment or output in that market—even if the particular withdrawn worker had been employed, he or she would be immediately replaced by an unemployed worker. From the perspective of the market as a whole, the opportunity cost of the withdrawn worker is zero—despite positive *average* earnings in that market.[47] This would imply that net present value is understated in the estimates presented above.

That employment and training programs may have indirect effects on the employment of other workers seems clear. What is not clear is how the effect could be measured for a small program like Supported Work,[48] and how it should be treated in benefit-cost analysis.[49] Previous benefit-cost analyses have approached indirect labor market effects differently.[50] Most previous studies, however, have assumed that wages measure the social value of output produced—either explicitly or implicitly assuming that there is neither displacement nor free labor.[51]

We have adopted this conventional assumption for two reasons. First, we have no basis for estimating indirect labor market effects or even knowing their direction. Second, indirect labor market effects depend ultimately on macroeconomic policy. The conventional assumption can be viewed as providing estimates of Supported Work's potential increase in output—provided aggregate demand is manipulated to take advantage of it. For example, Supported Work might increase the productivity of its participants, but if there were no increase in aggregate demand, there would be no corresponding increase in output in the economy as a whole. In this case, the no-displacement assumption could be viewed as providing estimates of the increase in potential output due to Supported Work. On the other hand, if participants' wages are increased for reasons not related to increased productivity or improved information, such as hiring on the basis of special relationships with employers or of credentials that are not related to productivity on the job, then ignoring displacement would overestimate Supported Work's contribution to both potential and actual output for the economy as a whole.

While we believe the conventional assumption is a reasonable one, it is clearly debatable and merits the sensitivity tests shown in table 8.9. Assuming that the opportunity cost of participants while they are enrolled in Supported Work is zero increases social net present value estimates by a relatively small amount—not surprising since forgone earnings are low, and the length of stay in Supported Work is relatively short. Although it has not been made in any empirical studies we are aware of,[52] the argument that control group earnings overstate opportunity costs could apply to the postprogram period as well. When the zero opportunity cost assumption is made for the postprogram period, net present value increases by between $18,000 and $22,000. This enormous increase is not surprising since even modest postprogram earnings of experimentals are a huge benefit when extrapolated far into the future under an assumption of no postprogram output in the absence of Supported Work. A program's efficiency is guaranteed if it

TABLE 8.9
Benchmark Estimates of Social Net Present Value and Changes
from It under Alternative Employment Assumptions
(1976 dollars)

	Target Group				All Groups
	AFDC	Ex-addict	Ex-offender	Youth	
Benchmark estimates	8150	4345	−3184	−1464	1543
Changes from the Benchmark Estimates under Alternative Assumptions					
Opportunity cost = 0					
In-program	+879	+1219	+1100	+974	+1047
Postprogram	+22111	+18957	+19611	+18490	+19872
Total	+22990	+20176	+20711	+19464	+20919
100% displacement					
In-program	−796	−26	−1	−283	−256
Postprogram	−9193	−819	−642	−29	−2666
Total	−9989	−845	−643	−312	−2922
50% displacement					
In-program	−398	−13	−1	−142	−127
Postprogram	−4597	−410	−321	−14	−1333
Total	−4996	−423	−322	−156	−1461

can induce lifelong shifts of workers from surplus to shortage labor markets.

If, on the other hand, Supported Work simply shuffles workers among jobs, increased postprogram output is zero, and benefits fall well short of costs for the program as a whole and for the AFDC target group; results for the other target groups are affected only slightly by assuming 100 percent postprogram displacement. During-program displacement would have relatively little impact on net present value because, as we have noted, value of output net of project cost is only slightly above the opportunity cost of labor.

Generally speaking, then, indirect labor market effects are an important issue in the evaluation of Supported Work only for the AFDC target group during the postprogram period. As has been indicated, applying the extreme alternative assumptions to the in-program period has relatively little impact on the overall net present value estimates (although they are large when one looks at months 1–27 by themselves). For ex-addicts, ex-offenders, and youths during the postprogram period, it is hard to accept the view that Supported Work shifted participants from surplus to shortage labor markets when there is little indication of increased postprogram employment or earnings gains. For the AFDC group during the postprogram period, the case is far from certain, but it is unlikely that all of the postprogram gains are offset by indirect effects arising from displacement. As Masters points out (1981), some of the increased postprogram earnings were the result of higher average wage rates, suggesting that there may have been some shift to higher wage labor markets. In any case, a displacement rate of more than 80 percent in both the in-program and post-program periods would be necessary for net present value to be negative. We conclude, therefore, that displacement is not likely to be of sufficient importance, by itself, to change the conclusion that social benefits exceed costs for AFDC.[53]

Value of Output   One problematic case of applying the resource cost approach to valuing benefits was in valuing in-program output at the alternative supplier's price for equivalent output. While the alternative supplier's price indicates the productivity of the Supported Work projects, it may not represent society's willingness to pay for the output. The traditional example of "make-work" where the alternative supplier's price and society's willingness to pay differ is the work crew that digs ditches only to fill them up again. While an alternative supplier would certainly charge to perform the same work, society would not ordinarily value this activity. As an estimate of the value of the output, however, the alternative supplier's price has important advantages. First, the alternative supplier's price is an easily defined concept that can be measured objectively. Second, the alternative supplier's price is arguably an upper bound on society's willingness to pay for the output—if willingness to pay exceeded the supply price, the output would have been purchased up to the point where they are equal.[54] Finally, an examination of the case studies of projects leads us to conclude that the benefit to society from the increased output was probably not far below the alternative supplier's price.[55]

Because the use of the alternative supply price as the estimate of value of output is nonetheless debatable, we test the sensitivity of the results to using what is probably a lower bound on the value of output: the revenue received by Supported Work for project output.[56] The assumption is simply that society must be willing to pay at least as much as customers actually paid for the output. Revenue averaged $2.51 per hour ($3,298 per year of service)—slightly over half the alternative supply price estimate. When revenue is substituted for the alternative supplier's price, social net present value is reduced by between $1,300 and $2,100 (depending on the average length of stay of the target group). This change is too small to change the conclusion that Supported Work is efficient for the AFDC and ex-addict target groups. The changes are large, however, if one looks only at the 1–27-

month observation period. For AFDC, for example, instead of depending on $800 in future benefits for net present value to be positive,
$2,800 is required. Thus, while the conclusion remains the same, it
depends more heavily on the existence of benefits beyond the measurement period.

Crime Reduced criminal activity turned out to be the most important benefit for the ex-addict target group, accounting for more than
80 percent of all social benefits (other than value of in-program output),
and was the basis for concluding that Supported Work is efficient for
that group. While we believe the benchmark estimates are reasonable,
valuing reduced criminal activity did require many assumptions that
are subject to debate.

Ideally, the value of crime reductions from the social perspective
should be measured by the amount society would be willing to pay to
bring those reductions about rather than by the resource cost savings
achieved. It might be argued that society's willingness to pay for crime
reductions is indicated by its expenditures on crime-reducing activities
alone, which suggests that there is no need to include estimates for
personal injury, property damage, or stolen property. While this implies that the benchmark estimates overestimate the social benefits of
reduced crime,[57] it is also possible to argue that the estimates underestimate benefits. First, the estimate for criminal justice system cost
savings includes only the estimated change in public costs because
private crime prevention activities have been ignored. Second, information is far from perfect—the technology of crime prevention, in
particular, is imperfectly understood. Finally, the social demand for
crime reduction may be expressed imperfectly through the political
system, a proposition supported by the level of public concern over
increases in crime.[58] Reduction in the psychological cost of crime may
be a substantial unmeasured benefit that may not be expressed through
expenditures on the criminal justice system, or even the estimates of
the value of property damage, personal injury, and stolen property.
Finally, some would argue that because it requires so many judgments,
no attempt should be made to value changes in criminal activity.
Rather, the change in criminal activity should be measured but not
valued—leaving it to users of the research to judge how much it is
worth.

Sensitivity tests in table 8.10 indicate what excluding all crime benefits, excluding half of all crime benefits, and including only criminal
justice system costs do to the results. For ex-addicts, estimates of changes
in net present value excluding all crime benefits show that society

TABLE 8.10
Benchmark Estimates of Social Net Present Value and Changes
from It under Alternative Crime Assumptions
(1976 dollars)

	Target Group		
	Ex-addict	Ex-offender	Youth
Benchmark estimates	4345	−3184	−1464
Changes from the Benchmark Estimates under Alternative Assumptions			
No crime benefits	−5177	+2874	+89
50% of crime benefits	−2589	+1437	+45
Justice system costs only	−1871	−87	+942

Note: Criminal activity was not measured for the AFDC target group.

would have to be willing to pay $800 per participant for the reduction in criminal activity if social benefits are to continue to exceed costs. If half of the estimated crime benefit is included, social benefits exceed costs by $1,800. Using reduced criminal justice system costs only as the crime estimate also leaves social net present value positive since they amount to about 60 percent of all measured social benefits from crime for ex-addicts. Estimated crime benefits for youths are sufficiently small that the results for them are insensitive to alternative assumptions. For ex-offenders, since crime "benefits" were estimated to be negative, excluding crime benefits *increases* net present value. If all crime benefits are excluded, remaining benefits still fall short of costs, but only by about $300. This reinforces our conclusion based on the extrapolation sensitivity tests that, although net present value is probably negative for ex-offenders, we are least confident in our conclusion for them.

Chance Sampling Variability

In contrast to analyses of specific program outcomes such as post-program earnings, benefit-cost analyses have not been concerned with the statistical confidence that can be placed in their results. Instead, they have used point estimates of program effects to compute benefits and costs without regard to possible sampling variability. The variance underlying the benefit-cost estimates could be quite high, especially when a large shadow price is multiplied by an outcome variable with a high variance. Ideally, estimates of benefits, costs, and net present value would be presented along with their statistical confidence intervals.

One difficulty in constructing confidence intervals is that the benefit and cost estimates are sums of products of outcomes and shadow prices. While the variances and covariances of the outcomes can be estimated, there is often no basis for estimating variances of shadow prices (to say nothing of their covariance with each other and the outcomes). It is nonetheless possible to assume that the shadow prices are fixed and compute the variance of the estimates of benefits and costs due to sampling variability in the outcome measures alone.

Because assessing the variance of all benefits and costs would be a major undertaking, attention will be focused on the sampling variability of crime benefits, which the preceding sensitivity tests showed are important to both the ex-addict and ex-offender results. Moreover, some of the categories of crimes have very high costs per arrest, so that estimates of crime benefits have high variances.

Table 8.11 presents the estimates of crime benefits and their 95 percent confidence intervals for each 9-month interview period and for each target group. The confidence intervals range between $680 and $1,065 on either side of the point estimate until months 28–36 when they increase because of the smaller samples. It may be noted that the estimates for ex-addicts are significantly different from zero at the 90 percent level in all periods except the 19–27-month period. This, combined with the fact that the benefits are positive in all periods, strengthens our confidence that Supported Work did produce a substantial crime benefit for this group. For youths, the point estimates and confidence intervals strongly support the conclusion that there are no crime benefits for Supported Work's youths.

For ex-offenders, however, the interpretation is more complicated. The crime benefit is negative in the first three periods, although a positive benefit is well within the statistical confidence interval. But in months 28–36, as noted above, the crime benefit appears to turn sharply positive. However, evidence suggests that this apparent reversal in crime benefits results from chance sampling variability, or from a change in the composition in the research sample rather than a delay in Supported Work's effect on crime. Recall that the evalua-

TABLE 8.11
Social Benefits of Reduced Crime, with 95 Percent Statistical
Confidence Intervals, by Target Group and Time Period
(1976 dollars)

Target Group	Months 1–9	Months 10–18	Months 19–27	Months 28–36
Ex-addict	777 ± 854	865 ± 762	73 ± 681	832 ± 983
Ex-offender	−267 ± 915	−121 ± 722	−715 ± 1064	1345 ± 1329
Youth	59 ± 924	−112 ± 845	165 ± 970	−169 ± 2117

TABLE 8.12

Social Crime Benefits, with 95 Percent Statistical Confidence
Intervals for Ex-offenders, by Cohort and Time Period
(1976 dollars)

Cohort	Sample Size[a]	Months 1–9	Months 10–18	Months 19–27	Months 28–36
18-month	636	−211 ± 1428	−523 ± 1115	—	—
27-month	742	−719 ± 1165	272 ± 1065	−932 ± 1353	—
36-month	292	1835 ± 3100	883 ± 1901	−23 ± 1480	1345 ± 1329

a The sample size is the maximum number of observations in the cohort; actual sample
sizes varied slightly from period to period because of missing data.

tion's differential follow-up implies that sample composition changes
over time.[59] Table 8.12 presents the ex-offender crime benefit estimates
for different cohorts defined by length of follow-up. The experimental-
control differences for each cohort vary considerably in sign and magnitude from period to period. This fluctuation and the wide statistical
confidence intervals suggest that much of the variation over time is
random. There does appear, however, to be a systematic difference
between the 36-month cohort and the others—for this cohort there are
substantial crime benefits in three out of four time periods. Whether
this too is the result of random effects is difficult to determine. We
can say, however, that the upturn in crime benefits shown in table
8.11 is highly uncertain and provides a poor base for extrapolation.

This examination of the confidence intervals around the crime benefits increases our confidence that the observed crime benefits for ex-
addicts are real and not the result of chance sampling variability, although the true benefit may differ in magnitude from the benchmark
point estimate. It does nothing to resolve the uncertainty about the
results for ex-offenders. The examination does, however, emphasize
the uncertainty surrounding the estimates of crime benefits and indicates that they should be used as indicators of the existence and
nature of crime benefits rather than as precise estimates of their magnitude.

Unmeasured Benefits and Costs

A number of potentially important benefits and costs have not been
quantified in the estimates presented above. In this section we indicate
what they are and assess the direction of the bias arising from their
omission.

Preferences for Work To have the unemployed working instead of
receiving welfare, many in society might be willing to pay more than

the value of output these new workers would produce. Political "work-fare" rhetoric and the existence of subsidized employment programs for disadvantaged workers provide some evidence of the societal demand for employment opportunities for disadvantaged workers. Because Supported Work was successful during the in-program period at putting all target groups to work and reducing welfare payments, omitting society's preference for work biases downward net present value estimates from the social and nonparticipant perspectives. To the extent that participants prefer work to leisure or nonmarket activities such as child care, a downward bias of estimates also may be present for the participant perspective.[60] The bias is largest for the AFDC group because of the postprogram increase in employment.

Redistribution of Income   Society's taste for income redistribution is clearly evident in the existence of welfare programs and progressive income tax laws. Whether society desires additional redistribution of the type brought about by Supported Work is an open question, but it seems likely that this would be viewed as a benefit (apart from the other program effects) by many members of society. Omitting this benefit, therefore, leads to an underestimate of net present value.[61] Since the amount redistributed was modest, however, the magnitude of this benefit is probably relatively small.

Reduced Family Disruptions   Poverty and its related ill effects are also disruptive to members of the immediate families of participants. To the extent that Supported Work increases employment and income, therefore, the benefits to immediate family members arising from any resulting increase in family stability may be substantial, however unquantifiable they may be.

Improved Health Status   Although information on participant health status was not collected, data on the number of doctor and hospital visits were collected and analyzed as part of the outcome analyses. For ex-addicts, ex-offenders, and youths, there was no evidence of a reduction in such visits, but for the AFDC participants there was some evidence of a reduction in doctor visits. This could have arisen because their health improved or because, having lost their Medicaid cards and having less free time due to increased employment, they were not as quick to go to the doctor. It is thus impossible to determine whether health status of this group was actually improved by Supported Work.[62]

Reduced Drug Use   We have included the reduced drug treatment cost as a resource saving (it turned out to be small), but we have not measured possible psychological benefits of reduced drug use. Recent survey data indicate that almost 60 percent of the population feels that in their own communities drug and alcohol abuse by young people is a serious problem (U.S. Department of Justice 1978, 277). Moreover, participants themselves may be happier if they are less dependent on drugs. The only evidence of reduced drug use, however, was for the ex-offender target group, so this unmeasured benefit must be weighed with the other uncertainties concerning the ex-offender results.

Forgone Nonmarket Production By limiting our measure of the cost of participant labor to the forgone output for *paid* work, the analysis ignores nonmarket production and increased work-related expenses. Forgone home production—especially child care—is a potentially important cost. To a large extent, the changes in the resource costs of child care are captured in the analysis, but there is no way of knowing whether children would be better off if cared for by their own mothers rather than by formal or informal child-care providers. However, given that eligibility requirements for participation of AFDC women in Supported Work ensure that children are of school age, such child-care issues are of less importance for this demonstration than they might be for programs for parents of younger children. Other work-related expenses, which include increased transportation, clothing, and meal costs, are also unmeasured costs to participants and to society, but they are probably relatively small.

In summary, the preceding discussion suggests that unmeasured costs are probably small relative to unmeasured benefits. Including unmeasured effects, therefore, would strengthen the conclusion based on measured benefits and costs that Supported Work is an efficient employment program for the AFDC and ex-addict target groups. Consideration of unmeasured effects adds to the uncertainty concerning Supported Work's efficiency for ex-offenders. For youths, the assessment depends entirely on the unmeasured benefits being sufficiently large to outweigh the costs.

Conclusion

The preceding analysis has gone to some length to present the methodology, test the sensitivity of results to important assumptions, and assess the magnitude of unmeasured benefits and costs so that the analysis would not convey a false sense of precision or finality. Our intention was not to arrive mechanically at an estimate of net present value that dictates an investment decision, but rather to identify what issues and program effects are important to consider, to provide a basis for weighing the relative importance of these effects, and to indicate where the greatest uncertainties lie. Thus, for example, identifying what assumptions are most critical to the results may well provide more insight than assigning a value to a given benefit or cost. Full use of the analysis, therefore, requires recognition of the sensitivity of the results of key assumptions, the relative roles of various benefit and cost components, and the potential importance of unmeasured effects.

Summary of the Results

The benefit-cost results indicate that, on average, Supported Work has been an efficient public investment. Measured benefits exceed costs from the perspective of society as a whole and of program participants. For nonparticipants, who bear the taxes required to fund the program, benefits fall slightly short of costs.[63]

The disaggregations of the overall results presented in the previous section, however, suggest that Supported Work has been more effective for some groups, and in some sites, than others. In particular, benefits appear to exceed costs—from the perspective of society as a whole and nonparticipants—for two target groups: AFDC recipients and ex-addicts. For the AFDC target group, this results largely from increased post-program earnings, while the reduced criminal activity of ex-addicts dominates the results for that group. When extrapolated future benefits are included, the overall results are positive for these two target groups, and sensitivity tests show that only a substantial altering of the bench-mark assumptions would change the results from positive to negative.

In contrast to the positive results for AFDC women and ex-addicts, the measured benefits fall well short of costs from the social and non-participant perspectives for the youth target group during the first 27 months after enrollment, and virtually no benefits were observed for youths in the postprogram period. For them, a decision to invest in Supported Work must depend on unmeasured benefits such as the desire to put youths to work for its own sake or to redistribute income to them.

The results for ex-offenders are ambiguous. The net present value for the first 27 months after enrollment is negative, and the estimate of future benefits varies considerably depending on the assumptions made in extrapolating observed program effects. While the evidence is inadequate to draw a firm conclusion, our own judgment is that measured benefits fall short of costs, and that for the overall ex-offender results to be positive, there must be substantial unmeasured benefits.

When the data are disaggregated by site, samples become too small to draw inferences with confidence. Nonetheless, the variation in social net present value is large enough to suggest that some differences in the effectiveness of Supported Work sites probably exist. Sites that performed well had (1) low net costs, resulting from greater use of relatively inexpensive but productive work projects where participants are placed in outside agencies and from lower overhead costs, and (2) substantial postprogram earnings gains. There is no evidence that large investments during the program result in higher benefits; to the contrary, higher net cost tends to be associated with lower program benefits. While there is some correlation between site and target group, differences in target groups served do not appear to explain fully site differences, and differences in site effectiveness do not seem to explain fully target group differences.

In addition to the analysis of benefits and costs to society as a whole and to nonparticipants, an assessment of the benefits and costs from the perspective of participants is also important, especially because Supported Work has intended distributional effects. The analysis indicated that the demonstration redistributed a modest amount of income to all groups served.[64]

Implications for Future Research

This analysis has suggested several ways in which the application of benefit-cost methodology to social programs can be improved. In particular, two features of this analysis were identified at the outset of the chapter as departures from the approaches used in most previous evaluations of this kind: the use of a comprehensive accounting framework and the inclusion of more types of benefits and costs than usual, valued according to a resource cost principle. These general techniques could easily be used in other evaluations of social programs.

A consistent accounting framework is essential to any benefit-cost analysis. In most benefit-cost evaluations of social programs, important distributional effects of programs are assessed separately from the accounting of social benefits and costs (if such effects are considered at all). A single accounting framework integrating both efficiency and distributional effects has several advantages. It allows both analysts and users of the research to identify at a glance not only a large number of individual benefits and costs, but also the distributional effects of the program. Equally important, it provides a convenient means for them to weigh the relative importance of various program evaluation issues and to assess interrelated program effects such as those of income, taxes, and public transfers. Above all, it assures that distributional issues are given as much attention—and are analyzed as rigorously in the evaluation itself—as economic efficiency issues.

The results of this analysis also indicate how important it is that social program evaluations look beyond traditional program outcome measures: changes in postprogram earnings and transfer program use. For example, the results for Supported Work ex-addicts indicate the need to include the value of crime-related benefits. Because of the high cost of crime, even small changes in criminal activity can generate benefits that may outweigh those from increased earnings.[65] The Supported Work results also show the importance of valuing in-program output. Net program costs would have been badly overstated if such an effort had not been made. In the evaluation, these (and the other benefits and costs) have been valued on the basis of the cost of supplying the resources used or saved and the output produced as a result of the demonstration. This approach has its limitations, particularly that it does not estimate social willingness to pay for program outcomes. However, the approach can be justified for social programs that have only marginal effects on the economy and, importantly, it allows potentially important benefits and costs to be valued in a known way and included directly in the analysis.

The sensitivity of the net present value estimates for all target groups to assumptions made in extrapolating benefits and costs into the future, and the uncertainty concerning whether the results for ex-offenders are positive or negative underscore the need for long-term follow-up data on a sample of substantial size. Whatever the research design and however large the sample, however, some uncertainty is unavoidable because evaluation follow-up must be ended at some point and because policymakers need analyses as soon as possible. While we have tried to make reasonable assumptions in making the benchmark extrapolation and have tested the sensitivity of the results to those assumptions, careful research on the methodology for estimating decay rates is clearly called for, not only for earnings but for other effects as well.[66]

This analysis, like all benefit-cost analyses we are aware of, is based on point estimates of benefits and costs without regard to variance of those estimates. As the analysis of the variance of crime benefits illustrates, examination of the statistical confidence intervals can be of help in assessing the credibility of estimates of benefits and costs. Greater emphasis in benefit-cost analyses on statistical confidence intervals not only for specific benefits and costs, but also for overall net present value, would, along with continued use of sensitivity tests, strengthen benefit-cost methodology and make assessments of the confidence that can be placed in its results far easier to make.

Finally, perhaps the greatest shortcoming of this and other benefit-cost analyses is their inability to identify the determinants of benefits and costs. The disaggregations presented above showed large variation in results across both target groups and sites. While we have attempted to offer some plausible reasons for the differences, we have been unable to draw any conclusions with confidence. Future evaluations should be designed to analyze the determinants of benefits and costs to provide national policymakers and local program operators guidance so that they can modify or eliminate unsuccessful program models and expand successful ones.

Appendix: Implications of Recent AFDC Results for the Benefit-Cost Analysis

An important aspect of the benefit-cost analysis of Supported Work was the estimation of future benefits and costs based on evidence from the last months of the observation period. For the AFDC target group, the future benefits of increased earnings and reduced transfer payments were extremely important to the overall findings. Extrapolating the earnings results for months 19–27 after enrollment—using an annual decay rate of 3 percent and an annual real discount rate of 5 percent—the extrapolated future earnings increase (that is, the increase after the observation period) was estimated to be about $8,200. The same extrapolation procedure yielded an estimate of more than $9,200 for the future benefit of reduced transfers. As a result, the net present value of the program for AFDC recipients was very high from the perspectives of both society and nonparticipants. However, the estimated loss of transfer income to participants was sufficiently large to cause net present value from their perspective to be negative—a result we attributed to a temporarily large welfare reduction during months 19–27.

Since the completion of the benefit-cost analysis, additional follow-up interviews were administered to the AFDC group, the results of which are reported in Masters (1981). It is not possible to update the benefit-cost analysis with these new data. Differences in this follow-up from the earlier data collection do not permit program effects to be estimated in the same way.[67] However, it is possible to estimate the key future benefits of increased earnings and reduced transfers using the additional follow-up data and then compare these estimates to the benchmark estimates in the benefit-cost analysis.

Masters reports an earnings increase of $511 over the nine months that, more or less, follow the 27 months of observation used in our analysis.[68] Using the same extrapolation procedure as before (that is, a 3 percent decay rate, a 5 percent discount rate, and 27-year time horizon, and all figures expressed in 1976 dollars), this implies an estimate of about $7,800 in increased future earnings. This is slightly less than our benchmark estimate of $8,200.

On the other hand, Masters's results for earnings show little decay over time. Nominally, earnings increased during the time covered by the additional follow-up and, adjusting for inflation, declined by less than 1 percent in real terms.[69] This is consistent with earnings differences observed between months 19 and 27 and suggests that the assumption of a 3 percent decay rate may be too high. For comparison, if an assumption of zero decay is used, the estimate of future earnings is roughly $10,200, which is substantially higher than the benchmark estimate.

The additional follow-up data enable us to estimate the future public transfer reductions. Using these estimates[70] and the benchmark extrapolation procedures, we estimate that the future reduction in transfer payments for AFDC, food stamps, and unemployment insurance is about $3,400. Additional findings by Masters suggest that the value of the reduction in other categories of transfers probably exceeds $1,000. This raises the estimate of future transfer payment reductions into the general vicinity of $4,500, half our benchmark estimate, which is about $9,000.

These rough figures do not affect our conclusions regarding the desirability of Supported Work for the AFDC target group from the perspective of both nonparticipants and society as a whole. The figures do suggest that the net present value estimate should be somewhat lower for nonparticipants, and perhaps for society, but the value remains highly positive nevertheless. However, these additional follow-up data do imply two changes in the results. First, they indicate that net present value for AFDC participants is positive. This is consistent with our view that the reduction in transfer payments was overestimated using the more limited follow-up data because of lags in the effects of earnings on welfare. Second, these changes in AFDC results also affect the findings for the program *as a whole* for the nonparticipant perspective, which indicated that nonparticipant benefits were approximately equal to costs. If the estimate of future reductions in transfer payments to AFDC recipients if $4,500 instead of the original estimate of $9,000, then nonparticipant benefits for the entire program fall short of costs by about $1,000 per participant. Participant net present value, already positive for the program as a whole based on the earlier data, would be increased correspondingly.

Notes

1 These studies are discussed by Barsby (1972), Hardin and Borus (1972), Schiller (1978), Somers and Wood (1969), and Stromsdorfer (1972). The work of Friedman (1977), who reported the findings of a benefit-cost analysis of a pilot Supported Work program in New York City run by the Vera Institute of Justice, was especially important to this evaluation.

2 Hardin and Borus (1972), Friedman (1977), and Mallar and Thornton (1978) also addressed both issues, though they include fewer components in their analyses.

3 Net present value is not the only benefit-cost criterion for judging the desirability of a program that has been evaluated. For an explanation of the net present value criterion and alternative decision criteria—internal rate of return and benefit-cost ratios—see Dasgupta and Pearce (1972, chap. 7).

4 Although customary, social net present value is an efficiency criterion only in the restricted sense of the Kaldor-Hicks extension of the Pareto criterion. If social net present value is positive, then it would be *possible* to make some people better off without making anyone worse off, *provided* the correct set of redistributions was made. The Kaldor-Hicks criterion does not require that the redistributions actually be made, and some people are undoubtedly worse off even though social net present value is positive. See Dasgupta and Pearce (1972, chap. 2) and Rothenberg (1975) for discussions of the alternative efficiency criteria and the controversy surrounding them.

5 It should be noted, however, that many participants are taxpayers. Indeed, one effect of the program is to increase tax payments of participants.

6 There are well-known theoretical difficulties, however, in using this perspective alone to judge the effectiveness of the program as a government investment; see Smith (1975).

7 This constraint also implicitly assumes that a dollar in the hands of participants is of equal social value to a dollar in the hands of nonparticipants. The analysis treats the social benefits of income redistribution as an unmeasured benefit—recognizing that nonparticipants probably believe that participants' marginal utility of income is higher than their own.

8 Since the analyses in chapters 4–7 report differences in regression-adjusted means, some of the estimates in this chapter will differ slightly from those of previous chapters.

9 As indicted in previous chapters, the 27-month sample consisted of approximately 3,025 individuals divided approximately evenly between experimentals and controls. A larger sample (4,665 individuals) was available and used for estimates for the first 18 months after assignment.

10 For further discussion of the theory of benefit-cost valuation, see Dasgupta and Pearce (1972, 44–50); Dasgupta et al. (1972, 42–46); and Sassone and Schaffer (1978, chap. 5). The use of a cost-saving approach to shadow pricing in benefit-cost studies of transportation and energy projects, which is similar to that used here, is discussed by Margolis (1970, 314–29).

11 As it turned out, participation of the control group in alternative employment and training programs was relatively limited.

12 Kemper and Long (1981) contains a detailed examination of these issues.

13 As discussed in Kemper and Long (1981), the amount of the Supported
Work budget that was incurred by government sources was about $10,700
because about $3,300 of the revenue from the sale of goods and services
produced on Supported Work projects offset part of this $14,000. See also
the fourth section of this chapter.

14 In public employment and training programs, these functions are normally
performed by the federal government; in the case of Supported Work they
were performed by MDRC, which was responsible for running the demonstration. The central administrative cost estimate excludes costs associated with carrying out the demonstration and the research that would
not be incurred by an ongoing federal program; see Kemper and Long
(1981) for details.

15 This figure should not be compared to an annual salary because (1) it
includes fringe benefits, and (2) participants' paid time averaged only 80.9
percent of enrollment time (years of service) because of inactivations, sus-
pensions, and other unpaid absences.

16 The averages reported in table 8.1 are lower because they include zeros for
the other three target groups.

17 The methodology used here was based on that developed by Friedman
(1977) and is fully documented in Kemper and Long (1981); for a discussion of the theoretical framework, see also Kemper and Moss (1978).

18 It also provides a direct measure of demand price—that is, willingness to
pay for the output.

19 Because the alternative supply price in many cases includes alternative
supplier management and overhead costs (appropriately for benefit-cost
purposes), this number is an overestimate of value of the additional output
attributable to participant labor.

20 It is interesting to note in this regard that the $1.69 per hour converts to
$2,221 per year, which is slightly higher than the $1,867 opportunity cost
of participant labor.

21 This estimate of postprogram earnings gains is an approximation. Because
individuals stayed in Supported Work different lengths of time, average
control group earnings had to be arbitrarily divided between the in-program
and postprogram periods. This division was made in proportion to the
average months enrolled during each 3-month period.

22 Taxes were adjusted for credits; of particular importance for this group is
the earned income tax credit.

23 An "other welfare" category was also included. It contained cash transfers
from miscellaneous small programs and those cases where the interview
respondents did not specify from which program these payments came.

24 Thornton and Long (1980) describe the estimation procedures in more
detail than can be provided here. Similar procedures were used by Thorn-

ton et al. (1979) to measure the crime-reduction benefit of the Job Corps program.

25 Members of the AFDC target group were not asked about their criminal behavior since such activity was believed to be relatively infrequent for that group (so program effects would have been undetectable). We have assumed that crime benefits were zero for this group.

26 This estimate is based on a study by Schore et al. (1979) of interview and official records data for a sample of 581 experimentals and controls.

27 Wesley G. Skogan provided us with access to these data. The personal injury and property damage costs include those associated with repair or replacement of damaged property, medical costs, lost time from work, and administrative costs for insurance.

28 This, of course, is a simplification because participants quite possibly could have been the victims of other participants in the absence of Supported Work, and they do pay taxes that support the criminal justice system.

29 In addition, differences in registrations with the U.S. Employment Service were valued by multiplying the estimated difference in mean number of registrations by the average cost of a registration.

30 One way to avoid these biases in a short-run evaluation might be to incorporate estimates of the returns to investments in human capital. This method was not adopted primarily because the inclusion of these estimates would lead to double counting of some earnings gains (the effects of alternative programs could not be eliminated from the direct measures of earnings).

31 The actual formula is somewhat more complicated, to account for discounting from the time of the base period to the initial observation period. See Thornton and Long (1980) for details.

32 The AFDC group was followed for only 27 months, so the 19–27-month results were used as the base.

33 If capital markets worked perfectly, the marginal rate of transformation of present goods into future goods of producers would be equated to marginal rate of substitution of consumers. This one rate would then be the appropriate discount rate for all government projects. In fact, for a variety of reasons, these rates are not equal, and the correct rate for a particular project will depend on the magnitudes of both rates, tax rates, capital market conditions, the method used to finance the project, how that method affects investment, and how the program itself affects capital formation (Bradford 1975; Mendelsohn 1981). Attempts to measure the correct discount rate are confounded by these problems. Typically, estimates of real rates of 3–6 percent per year are based primarily on estimates of the marginal rates of substitution in consumption, while real rates of 8–15 percent are based primarily on estimates of marginal rates of transformation in production. The federal government has adopted 10 percent annual real rate as its standard (Office of Management and Budget 1972). Previous studies of employment and training programs have used rates ranging from 0 to 12 percent (Kemper et al. 1981). Given this unresolved—and probably

unresolvable—controversy, this study uses a real discount rate within this range (5 percent) for benchmark estimates, and presents sensitivity tests using 3 and 10 percent rates.

34 For a different approach to analyzing the determinants of outcomes, which uses individual data on program experience, see Hollister et al. (1979).

35 Child-care costs were estimated to be about $350 per participant, about $200 of which was born by nonparticipants.

36 As with costs, we assumed that value of output per year of service was the same for all groups. There is some suggestive evidence, however, that it may have been higher for the AFDC group. See the analysis of differences in value of output across projects in Kemper and Long (1981).

37 The Wisconsin site was excluded from this comparison because of its extremely small sample.

38 Project case studies were not done at New York; hence the average net cost per year of service was used there.

39 Long's (1980) analysis suggests that the primary determinant of overhead cost per year of participant service is the scale of the Supported Work site.

40 This analysis is reported in some detail in Kemper and Long (1981).

41 The analysis was unable to distinguish between the hypothesis that program-supervised projects run by the Supported Work program are inherently less productive and several competing explanations for this difference: (1) more productive participants are more likely to be assigned to jobs in outside agencies; (2) jobs in service occupations are inherently more productive for Supported Work participants; (3) unmeasured costs imposed on the outside agencies (for additional administration, management, and nonlabor imputs) distort the comparison beween program- and agency-supervised projects; and (4) the sites that emphasized agency-supervised projects differed in some way (for example, more productive participants or better management) than the other sites. Our own judgment is that all of these explanations probably contribute in some degree to the observed difference, but that there are probably some inherent advantages in agency-supervised jobs.

42 Oakland, which also had low estimated net cost, was an exception, having high value of output on painting projects supervised by Supported Work staff.

43 Analysis using individual data to analyze the relation between the post-program earnings of participants and whether they worked in program-supervised or agency-supervised jobs while they were enrolled in Supported Work showed that, if anything, earnings were higher for participants in agency-supervised jobs. Thus, the type of projects associated with higher value of in-program output may also be associated with larger postprogram earnings gains. While there is limited available evidence, one possible mechanism explaining this association is the possibility of a transition upon graduation from Supported Work to a regular position within the agency.

44 Another possible explanation is differences in labor market conditions across sites. Unfortunately we were not able to test this hypothesis adequately

because of difficulties in developing a satisfactory measure of aggregate labor market conditions facing those in our sample.

45 Examination of experimental-control differentials in hours worked during the months 19–27 shows only two statistically significant differences at the site level of aggregation—a large positive effect for AFDC and a large negative effect for ex-offenders at Newark. Nonetheless, for AFDC, hours worked increased at five or six sites; results for the other target groups were mixed, with some sites positive and others negative. Interestingly, no site was successful in increasing the hours worked of both AFDC women and the other, predominantly male, target groups it served. Although samples at this level of disaggregation are too small to draw firm conclusions, this suggests that site differences may be less important than target group differences in explaining increases in postprogram earnings.

46 Representative of this literature are articles by Bassi and Fechter (1979), Nathan et al. (1978), Johnson and Tomola (1977), Wiseman (1976), and Ashenfelter and Ehrenberg (1975). For two useful reviews, see Borus and Hamermesh (1978) and Fechter (1975).

47 Of course, if Supported Work simply placed the participant back in the same market, then the case of displacement described above applies. In order for the zero opportunity cost case to differ from the displacement case, Supported Work must shift participants from surplus labor markets to shortage markets where they will expand output rather than displace employed workers.

48 For a large program (relative to the labor market), such effects might be large enough to measure. The Employment Opportunity Pilot Projects were intended, in part, to estimate such effects.

49 For discussions of the treatment of indirect labor market effects in the evaluation of employment and training programs, see Johnson (1979) and Kemper (1980).

50 Borus (1964) assumed that the opportunity cost of participant labor while enrolled in MDTA training was zero, making the argument that participants could easily be replaced on the unskilled jobs they left, and Borus et al. (1970) used a zero opportunity cost in one of their alternative estimates. Haveman (1978) assumed that the output produced by the Dutch sheltered workshops he evaluated displaced a maximum of 30 percent of the regular workers who would have produced the output and constructed an estimate of this cost to society.

51 Representative of such studies are Cain (1967), Cain and Stromsdorfer (1968), Stromsdorfer (1968), Sewell (1971), Hardin and Borus (1972), Friedman (1977), and Thornton et al. (1980).

52 Johnson (1979) does raise this as a theoretical issue.

53 We also tested the sensitivity results to the assumptions that wages exceeded the value of output produced for those employed in jobs subsidized by CETA or WIN. Making such an assumption had little effect on our results, since there was little experimental effect for any target group on jobs respondents reported to be CETA/WIN positions.

54 The assumptions required for the supply price to exceed society's willingness to pay—most notably the assumed rationality of the political process
   in the transmission of society's demand—may not hold. See Kemper and
   Moss (1978) and Kemper and Long (1981) for a discussion of these issues.

55 This conclusion is based on a number of assumptions, the most important
   of which is the assumption just discussed that there was no displacement.

56 While part of the funding for the sites came from the Manpower Demonstration Research Corporation, each site was required to raise a substantial portion of its funding from local sources. In several cases this was
   done by selling goods and services produced by Supported Work projects.
   In these cases, the revenue is a lower bound for the value society places
   on in-program output per se as long as purchases are not made for char-
   itable reasons.

57 The crime benefit estimates would also be too high if long-run average
   costs exceed long-run marginal costs, since average costs were used to
   estimate shadow prices.

58 Data gathered as part of the national crime survey indicated that approximately 50 percent of the people have "changed or limited their activities
   in the past few years because of crime" (U.S. Department of Justice 1978,
   215).

59 See chapters 3–7 for a discussion of this feature of the evaluation. Essentially, the early enrollees were followed for the longest period of time, and
   it appears that they systematically differed from the later enrollees.

60 To the extent that participants value leisure highly, the bias could be in
   the opposite direction. Participants' increase in income overestimates their
   increased well-being because it ignores this foregone leisure. A growing
   body of literature suggests, however, that the poor do want to work (see,
   for example, Goodwin 1972). Moreover, the demonstrated willingness of
   AFDC women to go to work in the face of rather large disincentives in
   lost welfare benefits and increased taxes is rather strong evidence of their
   own preference for work over welfare, which is supported by the interviews
   with selected participants reported by Danziger (1981). While we believe
   that participants do not value foregone leisure highly, it can be argued that
   we have not measured a participant and social cost. In the extreme, work
   could be viewed as punitive for welfare recipients and so participants are
   made worse off by Supported Work.

61 As noted above, although they have not been valued, the redistributive
   effects have been measured through the use of participant and nonparticipant perspectives in the analysis. For further discussion of the relationship between the efficiency and distribution effects of public programs, see
   Weisbrod (1968).

62 One unmeasured cost of Supported Work was an increase in job-related
   doctor and hospital visits. While those visits covered by Medicaid are
   included as a cost to nonparticipants and a benefit to participants, a full
   accounting of the social benefits and costs of changes in doctor and hospital
   visits is beyond the scope of analysis.

63 The results based on the original data are that nonparticipant benefits are about equal to costs, but as discussed in the appendix to this chapter, further follow-up data for the AFDC target group analyzed by Masters suggest that nonparticipant benefits fall short of costs.

64 The data on which this study was based showed a large reduction in transfer payments which we believed overestimated the long-run reduction in transfer payments. Masters' more recent evidence supports this interpretation and suggests that for the AFDC target group, too, participant benefits exceed costs. (See the appendix to this chapter.)

65 The evaluation of Job Corps by Thornton et al. (1980) is another illustration of the potential importance of crime benefits for employment and training programs.

66 This issue is also addressed by Masters (1981).

67 The additional follow-up interview was administered at one point in time—September to November 1979. Thus, unlike the original interview data, this covers different periods of time since enrollment, depending on the participant. In addition, there are differences between the sample for the additional follow-up interview and that for earlier interviews.

68 See Masters (1981, Table B-2) on the effects for the AFDC group. The results reported in this table are experimental-control differences similar to those used for the benefit-cost analysis. The results are very similar to those discussed in detail by Masters.

69 This computation was made using data from Masters (1981, Table B-2) correcting for inflation with the GNP price deflator. In the text of his paper, Masters assumes that the experimental effect on earnings declines to zero at Atlanta but remains constant in real terms at the other sites. This approach yields an estimate of total discounted earnings gains intermediate between the two presented in this appendix.

70 See Masters (1981, Table B-3).

9 *Judith Gueron*

Lessons from Managing
the Supported Work Demonstration

The Supported Work program was implemented with a number of explicit and implicit objectives: as a demonstration to examine the feasibility of replicating the program model under different conditions; as a social experiment to test the utility of that model; as a demonstration of the feasibility of using an experimental design to study an employment program; and as a demonstration of a new technique for the management and oversight of large-scale, private and publicly funded research efforts.

This chapter describes how the newly created oversight agency—the Manpower Demonstration Research Corporation (MDRC)—approached meeting the first three objectives. An understanding of MDRC's activities and philosophy is important to a determination of the replicability of the project's results. MDRC's operational experience also provides lessons relevant to the fourth objective: the organization of large-scale experiments and the oversight and management of categorical programs.

At an early stage in the planning, the MDRC board and the funders specified the following questions as the knowledge objectives of the Supported Work project:

1. How effective is Supported Work in increasing the long-term employment and earnings of participants and in reducing welfare dependency, criminal activities, or drug abuse?
2. What target populations benefit most from the program?

3. What does the program cost? To what extent does it produce valuable goods and services? How do the program's costs compare to its measurable benefits?
4. What local conditions, administrative auspices, and implementation strategies seem to be most conducive to success?
5. What characteristics of the program model have the greatest impact on participant performance and behavior?

These questions and the strategies developed to answer them reflect a dual conception of the endeavor as both a demonstration and an experiment. This was to dominate most of the decisions made in the demonstration and MDRC's direction in managing both the operations and research of the program.

On the one hand, the project set out to determine the feasibility of replicating a particular program model under different local circumstances; it thus sought to provide a real world test to uncover administrative, legal, or other obstacles to the program's successful implementation. On the other hand, it was also a social experiment in that the impact questions were to be answered using rigorous techniques and a controlled environment. In particular, for the first time on a large scale, an employment program would be tested using a control group obtained by random assignment.

Prior to Supported Work, a small number of large-scale social experiments had demonstrated that this method was feasible for evaluating individuals' responses to alternative test treatments. However, these earlier efforts—for example, the negative income tax, health insurance, and housing demand experiments—tested variations in economic incentives: treatments which could be exactly defined by a small number of parameters (guarantee levels, tax rates, coinsurance requirements, etc.), and tightly controlled and administered by the research contractors. With some exceptions, the experimenters delivered money or jiggled payment structures; they did not provide "services" or "programs."

The Supported Work experiment was distinctly different. In 15 different locations, it tested a multidimensional program model which included some features that were uniform across sites and others that were not capable of rigorous control (for example, leadership and supervision). Some were dependent on local conditions (such as the nature of in-program worksites and postprogram work opportunities), or so critical to management style and administration that their standardization might compromise the viability of program operations (the assignment of workers to worksites and detailed personnel policies).

Moreover, because of the complexity of the overall Supported Work treatment, there was a continued concern that overspecification during the experimental period might limit the relevance or generalizability of the findings to a postprogram real world.[1] Thus, in the Supported Work project, the feasibility of social experimentation was to be tested in a new way.

One result of the project's dual demonstration and experimental functions was a certain tension between the two. In order to ensure the integrity of an experiment that would pool data from up to 10 different sites, local programs had to share certain core characteristics. However, it was argued that, in order to operate effectively, "the local directors must be given adequate flexibility to develop their programs along lines suitable for the populations employed, the local conditions, and their personal styles and objectives."[2] Excessive control and specificity, while possible in a demonstration period, would not be replicable in the future. Thus, for reasons of realism, feasibility, and subsequent generalizability, the delivery of the Supported Work treatment was not put in the hands of researchers but of local Supported Work corporations.

The resulting large number of organizations involved in the demonstration and the complexity of Supported Work's design seemed to necessitate an independent decision-making body responsible for carrying out the multiple objectives and answering the research questions listed earlier. The tasks to be addressed covered several distinct major areas of activity: the development and implementation of the research design; the specifications of the program model and its adequate implementation to ensure a reasonable test of the program's effectiveness and replicability; the resolution of conflicts in achieving these two functions; and the overall conduct of the demonstration in a financially responsible and cost-effective manner. Furthermore, these responsibilities were to be carried out over a 5-year period, in the context of 15 separate Supported Work corporations, and on a scale that was, at that time, unprecedented in employment and training research. Finally, the funding consortium assembled for the national demonstration included a total of six federal agencies and a major private foundation, each with its separate interests and priorities.[3]

During the formative stages of the Supported Work project, an advisory committee was established to guide the participating funding agencies. Composed of individuals with knowledge and expertise in social policy and research in employment and welfare programs, the committee considered the appropriate administrative techniques for managing the project, taking into consideration the lessons from prior demonstration efforts.[4] In the past, the results from large-scale research demonstrations of employment initiatives had proved disappointing for several reasons. It had been difficult to isolate projects from political pressures, to maintain within them a consistent focus and design, to discipline individual program operators, to control project costs, and to coordinate operational and evaluation priorities in the context of the project's overall knowledge development objectives.[5] The result was little in the way of hard findings, reflecting the design breakdowns which characterized these evaluations.

To avoid these pitfalls and their probable exacerbation in an environment of multiple funders and reporting requirements, the committee and funding agencies agreed on the need for a new administrative mechanism, one which would be charged with coordinating and managing the implementation of the operational and research designs on behalf of the sponsoring agencies. They further agreed that this organization must be given both sufficient independence and authority to carry out this mandate, while still operating under the policy guidance of the funding consortium and a board of directors.

The remainder of this chapter describes how the Manpower Demonstration Research Corporation interpreted this mandate and the role that it played in the implementation of the Supported Work experiment.[6]

MDRC's Structure

MDRC was established in 1974 as a private nonprofit corporation with a 10-member board of directors composed primarily of academics and a small staff of program managers and researchers drawn from the Ford Foundation, the Vera Institute of Justice, and the New York City government.[7] Its president was William J. Grinker, the Ford Foundation program officer responsible for developing the Supported Work Demonstration under Ford Foundation vice-president Mitchell Sviridoff. From the outset, the board paid particular attention to the development of the research focus of the demonstration, recognizing that one of their major responsibilities was to weigh and to define the limits of applied research in an operational setting. This included the development of a research agenda that addressed key policy concerns: assessing alternative research designs; defining the target populations; determining the demonstration's operating policies; and most critically, arbitrating the conflicting research and operational priorities in a manner that would protect the validity of the evaluation while not overly constraining or hindering program operators.

Another responsibility centered on MDRC's position vis-à-vis the project's funders. MDRC has sometimes been called an "intermediary" corporation in that it stands between the sponsoring agencies and the local programs and other subcontractors in their execution of the day-to-day objectives of the funders. While yet maintaining its independent stance, MDRC went to unusual lengths to ensure that its funders were both informed and consulted. One mechanism used to assure agency input was their representation in all board meetings. Within this framework, the federal agencies and the Ford Foundation guided and shaped critical decisions, while also showing an unusual ability to go beyond narrow agency interests to recognize the mutual benefits in achieving a balanced response to project alternatives.

The structure of the Supported Work experiment demonstrated the complex management functions MDRC undertook. While MDRC had oversight and fiduciary authority for the total effort, a good part of the research and all of the local operations were conducted by separate organizations, the 15 local sites and Mathematica Policy Research (MPR), under contract to MDRC.[8] This separation was not accidental. MDRC was conceived as a vehicle to manage, not to implement, the demonstration and its research and operations. Further, it was important that local operations be put in the hands of agencies resembling potential future service deliverers.

MDRC's responsibilities fell into three key areas: designing the program model and assuring its satisfactory implementation; developing the research design and implementing it with precision; and putting into place effective monitoring and management information systems. To accomplish these tasks, MDRC organized itself into two main divisions: an operations or program monitoring staff under Gary Walker, who had run the first Supported Work program for the Vera Institute, and a research staff directed by the author, an economist with a background in welfare research. An information service and fiscal staff provided support services to both units.

Most critical to MDRC's vision of its mandate was the fact that these two core staffs did not have distinct spheres of influence. Rather, the organization saw as an essential precondition of its success the integration of the research and operational activities to achieve its overall corporate mission: the establishment and oversight of an operating program in a manner that would optimally test its utility and replicability. This concept did not include a separate operational role per se for MDRC. Rather, the corporation measured its effectiveness by the extent to which it could avoid the disintegration and fragmentation of the program and research designs exhibited by prior research/demonstration efforts.

The manner in which this approach was put into practice is summarized in table 9.1, which indicates the extent to which operations

TABLE 9.1
Summary of MDRC Activities in the Supported Work Demonstration

Activity	Degree of Participation, by Staff Unit	
	Operations	Research
Program Design and Monitoring		
Develop operating guidelines	X	X[a]
Select local sites	X	X[a]
Develop site contracts	†	X
Monitor site performance against contract: budget, unit cost, performance standards, satisfaction of reporting requirements, implementation of program guidelines, cooperation with research requirements	†	0
Oversee site audits	†	0
Develop response to contract failures	X	X
Provide technical assistance	†	0
Approve proposed worksites	†	0
Interpret program guidelines	†	0
Research Design and Implementation		
Identify research questions	X	†[a]
Design research strategy	0	†[a]
Select impact and benefit-cost subcontractor	0	†
Oversee performance of impact and benefit-cost subcontractor	0	†
Develop process analysis plan	X	†
Collect process information on sites	X	X
Prepare process/documentation reports	X	†
Analyze program costs	X	†
Prepare final report	X	†[a]
Systems Design and Implementation		
Design management information system	X	X[a]
Design fiscal reporting system	X	X[a]
Monitor site delivery of management and fiscal data	X	0
Other		
Prepare quarterly progress reports to funders	X	X
Prepare annual reports on the demonstration	X	X

Key: † Lead responsibility.
  X Participated actively.
  0 Did not participate or minor role.
a With the participation of Mathematica Policy Research, the impact contractor.

and research personnel participated in each MDRC task, including which, if either, had lead responsibility. To understand how this high degree of joint input and decision-making functioned in practice and the critical role it played in reaching the demonstration's objectives, it is important to go beyond the table to several key examples.

The Experimental Design

The inability of past employment program evaluations to produce reliable and conclusive findings has been attributed primarily to three issues: the absence of an appropriate control group, the small size of the research sample, and the inadequate length of follow-up. In designing the Supported Work evaluation, MDRC and MPR researchers, the board, and the funders sought to avoid these pitfalls.

The first problem was dealt with during the planning phase, prior to site selection, when Supported Work's designers specified that random assignment would be used to assign samples of individuals either to participate in Supported Work or to become members of a control group. Thus, local program operators knew, at the time they were selected and funded, that random assignment was an essential condition and, in their contracts, they accepted to participate on these terms. However, since program operators had initially criticized this procedure as unfair and an interference in their control of hiring practices, its successful implementation required some mechanism to monitor compliance (which was developed by MPR) and an oversight staff unyielding in its rejection of attempts to circumvent this procedure. The commitment of the MDRC operations staff to the project's research priorities resulted in a virtually problem-free resolution of this issue.

The other two issues proved more challenging. The experiment's designers sought a sample size sufficiently large to provide a good prospect of detecting the anticipated postprogram effects at statistically significant levels, and a follow-up period adequate to allow the determination of postprogram effects. Both were constrained by a known and fixed research budget, and unknown and difficult-to-predict site performance levels and data collection costs.[9]

After extensive negotiations, an initial plan resolving the sample size was worked out within the budget ceiling, calling for a baseline sample of 5,400 individuals drawn from eight sites with part of the sample followed for up to 30 months after random assignment.[10] While this represented the maximum amount of data thought purchasable within the research budget, both MPR and MDRC remained concerned about the adequacy of the sample size and length of follow-up. This, plus the uncertainties underlying the cost estimates and concern over the ability of the interviewers to find and follow these particularly difficult populations for the required number of years, led the project researchers and managers to adopt a flexible sequential design methodology. This strategy allowed the sample size and its allocation across sites, target groups, and time periods to be periodically reevaluated to determine whether improvements or changes were needed. It also offered an opportunity to extend the follow-up period if survey unit costs were brought below projected levels, as they eventually were.

The sequential design, so important to the experiment, was made possible and suggested by several special features of the Supported Work project. First, in contrast to previous large social experiments, where all sample members were enrolled at the start, Supported Workers and controls were continually recruited; as previous experimentals left the program after their maximum of 12 or 18 months, they were replaced by new employees. Thus, the fact that a temporary, operational employment experience was provided, not an ongoing transfer payment or subsidy, meant that the sample build-up could be continuous, constrained only by the availability of job slots.

Second, the tentative sample plan and budget were based on a number of assumptions about program growth and operations. Random assignment was limited to certain time periods at specific demonstration sites, depending on the sites' expected enrollment levels of the different target populations and on projected no-show and turnover rates of the participants. It was anticipated, however, that some sites would face unexpected start-up problems, and that MDRC might have to reallocate the sample among sites or add to, or make substitutions for, planned survey sites.[11] Therefore, as actual information became available on program growth rates and other key indices, these were fed into MPR's sample generation model, allowing for both recalculation of the survey budget and up-to-date information on possible sample shortfalls. As a result, MDRC was able to direct expansion activities for certain target groups, to substitute several nonsurvey for planned survey sites, and to take steps to assure that survey sites reached the required operating size.

To a greater extent than anticipated, this type of reshuffling became a constant feature of MDRC staff's program management and review. Not only questions of local program capacity and performance were involved, but external events, such as local funding difficulties, which created bottlenecks at several sites. Many times throughout the demonstration, MDRC had to provide additional or stopgap funding for a critical survey site in order either to keep it operational or assure its continuation at the size required to generate the research sample. One example of such an obstacle was an unexpected delay at the AFDC sites in obtaining special waivers of the Social Security Act which were necessary both for the operations of these sites and for their funding. The resulting stalled intake of AFDC participants prompted MDRC to add a major new demonstration site, New York City, to expand survey activities to 10 sites, and to request that certain other sites also add AFDC participants.[12]

The funding of back-up nonsurvey sites and the existence of adequate resources (which MDRC could use to offset sample shortfalls) proved critical to the establishment of the research sample, given the experiment's requirement that the sites achieve certain levels of local funding and their difficulty in gaining solid and long-term CETA commitments. The ability of the funding agencies and, most critically, of the Department of Labor to assure long-term adequate resources was essential to the success of both the program and the research.

Over the four years of field interviewing, substantial cost savings permitted a revision of the interviewing plan, including an expansion of the baseline sample to 6,500 individuals; an extension of the follow-up period to a maximum of 36 months; and an increase in the number of individuals receiving each follow-up interview. The field interviewers succeeded in meeting their target interview completion rates and demonstrated that it was feasible to conduct a longitudinal study of the disadvantaged populations served by Supported Work. An analysis of the nature of sample attrition concluded that the interview results did not suffer serious bias from this source.[13]

However, while a flexible design was critical to the successful implementation of the research design, it was not sufficient alone to ensure delivery of the research sample. Implementing the design required close coordination between both MDRC and MPR research staffs, and the research and operations arms within MDRC itself. Further, it presupposed a management vehicle committed to the research design, sensitive to the program operator's concerns, able to act flexibly and quickly, and in control of the purse strings. Thus, the joint operations and research input of MDRC's staff (as noted in table 9.1) was evident in a number of ways.

Initial site selection, for example, was based in part on an assessment of each local entity's ability to generate the research sample and the unit costs of interviewing in particular geographical locations, as well as questions of operational capacity. Site contracts reflected the planned sample allocation, and, if sites fell short on contract targets for intake, slot build-up, or the generation of local revenues, the MDRC response reflected both operational assessments and research needs. Depending on the ability of a site to alter its performance and the impact of any action on the research sample, MDRC could give more technical assistance or funds, adjust the contract targets, or even close the site. The fact that the operations and research staffs worked together contributed to a useful balancing of perspectives.

Joint judgments were continually required in other ways if the operators were to gain sufficient leeway to meet crises, while yet maintaining the integrity and yield of research data. Because operations staff had been initially involved in the development of the sequential research design and had worked with the sites in its implementation, they could make adjustments rapidly when problems became apparent. Moreover, close relationships between MDRC and MPR researchers led to MDRC's heightened awareness of the importance of operational parameters and the need to propose or ratify a new direction quickly, if required. Finally, the fact that MDRC was the major funding source for the local programs gave it the critical leverage to impose changes or correct violations of research conditions at each site when necessary.

Standardization and Variation in the Program Model

As noted earlier, the Supported Work project was a conscious compromise between conflicting pressures for standardization and local flexibility. Early in the demonstration, the MPR principal investigator proposed the following criteria as a basis for determining which program features would be rigidly standardized and which subject to less stringent control. Those to be standardized were the ones which:

1. could be expected to produce statistically significant differences in major behavioral hypotheses.
2. were measurable and monitorable.
3. were amenable to control without unduly constraining or disrupting local operators.
4. could be controlled in any subsequent national program.

Four areas of program design met all of these conditions: eligibility criteria; the wage, bonus, and benefit structure; the maximum treatment period (where variations of 12 and 18 months were permitted); and intake procedures (where random assignment was imposed). For each of these criteria, clear program regulations were drafted during the planning period, and site selection was conditional on a site's agreement to implement these policies.[14]

Finally, MDRC issued guidelines and monitored the application of a number of other program dimensions that were considered fundamental to the concept or character of Supported Work but did not meet the criteria for uniform standardization:

worksite characteristics
nature of supervision
graduated stress
peer support
use of ancillary support services
design of AFDC diversion
regulations on terminations, promotions, and transfers
local funding requirements
job placement activities
average cost per person-year

While the major research questions of the Supported Work experiment—Does Supported Work work? For whom? At what cost?—were addressed by the experimental design comparing participants with a "nontreatment" control group, the experiment's planners and funders were also interested in finding out what particular characteristics of the program or the environment and administrative structure had the greatest effect on performance and behavior. They were interested in lessons about program design and redesign that might improve any subsequent Supported Work expansion or help in the general understanding of the design of employment programs. Two strategies were followed: a qualitative documentation effort implemented by MDRC and a statistical process analysis conducted by MPR.

One strategy was rarely implemented: the systematic variation of discrete program elements among sites or the random assignment of participants to different program features within sites. The MDRC board of directors and staff had argued against this approach for a number of reasons. First, after exhaustive study, there was skepticism that a variation at one or two sites could provide conclusive information on its usefulness, especially given the many other uncontrolled differences among sites. Second, the specific suggestions offered by MPR were considered impractical—for example, providing similar placement services to controls and experimentals in order to test this component's contribution to overall outcomes.[15]

Finally, there was intense concern that excessive research demands might push the local programs too hard, thereby endangering the possible success of the overall operation. A higher wage variation might cut down postprogram placements or raise operating costs beyond local funding capacities; random assignment to work positions might interfere with productivity or a program's ability to interest work sponsors so as to impair its capacity to provide the basic program treatment. Consistently, the MDRC board argued that it was critical not to jeopardize the researchers' ability to address the basic question about Supported Work's efficacy, even if this meant giving up an opportunity to obtain evidence on more refined questions.

One of the two alternative strategies—documentation of the in-program experience—proved useful in interpreting the experimental and Management Information System (MIS) findings and has informed the assessment of program components. The second strategy—an extensive quantitative process analysis which sought to identify the key components of the program treatment and to measure statistically their impact on in-program and postprogram performance—was both more difficult and less informative than anticipated. Although it, too, was based on management data, the construction of the required data files proved complicated and time-consuming, and the absence of random assignment made it difficult to determine whether the statistically significant relationships that were found represented real differences or manifestations of selection bias. Finally, the data, while extensive, probably did not capture variations in the components that were critical to program success (for example, the quality of supervision or the extent of the implementation of graduated stress).[16] Of course, to the extent that the critical program features could not be effectively defined or measured, an attempt at experimental analysis, with systematic variation and random assignment, would also have been of limited usefulness.

As the above discussion indicates, the resolution of issues on program standardization and variation was based on both operational and research concerns and proved to be an area of active board and funder involvement. This careful balancing of operational and research perspectives extended beyond the design phase to become the basis for jointly developed site operating guidelines and contracts, reflecting the advantages of an oversight structure designed to weigh the relative merits of the pleas of local operators and project researchers.

Managing the Research Contractor

In contrast to its attitude toward the sites—where the extent of MDRC intervention was tempered by an interest in assuring a replicable test of site capability—the philosophy vis-à-vis its major research contractor, MPR, was one of active oversight and collaboration to assure the best possible research products within the available budget and timeframe. The MPR/Poverty Institute team, led by the principal investigator, Robinson Hollister, brought to the effort extensive experience in social policy research, particularly on the various negative income tax experiments. Throughout Supported Work's life, this team demonstrated a consistent capacity to apply this know-how flexibly in the interest of achieving an optimal research design and product.

Because of the obvious technical strength and seasoned judgment of the research group, MDRC's oversight role rarely involved methodological disputes. Instead, attention focused on the allocation of the research budget among analysis and survey activities, the detailed review of the use of project resources, examination of the relative importance of different policy questions, the detailed specification and review of project reports, communication of research needs to the sites and site data to the MPR team, and the identification and resolution of conflicts between research demands and site operational constraints. MDRC staff conducted regular review sessions with MPR staff to monitor progress and explore problems. To clarify expectations and promote their execution, MDRC negotiated detailed contracts, including survey performance objectives and report coverage.

The nature of this oversight can be highlighted by several examples. First, early in the project, MPR submitted a 5-year budget that was three times the limit on which it had been awarded the contract. The MDRC board of directors and staff were adamant on holding the budget at the $7.5 million ceiling (in 1975 dollars) and worked intensively with MPR to develop an acceptable alternative.[17] This process resulted in the formulation of the sequential design, discussed earlier, which led to a continuing joint MDRC-MPR reassessment of the potential yield of the survey effort and the optimal allocation of the overall research budget among competing priorities.

The MPR agenda included an impact analysis, a benefit-cost analysis, and the quantitative process analysis. The MDRC board of directors was particularly interested in the objectives, design, and quality of the impact study. However, board concern about an overreliance on the benefit-cost analysis led to persistent review, for example, of the proposed methodology for valuing the in-program output of Supported Workers. Board skepticism about the yield of the process analysis led to a continued effort to limit the funds going toward this unexpectedly resource-intensive effort. As also discussed earlier, there was extensive review of MPR's proposed systematic variations, which were rarely implemented.

Finally, MDRC paid particular attention to the clarity and comprehensiveness of the demonstration's reports. This included participation in the development of report outlines and the detailed review of the final products by staff, by the MDRC board, and by funding agency representatives.

A notable achievement of the demonstration was the completion of the research within its original cost-frame. In the author's view, several factors probably were most critical to carrying out this massive survey effort within budget and surpassing its initial goals. First, while the survey and research contracts were written on an annual basis, the selection of a contractor had been made in the context of a 5-year budget which set a firm ceiling on total research resources. This inflexible ceiling promoted the clear interest and commitment of survey managers in squeezing the maximum out of available resources. Second, this commitment was enormously strengthened by the fact that the survey firm also held responsibility for the data analysis. While the research team, from the beginning, was concerned about the adequacy of the sample size and applied continuing pressure to obtain the maximum and best quality data, they knew also that budget overruns on the survey would have to be met with resources targeted toward later data analysis. As a result, MPR had many incentives to perform well on the survey and showed great ingenuity in, and commitment to, doing so.

Third, throughout the project, MDRC negotiated each annual contract carefully to assure its conformance with the 5-year resource constraint. Because of the early and real emphasis on limited project funds, the survey budget was continually monitored and reestimated. As a side effect, any savings were clearly identified and speedily reallocated to additional field activities, aiding in the success of the sequential design strategy.

Finally, any 5-year plan for a major social experiment can only be a relatively broad blueprint of activities and products. The details remain to be filled in as the circumstances and requirements of the activity unfold, requiring an ongoing process of optimization. The relatively secure funding and apolitical origin of the project, combined with the ongoing close involvement of the funding agencies and their confidence in MDRC, gave MDRC substantial flexibility to restructure

MPR's tasks and schedule in an ongoing effort to achieve the project's long-term objectives within its resources.

The Generalizability of Supported Work's Results

An assessment of the wisdom of the Supported Work design and the usefulness of its findings lies beyond the scope of this chapter. These should understandably be judged by someone less directly involved than the author. However, some observation is in order about the way in which the project's design and oversight affect our ability to make inferences from the experiment's findings.

The aim of social experimentation is to produce findings generalizable or relevant to a nonexperimental program serving the larger eligible population. In the Supported Work Demonstration, random assignment, high interview completion rates, and quality data suggest confidence that the results accurately reflect the impact of that experiment. Whether or not these achievements can be replicated in a subsequent ongoing program depends on how typical were the participants, the operating environment, and the sites. In Supported Work, the operating agencies, the program sites, and the research sample were not chosen at random from the relevant populations of alternative or eligible candidates. Moreover, despite efforts to follow procedures likely to be replicated in an expanded program, the experimental mode involved some necessary distortion: small scale, extensive central monitoring and technical assistance, a focus on the start-up period, and possible Hawthorne effects.

Turning first to those factors unrelated to MDRC's activities, the generalizability of the findings is affected by the approach used to select the study sample and the particular economic and programmatic environment in which the demonstration was implemented. As noted earlier, to keep research costs in line within an already large budget, random assignment was conducted at the point where individuals were offered a job in the Supported Work program; it was not carried out on a representative sample of potential program eligibles. As a result, the experiment does not provide an estimate of what percent and what subset of individuals meeting the eligibility criteria would be interested in participating in a national program. An expanded program might reach different individuals and have different impacts.

Further, the Supported Work experiment was conducted under specific economic conditions and in a period when a large number of alternative employment services, operated under the Comprehensive Employment and Training Act and Work Incentive Program, were available. The importance of the changing unemployment rate is discussed elsewhere in this volume. Potentially as important is the fact that the controls could and did avail themselves of the full array of alternative existing programs. As a result, the impact findings measure the marginal change that would follow Supported Work's introduction in an environment of specific available alternative programs. A change in that environment would alter the opportunities available to controls and Supported Workers, with unclear impacts on the program's measured effectiveness.

The selection of sites could be another factor limiting the generalizability of the results. One criticism of prior social experiments was their exclusive focus on a very small number of sites. Despite their attempts to model or simulate national conditions, there has been suspicion that the findings they produced were idiosyncratic. The designers of the Supported Work experiment used a different approach, taking the research sample from a substantial number of sites and pooling all data in the analysis. It was hoped that the 10 survey sites would thus approximate the variety of operating experiences and local conditions of a national program, and that the cross-site average would be a reasonable estimate of such a program's effect. The importance of this issue is suggested by the observed variation in program effectiveness at the different sites, discussed elsewhere in this volume. While the MPR analysis generally assumes that the all-site average provides the best estimate of the program's impact, a case could be made for other choices. (This would be particularly true if specific program or site dimensions could be identified as clearly related to improved outcomes—which was not the case—or if these features could realistically be controlled in a subsequent program.)

Yet another factor to be considered is that, in any experimental test of an operating program, there is a certain tension between giving the program model the best chance of working and providing a realistic level of service. Two offsetting factors were at work in the Supported Work experiment. On the one hand, site selection was based on demonstrated or suggested expertise, and MDRC provided technical assistance in training the fledgling managers in the essential concepts of Supported Work and their implementation. On the other side, there was substantial evidence of an operational learning curve, with the sites taking several years to reach their maximum performance levels on operational indicators as diverse as attendance rates, postprogram job placements, and unit cost.[18] There is also evidence that some of the sites were of very poor quality (two of the 10 were closed either permanently or temporarily during the experimental period).

The research nature of the project also hindered inference from the experiment. The sites were both subject to extensive control and yet given unusual freedom to experiment. Detailed uniform fiscal and management information data systems allowed MDRC to monitor aspects of program performance never evaluated in most employment programs: real unit costs, eligibility, attendance rates. Feedback from this monitoring undoubtedly improved program performance. On the other hand, sites were allowed to implement some innovative work-sites, which proved to be extremely costly and probably diverted scarce management resources.

On balance, the author concludes that, while competitive site selection and technical assistance did serve to speed the sites along the learning curve, this was a positive outcome, since it permitted the demonstration to measure ongoing rather than start-up performance. In addition, while explanations for the wide outcome variations by site remain unclear, the diversity itself suggests that a multisite experiment was a wise idea, providing both a reliable estimate of average impact and a tentative estimate of the range of outcomes that could be anticipated in an expanded program.

A final judgment on the appropriateness of the management decisions and directions taken by MDRC must be made by others. However, the author would argue that, while individual judgments or decisions may be considered faulty, the concept of a unified management structure, jointly responsible for operational and research activities, has proven itself and was, for Supported Work, an essential part of the project's success.

Notes

1 While this issue also arose in the income maintenance and other prior experiments, the ease of defining and standardizing those treatments made their uniform replication and expansion plausible. The exact duplication of an employment program is more complex. By way of analogy, a health experiment that tested the effectiveness of medical care or a housing experiment that tested the quality of construction and building management policies would encounter some of the dilemmas faced during the Supported Work design period.

2 See MDRC (1976, 88). Also see Gueron (1980).

3 The seven original funding agencies and their respective contributions to the 4-year demonstration and 5-year research effort were: the Employment and Training Administration, U.S. Department of Labor, the lead agency administering the program from the federal level ($26.9 million); the Law Enforcement Assistance Administration, U.S. Department of Justice ($10.0 million); the National Institute on Drug Abuse and the Office of Planning

and Evaluation, U.S. Department of Health, Education, and Welfare ($3.8 and $3.1 million, respectively); the Office of Policy Research and Development, U.S. Department of Housing and Urban Development ($1.3 million); the Economic Development Administration, U.S. Department of Commerce ($0.1 million); and the Ford Foundation ($4.3 million). An additional $32.9 million was raised by the program operators from the sale of goods and services, locally generated grants, or the diversion of AFDC benefits, for a total project budget of $82.4 million.

4 The committee members were Eli Ginzberg, Robert Lampman, Richard Nathan, Robert Solow, Gilbert Steiner, and Phyllis Wallace.

5 For example, one study characterized a series of prior Department of Labor–managed demonstrations as suffering from a "lack of consistent management and oversight between sites and inadequate coordination between program operators and research and evaluation contractors" (Lowry & Associates 1980, 3: xii).

6 This discussion draws on MDRC (1976, 1980). For a detailed description of the origins of MDRC, see Brecher (1978).

7 The MDRC board of directors was composed of the six members of the advisory committee plus Anthony Downs, Ernest Green, Alan Kistler, and Wayne Thompson.

8 Both the impact and benefit-cost analyses were contracted to MPR, which in turn subcontracted with the Institute for Research on Poverty, University of Wisconsin, for assistance in the impact analysis.

9 Out of the total $82.4 million project budget, $66.4 million went for program operations; $3.6 million for MDRC oversight and research activities; and $12.4 million for contracted impact, benefit-cost, and data collection work.

10 The sample was to be evenly divided among participants and controls and to include 1,800 ex-addicts, 1,500 AFDC women, 1,350 ex-offenders, and 750 youths.

11 This was possible because the survey had not begun simultaneously at all sites. Fortunately, there was an early decision, for both budget and research reasons, to separate program start-up from survey start-up. Program planners wanted to avoid a concentration in the research on participants enrolled in the program during the start-up first year. Thus, while operations began at 13 sites in March 1975, the survey began at one site in April 1975 and was scheduled to phase in at the others over the next 12 months.

12 A critical result of the delay in AFDC intake was the shortened period of follow-up available for that target group. Under the basic project budget, the AFDC sample received a maximum of only 27 months of follow-up. Supplemental funding was subsequently made available to extend the follow-up period.

13 For an analysis of attrition bias, see Brown (1979). For final interview completion rates, see Jackson et al. (1979).

14 Some of these features proved difficult to implement (for example, rigid eligibility verification); others encountered legal obstacles (for example,

fringe benefits varied somewhat among sites to satisfy local legislation on unemployment insurance coverage); and others encountered some site reluctance and were subject to close MDRC monitoring (for example, enforcing the mandatory graduation policy).

15 The discussion focused on three specific proposals put forward by the MPR and Wisconsin researchers: testing a higher wage level at two sites; testing the importance of job-placement services by having two or three Supported Work programs supply these services to members of the control group; and assessing the importance of crew work versus single placement in host agencies by randomly assigning Supported Workers to these two types of work settings. While the debate centered on these alternatives, similar arguments would probably have been made against other comparable interventions. An exception is the systematic variation in program duration, which was implemented, and the conscious selection of certain sites that provided a natural variation in administrative structures and environmental conditions.

16 Alice Rivlin notes how similar problems in defining the critical dimensions of program treatment occurred in the planned variation in education experiments. She also suggests that currently we are simply not knowledgeable enough to carry out experimental analyses of the components of complex service-delivery models. See "How Can Experiments Be More Useful?" *AER: Papers and Proceedings* (May 1974): 346–54.

17 MPR's original budget called for the random assignment of individuals on file at the many referral agencies. Roughly 20,000 Supported Work eligibles would have been identified and referred to the program or the control group and followed in subsequent interviews. This approach would have provided findings on the size and nature of the potential pool of program enrollees, as well as on the eventual participants. The final design cut the sampling frame back to individuals referred to the local programs who were found to satisfy all eligibility and any other minimal criteria. While this change made it more difficult to estimate the interest in and impact of an *expanded* Supported Work program, it simplified the measurement and presentation of the program's impact on participants, since this was directly available from a comparison of all experimentals and controls.

18 This is somewhat analogous to the "limited duration" criticism leveled against the NIT (Negative Income Tax) experiment findings. While Supported Work did provide the duration of treatment that would be available in an ongoing program—something not possible in the NIT tests—it faced the problem of assuring that the quality of service provided during the start-up phase accurately reflected a likely ongoing program—a problem not faced in the NIT experiments as a result of their relative operational simplicity. Since almost all of the sample was enrolled in the first two years, MDRC argued that some technical assistance was essential to assure that the programs developed rapidly enough to give a fair test of the Supported Work model.

10 *Eli Ginzberg, Richard Nathan, and Robert Solow*

The Lessons
of the Supported Work Demonstration

This chapter discusses the principal policy lessons of the Supported Work Demonstration. It first describes the groups that helped launch the demonstration, highlighting the factors that make it different from other efforts to provide training and jobs for hard-core disadvantaged persons.

The second section discusses the uses of research in the formulation of social policy. It deals with issues that arise when a democratic society seeks to respond to social needs without adequate knowledge of their underlying causes and a clear understanding of what types of programs will be most effective. It discusses how the results of the Supported Work Demonstration contribute to the resolution of both issues.

The third and concluding section deals with how the lessons from the Supported Work Demonstration can be applied to policy in the context of contemporary federal, state, and local relationships.

The Development and Operation of the Demonstration

When the Supported Work program was launched early in 1974, national policymakers had been engaged for over forty years in various short-term and long-term programs to assist the unemployed and the poor. In the New Deal period, the federal government introduced unemployment insurance for laid-off workers, work relief for the long-term unemployed, and welfare for households where the father had died. In the early post-World War II period—from about 1945 to 1962—the federal government turned away from assistance in the form of work relief and relied instead on an enlarged and improved transfer payment system to provide benefits to families lacking income from employment. Even after this shift, however, Congress did provide appropriations for public works to help cushion the effects of recessions.

With the end of the 1962 recession, it became apparent that most skilled workers were able to find employment without federal assistance. To deal with the problems of those skilled workers unable to find jobs, Congress adopted the Manpower Development and Training Act in 1962, and in the 12 ensuing years annual spending for employment and training activities rose rapidly.

The federal government in the mid-sixties became increasingly aware of the problem of a large pool of marginal workers. The problem they faced no longer was a slow economy, but lack of skills, education, and work experience and, additionally, discrimination toward some of the people in this group since many of the most disadvantaged persons of working age were members of minority groups.

Structurally unemployed persons represented an increasingly critical social problem. Their numbers were growing even as the nation was experiencing the longest period of economic expansion in its history (1961–1969). At the same time, another social problem began to assume larger proportions: the number of women and children receiving welfare payments under the Aid to Families with Dependent Children (AFDC) program. The reasons for this increase, still not completely clear, appear to include the civil rights movement and the antipoverty and community action programs of the 1960s, which caused many disadvantaged people to become aware of their entitlement to assistance.

Even after 12 years of expanded employment and training efforts (1962–1974), senior federal officials found to their dismay that they had gathered little knowledge on the effectiveness of social programs. They were especially troubled and perplexed by their failure to counteract the continuing steep rise in the welfare population.

Policymakers and program specialists in the executive branch were not alone in their growing awareness of the lack of data. Questioning had intensified about whether increasingly expensive training programs could justify the money being spent on them. In the early years of the Nixon administration, deputy secretary of the Treasury, Charles Walker, one of the foremost critics of employment and training programs, contended that the national unemployment rate had been lowered by only about .003–.004 percent by an outlay of some $40 billion for these programs. Although there was little basis in fact for such an estimate, if the test of manpower programs is to be found in declining unemployment rates, the basic point could not be ignored.

Against this background, a growing group of members of Congress, bureaucrats, academicians, and others became concerned about the need to develop ways to test the effectiveness of social programs. They wanted to move beyond impressions and anecdotes to facts and findings that could stand the test of rigorous analysis and comparison. This new mood helps to explain the good response that Mitchell Sviridoff, vice-president for national affairs for the Ford Foundation, received when he visited several federal departments and agencies in 1973 to determine whether they were interested in joining with the foundation to replicate on a large scale a seemingly very successful jobs program that the Vera Institute of Justice had operated in New York City.[1] At the outset, the Vera demonstration of the "supported work" program was limited to helping former drug addicts to enter or reenter the job market and become self-supporting.[2] Sviridoff suggested that this approach be tested on a larger scale with other groups besides ex-addicts.

Sviridoff received strong support from two Labor Department officials—William Kolberg, assistant secretary for manpower, and Howard Rosen, director of the Office of Research and Development. With the Department of Labor willing to become the lead agency, the departments of Health, Education, and Welfare (HEW), Housing and Urban Development (HUD), and Justice agreed to join in providing funds for a national Supported Work Demonstration.

Sviridoff then confronted a problem. A collaboration between a foundation and several federal agencies requires an unusually high degree of cooperation among many actors, something that is extremely difficult to achieve when several government agencies are involved. To help achieve such cooperation, Sviridoff assembled an advisory group of six academicians early in 1974 to serve as consultants at monthly meetings of a task force to plan for the new project. In May 1974, by which time broad support for the demonstration had developed, this advisory group was transformed into a corporation, the Manpower Demonstration Research Corporation (MDRC). It was widely believed that such an intermediary organization was needed to plan and run a rigorous test of the Supported Work concept. MDRC's task was to link and keep together all of the participating agencies, manage the demonstration, and oversee the research.

It soon became clear that two components were essential to MDRC's success. MDRC was both a new organization and was facing a new kind of task. Strong leadership and follow-through were needed, along with the sustained involvement of an advisory group that could contribute to the policy development process and the research planning.

William Grinker, named in May 1974, as the first president of MDRC, and the MDRC board faced many challenges—including winning and holding the trust of the funding agencies; setting standards for the demonstration sites without inhibiting their capacity to innovate; ensuring the responsiveness of site directors to the needs of the research effort; and avoiding confrontations with local politicians and community and business groups, even if it became necessary to close down sites that failed to meet the required standards. The fact that MDRC largely accomplished these tasks is a tribute to the competence of Grinker and the staff he assembled at MDRC.

Members of the MDRC board of directors were highly involved in the Supported Work Demonstration. Individually and in subcommittees, they were engaged in MDRC's work on a continuing basis. By phone, written communication, and attendance at meetings, they worked with the president and key staff members on problems where their experience was relevant. In effect, the board served as a group of in-house consultants to the president and his senior staff.

One event helps illustrate the role of board members. The federal government and the Ford Foundation had budgeted $7.5 million for the 5-year Supported Work research effort and an additional $2.5 million for a management information system. When Mathematica Policy Research, Inc., which had won the competition as the research contractor, submitted its budget, the total exceeded $22 million, three times the amount allotted to this task. Members of the board entered into intensive negotiations with Mathematica Policy Research, offering detailed suggestions for redesigning the research analysis to bring it down to budget, which was done.

In another important development, Robert Lampman, one of the original board members, warned his colleagues that a null hypothesis was likely to be substantiated for Supported Work. That is, he felt that the odds were against uncovering a measurable impact, either in terms of gains in income or an increase in employment for the four target groups participating in Supported Work. Lampman said that when persons with severe employment handicaps and disabilities are singled out for remediation, positive and lasting effects are not likely. The odds in favor of the null hypothesis were even greater in this case, he thought, since the four groups chosen were from among those least likely to succeed in the labor market—long-term AFDC recipients, former drug addicts, ex-offenders, and high school dropouts, many with criminal records.

In the end, the research found measurable positive effects for the AFDC group and smaller but still positive effects for the ex-addicts. Lampman's warning, however, put the board and senior staff on guard against becoming overconfident. The corporation established and adhered to basic objectives: to discover whether Supported Work was making a difference; to determine which groups it worked for; and, if it did work, to find out why. MDRC was equally interested in learning whether and why Supported Work would *not* work for some groups. Neither the staff nor the board made any assumptions about the greater likelihood of success for any one or several of the target groups. The objective was to secure valid findings.

Several important organizational lessons can be extracted from this demonstration. The first was that it was possible to design and carry out, over a 5-year period, a complicated undertaking involving a private foundation and several federal departments. Between 1974 and 1980, three different presidents occupied the White House. There were three congressional elections, and there was a high rate of turnover in the cabinet and subcabinet positions most relevant for the demonstration. Fortunately, a number of the senior career officials in the federal establishment remained in their posts. The continuing commitment of the Ford Foundation reassured new federal officials that the Supported Work Demonstration was a significant and professionally managed project worth seeing through to its conclusion.

A second and more substantive lesson was that Supported Work could be fitted into the interstices of the labor market. During the early months, when representatives of the Ford Foundation and the federal agencies as well as academic advisors were exploring the likely costs and benefits of the demonstration, a consensus was reached that if the national unemployment rate rose to 6 percent or higher, the Supported Work Demonstration should be postponed. Those concerned felt that the necessary number of Supported Work job positions could not be found in communities where considerable numbers of experienced workers were unemployed.

This self-imposed limitation proved unduly pessimistic. Even though Supported Work was launched at a time when the unemployment rate reached its highest level since World War II—8 percent when most local operations began in early 1975—the program did not arouse significant community opposition in any of the sites. The most likely reason is that it was not a large program, with a typical local operation having from 80 to 150 job slots. The relatively small number of work assignments helped to avoid the problem of major opposition from politicians, trade unions, or the recently unemployed. A large expansion of the Supported Work program for very disadvantaged workers could, however, cause these kinds of problems.

The reasons for the successful implementation of the Supported Work Demonstration can be summarized as follows:

1. The critical role of the major foundation, in this case the Ford Foundation, which was able and willing to offer significant support.
2. The active interest and involvement of a number of federal government agencies.
3. The role of the academicians, especially during the formative period, in helping to design the research effort.
4. The importance of establishing an intermediary organization such as MDRC, with a strong president, to oversee and manage the demonstration.
5. The selection of capable contractors, such as Mathematica Policy Research and the Institute for Research on Poverty at the University of Wisconsin. These organizations executed their complex research assignments with professional skill and distinction.
6. Strong in-house capacity at MDRC for operations, management information systems, finance, and research.

A number of important findings, reviewed in other chapters in this volume, were obtained from the demonstration. Supported Work proved to be a successful intervention in the case of a significant number of the women who were previously long-term AFDC dependents. Three years after Supported Work, many in the experimental group were still working; some had been able to leave the relief rolls, and others received smaller public assistance grants. The benefit-cost ratio for this group was highly favorable. In the case of disadvantaged youths and ex-offenders, no lasting positive results could be ascertained. For the ex-addict group, the results were mixed. While Supported Work appears to have contributed to a reduction in their criminal activity, participation did not clearly raise this group's employment and income levels significantly above those found for the control sample.

The most important substantive finding from Supported Work relates to social policy. Throughout the 12-year period (1962–1974) when the federal government was experimenting with employment and training programs, groups at the end of the queue, such as those assisted by Supported Work, had been neglected. Most programs leaned toward the selection of the workers most likely to succeed from the pool of the unemployed. Supported Work, in essence, demonstrated that society need not acquiesce to the existence of a permanently disadvantaged group of citizens. There are ways that some of these individuals can be reached; they can be assisted in a way that will enable them to earn a livelihood so that they and some of their children can escape from what is often otherwise a dead-end track.

This important substantive lesson for social policy came at a turning point in the nation's history. The board of MDRC proposed in 1980 that the Secretary of Labor recommend an amendment to the Comprehensive Employment and Training Act (CETA) to make Supported Work a national program. He should, the board suggested, seek funding to double the program's size, and establish and fund a new organizational mechanism to oversee the expanded program, replacing MDRC. But the new administration had other priorities. CETA, which had a limited impact on the problems of the hardest-to-employ, became a target for curtailment. In this new climate, Supported Work clearly was not to be institutionalized at the national level.

Fortunately, this was only part of the outcome. Other recent developments are more positive. Eleven Supported Work sites are still operating two years after the demonstration ended; the outlook is favorable for their continuation. Even more important, the lessons from Supported Work have become widely diffused and are being studied by many state and local officials confronted by reductions in federal spending for social welfare and training programs. Two states, Massachusetts and California, have passed legislation funding an expansion of Supported Work. As this chapter is written (July 1982), MDRC's staff is consulting with a number of states—including West Virginia, Arkansas, New Jersey, Maryland, and California—to help them design or evaluate work-welfare programs focusing on the AFDC population. The lessons from Supported Work have also served to shape other demonstration programs, including one now in operation by MDRC for the mentally retarded.

Certainly the hardest-to-employ will not disappear. What we cannot be certain of, however, is the scale of future efforts needed to help equip them for the labor market. Supported Work has shown that one large, important group can be assisted—individuals receiving AFDC payments. Even in this period of reduced federal financial support for social programs, state governments are addressing this task with more knowledge than was previously available.

There is also hope for private funding to follow up on the lessons of the Supported Work Demonstration. One of the strengths of a highly pluralist political system is that new knowledge and alternative sources of funding can take up some of the slack when the federal government retrenches. In addition, the lessons of the Supported Work Demonstration for the application of social research provide lessons for the future. We turn now to these lessons.

Implications for Social Research

For the purposes of this analysis, three characteristics of the experimental results of Supported Work are significant:

1. The evidence of improvement for different target groups was mixed.
2. The outcome was not predicted. For example, it was not obvious in advance that Supported Work would prove most successful for the AFDC group.
3. The experiment had clear implications for social policy.

One can imagine that all or nearly all social experiments would share the first two of these characteristics, but that in some social experiments, the policy implications might not be so clear. For Supported Work, the evidence warranted the conclusion that Supported Work should be tried on a national scale for AFDC mothers. One can argue about the proper scale and organization of the next step, but hardly about the desirability of going further.

Experience shows, however, that new developments and major shifts in social policy have little to do with actual advances in knowledge in the social sciences. The direction of policy responds to much deeper forces—historical commitments, political developments, ideological trends, and shifts in the balance of power among social classes. Social science does not initiate changes on such a broad scale, nor can it be used to resist a particular policy that has strong support despite social science findings suggesting that it is unlikely to succeed. Neither the Manpower Development and Training Act of 1962 nor the CETA legislation of 1973 gives much evidence that their authors had drawn from the accumulation of knowledge about labor markets and labor market participants. Nor could one argue that the shift under Reagan to the "workfare" concept was based on new scientific insights. That shift came about because of a change in national attitudes toward the poor and disadvantaged, as well as a reaction to the perceived failure of the employment and training programs of the past two decades. Even in the case of macroeconomic (fiscal and monetary) policy, where the relationship between analysis and action is clearer, the true connection has usually been indirect. Thus, when it comes to major directions and redirections of policy, the record of having and using social science knowledge is not a very good one; the lag in the impact of social science knowledge on policy is usually long.

In most cases, the political process refers hard issues to the scientific community for evaluation only when there is a serious lack of knowledge available for clear, definitive judgment. This is true of the natural scientific questions that are referred to the National Academy of Sciences, as it was of the employment questions that came within the purview of MDRC. If it were possible for a reasonably clear judgment to be made, based in full or in part on scientific knowledge, the Congress or the executive branch would have learned about it through the normal course of hearings and consultations. There would be no need to undertake a demonstration project or an Academy study.

Social experimentation and demonstration projects (and more conventional modes of social research) ordinarily have their primary role within a particular system and tradition of government policy. In that context, their function is like that of science in general: to refine estimates of numerical parameters; to choose between serious competing hypotheses; to test new ideas. The negative income tax experiment taught us something about the responsiveness of labor supply to lump-sum subsidies and marginal tax rates. However, support for the negative income tax disappeared before the new knowledge could be evaluated, let alone before it could have any practical effect on the design of new programs. Nevertheless, the knowledge gained about labor supply is not wholly lost. It will be useful in other contexts. And if the negative income tax idea comes up again on the nation's policy agenda, this country will be a little bit ahead.

Supported Work illustrates these points. Lampman's warning about the overwhelming likelihood that the null hypothesis would be accepted was on the mark. If there were any clear-cut solutions to the employment problems of the disadvantaged, they would have long since been legislated. Further, it is almost inevitable that policy-relevant social experiments will be seeking what are at best small effects. That is what the Supported Work experiments found: small effects, one of which—the results for AFDC mothers—seemed strong enough to warrant a policy shift. So far, this shift has not taken place. The Supported Work idea has not been adopted on a broader scale, largely because the mood of the country changed in the course of the Supported Work research. However, the positive knowledge will be available and pertinent for some time, and even the negative knowledge may help in the future to limit the sort of extreme and untested claims that sometimes prevail in both social science and social policy.

This view of the nexus between social experiments and social policy, together with the Supported Work experience, suggests certain hypotheses about the planning and operation of social experiments and demonstration projects in general. The most important of these stems from the strong likelihood, previously stated, that the effects to be captured and measured from social experiments are small and complex. It is essential, therefore, that experiments be carefully designed, thoroughly planned, and finely tuned. Large samples will undoubtedly be necessary; otherwise, there will be a low probability that treatment effects will be distinguishable from background noise, even if those effects are truly present.

To go further, even with large—and expensive—samples, a strategy of random assignment to experimental and control groups will always be desirable, often essential. Because program operators understandably do not want to deny access or treatment to half of a program's referrals, the control group concept generally will meet skepticism or resistance. It is, however, a key research issue.

The point that it is worth working for and, if necessary, pressing hard for the best achievable experimental design is underscored by the fact that the Supported Work experimental sites were spread out geographically, in locations with quite different sorts of economies. Inevitably, the postprogram experiences of Supported Work participants were powerfully influenced by conditions in the local labor markets; these variations probably would have swamped the effects of Supported Work in many instances. Only the control group strategy—the fact that the behavior of participants could be measured against the benchmark of the behavior of a randomly chosen group exposed to exactly the same local labor market and year-to-year variations in it—held promise of reliable results on a widespread or general basis.

The next best alternative in social experiments and demonstrations is usually a "comparison group"—the experience of a "similar" neighborhood or city or other unit of comparison. Although cost or other factors sometimes require this approach, it is bound to be inferior to an explicit control group strategy.

These considerations also emphasize the importance of rigidly adhering to the standard of objectivity. All those involved in the Supported Work Demonstration wanted it to succeed. The board, staff, and the program operators in the field had to keep reminding themselves that it probably would not. The most important reason for the need for objectivity is that there is always pressure from the policy apparatus to come up with *something* when the true effects are likely to be small; it is often too easy to bias the results or the interpretation of the results in the desired direction.

This last point calls attention to another pitfall in the research and demonstration process. Any substantial demonstration effort directed at problems in the area of human resources is likely to be decentralized in operation. Program operators will be dispersed at experimental sites. Geographic dispersal of sites is likely both for political reasons (to spread participation and its benefits among many constituencies) and for design reasons (to achieve controlled variety in treatment and setting). Research, on the other hand, is necessarily centralized, although, of course, the research organization may need representation at the sites. The contrast between centralized research and decentralized operations suggests organizational strains and problems.

But the issue goes deeper. There is a built-in conflict of interest between program operators and researchers. Operators want to get on with their programs, usually for the sake of the treatment and immediate benefits that the program yields, as well as for professional satisfaction. Researchers have other goals—uniform data and strict attention to the design of the experiment (and, of course, like everyone else, personal achievement). Thus, the priorities of the operator and the researcher will often clash. Operators will see ways of improving the program; researchers will resist them because such "tinkering" alters the design. Researchers will want data protocols that operators may regard as an unnecessary or bureaucratic imposition in conflict with the program's objectives and smooth operation. In this setting, the cards are stacked in favor of the program operators, who have the local knowledge and the advantage of full-time, on-the-scene involvement. The operator makes things happen, while the researcher is more removed from the action, limited to observation and data collection.

In this situation, the researcher deserves support. It is essential that research requirements become an integral part of an experiment from the beginning, and management's powers must be mobilized to back up legitimate research demands throughout the demonstration. In the Supported Work case, this was accomplished by making MDRC the paymaster for individual sites, interposed between them and the funding agencies. While that approach seemed to work, so simple a prescription will not always be possible. The point, however, is that some mechanism is needed to ensure that the research design is not compromised by locally originated variations.

Clearly, the planning and execution of social experiments and demonstrations is a complicated business. It is expensive and takes skill and organization to assemble key components and to refine them. The development of this kind of capability within organizations should therefore be encouraged, for it cannot be efficient to whip it together on an ad hoc basis each time a major experiment or demonstration is desired. How such capability might be built and kept resilient is a concern of the next section. This section first considers the organizational implications for national policy of the successful implementation of a Supported Work program for AFDC recipients.

The Role of the Federal Government

To assess the organizational lessons of the Supported Work Demonstration, it is necessary first to review briefly how the two major types of domestic public programs in the United States—income-transfer and service programs—have evolved and become interconnected. The most important relationship for this analysis is that between income-transfer programs for the welfare population and job and training programs for this same population. Over the past 20 years that relationship has been one of fits and starts and of frustration on the part of national policymakers.[3]

In 1962 the theme of the Kennedy administration's policies toward the welfare population was "service." The concept enunciated by Health, Education, and Welfare secretary Abraham Ribicoff was that service, rather than money, would help "to move persons off the assistance rolls, and enable others to attain a higher degree of self-confidence and independence."[4]

Despite changes made in the law to promote social services during the Kennedy administration, the continued growth of the welfare rolls in the early sixties led to a harder line five years later in 1967 welfare legislation. At that time, emphasis was placed on a specific type of service—employment and training assistance—in combination with a work requirement. Wilbur Mills, the principal author of the 1967 amendments, pressed for and won enactment of a strengthened work requirement for the AFDC program. The 1967 act created the Work Incentive Program (WIN) as the mechanism to carry out the AFDC work requirement.

Since 1967, there has been continued jockeying on the work requirement, which is—or is supposed to be—the connecting link between welfare and employment and training programs. The Nixon administration, as part of its family assistance welfare-reform effort, called for further tightening of the work requirement. These changes were enacted in 1971, although the features of Nixon's plan applying to the benefits of welfare families were not enacted. President Reagan moved still further in the direction of a work requirement with his proposal for "workfare," which was adopted by Congress on a trial basis in 1981. Workfare requires the assignment of employable welfare recipients to jobs for as many hours as are needed to "work off" their welfare benefits.

In essence, the Supported Work program, like workfare, is a way to connect income-transfer and service programs for the AFDC population. This population is made up largely of women of working age, who are not disabled and who are single heads of households with young children. The fact that the AFDC group benefited most from Supported Work has major implications for future programs dealing with this population.

The original rationale for extensive federal financial involvement in Supported Work was to conduct a rigorous test of this idea. Presumably, if it proved successful for one or more of the target groups, it would be applied more widely. But what level of government should implement a successful national Supported Work program? The question is a complicated one in the current setting, in which domestic programs are increasingly being devolved to the state and local governments under block grant programs.

One of the most important block grants, which was enacted in 1973 just as the Supported Work Demonstration was getting underway, was for employment and training. When the Supported Work Demonstration ended eight years later, the policy climate under the Reagan administration had become, if anything, even more inhospitable toward the idea of employment and training and other service programs administered or highly influenced by the national government. One would expect that Supported Work, if it worked, would be expanded, not by the federal government, but by states and localities.

There is, however, a good case to be made for taking the contrary position—that a Supported Work program on an expanded scale should be adopted as a national program. When it became clear that the program was most effective for welfare mothers, supporters of a national program could argue that, in light of the national emphasis on moving able-bodied persons into jobs, Supported Work should be adopted as a national government initiative.

The issue involved here—centralization versus decentralization—is one that has been debated for a long time. The most widely accepted position in the recent past has been that the national government should be responsible for income-transfer programs for welfare recipients, while service programs—including those for employment and training services—should be operated by states and on the local level.

This was the basic division of responsibility advocated by the Nixon and Ford administrations and, to a lesser extent, by the Carter administration. The National Governors' Association and the U.S. Advisory Commission on Intergovernmental Relations have taken the same stand.

The Reagan administration, however, has departed from this prevailing viewpoint, arguing that the full responsibility for income-transfer payments to working-age, able-bodied persons (that is, AFDC) should be turned over to the states. If the Reagan view prevails, the question of the relationship between Supported Work and welfare is an easy one to answer. Both responsibilities—for income transfers and employment and training services for the AFDC population—would be given to the states.

But should federal policy revert to the position of the Nixon, Ford, and Carter administrations and that of the governors, the issue becomes more complex. If welfare payments to able-bodied adults with children are fully, or almost fully, financed by the national government, one can argue that the administrative responsibility for these payments also should be. assigned to the federal government. A split where one level of government pays for the benefits and another makes the actual payments undermines accountability and efficient management.

Furthermore, under a federally structured or federally administered system where working-age welfare recipients are also subject to a strong work requirement, a case can be made that the federal government should be, in substantial measure, responsible for providing work and training opportunities for this population.

There is no easy answer for these organizational issues. The issue of centralization versus decentralization for the working-age welfare population has been around for a long time. It is likely to continue to be an important issue for American social policy, rather than being decided by assigning clear and full responsibility for the AFDC population to one level of government, either federal or state.

The discussion so far has dealt with the organizational issues of Supported Work from an operational point of view. As indicated earlier, one needs to separate the organizational issues for Supported Work as an operating program from the organizational issues involving the Supported Work Demonstration as a research undertaking. We see a clearer picture as regards the latter issue. We believe demonstrations such as this one should be conducted centrally and the findings made available nationally. There is a strong justification for centralizing knowledge building and research for social programs. Creative talent and research expertise are in short supply. As has been demonstrated in this chapter, the large samples necessary for demonstration projects to produce significant results are expensive and cannot be put in place for many different programs at the same time. Most of the money spent on the Supported Work Demonstration came from the federal government. Ideas like Supported Work should be tested in this way before billions are invested in new programs. It is essential that such tests be uniformly structured and administered in different locations and often with different target groups.

For these reasons, we believe that policymakers, especially those concerned with reducing the welfare rolls and moving long-term unemployed persons into the labor market, should consider the creation of an organizational entity at the national level that can test and disseminate information about new approaches for achieving these objectives. There are precedents for doing this in a number of other areas of domestic policy, such as the National Institutes of Health and Mental Health. There are also national institutes, which have been established more recently, for education, corrections, and drug abuse control. Two purposes should be sought by such an organization in the employment and training field: (1) to test new ideas and disseminate information about the results; and (2) to encourage and support existing programs that demonstrate a capacity to reach and aid the most disadvantaged persons, while at the same time reducing their dependency on public assistance.

This is, we believe, an appropriate role for the federal government. It is also an activity that can benefit from the counsel and involvement of people outside government—academicians, businessmen, labor leaders, the voluntary sector. For it is an endeavor intricately related to the needs of the labor market, as well as to the social concerns and moral responsibilities of the nation.

Notes

1 Vera Institute of Justice is a private, nonprofit corporation that develops and tests new approaches to social problems in New York City.
2 Chapter 3 in this volume presents a detailed definition and description of the Supported Work program.
3 See Steiner (1971, chap. 2).
4 Ibid., 36.

Appendix
References
Index

Appendix

TABLE A.1

Means of Control Variables Used in Regressions

(Standard deviations of continuous variables are in parentheses)

	Target Group			
	AFDC Recipient	Ex-addict	Ex-offender	Youth
Experimental group	0.510	0.527	0.486	0.478
Amount of follow-up data[a]				
27 months	0.221	0.503	0.562	0.488
36 months	n.a.	0.261	0.157	0.147
Pressured by agency to apply to				
program	0.141	0.122	0.135	0.065
Site				
Atlanta	0.109	n.a.	n.a.	0.093
Chicago	0.173	0.232	0.153	n.a.
Hartford	0.080	n.a.	0.115	0.446
Jersey City	n.a.	0.396	0.097	0.225
Newark	0.180	n.a.	0.188	n.a.
New York	0.343	n.a.	n.a.	0.159
Oakland	0.096	0.091	0.235	n.a.
Philadelphia	n.a.	0.282	0.093	0.077
San Francisco	n.a.	n.a.	0.119	n.a.
Wisconsin	0.019	n.a.	n.a.	n.a.
Area unemployment rate during		9.489	8.633	7.490
follow-up period[b]	n.a.	(2.562)	(1.909)	(2.684)
Complies with formal program				
eligibility criteria	0.849	0.777	0.830	0.732
Age				
19 or older	n.a.	n.a.	n.a.	0.403
21–25	n.a.	0.383	0.422	n.a.
26–35	0.514	0.429	0.317	n.a.
36–44	0.266	} 0.125	} 0.069	n.a.
45 or older	0.093			n.a.
Male	n.a.	0.805	0.943	0.862
Race/Ethnicity				
White, non-Hispanic	0.046	0.134	0.073	0.060
Hispanic	0.121	0.081	0.089	0.155

(Continued on following pages)

TABLE A.1 (Continued)
Means of Control Variables Used in Regressions
(Standard deviations of continuous variables are in parentheses)

	Target Group			
	AFDC Recipient	Ex-addict	Ex-offender	Youth
Years of education				
9–11	0.537	0.582	0.607	} 0.848
≥ 12	0.305	0.279	0.269	
Time since last enrolled in school[a]				
1 year	n.a.	n.a.	n.a.	0.367
1–2 years	n.a.	n.a.	n.a.	0.267
Reason left school[a]				
Expelled	n.a.	n.a.	n.a.	0.155
Trouble with law	n.a.	n.a.	n.a.	0.145
Wanted a job	n.a.	n.a.	n.a.	0.287
Number of persons in household	3.742	3.596	3.837	4.923
	(1.638)	(2.283)	(2.280)	(2.563)
Number of dependents				
1	n.a.			
2	0.264	} 0.390	} 0.190	} 0.102
3 or more	0.371			
Currently married	n.a.	0.498	0.119	n.a.
Any children 12 or younger	0.807	n.a.	n.a.	n.a.
Raised by[a]				
One parent	n.a.	n.a.	n.a.	0.564
Two parents	n.a.	n.a.	n.a.	0.347
Currently living with parents[a]	n.a.	n.a.	n.a.	0.701
Any food stamps or welfare last month	n.a.	0.498	0.316	0.343
Total income last month[c]	388.36	228.97	94.10	120.15
	(139.23)	(234.23)	(147.96)	(132.74)
Earnings last month[c]				
Any	0.198	0.493	0.350	0.572
Amount	20.21	100.08	46.20	67.24
	(61.80)	(171.16)	(100.09)	(98.44)
Unemployment compensation last month[c]				
Any	0.021	0.050	0.029	0.028
Amount	4.14	15.82	6.31	5.08
	(33.49)	(73.68)	(41.83)	(33.60)
Welfare last month[c]				
Any	n.a.	0.413	0.168	0.131
Amount	283.69	87.78	23.93	22.30
	(112.91)	(116.66)	(65.37)	(67.34)

(Continued on following pages)

TABLE A.1 (Continued)
Means of Control Variables Used in Regressions
(Standard deviations of continuous variables are in parentheses)

	Target Group			
	AFDC Recipient	Ex-addict	Ex-offender	Youth
Food stamps last month[c]				
Any	0.928	0.333	0.213	0.252
Bonus value	71.87	20.08	12.43	20.04
	(43.65)	(34.98)	(29.22)	(38.80)
Other unearned income last month[c]				
Any	0.077	0.040	n.a.	0.041
Amount	8.44	9.21	5.22	5.49
	(41.14)	(61.64)	(37.49)	(31.35)
Weeks worked in prior year	3.368	10.165	5.560	9.359
	(8.840)	(14.105)	(9.971)	(11.684)
Length of longest job ever held				
12 months or less	0.287	0.393	0.513	0.696
More than 12 months	0.547	0.550	0.365	0.075
8 or more weeks of job training in prior year[d]	0.081	0.091	0.190	0.109
Years on welfare				
4–7	0.369	n.a.	n.a.	n.a.
≥ 7	0.575	n.a.	n.a.	n.a.
Used any drugs (other than marijuana)	n.a.	0.980[c]	0.647	0.233
Used heroin regularly but not cocaine regularly	n.a.	0.733	⎱ 0.316	n.a.
Used heroin regularly and used cocaine regularly	n.a.	0.124	⎰	n.a.
Used cocaine[c]	n.a.	0.679	0.411	0.129
Used alcohol daily[c]	n.a.	0.115	0.084	0.058
Months of prior cocaine use	n.a.	21.970[c]	10.771[a]	n.a.
		(45.103)	(29.673)	
Months of prior heroin use	n.a.	76.384[c]	21.992[a]	n.a.
		(67.875)	(41.207)	
Drug treatment in last 6 months				
In treatment	n.a.	0.886	0.117	n.a.
In methadone maintenance	n.a.	0.482	n.a.	n.a.
In drug free	n.a.	0.217	n.a.	n.a.
In treatment involuntarily	n.a.	0.258	n.a.	n.a.
Best friend does not use drugs and is not involved in crime[a]	n.a.	0.739	n.a.	0.814
Many addicts in neighborhood[a]	n.a.	0.540	n.a.	0.323

(Continued on following page)

TABLE A.1 (Continued)
Means of Control Variables Used in Regressions
(Standard deviations of continuous variables are in parentheses)

	Target Group			
	AFDC Recipient	Ex-addict	Ex-offender	Youth
Ever arrested	n.a.	0.891	n.a.	0.542
Number of arrests	n.a.	8.255	8.910	2.250
		(11.083)	(12.744)	(5.305)
Weeks in jail in last 2 years				
> 26	n.a.	n.a.	0.622	n.a.
Time since incarcerated				
1–2 months	n.a.	⎫0.291	n.a.	⎫0.174
3–12 months	n.a.	⎬	⎫0.337	⎬
> 12 months	n.a.	0.412	⎬	0.112
On parole or probation[e]	n.a.	0.488	0.739	0.275
Maximum number of cases in regression	1351	974	1458	861

Note: These figures apply to those sample members who completed a baseline, 9-month, and 18-month interview. Means of these variables will vary slightly from one set of regressions to another because of slightly different sample sizes for analyses of various outcome measures. They may also vary from those presented in the text because the above means were obtained from actual analysis samples as opposed to potential samples based on interview completions.

a These variables were included only in regressions to estimate subgroup effects for individuals with the various attributes.

b Area unemployment rate was ultimately excluded from regressions because of its high correlation with the site variables.

c These variables were included only in regressions where the dependent variable was the postenrollment value of the same.

d This variable was included only in employment-related regressions.

e This variable was included only in regressions where indicators of drug use and criminal activities were the dependent variables.

n.a. Not applicable.

References

Abelson, H., P. Fishburn, and I. Cisin. 1977. *National Survey on Drug Abuse: A Nationwide Study—Youth, Young Adults, and Older People*, Vol. 1. Rockville, Md.: National Institute on Drug Abuse.

Adams, A., and G. Mangum, with W. Stephenson, S. Seninger, and S. Mangum. 1978. *The Lingering Crisis of Youth Unemployment*. Kalamazoo, Mich.: W.E. Upjohn Institute for Employment Research.

Ajemian, S., J. W. Frees, and E. Stromsdorfer. 1981. "Minnesota Work Equity Project: Second Interim Report, A Summary of Findings." Cambridge, Mass.: Abt Associates, Inc.

Ashenfelter, O. 1974. "The Effect of Manpower Training on Earnings: Preliminary Results." *Proceedings of the 27th Annual Meeting of the Industrial Relations Research Association* (December).

Ashenfelter, O. 1978. "Estimating the Effect of Training Programs on Earnings." *Review of Economics and Statistics* 60 (February): 47–57.

Ashenfelter, O., and R. Ehrenberg. 1975. "The Demand for Labor in the Public Sector." In *Labor in the Public and Nonprofit Sectors*, edited by D. S. Hamermesh, 55–78. Princeton, N.J.: Princeton University Press.

Auerbach Associates. 1973. *Lowering Artificial Barriers to Public Employment of the Disadvantaged: The Welfare Demonstration Program and Institutional Change*. Philadelphia: Auerbach Associates.

Azrin, N. 1978. "The Job-Finding Club as a Method for Obtaining Employment for Welfare-Eligible Clients: Demonstration, Evaluation, and Counselor Training." A Final Report to the U.S. Department of Labor, Grant No. 51-17-76-04. Anna, Ill.: Mental Health and Development Center, July 28.

Ball, J. 1977. *Implementing Supported Work: Job Creation Strategies during the First Year of the National Demonstration*. New York: Manpower Demonstration Research Corporation.

Barsby, S. L. 1972. *Cost-Benefit Analyses and Manpower Programs*. Lexington, Mass.: D.C. Heath.

Barton, P., and B. Fraser. 1978. "Between Two Worlds: Youth Transition from School to Work, Vol. 3, New Research and Measurement." Center for Education and Work. Washington, D.C.: U.S. Department of Commerce, PB-286-844.

Bass, U., and J. Woodward. 1978. "Skills Training and Employment for Ex-Addicts in Washington, D.C.: A Report on TREAT." Washington, D.C.:

U.S. Department of Health, Education, and Welfare, National Institute on Drug Abuse.

Bassi, L., and A. Fechter. 1979. "The Implications for Fiscal Substitution and Occupational Displacement under an Expanded CETA Title VI." Washington, D.C.: Urban Institute (February).

Becker, G. S. 1968. "Crime and Punishment: An Economic Approach." *Journal of Political Economy* 76 (March/April): 169–217.

Becker, H. S. 1963. *Outsiders: Studies in the Sociology of Deviance.* New York: Free Press.

Bishop, J. 1979. "The General Equilibrium Impact of Alternative Antipoverty Strategies." *Industrial and Labor Relations Review* 32(2) (January).

Block, M. K., and R. C. Lind. 1975. "Crime and Punishment Reconsidered." *Journal of Legal Studies* 4 (January): 241–47.

Blumstein, A., J. Cohen, and D. Nagin, eds. 1978. *Deterrence and Incapacitation: Estimating Effects of Criminal Sanctions on Crime Rates.* Washington, D.C.: National Academy of Sciences.

Boland, B. 1973. "Participation in the Aid to Families with Dependent Children Program (AFDC)." In U.S. Congress Joint Economic Committee, Subcommittee on Fiscal Policy, Studies in Public Welfare, Paper No. 12 (Part 1), *The Family, Poverty, and Welfare Programs: Factors Influencing Instability.* Washington, D.C.: U.S. Government Printing Office.

Borus, M. E. 1964. "A Benefit-Cost Analysis of the Economic Effectiveness of Retraining the Unemployed." *Yale Economic Essays* 4:371–429.

Borus, M. E. 1972. *Evaluating the Impact of Manpower Programs.* Lexington, Mass.: Lexington Books.

Borus, M.E., and D. S. Hamermesh. 1978. "Study of the Net Employment Effects of Public Service Employment—Econometric Analyses." In *Job Creation through Public Service Employment*, Vol. 3, Commissioned Papers, Report No. 6, 89–149. Washington, D.C.: National Commission for Manpower Policy.

Borus, M. E., J. P. Brennan, and S. Rosen. 1970. "A Benefit-Cost Analysis of the Neighborhood Youth Corps: The Out-of-School Program in Indiana." *Journal of Human Resources* 5 (Spring): 139–59.

Bradford, D. F. 1975. "Constraints on Government Investment Opportunities and the Choice of Discount Rate." *American Economic Review* 55 (December): 887–99.

Brecher, E. 1978. *The Manpower Demonstration Research Corporation: Origins and Early Operations.* New York: The Ford Foundation.

Brown, R. S. 1979. "Assessing the Effects of Interview Non-Response on Estimates of the Impact of Supported Work." Princeton, N.J.: Mathematica Policy Research.

Brown, R. S. 1980. "The Effects of Length of Time Spent in Supported Work on Program Impacts." In *The Impact of Supported Work on Young School Drop-outs*, edited by R. A. Maynard. New York: Manpower Demonstration Research Corporation.

Brown, R. S., and R. A. Maynard. 1981. "The Effects of Length of Time Spent in Supported Work on Program Impacts for the AFDC Target Group." In *The Impact of Supported Work on Long-Term Recipients of AFDC Benefits*, edited by S. Masters and R. A. Maynard. New York: Manpower Demonstration Research Corporation.

Brown, R. S., and A. Mozer. 1981a. "The Effect of Length of Time Spent in Supported Work on Program Impacts." In *The Impact of Supported Work on Ex-offenders*, edited by I. Piliavin and R. Gartner. New York: Manpower Demonstration Research Corporation.

Brown, R. S., and A. Mozer. 1981b. "The Effect of Length of Time Spent in Supported Work on Program Impacts for Ex-addicts." In *The Impact of Supported Work on Ex-addicts*, edited by K. Dickinson and R. A. Maynard. New York: Manpower Demonstration Research Corporation.

Brown, R. S., and J. Schore. 1981. "Assessing the Effects of Interview Non-Response on Evaluation Results for the Ex-offender Target Group." Appendix B in *The Impact of Supported Work on Ex-offenders*, edited by I. Piliavin and R. Gartner. New York: Manpower Demonstration Research Corporation.

Cain, G. G. 1967. "Benefit/Cost Estimates for Job Corps." Discussion Paper 9-67. Madison: Institute for Research on Poverty, University of Wisconsin.

Cain, G. G., and E. W. Stromsdorfer. 1968. "An Economic Evaluation of Government Retraining Programs in West Virginia." In *Retraining the Unemployed*, edited by G. G. Somers. Madison: University of Wisconsin Press.

California Council on Criminal Justice. 1973. *Direct Financial Assistance to Parolees Project*. First progress report (February).

Clark, K. B., and L. H. Summers. 1978. "The Dynamics of Youth Unemployment." Working Paper No. 274. Cambridge, Mass.: National Bureau of Economic Research (August).

Classen, K. 1977. "The Effect of Unemployment Insurance on the Duration of Unemployment and Subsequent Earnings." *Industrial and Labor Relations Review* 30 (July).

Cloward, R., and L. Ohlin. 1960. *Delinquency and Opportunity*. Chicago: Free Press.

Cohn, R. M. 1978. "The Effect of Employment Status Change on Self-Attitudes." *Social Psychology* 41:81–93.

Cook, P. J. 1975. "The Correctional Carrot: Better Jobs for Parolees." *Policy Analysis* 1 (Winter): 11–54.

Dale, M. W. 1976. "Barriers to the Rehabilitation of Ex-offenders." *Crime and Delinquency* 22 (July): 322–37.

Danaceau, P. 1973. "Methadone Maintenance: The Experience of Four Programs." Washington, D.C.: Drug Abuse Council, Inc. (May).

Danziger, S. 1981. "Postprogram Changes in the Lives of AFDC Supported Work Participants: A Qualitative Assessment." *Journal of Human Resources* 16 (4) (Fall).

Dasgupta, A. K., and D. W. Pearce. 1972. *Cost-Benefit Analysis: Theory and Practice*. London: Macmillan and Co.

Dasgupta, P., A. Sen, and S. Marglin. 1972. *Guidelines for Project Evaluation.* New York: United Nations.

Dembo, R. 1971. "Recidivism: The Criminal's Reaction to Treatment." *Criminology* 8 (February): 345–56.

Diamond, D., and H. Bedrosian. 1970. "Industry Hiring Requirements and the Employment of Disadvantaged Groups." New York: New York University School of Commerce.

Dickinson, K. 1979. "Social Cost Indexes of Drug Use." Princeton, N.J.: Mathematica Policy Research.

Dickinson, K. 1980. "Indexes of Drug Use Based on Data from the National Supported Work Demonstration." Princeton, N.J.: Mathematica Policy Research (May).

Dickinson, K. 1981. "Supported Work for Ex-addicts: An Exploration of Endogenous Tastes." *Journal of Human Resources* 16 (4) (Fall).

Dickinson, K., and R. A. Maynard. 1981. *The Impact of Supported Work on Ex-addicts.* New York: Manpower Demonstration Research Corporation.

DiPrete, T. 1978. "Unemployment over the Life Cycle: Probability Models of Turnover." PB-287-953. Washington, D.C.: U.S. Department of Commerce.

Durkheim, E. 1951. *Suicide.* Glencoe, Ill.: Free Press.

Duvall, H., B. Locke, and L. Brill. 1963. "Follow-up Study of Narcotic Drug Addicts Five Years after Hospitalization." *Public Health Reports* 78:185–93.

Ehrenberg, R., and J. Hewlett. 1976. "The Impact of the WIN-2 Program on Welfare Costs and Recipient Rates." *Journal of Human Resources* 11 (Spring).

Ehrenberg, R., and R. Oaxaca. 1976. "Unemployment Insurance, Duration of Unemployment, and Subsequent Wage Gain." *American Economic Review* 66 (December).

Ehrlich, I. 1973. "Participation in Illegitimate Activities: A Theoretical and Empirical Investigation." *Journal of Political Economy* 81 (May/June): 521–65.

Elliot, D., and B. Knowles. 1978. "Social Development and Employment: An Evaluation of the Oakland Work Experience Program." In *Conference Report on Youth Unemployment: Its Measurements and Meaning.* Washington, D.C.: U.S. Department of Labor.

Erickson, R., W. J. Crow, L. A. Zurcher, and A. V. Connett. 1973. *Paroled But Not Free.* New York: Behavioral Publications.

Evans, R., Jr. 1968. "The Labor Market and Parole Success." *Journal of Human Resources* 3 (Spring): 201–12.

Farber, D. J. 1971. "Highlights—First Annual Follow-up: 1968 Jobs Contract and Noncontract Program." Washington, D.C.: U.S. Department of Labor Study.

Fechter, A. E. 1975. *Public Employment Programs.* Washington, D.C.: American Enterprise Institute for Public Policy Research.

Feeley, M. 1974. *Final Report on the Parolee Integration Project.* Hartford, Conn.: Department of Correction.

Fleisher, B. 1966. "The Effect of Income on Delinquency." *American Economic Review* 56 (March): 118–37.

Freeman, R., and D. Wise. 1980. *Youth Unemployment: Summary Report.* Cambridge, Mass.: National Bureau of Economic Research.

Friedman, L. S. 1977. "An Interim Evaluation of the Supported Work Experience." *Policy Analysis* (Spring): 144–70.

Friedman, L. 1978. *The Wildcat Experiment: An Early Test of Supported Work.* New York: Vera Institute of Justice.

Funke, G. 1979. "Unemployment and Crime: A Socioeconomic Approach." In *Crime and Employment Issues.* Washington, D.C.: American University Law School, Institute for Advanced Studies in Justice.

Gay, R., and M. Borus. 1980. "Validating Performance Indicators for Employment and Training Programs." *Journal of Human Resources* 15 (1) (Winter): 29–48.

Geraci, V., and C. King. 1981. "Employment and Training Program Performance: Long Term Earnings Effects and Short Term Indicators." Austin, Texas: Center for the Study of Human Resources.

Ginzberg, E. 1980. "Overview: The $64 Billion Innovation." In *Employing the Unemployed*, edited by E. Ginzberg. New York: Basic Books.

Glaser, D. 1964. *The Effectiveness of a Prison and Parole System.* Indianapolis: Bobbs-Merrill.

Goldman, B. S. 1981. *Impacts of the Immediate Job Search Assistance Experiment.* New York: Manpower Demonstration Research Corporation.

Goldstein, J. 1972. *The Effectiveness of Manpower Training Programs: A Review of Research on the Impact on the Poor.* Washington, D.C.: U.S. Government Printing Office.

Goodwin, L. 1972. *Do the Poor Want to Work?* Washington, D.C.: The Brookings Institution.

Gramlich, E. 1976. "Impact of Minimum Wages, Employment and Family Incomes." *Brookings Papers on Economic Activity* (2): 409–461.

Greenberg, S., and F. Adler. 1974. "Crime and Addiction: An Empirical Analysis of the Literature, 1920–1973." *Contemporary Drug Problems* 3 (Summer).

Gueron, J. 1980. "The Supported Work Experiment." In *Employing the Unemployed*, edited by E. Ginzberg. New York: Basic Books.

Hardin, E. 1969. "Benefit-Cost Analyses of Occupational Training Programs: A Comparison of Recent Studies." In *Cost-Benefit Analysis of Manpower Policies*, edited by G. G. Somers and W. D. Wood. Kingston, Ont.: Industrial Relations Centre, Queen's University.

Hardin, E., and M. E. Borus. 1972. *Economic Benefits and Costs of Retraining Courses in Michigan.* East Lansing: Michigan State University.

Haveman, R. H. 1978. "The Dutch Social Employment Program." In *Creating Jobs: Public Employment Programs and Wage Subsidies*, edited by J. L. Palmer. Washington, D.C.: The Brookings Institution.

Haveman, R. H., and J. Margolis, eds. 1983. *Public Expenditure and Policy Analysis.* Boston: Houghton Mifflin Co.

Heckman, J. 1976. "The Common Structure of Statistical Models of Truncation, Sample Selection and Limited Dependent Variables and an Estimator for Such Models." *Annals of Economic and Social Measurement* 5 (Fall): 475–92.

Heinecke, J. M. 1978. "Economic Models of Criminal Behavior: An Overview." In *Economic Models of Criminal Behavior*, edited by J. M. Heinecke. New York: North Holland.

Hindelang, M. 1978. "Race and Involvement in Common Law, Personal Crimes." *American Sociological Review* 43:93–109.

Hollister, R. G., Jr., P. Kemper, and J. Wooldridge. 1979. "Linking Process and Impact Analysis: The Case of Supported Work." In *Qualitative and Quantitative Methods in Evaluation Research*, Vol. 1, edited by T. D. Cook and C. S. Reichardt. Beverly Hills, Calif.: Sage Publications.

Jacks, J. 1973. "The Public Vocational Rehabilitation Program and the Drug Abuser." In *Drug Dependence and Rehabilitation Approaches*, edited by R. Hardy and J. Cull. Springfield, Ill.: Thomas.

Jackson, R., D. Kueter, and R. Pannell with B. Phillips. 1979. "Survey Procedures and Field Results in the Evaluation of the National Supported Work Demonstration." Princeton, N.J.: Mathematica Policy Research (July).

Jackson, R., J. Mattei, R. A. Maynard, and J. Wooldridge. 1978. *The Supported Work Demonstration's Research Sample: Characteristics at Enrollment*. Princeton, N.J.: Mathematica Policy Research.

Johnson, G. E. 1979. "The Labor Market Displacement Effect in the Analysis of the Net Impact of Manpower Training Programs." In *Evaluating Manpower Training Programs*, edited by F. Block. Greenwich, Conn.: JAI Press.

Johnson, G. E., and J. D. Tomola. 1977. "The Fiscal Substitution Effect of Alternative Approaches to Public Service Employment Policy." *Journal of Human Resources* 12 (Winter): 3–26.

Kemper, P., and P. Moss. 1978. "Economic Efficiency of Public Employment Programs." In *Creating Jobs: Public Employment Programs and Wage Subsidies*, edited by J. L. Palmer. Washington, D.C.: The Brookings Institution.

Kemper, P. 1980. "Supported Work Evaluation Supplementary Paper: Indirect Labor Market Effects in Benefit-Cost Analysis." Princeton, N.J.: Mathematica Policy Research.

Kemper, P., and D. A. Long. 1981. *The Supported Work Evaluation: Technical Report on Value of In-Program Output and Costs*. New York: Manpower Demonstration Research Corporation.

Kemper, P., D. A. Long, and C. Thornton. 1981. *The Supported Work Evaluation: Final Benefit-Cost Analysis*. New York: Manpower Demonstration Research Corporation.

Kerachsky, S., D. Horner, and A. Mozer. 1979. "The Quality of Self-Reported Data on AFDC Payments." Princeton, N.J.: Mathematica Policy Research (May).

Kesselman, J. R. 1978. "Work Relief Programs in the Great Depression." In *Creating Jobs: Public Employment Programs and Wage Subsidies*, edited by J. L. Palmer. Washington, D.C.: The Brookings Institution.

Ketron, Inc. 1978. *Differential Impact Analysis of the WIN II Program.* Wayne, Pa.: Ketron, Inc.

Ketron, Inc. 1979a. *Differential Impact Analysis of the WIN II Program,* Final Report. Wayne, Pa.: Ketron, Inc. Prepared for the Employment and Training Administration, U.S. Department of Labor, under Contract No. 55-42-77-01.

Ketron, Inc. 1979b. *The Long-Term Impact of WIN II: A Longitudinal Evaluation of the Employment Experiences of Participants in the Work Incentive Program.* Wayne, Pa.: Ketron, Inc. Prepared for the U.S. Department of Labor under Contract No. 55-42-77-02.

Ketron, Inc. 1980. *The Long-Term Impact of WIN II: A Longitudinal Evaluation of the Employment Experiences of Participants in the Work Incentive Program.* Wayne, Pa.: Ketron, Inc.

Lamb, R., and C. Mackota. 1973. "Using Work Therapeutically." In *Drug Dependence and Rehabilitation Approaches,* edited by R. Hardy and J. Cull. Springfield, Ill.: Thomas.

Lax, E. 1980. "Succeeding or Not in Supported Work: How Participants Perceive the Program." New York: Manpower Demonstration Research Corporation.

Lefkowitz, B. 1976. *Highlights of Site Activities during the Planning Period for the Supported Work Demonstrations.* New York: Manpower Demonstration Research Corporation.

Lemert, E. M. 1964. *Human Deviance, Social Problems and Social Control.* Englewood Cliffs, N.J.: Prentice-Hall.

Lettre, M. A., and A. M. Syntax. 1976. *Application of JUSSIM to the Maryland Criminal Justice Planning Process.* Towson, Md.: Maryland Governor's Commission on Law Enforcement and the Administration of Justice.

Long, D. A. 1980. "An Analysis of Expenditures in the National Supported Work Demonstration." Princeton, N.J.: Mathematica Policy Research.

Long, D. A., C. Mallar, and C. Thornton. 1982. "Evaluation of the Benefits and Costs of the Job Corps." *Journal of Policy Analysis and Management* 1 (1) (Fall).

Lowenthal, M. 1971. *Work and Welfare: An Overview.* Boston: Social Welfare Regional Research Institute, Boston College.

Lowry, J. H., and Associates. 1980. *Analysis of Functions with Youth Demonstrations,* Volume 3 of *Determining the Viability of Intermediary Non-Profit Corporations for Youth Programming.* U.S. Department of Labor, Office of Youth Programs, Employment and Training Administration.

Maddala, G., and L. Lee. 1976. "Recursive Models with Qualitative Endogenous Variables." *Annals of Economic Measurement* 5 (Fall): 525–46.

Mahoney, J. 1979. "Youth Unemployment and Other Issues Affecting Violence Levels." In *Crime and Employment Issues.* Washington, D.C.: American University Law School, Institute for Advanced Studies in Justice.

Mallar, C. D., and C. V. D. Thornton. 1978. "Transitional Aid for Released Prisoners: Evidence from the LIFE Experiment." *Journal of Human Resources* 13 (Spring): 208–36.

Manpower Demonstration Research Corporation (MDRC). 1976. *First Annual Report on the National Supported Work Demonstration.* New York: MDRC.

Manpower Demonstration Research Corporation (MDRC). 1978. *Second Annual Report on the National Supported Work Demonstration.* New York: MDRC.

Manpower Demonstration Research Corporation (MDRC). 1980. *Summary and Findings of the National Supported Work Demonstration.* Cambridge, Mass.: Ballinger.

Margolis, J. 1970. "Shadow Prices for Incorrect and Nonexistent Market Values." In *Public Expenditures and Public Policy,* edited by R. H. Haveman and J. Margolis. Chicago: Markham.

Masters, S. H. 1981. "The Effects of Supported Work on the Earnings and Transfer Payments of Its AFDC Target Group." *Journal of Human Resources* 16 (4) (Fall).

Masters, S. H. 1979. "Using Social-Security Data to Check for Possible Bias in the Earnings Effects of Supported Work, as Estimated with Interview Data." Madison: Institute for Research on Poverty, University of Wisconsin.

Masters, S. H., and T. McDonald. 1981. "Postprogram Effects of Supported Work for the AFDC Target Group." New York: Manpower Demonstration Research Corporation.

Masters, S. H., and R. A. Maynard. 1981. *The Impact of Supported Work on Long-Term Recipients of AFDC Benefits.* New York: Manpower Demonstration Research Corporation.

Maynard, R. A. 1980. *The Impact of Supported Work on Young School Dropouts.* New York: Manpower Demonstration Research Corporation.

Maynard, R. A., E. Cavin, and J. Schore. 1982. "Postprogram Impacts of Supported Work for Young School Dropouts: Results from a Follow-up Survey." Princeton, N.J.: Mathematica Policy Research.

MDRC. *See* Manpower Demonstration Research Corporation.

Mendelsohn, R. 1981. "The Choice of Discount Rates for Public Projects." *American Economic Review* 71 (March): 239–41.

Merton, R. 1938. "Social Structure and Anomie." *American Sociological Review* 3 (October): 674–82.

Metcalf, C., and J. Behrens. 1975. "Proposed Changes in the Supported Work Sample Allocation." Princeton, N.J.: Mathematica Policy Research (August).

Nathan, R. P., R. F. Cook, J. M. Galchick, and R. W. Long. 1978. "Monitoring the Public Service Employment Program." *Job Creation through Public Service Employment,* Vol. 2, Report No. 6. Washington, D.C.: National Commission for Manpower Policy.

National Academy of Sciences. 1974. *The Use of Social Security Earnings Data for Assessing the Impact of Manpower Training Programs.* Washington, D.C.

National Commission for Employment Policy. 1979. *Expanding Employment Opportunities for Disadvantaged Youth,* Report No. 9. Washington, D.C.

National Institute on Drug Abuse. 1978. *The Wildcat Experiment: An Early Supported Work Test in Drug Abuse Rehabilitation,* by L. N. Friedman. Washington, D.C.: U.S. Government Printing Office.

O'Donnell, J. 1969. *Narcotics Addicts in Kentucky*. Washington, D.C.: U.S. Government Printing Office.

O'Donnell, J., H. Voss, R. Clayton, G. Slatin, and R. Room. 1976. *Young Men and Drugs—A Nationwide Survey*. Rockville, Md.: National Institute on Drug Abuse.

Office of Management and Budget. 1972. "Discounted Rates to Be Used in Evaluating Time Distributed Costs and Benefits." Washington, D.C. (March 27).

Ohls, J., and G. Carcagno. 1978. "Second Year Evaluation Report for the Michigan Private Employment Agency Job Counselor Project." Project Report PR-78-08. Princeton, N.J.: Mathematica Policy Research.

O'Neill, D. M. 1973. *The Federal Government and Manpower*. Washington, D.C.: American Enterprise Institute.

Osterman, P. 1978. "Youth, Work and Unemployment." *Challenge* (May/June): 69–69.

Perry, C., B. Anderson, R. Rowan, and H. Northrup. 1975. *The Impact of Government Manpower Programs*. Philadelphia: University of Pennsylvania Press.

Piliavin, I., and R. Gartner. 1979. "Assumptions and Achievements of Manpower Programs for Offenders: Implications for Supported Work," Institute for Research on Poverty Discussion Paper 541–79. Madison: University of Wisconsin.

Piliavin, I., and R. Gartner. 1981. *The Impact of Supported Work on Ex-offenders*. New York: Manpower Demonstration Research Corporation. (January).

Platt, J., and C. Labate. 1976. "Recidivism in Youthful Heroin Offenders and Characteristics of Parole Behavior and Environment." *The International Journal of the Addictions* 11 (4): 651–57.

Preble, E., and J. Casey. 1969. "Taking Care of Business: The Heroin User's Life on the Street." *The International Journal of the Addictions* 4: 1–24.

Prescott, E., W. Tash, and W. Usdane. 1971. "Training and Employability: The Effects of MDTA on AFDC Recipients." *Welfare in Review* (January/February).

Ragan, J. 1977. "Minimum Wages and the Youth Labor Market." *Review of Economics and Statistics* 59 (May): 129–36.

Reckless, W. C., and S. Dinitz. 1967. "Pioneering with Self-Concept as a Vulnerability Factor in Delinquency." *Journal of Criminal Law, Criminology and Police Science* 58 (December): 515–23.

Reid, W. J., and A. Smith. 1972. "AFDC Mothers View the Work Incentive Program." *Social Service Review* 46.

Rence, C., and M. Wiseman. 1978. "The California Welfare Reform Act and Participation in AFDC." *Journal of Human Resources* 13 (Winter).

Ritter, M. K., and S. K. Danziger. 1983. "Life After Supported Work for Welfare Mothers." New York: Manpower Demonstration Research Corporation.

Rivlin, A. M. 1974. "How Can Experiments Be More Useful?" *American Economic Review: Papers and Proceedings* 64 (May): 346–54.

Rossi, P., R. Berk, and K. Lenihan. 1979. "Money, Work and Crime." Paper presented at the 1979 annual meeting of the American Sociological Association, Boston.

Rothenberg, J. 1975. "Cost-Benefit Analysis: A Methodological Exposition." In *Handbook of Evaluation Research*, Vol. 2, edited by M. Guttentag and E. Struening. Beverly Hills, Calif.: Sage Publications.

Ruth, H., J. Behrens, and C. Metcalf. 1980. "Issues in Program Design and Sampling Strategy for the National Supported Work Demonstration." Princeton, N.J.: Mathematica Policy Research (March).

Sassone, P. G., and W. A. Schaffer. 1978. *Cost-Benefit Analysis: A Handbook*. New York: Academic Press.

Schiller, B. R. 1978. "Lessons from WIN: A Manpower Evaluation." *Journal of Human Resources* 13 (Fall): 502–23.

Schiller, B. R., Camil Associates, D. Miller and W. Cameron, and Ketron, Inc. (M. Temple and D. Howe). 1976. *The Impact of WIN II: A Longitudinal Evaluation*. Prepared for the Office of Program Evaluation, Employment, and Training Administration, U.S. Department of Labor, and for the Social and Rehabilitation Service, U.S. Department of Health, Education, and Welfare, under Contract No. 53-3-013-06.

Schore, J., R. A. Maynard, and I. Piliavin. 1979. "The Accuracy of Self-Reported Arrest Data." *Proceedings of the American Statistical Association*.

Schur, E. M. 1971. *Labeling Deviant Behavior*. New York: Harper and Row.

Semo Scharfman, V. 1981. "The Supported Work Youth Variation: An Enriched Program for Young High School Drop-Outs." New York: Manpower Demonstration Research Corporation.

Sewell, D. O. 1971. *Training the Poor: A Benefit-Cost Analysis of Manpower Programs in the U.S. Anti-Poverty Program*. Kingston, Ont.: Industrial Relations Centre, Queen's University.

Shapiro, H. 1978. *Waiving the Rules*. New York: Manpower Demonstration Research Corporation.

Shapiro, H. 1979. *Paying the Bills*. New York: Manpower Demonstration Research Corporation.

Shapiro, H. 1981. *Setting Up Shop*. New York: Manpower Demonstration Research Corporation.

Simpson, D., L. Savage, G. Joe, R. Demaree, and S. Sells. 1976. *DARP Data Book: Statistics on Characteristics of Drug Users in Treatment during 1969–1974*. Fort Worth, Texas: Institute for Behavioral Research, Texas Christian University.

Singell, L. 1967. "An Examination of the Empirical Relationship between Unemployment and Juvenile Delinquency." *American Journal of Economics and Sociology* 26:377–86.

Sjoquist, D. L. 1973. "Property Crime and Economic Behavior: Some Empirical Results." *American Economic Review* 63 (June): 439–46.

Smith, J. P. 1975. "A Critique of Tax Based Cost-Benefit Ratios," Paper P-5573. Santa Monica, Calif.: The Rand Corporation.

Solon, G. 1979. "Labor Supply Effects of Extended Unemployment Benefits." *Journal of Human Resources* 14 (Spring).

Somers, G. G., and W. D. Wood. 1969. *Cost-Benefit Analysis of Manpower Programs*. Kingston, Ont.: Industrial Relations Centre, Queen's University.

Soothill, K. 1974. *The Prisoner's Release: A Study of the Employment of Ex-prisoners*. London: George Allen and Unwin.

Steiner, G. Y. 1971. *The State of Welfare*. Washington, D.C.: The Brookings Institution.

Stephens, R., and E. Cottress. 1972. "A Follow-up Study of 200 Narcotic Addicts Committed in Treatment under the Narcotic Rehabilitation Act (NARA)." *British Journal of Addiction* 67: 45–53.

Stromsdorfer, E.W. 1968. "Determinants of Economic Success in Retraining the Unemployed." *Journal of Human Resources,* 3 (Spring): 139–158.

Stromsdorfer, E. W. 1972. *Review and Synthesis of Cost-Effectiveness Studies of Vocational and Technical Education*. Columbus, Ohio: ERIC Clearing House on Vocational and Technical Education.

Sullivan, C. E. 1971. "Changes in Correction: Show or Substance?" *Manpower* 3 (January): 2–7.

Sutherland, E. 1947. *Principles of Criminology*. Philadelphia: Lippincott.

Taggart, R. 1972. *The Prison of Unemployment*. Baltimore: Johns Hopkins Press.

Tharp, R. G., and R. J. Wetzel. 1969. *Behavior Modification in the Natural Environment*. New York: Academic Press.

Thornton, C., and D. A. Long. 1980. "The Supported Work Evaluation: Valuing Behavioral Outcomes." Princeton, N.J.: Mathematica Policy Research.

Thornton, C., D. A. Long, and C. Mallar. 1980. "A Comparative Evaluation of the Benefits and Costs of Job Corps after 18 Months in Post-Program Observation." Princeton, N.J.: Mathematica Policy Research (May).

Thornton, C., C. Mallar, and D. A. Long. 1979. "Estimating the Social Value of Changes in Criminal Behavior: Crime Reduction Benefits of Job Corps." *Proceedings of the American Statistical Association* Social Statistics Section.

U.S. Department of Health, Education, and Welfare. 1978. National Institute on Drug Abuse, *Statistical Series: Series F, Executive Report, April 1978*. Washington, D.C.

U.S. Department of Justice. 1978. *Sourcebook of Criminal Justice Statistics 1977*. Washington, D.C.: Law Enforcement Assistance Administration.

U.S. Department of Labor. 1979. *Employment and Training Report of the President*. Washington, D.C..

U.S. Department of Labor, Employment and Training Administration. 1977. *Implementing Welfare-Employment Programs: An Institutional Analysis of the Work Incentive Program*, R&D Monograph 78.

Utah, State of, Department of Social Services, Office of Evaluation. 1977. *Review of the Work Experience and Training Program of the Assistance Payments Administration*.

Vera Institute of Justice. 1975. *Third Annual Report on Supported Employment*. New York: Vera Institute.

Vera Institute of Justice. 1977 *Operating Plan for Vera's Study of Employment and Crime.* New York: Vera Institute.

Weisbrod, B. A. 1968. "Income Redistribution Effects and Benefit-Cost Analysis." In *Problems in Public Expenditure Analysis,* edited by S. B. Chase. Washington, D.C.: The Brookings Institution.

Westat, Inc. 1979. "Continuous Longitudinal Manpower Survey, Special Report No. 1" (draft). Rockville, Md.: Westat, Inc. (March).

Wiseman, M. 1976. "Employment as Fiscal Policy." *Brookings Papers on Economic Activity* (1).

Index

Addicts, ex-addicts: design and implementation of research, 12–13, 27, 36, 39, 41, 44; eligibility criteria, 19; model program for, 51, 53, 57, 59, 65; work projects, 60; job-search assistance, 73–74; experience of program participants, 82–83; impact of program on, 136–71; characteristics of program, 138–43; experiences of employers, 144–46; employment and earnings, 147–59; drug use, effects of program on, 159–71; crime-related outcomes, 162–68; benefit-cost study, 250, 255–59, 263, 274; criminal activity reduced, 270–71

Advocap, Inc., Wisconsin, 14

Aid to Families with Dependent Children: design and implementation of research, 12, 24, 36, 39, 41, 43–46, 294; eligibility criteria, 19; model program for, 52–53, 57–59, 65–66; work projects, 60–64; job-search assistance, 72–74, 119–20; experience of program participants, 82–87; impact of supported work analyzed, 90–132; characteristics of research, 94–105; analytic approach to study, 105–8; impact of program, 108–18, 121–24, 128–31; employment and earnings, 109–21; employment in public sector, 119–20; benefit-cost analysis, 241, 243–45, 255–59, 263, 274, 277–78, 306, 310–13, 316–18; workfare, 312, 316–18. *See also* Work Incentive Program

Alameda County, California, Peralta Service Corporation, 14

Arkansas, Supported Work Program, 311

Atlanta, Georgia: Preparation for Employment Program, 14; model program in, 52, 56–58, 64, 66, 68, Visiting Nurses Association, 58; work projects, 60; categories of project time, 61–63; job-search assistance, 71, 73; experience of program participants, 81–82; AFDC, characteristics of research, 94–99, 101–3, 113–14, 119, 127; youth, impact of program, 206–8, 213, 225, 228, 231, 234; benefit-cost study, 260–62

Ball, Joseph, 34

Barth, Michael, 11n

Benefit-cost study, 28–33, 239–85; AFDC, 241, 244–45, 255–59, 263, 274, 277–78; criminal activity, effects of, 241, 247–49, 255–59, 263–64, 268–69; methodology and results, 242–54; child care, 244–45, 255; drug abuse, 250, 255–58, 263, 274

Brown, Randall, 36

California: ex-offenders, 190; Supported Work Program, 311. *See also* Oakland, California

Carter, James Earl, 318

Chicago: Options, Inc., 14; local programs developed, 57–58, 66, 70; work projects, 60; categories of project time, 61–63; job-search assistance, 73; experience of program participants, 81–82; AFDC, characteristics of research, 94–99, 101, 102–3, 113–14, 127–28, 130; ex-addicts, 144, 147; ex-offenders, 178; benefit-cost study, 260–61

Child care: impact on working mothers, 92, 123–24; benefit-cost study, 244–45, 255

Community Help Corporation, Jersey City, New Jersey, 14

COMPOSED BY IMPRESSIONS, INC., MADISON, WISCONSIN
MANUFACTURED BY EDWARDS BROTHERS, INC., ANN ARBOR, MICHIGAN
TEXT AND DISPLAY LINES ARE SET IN TIMES ROMAN

Library of Congress Cataloging in Publication Data
Main entry under title:
The National Supported Work Demonstration.
Bibliography: pp. 327–338.
Includes index.
1. Hard-core unemployed—United States—Addresses,
essays, lectures. 2. Public service employment—
United States—Addresses, essays, lectures.
I. Hollister, Robinson G. II. Kemper, Peter, 1944–
III. Maynard, Rebecca A.
HD5708.85.U6N37 1984   331.12′042   83-40266
ISBN 0-299-09690-4